WITH THE RANK AND PAY OF A SAPPER

With the Rank and Pay of a Sapper:

the 216th (Nuneaton) Army Troops Company,
Royal Engineers, in the Great War

By James Sambrook

'The Lord he created the Engineer,
Her Majesty's Royal Engineer,
With the rank and pay of a Sapper.'
(Kipling)

Paddy Griffith Associates
Nuneaton, 1998

To the memory of the men of the 216th Company R.E.

Published by
Paddy Griffith Associates
22 Callendar Close, Nuneaton,
Warwickshire CV11 6LU, England
1998

ISBN number 0 9521488 3 8

A catalogue record for this book is availble from the British Library

Printed by Warwick Printing Company Ltd.

Table of Contents

Frontispiece: Arthur Sambrook's drawing of Germans advancing towards part of the Amiens Defence Line, 30 March 1918.

Introduction by Paddy Griffith

Author of 'Battle Tactics of the Western Front, 1916-18'

James Sambrook is an established editor and biographer of eighteenth- and nineteenth-century literary figures; but he has now written a masterly 'biography' of a twentieth-century military unit. In so doing he has displayed the same sensitivity that normally informs his literary criticism; but he has added an extra stratum of military expertise which ensures that this book is far more than just another dilettante literary promenade along the Western Front. Indeed, it is not about 'Literature with a capital L' at all; but about the humbler but surely far more important type of 'small l' literature which is written by ordinary men in their letters and diaries at the time, or in their informal subsequent 'war memoirs' intended to enlighten their grandchildren. As such it offers a rare insight into the thoughts and experiences of quite a high proportion of the rank and file within a single company at the front. It therefore bridges the crucial gap between the subjective personal impressions of one particular individual, and the clipped official narrative of what the distant high command believed his unit was thought to be supposed to be doing.

From the local point of view this book certainly adds an important chapter to Nuneaton's civic history, since the 216th Company was recruited under official municipal arrangements and mainly from local volunteers. Many of the places of significance to its initial phase of training can still be seen in Nuneaton today, although it often takes quite a leap of imagination to visualise them as they were in 1915, rather than as they have become in 1998.

More generally, however, Jim Sambrook's book is about the experiences of Royal Engineers in the Great War, and in fact it is the first full history ever written about a company of 'Army Troops', as opposed to 'Field' engineers. The RE field companies were employed on general duties within the front line trenches; but the 'Army' companies were more specialised and focussed upon more strategic tasks. They constituted one among the many novel technical élites which this war called into being, and no student of the birth of modern warfare should ignore their contribution.

Our image of the British army on the Western Front is nevertheless dominated by the massed battalions of infantry, which provided about a third of all those serving in the BEF at any given time.[1] The infantry paid a disproportionately heavy price, suffering some 86 per cent of the total British casualties in France and Belgium (including killed, missing and prisoner; but mostly wounded). This sacrifice is made doubly poignant by the particularly squalid and inglorious conditions in which so many died, often with no known grave. It is trebly poignant to reflect that a very high proportion of those who went into this holocaust did so with at least initial enthusiasm, as hostilities-only volunteers rather than as either professional soldiers or as conscripts.

The present book, however, is not about the long-suffering infantry but about the sappers, who normally enjoyed a much easier time. The Royal Engineers suffered only 2.5 per cent of the BEF's total losses on the Western Front, although they contributed some eight or nine per cent of the army's total manpower at any given time. For each infantryman at the front, therefore, there was an exceptionally high chance of becoming some sort of a casualty, sooner or later; whereas for the engineer the chance of being made casualty stood on average at around one in three.[2] The infantry itself was not unaware of this disparity, since large numbers of them were often turned out at inconvenient moments to do labouring tasks under engineer supervision – when any non-appearance of the engineer supervisors would be greeted with particularly scathing disdain. Many of the engineers also enjoyed rates of pay that were significantly higher than those of the infantry, and as Jim Sambrook's annals of the 216th (Army Troops) Company abundantly reveal, they often contrived to find comfortable billets outside the firing line, all complete with the rare luxury of plentiful firewood as well as more than a little liquid refreshment for the relaxing time which followed each day's hard work.

We should certainly not, however, dismiss the sappers as irrelevant parasites, or some sort of stodgy rear-echelon auxiliary to the main task of defeating the Kaiser's threatening hordes. On the contrary, the Royal Engineers on the Western Front played a truly crucial part in the radical modernisation of the art of war which took place within four short years. There was apparently no end to the diversity of tasks that they were called upon to undertake, which included the foundation of half a dozen innovative new arms, corps or services. Quite apart from fulfilling their traditional responsibilities such as fortification, mining and bridging – each of which was itself technically revolutionised between 1914 and 1918 – the engineers played an absolutely central part in the development of military aviation, gas warfare, the tank, field survey (and hence the accuracy of long range artillery fire), trench railways and all signals. This list includes quite as many offensive as defensive technologies, and so one should not imagine that the engineers were in any way confined to a static role. Indeed, the Australian General Monash, who had been a civil engineer before the war, once memorably quipped that the assault of an enemy defensive system under the conditions of 1917-18 was 'simply a problem of engineering'.[3]

The whole phenomenon of the Western Front was, after all, essentially a siege conducted on a scale that the great Vauban could never have imagined in even his craziest futuristic dreams (or nightmares). It was therefore natural that the Royal Engineers should play a particularly important part in it, and in the event their sheer numbers, at about one for every five infantrymen at any time, turned out to be unexpectedly gigantic. In the days of Wellington, who was an infantryman, the British army had included scarcely 3,000 engineers for roughly 90,000 infantry, making a ratio of about one in thirty.[4] Yet in the days of the cavalryman Haig it was clear that things were being arranged very differently indeed.

The engineers had traditionally always been the most scientifically-minded of all the branches of the army, and tended to enjoy the closest links with advanced civilian technologies, and even with universities. In the higher research and development of new weapons such links were obviously of very great importance; but it should also be remembered that there was a similarly strong cross-fertilisation from civilian technology at humbler levels of activity. Men transferred easily from deep coal mines to the web of relatively shallow tunnels beneath Vimy ridge or Messines. Draughtsmen who normally drew machine tools found little difficulty in designing pill boxes or accurate maps. Carpenters were at a premium for building huts or furnishing dugouts, while expert plumbers were essential for maintaining the army's water supply. We tend to think of the trenches as eternally wet places where there was never any shortage of water; but of course there had to be special provision of water that was both drinkable and readily available at the points where it was needed. It almost always created a major headache in the logistic planning for operations.

The present study of the Nuneaton engineers demonstrates that even the humblest members of the Corps were often men who had already established themselves in specialised civilian trades or skills, who could not therefore be considered as mere cannon-fodder. They constituted an 'aristocracy of labour', regardless of whether they were in or out of uniform; and they could perform invaluable services for the BEF in many fields that the relatively unskilled infantrymen normally could not master. The engineers represented a technical élite whose members were deliberately sheltered by the high command from the worst risks to life and limb, because of their scarce and precious expertise. In common with staff officers or aviators they could not be replaced easily, and so they enjoyed many privileges and even indulgences; but their contribution to victory was also commensurably high.

The 216th Company itself was composed of volunteers raised under a Kitchener scheme of early 1915,[5] after the initial enthusiasm had passed but before grinding attrition would forever change the way this war was viewed. The company was drawn almost entirely from the Nuneaton area, just as its contemporary 214th Company was drawn from Coventry and the 230th from Tottenham. This system of local recruiting ensured a strong 'family' feeling among its members, who often enjoyed the rare military privilege of living at home, still dining in their mothers' kitchens, during the first weeks of their training. They were Nuneaton artisans first and foremost, and soldiers only as an afterthought. This community of background helped them to forge a natural bond among themselves which persists among some of their offspring down to the present day. Professor Sambrook is himself the son of one of the engineers of the 216th company, and remains in touch with a number of other sons or daughters of his father's comrades.

The 'family' atmosphere surrounding the 216th Company doubtless helps explain its relatively slow accumulation of military skills and attitudes, although its relatively leisurely progress to the front was in part due to its status as a 'Fortress' or 'Army Troops' company, which meant that it was designated for use in more rearward areas. It was 'blooded' in the battles near Vimy in early 1916, and it narrowly missed the battle of the Somme soon afterwards. In 1917 it was employed on many diverse tasks in the area of Ypres. Like a fine wine, however, the length of its maturation unquestionably helped to ensure that the final product was of the highest possible quality. In the improvised last ditch defence against the high tide of the German March offensive in 1918 it so happened that the Nuneaton 216th Company formed part of Carey Force, acting as infantry, and it was Carey Force which finally held the line near Villers Bretonneux (thereby effectively winning the whole war, as was acclaimed in the House of Commons by none less than the Prime Minister himself!).

On a more strictly engineering plane, the 216th Company excelled itself during much of 1918 as an élite bridge-building organisation in the area of the Somme, first in Gough's ill-fated Fifth Army and then in Rawlinson's spearhead Fourth Army. It specialised in building the new heavy steel girder bridges that had been developed during the war, including the Hopkins bridge, direct predecessor to the more famous Bailey, which could be erected very quickly and could carry exceptionally heavy loads, such as tanks. An ample supply of these bridges was therefore essential to operations, particularly as the war became more mobile when first the Germans made a deep advance in the spring, and then the British made a still deeper counter-advance in the autumn. During all this coming and going the 216th Company was constantly called upon to build, demolish and then re-build bridges over the numerous rivers and canals that criss-crossed the whole area. Its services were of direct and timely utility to the generals in a way that could scarcely have been foreseen during training in 1915, when the company had proudly built pontoons out of wooden barrels on the ornamental lake in Buxton.

All this, and much more, is carefully catalogued in the present book. There is an excellently comprehensive appendix on the technicalities of bridging equipment – but the bulk of the text is filled with tales of trench life and trench people, as seen from a perspective that is rather different from the normal.

Notes

1. Statistics from *Abstract of Official Statistics of the military effort of the British Empire during the Great War, 1914-20* (HMSO, the War Office, London 1922)
2. 216th Company, however, would suffer at least 69 casualties during the war out of a nominal establishment of 138 (ie exactly fifty per cent).
3. Cited in P Firkins, *The Australians in Nine Wars* (Hale, London 1972), p.130.
4. Figures derived from SJ Park & GF Nafziger, *The British Military, its system and organization 1803-1815* (RAFM, Cambridge, Ontario 1983).
5. For all aspects of the 'New Army' phenomenon, see Peter Simkins, *Kitchener's Armies* (Manchester University Press, 1988).

Author's Preface

Near the end of his life, in the late 1970s, my father wrote down some reminiscences of his service with the locally-raised company of Royal Engineers during the Great War. About the same time, his friend and former comrade-in-arms, Arthur Daulman, also wrote his wartime reminiscences. Both of them consulted, as a memory aid, a diary kept between 1915 and 1919 by another friend and former comrade, Frank Hextall. My father's (unfinished) account was written not for publication but for the possible amusement of his grandchildren. Years after the deaths of all three men, when I had retired from work entirely unconnected with military history, I attempted, for my own amusement, to fill in a background to my father's reminiscences. I was not able so late in the day to find many more memorabilia of men who served in the Nuneaton Royal Engineer Company: apart from a brief diary by Sapper Walter Woodfield (now in the possession of his granddaughter, Mrs Dewell), some information about Sapper Thomas Henry Wright, communicated by his nephew, Harry Harrison, and, finally and most importantly, a cache of letters written by Sergeant Charles Streather, kept by his parents, and fortunately preserved by his daughter, Beryl Kerby. Printed sources, including newspapers and war histories, and the Company War Diary (preserved in the Public Record Office) provided useful, if patchy, additional information.

Gradually it appeared to me that this material might be sufficient to make a narrative that would interest more readers than myself. A remarkably large attendance at the unveiling in 1995 of a plaque in Nuneaton Council House to commemorate the raising of the local Royal Engineer Company eighty years earlier was evidence of considerable local interest in what, on any reckoning, is an honourable episode in the Borough's history. Though the Great War histories of a few Field Companies, R.E., have been published, and the R.E. 'Special' (i.e. Gas) Brigade and the Tunnellers have their published histories too, I am not aware of any history of an Army Troops Company, R.E., in print. The following narrative may therefore fill a small gap on military history shelves beyond the locality where the 216th (Nuneaton) Army Troops Company was raised.

This history is constructed out of partial accounts, originally written for very different audiences at different times in different styles. My father's was intended for his grandchildren; Arthur Daulman's (reproduced in typescript and deposited by him in a few libraries) was intended for a small public audience. For both men the Great War was sixty years distant and could be seen with all the ironies of hindsight; also, in both men memory was a sieve which for the most part retained the happy moments when they were free of the war machine. Frank Hextall's diary was a list of dates and places with jottings only to prompt his own memory. Charles Streather's letters home arose immediately and authoritatively from his day-to-day activities in the war; they were shaped by his happy acceptance of the responsibilities of N.C.O. rank; they were self-censored by his desire that his parents should not worry about him. The official War Diary (which the War Office required all unit commanders to keep) was a daily brief summary of the Company's work intended for the information of higher authorities, eventually to be filed and forgotten, or lost. Most of my sources are partial in another sense. My father's account was never completed; not all of Charles Streather's letters to his parents survive; the Company War Diary exists only from July 1917 onwards: Nuneaton newspapers which are full of the Company's doings for the first year of its existence mention it very little after early 1916.

A full, well-balanced history could, perhaps, have been written forty, thirty, even twenty years ago, when former members of the Company were alive. This one has been written now in the belief that it is not too late to put something on record, and in the hope that the sum of its limitations will not be a minus quantity.

I thank the following institutions for granting me access to material in their archives: the Public Record Office, the Imperial War Museum, the Royal Engineers' Library at Chatham, the Australian War Memorial, Birmingham University Library, and Nuneaton Public Library. I thank the Public Record Office for permission to quote from the War Diaries of the 216th Company, R.E. (WO95 / 484: Crown Copyright), and some other war diaries. I thank the Australian War Memorial for permission to quote from Chief Engineer War Diaries (AWM4 14 / 4, reels 334, 341). Among the staff of those and other libraries who have provided information or corrected my errors I thank Alison Gaukroger, Alan King, Maggie Magnuson, Eleanor Nannested, and Peter Simkins. I also acknowledge gratefully the help given to me by the kin of men in the Nuneaton Company: in particular, Mrs Dewell, Mrs Beryl Kerby (née Streather), Colonel H.C.B.Cook, O.B.E., Roger Daulman, J.P., Harry Harrison, Geoffrey Hextall, and Tony Parratt. My heartfelt thanks also to Harry Harrison for drawing the maps, and to Paddy Griffith, whose professionalism steered me away from at least some of the worst blunders of my amateurishness.

J.S., Southampton 1998

List of Illustrations

List of Maps

Chapter One: Nuneaton, March to August 1915

The Lord he created the Engineer,
Her Majesty's Royal Engineer,
With the rank and pay of a Sapper.

Nuneaton's Company of Royal Engineers was made not by Kipling's Lord but by Lord Kitchener, Secretary of State for War, and Alderman W.T.Bates, Mayor of Nuneaton. Nuneaton men had joined the rush in response to Kitchener's call for volunteers at the beginning of the war, so that before the end of October 1914 the number of the town's recruits to Kitchener's 'New Army' was equivalent to two battalions (including more than a thousand men who enlisted in the first week of September), but no specific 'Pals' Battalion' of infantry, similar to those raised by civic pride and patriotism in other English towns, was recruited in Nuneaton. By 1915, static trench warfare on the Western Front revealed a shortage of support units, especially artillery and engineers, so, in late January and early February, the War Office made a renewed appeal to the 'pals' battalion' sentiment by sending to local authorities up and down the country a 'shopping list' of the kinds of units now required for the Army. Nuneaton Borough Council having chosen the engineers, the Mayor was authorised (30 March 1915) to raise a company to be known as the 216th Fortress Company, Royal Engineers (Nuneaton); the Borough Council was required to provide uniforms (made by local clothing firms), feed, pay, and lodge the members of this company, but these costs would be eventually refunded by the War Office. The Mayor was given authority to nominate a Commanding Officer; his choice fell on Mr F.C.Cook, the Borough Surveyor, a willing volunteer; the Council agreed to give him leave of absence for as long as the Army needed him; the War Office granted him a temporary commission as a captain on 14 April.[1]

Similar arrangements were being made all over England in response to the War Office 'shopping list', for the 216th was only one of forty-eight Royal Engineer companies raised locally during 1915 by town councils, among them Nuneaton's near neighbours Rugby and Coventry. These companies were mostly officered by passably healthy civilian engineers who had practical experience in supervising engineering work of some kind or another. Knowledge of soldiering was to be acquired later, though Captain Cook was not devoid of military experience, for he had been a sergeant in the Territorials, also Commandant of the Nuneaton Church Lads' Brigade before 1900, and, more recently, Commandant of the Nuneaton Citizens' Training Corps.[2] He was forty years old in 1915: well above the average age for an Army captain.

At the time the Nuneaton Company was formed, the war was more than seven months old. The country had taken note of Lord Kitchener's demand for volunteers on the famous poster, with fierce eyes, tragic moustache and a peremptory gloved finger pointing directly at the poor guilty shirker, proclaiming that the army 'wants YOU', and Nuneaton's patriotic newspapers had added their shrill reinforcement. The *Nuneaton Observer*, for instance, announced the outbreak of war with the headline: 'St. George and the Dragon. Europe's United Fight against the Mad Dictator. Britain Unsheathes the Sword in a Just Cause. King and Country's Call to Nuneaton's Young Men.' Every local newspaper published a weekly 'Roll of Honour' listing names of the latest recruits. Recruiting advertisements assured Nuneaton's young men that, if they enlisted, they would command their country's gratitude after the War and be looked up to and respected because they answered their country's call. No man could win a Victoria Cross by staying away from the recruiting office. 'The Regiments at the Front are covering themselves with Glory.' 'Enter your name today on the Nation's Roll of Honour and do your part. God save the King.'[3]

The kind of glory that many men were covered in was revealed by the accompanying reports of Nuneaton men (regulars, reservists, Territorials, mostly in the Royal Warwickshire Regiment) killed and missing on active service in places whose names would become miserably familiar over the next four years. The war had not ended by Christmas 1914, as many had predicted; but the British High Command, with the notable exception of the Secretary of State for War, Earl Kitchener himself, still imagined that it would be a short contest, characterised by movement and a knock-out blow. On 22 January 1915 Sir Douglas Haig, commanding the British First Army in France, told *The Times* military correspondent that as soon as his artillery were supplied with ample ammunition 'we could walk through the German lines at several places'.[4] The generals were confident that a really strong frontal assault would bring swift victory in 1915, but in retrospect it is clear that on the Western Front, where facing lines of strongly defended trenches ran from Switzerland to the North Sea, the war had reached stalemate. The High Command were slow to realize that the struggle on the Western Front was primarily a monstrous siege operation: an engineers' war.

Nuneaton's recruiting office was in the Law Courts / Police Station building on the corner of Coton Road and Chapel Street. The recruiting officer was Major George McMullen, ex-Indian Army, 59 years old, and lodging at the Windsor Temperance Hotel; his son was serving with the Army in France.[5] There were recruiting offices also in Atherstone and Bedworth. Most men enlisted in the Royal Warwickshire Regiment, but many other units also found recruits in Nuneaton, despite the local papers' incessant complaints about 'shirkers' who would not come forward to answer the appeal of King and Country. For instance, though Arthur Daulman, Wilf Cox, and Ernie Addison came out of the recruiting office as Royal Engineers of the 216th Company, they had entered it with the intention of joining the Scottish Rifles, influenced, said Daulman, by 'the Scots uniform and jaunty headgear'.

Men too old or medically unfit for enlistment in the regular armed forces of the Crown could enrol in the Nuneaton Citizens' Training Corps and so join the million or so men in similar units up and down the country receiving instruction in musketry and drill. For youngsters, aged between 16 and 19, there was a Nuneaton Junior Citizens' Training Corps, launched in the hall of the King Edward VI Grammar School on 23 November 1914, on the motion of Charles Streather, a recent old boy, now a pupil-teacher at Queen's Road Council School. He said 'there were many youths about who, although willing and eager to join the army, were not yet old enough. In case of sudden attack these would at present be useless,

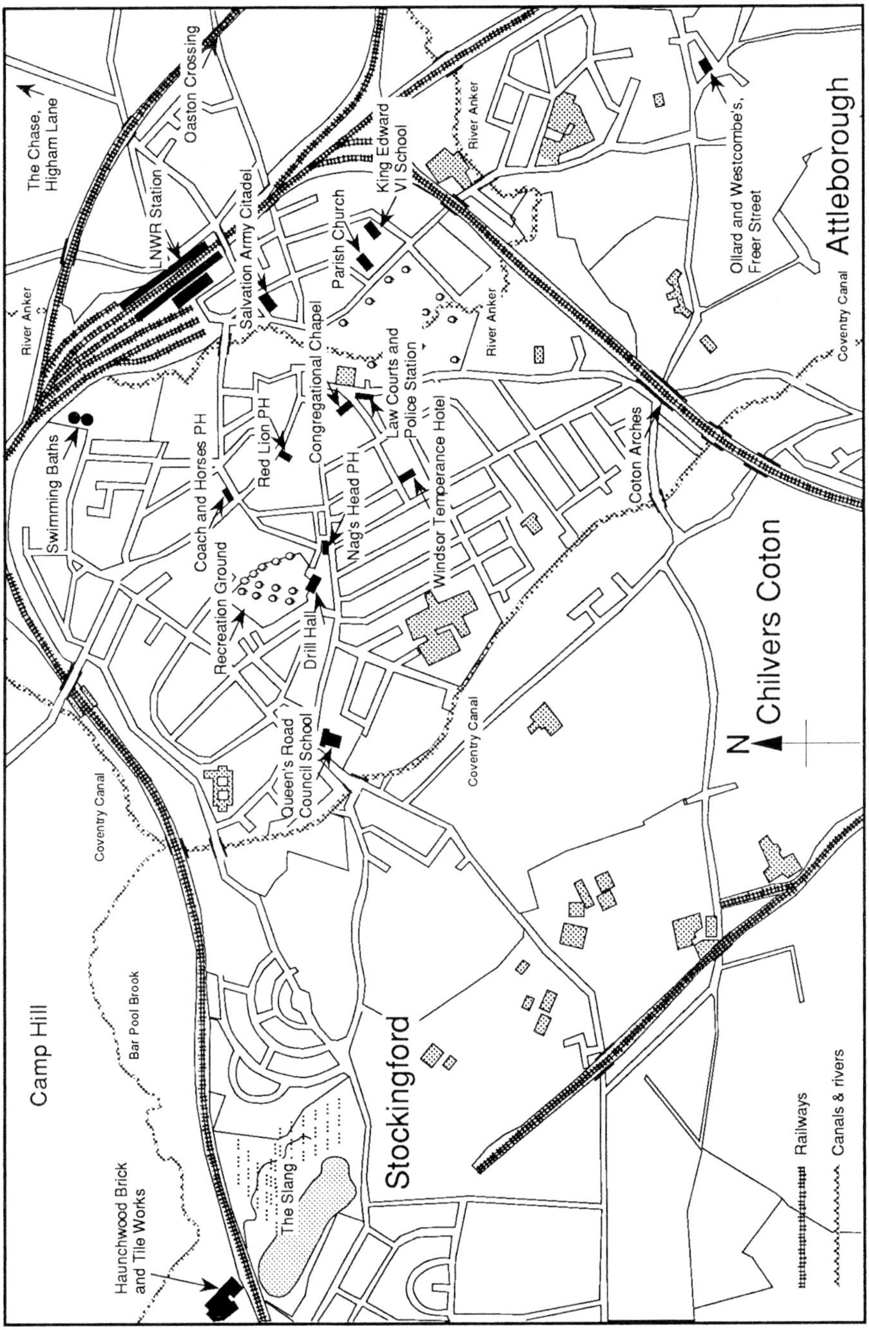

Map 1: Nuneaton

but with organisation and drilling they would soon make valuable units of defence. Again would it not be much better, not only for the army but for the recruits themselves, if by the time they were old enough to enlist, they had already become fairly proficient in their work.' Streather already had a list of nearly a hundred boys and had been promised the use of two halls and a miniature rifle range.[6] As we shall see, the age-rule for enlistment into the real army proved, in practice, to be more elastic than was assumed in the age-range of the Junior Citizens' Training Corps.

The real soldiers most plain to view in Nuneaton during the early months of the war were three regular infantry battalions belonging to the 86th Brigade (29th Division): the 2nd Royal Fusiliers, the 1st Royal Dublin Fusiliers, and the 1st Lancashire Fusiliers. They had been brought home from India to be acclimatised, presumably for France, but their eventual destination proved to be Gallipoli; they were billeted in Nuneaton from January to March 1915. Arthur Daulman recalls: 'The Dubliners were at daggers drawn, bayonets drawn would be more appropriate, with one of the other battalions and they were indeed drawn in the Red Lion pub. The fracas was only put under control with difficulty.' They were not the only ones out of control, for he also recalls that 'Alderman Melly got into trouble at this time when he drove his gig through the ranks of marching men. The air was blue and he was in danger of being tipped up. He was subsequently fined £25.'

April saw the publication of an advertisement addressed 'To the Men of Nuneaton, Atherstone, and Bedworth', signed by the Mayor and Captain Cook, announcing that 'The War Office have authorised the raising of a Local (Fortress) Company of Royal Engineers for the New (Fifth) Army. 105 Non-Commissioned Officers and men are required immediately for the following trades: Shoeing and Carriage Smiths, Drivers, Blacksmiths, Bricklayers, Carpenters, Clerks, Draughtsmen, Electricians, Engine Drivers, Fitters and Turners, Surveyors, Masons, Harness Makers, Platelayers, Plumbers, Wheelwrights.' The Mayor appealed confidently to the men of Nuneaton and district to join the Company 'and so effectively serve their King and Country in this Hour of Britain's Greatest Need. God Save the King.' The *Nuneaton Chronicle* backed this appeal with psychological speculations in an editorial on 16 April: 'Nuneaton, Bedworth and the surrounding districts have responded nobly to the Country's Call, but there are still men amongst us who have delayed to answer for reasons which can only be described as psychological. That is to say their hearts have insistently urged them to face their responsibilities as members of the glorious Empire to which they belong, but their minds have shrunk from becoming merely a numbered unit in the vast Kitchener's Army. These men have been ready and willing to defend the honour of England, but they wanted to feel they were doing something for their own friends and relatives here in Nuneaton. The opportunity now presents itself.'

The first two recruits were Sapper Joe Webster, a bricklayer, and Driver Bill Orrill; the next two were Wilf Cox and Ernie Addison, who both worked in signal-boxes at Nuneaton L.N.W.R. station; the fifth, as shown by his regimental number 92685, was Arthur Daulman, apprentice weaver at Ollard and Westcombe's factory in Freer Street, Attleborough. Daulman was a few weeks short of his seventeenth birthday, Cox was seventeen, and Addison eighteen, so they were all under the statutory minimum age of nineteen. Arthur Daulman recalled: 'First came the medical examination by Dr Nason, our family doctor, who did not spend much time on me. Then we were sworn in by the recruiting sergeant. He it was who probably had my shilling [the one the writer imagined would be given to each recruit]. At this time Capt. Cook entered and said: "Which is Daulman out of you three?" "Me sir." "How old are you?" "19." "Oh, all right." But I later found out that he had learnt that I was 16, because Mr Wells [the manager at Ollard and Westcombes] phoned down and told him. Gert Saunders in the warehouse overheard the conversation and told me. When I got back home I told my mother and father. I can't print what my father said. He had been in the old Volunteers for many years and had attended thirteen camps in Stoneleigh. He never stopped me, although he could have done.' (The 'old Volunteers' were government-funded, locally organized, units in which civilians were given military training; they were absorbed into the new Territorial Army when this was formed in 1908).

Another nineteen men joined the 216th Company, R.E. in the week to 23 April: Frank Adams, Billy Barratt, Len Brooks, Fred Duckering, Bill Higham, Charles Lathbury, Len Marriott, Fred Mobbs, Joe Moreton, Tom Norman, James Parton, Herbert Ross, Ernest Shade, Albert Taylor, Arthur Taylor, Harry Trevis, Sol Walker, John Wheway, and Alf Wiggins. The *Nuneaton Observer* praised these and the thirty other men who joined other army formations that week[7]. It made much of one in particular, proclaiming in its usual style: 'Nuneaton's manhood who interest themselves in football have a great example to follow this week. "Billy" Barratt, the famous left back of Nuneaton Town, has enlisted in the local Fortress Company of Engineers. After he has helped Nuneaton to win the shield he is going to help the British Empire win the greatest of all wars. The best tribute to "Billy" Barratt's popularity will consist in him being followed to the recruiting station by 100 men. . . . There is a glory and honour in being able to serve the nation in this the greatest crisis in history.' Nuneaton Town Football Club did, indeed, win the Birmingham Combination Shield that season. Their last match (a 5-2 victory) was at home on 1 May: Barratt scored two penalties and delivered a recruiting speech to the enthusiastic crowd at the end of the game: he said that Captain Cook had asked him to call for recruits to the Nuneaton Fortress Company and that the men especially wanted were blacksmiths, carpenters, plumbers, bricklayers, and masons[8].

On 22 April the second battle of Ypres began with a German poison-gas attack. 25 April saw the first landings at Gallipoli, when, in the space of two days, the 1st Royal Dublin Fusiliers lost all but four of their officers and over 550 men, and the other two battalions recently billeted in Nuneaton lost half their officers and over a third of their rank and file. Meanwhile, the Nuneaton Royal Engineer Company began drilling every morning and afternoon in the Drill Hall on the Recreation Ground, under Acting Sergeant Major Mitchinson (nicknamed 'John' or 'Mitch'), a regular reservist recalled to the colours at the outbreak of war. He had joined the army in 1899, entering the Royal Field Artillery; he was promoted to sergeant in 1902 and transferred to the 1st Life Guards. He was placed on the Reserve in 1909 and joined the Birmingham City Police Force. On his recall he was posted to the Warwick depot as a drill instructor, so when he joined the 216th R.E. in

April 1915 he was wearing the Royal Warwickshires cap badge. He had the unusual distinction among British soldiers of having seen the Kaiser, because, during his service in the Life Guards, he had ridden in an escort for the German Emperor as well as for several other crowned heads[9]. Arthur Daulman called him a strict disciplinarian. 'He fancied himself', said my father. It was likely to be an uneasy conjunction between this product of Edwardian military pageantry, the civilian workers and craftsmen turned soldiers now under his command, and, in France, the realities of a kind of warfare neither of the parties had ever dreamed of.

Before the middle of May another 35 local men had joined the 216th R.E. They were Cyril Anderton, Frank Arnold, Harry Ashley, John Barker, George Baxter, William Benson, John Collins, George Copson, Frank Cox, Alfred Evans, Ernie Fenn and his brother Sim, Frederick Follet, Charlie Harris, David Harrison, George ('Dick') Harvey, Frank Hextall, Sam Hollis, Allen Hughes, Harry Ludford, George ('Cubby') Marston, C.T.Montgomery, Fred Moore, Percy Phillips, Edwin Pullen, George Reader, Herbert Rees, Arthur Sambrook, Walter Shelmerdine, Fred Sherriff, Ernest Stone, Charlie Streather, Bill Toogood, Dick Townsend, and Alfred Wade. Streather had been the prime mover in the foundation of the Nuneaton Junior Citizens' Training Corps six months earlier; he was now old enough officially to join the army. The *Nuneaton Chronicle* observed happily: 'The total strength of the Company is now 61. It is satisfactory to notice that carpenters have commenced to come forward, and that six are already enrolled. Men of this trade are still required to complete the establishment, as are blacksmiths and masons. There are also vacancies for a harness maker, plasterer, slater and wheelwright. Men are being served out with uniform and equipment immediately they join, and there is every reason to believe that (with the possible exception of masons) the Company will be brought up to full strength without the necessity of an appeal outside the Nuneaton Recruiting Area.' The uniform was regulation khaki, including a soft cap with flat crown: steel helmets would not be issued for over a year. Individual equipment included a Lee Enfield rifle, back pack, leather pouches, water bottle on the right, haversack on the left, bayonet in frog also on the left, under the haversack.

One of the carpenters who had recently come forward was Arthur Sambrook. His number was 92725, indicating that he was the 45th man to join; his enlistment was recorded in the *Nuneaton Observer*'s weekly 'Roll of Honour' on 14 May, along with the names of fifteen other new recruits to the Company. The column reporting these names was headed: 'Avenge the Lusitania! Remember the Verdict — Wilful Murder against the Emperor of Germany.' Vengeance was probably far from my father's mind when, on 8 May, at the age of seventeen years and six weeks and with two years' experience as a carpenter's apprentice with the building firm of G.E. and W.Wincott (working hours 6 – 5.30 weekdays and 6 – 12 Saturdays), he went along Coton Road to call upon Major McMullen, be enlisted in the 216th R.E. and, he recalled, receive 'the Woodbine and match that McMullen presented to every accepted recruit'.

A Woodbine and a match was a poor substitute for the King's shilling, but was perhaps an appropriate induction into a war where tobacco bulked large. For

2. *Company Sergeant Major Mitchinson: Sergeant in the 1st Life Guards, 1902-1909; recalled on the outbreak of war to be drill instructor at the Royal Warwickshire depot; C.S.M. 216th Company from its formation to the end of the war.*

Band Stand: Sappers Streather, Phillips, Montgomery, Hughes, Ashley, Ludford, Cox (F), Harris, Lathbury, Marston, Marriott, Anderton, Harvey, Mobbs, Toogood, Fenn (E. H.), Reader, Harrison, Townsend, Hollis, Walker, Webster.

Second Row: Sappers Duckering, Benson, Taylor (A. J.), Stone, Wade, Higham, Baxter, Shade, Parton, Shelmerdine, Evans, Orrill, Brookes, Daulman and Barker.

Third Row: Sappers Sherriff, Cox (W. J.) Fenn (S), Arnold, 2nd Corpl. Seymour, Col. Sergt. Maj. C. G. Mitchinson, Capt. F. C. Cook, Corpl. Wheway, 2nd Corpl. Lee, Sappers Hextall, Copson, Sambrook.

Front Row (Seated): Sappers Follett, Addison, Keen, Pullin, Trevis, Adams.

3. *Early recruits to the 216th Company* Midland Daily Tribune, *31 May 1915.*

instance, the *Nuneaton Chronicle* had for some months been publicising a subscription fund for sending out parcels of what it called 'the soothing weed' to the British Army. It explained: 'The French people have been very generous to Tommy Atkins in regard to "Smokes", but Tommy dislikes their cigarettes. He says they have no "bite" in them. He longs for the British "fag".' The *Chronicle* published weekly a list of subscribers, one of whom was Captain Cook, whose five shillings would have provided twenty ounces of pipe tobacco and a hundred 'Kitchener' brand cigarettes. It also published extracts from an article in *The Lancet* upon the 'psychophysicological' benefits of smoking in allaying 'the restlessness and muscular irritability engendered by mental and physical fatigue'[10].

My father was sent to the Drill Hall in the Recreation Ground, the Company Headquarters, to see Capt Cook. On his way there he fell in with a friend who had also just enlisted; he was George Harvey (known as 'Dick'), an old Grammar-School boy and son of a local pawnbroker; before enlistment he was the articled pupil of a Nuneaton architect. The two lads were kitted out together with uniforms and equipment, for though the earliest members of the Company had at first drilled wearing their own clothes, uniforms and kit were now available; these were in the charge of John Wheway, promoted to corporal, as quartermaster. C.S.M. Mitchinson came into the stores while the latest recruits were there and did not like the way Harvey and Sambrook were lounging about, 'judging from his very impolite remarks when he welcomed us to the army', said my father.

The only other N.C.O.s in the Company at that time were two regular R.E. 2nd corporals (a rank peculiar to the Royal Engineers, intermediate between lance corporal and corporal) named Lee and Seymour. When the Company came to full strength both men were promoted to sergeant, as, too, was Wheway; at the same time a number of sappers became lance corporals. Lee had charge of numbers 1 and 2 sections, constituting the right half-company, and Seymour numbers 3 and 4 sections, constituting the left half-company; there was also a headquarters section, which included company headquarters and (still to arrive) the company's, mostly horsed, transport. Seymour had been in France in 1914 but was sent home with shell shock. He was 'stout and amiable' and 'a bit of a lad', said my father. A group photograph (illustration 3), published in the *Midland Daily Tribune*, miscaptioned '215th Company', portrays Captain Cook, flanked by his four N.C.O.s and 51 of the 60 or more local men who had joined by 14 May, all described as sappers though some, we know, were pioneers or drivers.

The group photograph shows a Sapper William Keen who does not figure in the Nuneaton newspaper 'Rolls of Honour'. Later recruits listed in those rolls down to 11 June are named as: Percy Bailey, William Berry, Fred Bott, John Brunt, Tom Burdett, Cecil Capet, Alf Chamberlain, Mike Cuffe, Dennis Douglas, William Dyer, Fred Earp, George Harris, Isaac Jackson, Samuel Kinsey, George Lago, George Lowndes, Frank Moore, Enderby Parratt, Albert Reynolds, Bill Rogers, Roland Shepherd, Frank E.Smith, Emanuel Taylor, Albert Thomas, Samuel Ward, Arthur Walters, Jack Williams, Walter Woodfield, and Thomas Wright: twenty-seven in four weeks. William Keen, Cuffe, Lago, and Shepherd, like Baxter and Follett before them, came from Tamworth and thus were not strictly local men. Dodds the boxer, subject of an anecdote to come, also enlisted, though his name seems not to have been printed in the newspapers.

Sapper Jack Williams's enlistment was remembered by his comrades. The Company was about to march off to attend a military funeral in Nuneaton Parish Church when, as Arthur Daulman recalled, Williams 'appeared on the scene obviously the worse for drink. He had come from the Police Station where he had been to attest, that is, to join up. It was early days and we probably wanted to make a bit of a show, so an angry sergeant-major greeted him menacingly with "I'll see you in the morning". The confrontation took place the following morning, the sergeant-major opening with "We tame lions in the army". "We eat the buggers where I come from" came the reply. They both came from Brummagem and were never the best of friends after that.'

The *Nuneaton Observer* on 28 May noted a preponderance of married men among recent recruits and complained that the single men of the town were not doing their duty: 'Unless they quickly rally to the Colours they will have justified the title of "slackers"'. On 11 June it put its journalistic weight behind a forthcoming great demonstration in Riversley Park by women who had relatives at the war or in training. 'Rich and poor alike will take part in the event'. It is hoped that this will 'shame the slackers' and persuade them to join up. 'A gigantic British army would strike terror into the Germans.' In the same issue it was able to report that the strength of the 216th (Fortress) Company, R.E., was 86 (exclusive of officers) and that there were vacancies for only sixteen more men: 'Five masons are wanted, and also a harness-maker and a few carpenters'. Two weeks later the Company was still ten men short and Captain Cook made a personal appeal in the newspapers' correspondence columns. He explained that it would be easy to fill these vacancies from other districts, but he wanted local men: 'It would be a sorry task to have to appeal personally to young men to fulfil what is surely a patriotic obligation, and I earnestly hope that this week end will see the Company brought up to full strength by the enlistment of the men we want, viz. Nuneaton men'. As masons were thin on the ground in Nuneaton he would happily take bricklayers instead. This last push recruited Sappers J.Briddon, C.E.Elsworth, C.Freeman, Harry Holt, R.Poulton, and J.E.Sewell, and Driver F.C.Toogood

By now Captain Cook had the services of two newly commissioned second-lieutenants, named Knox and Smith. Kenneth Knox, 31 years old, well-built and over six feet tall, was the son of Jimmy Knox, director of the Haunchwood Brick and Tile Company, who lived in some style in a large house, 'The Chase', on the edge of the town in Higham Lane. Six sons of this family became army officers in the Great War. At the outbreak of the war Kenneth and his brother Cecil were working as engineers on railway construction in Alberta; both men came home and enlisted in different companies of Royal Engineers. Cecil went on to win the Victoria Cross and Kenneth the Military Cross; both survived the war. Their eldest brother, James, a veteran of the South African War, was to rise to the rank of Lieutenant Colonel in the Royal Warwickshire Regiment and win the D.S.O. before being killed in France. Ronald, the last of the brothers to be commissioned and the first to die, was killed in France in December 1915 with a tunnelling company of

Royal Engineers. Two other brothers also joined the armed services and, like Kenneth and Cecil, came back from the war alive.

Lieutenant Harry Foster Smith had a more sheltered background than Kenneth Knox, for he came to the Nuneaton Company direct from Birmingham University Officer Training Corps. He had entered the University in 1913, from Birmingham Municipal Technical School, and begun a non-degree course in Engineering, which he broke off after a year and a half in order to join the army; he was commissioned on 29 May 1915, aged 21. Arthur Daulman writes that he 'was rumoured to be the son of Gypsy Smith, a noted reverend [fortune-teller]. He had a sallow complexion which was perhaps his only link with the gypsies. In contrast to Knox he was quiet and reserved and held Cook in great awe. There was no coming in early from work no matter what the conditions were like when Smith was in charge, so great was his fear of what Cook might say. Coming back from a route march he fainted in front of Dr Nason's in the High Street. Knox, coming in cold and wet in France, was told that Cook wanted to see him straight away. He replied "I'll come when I'm ready" and went to change and bath.'

There is no reason to suppose that the officers of the 216th R.E. were unpopular, but they do not figure largely in the recollections of their men. The sapper took his orders from and occasionally joked with his section sergeant: officers belonged to a distinct and different social class. All three officers would have spent some considerable time away from Nuneaton, receiving technical instruction in military engineering, horsemanship, and drill on short courses at the old R.E. training centre at Chatham or the one newly established at Newark.

Even so, the two young lieutenants at first joined the men in the physical training, marching, and drill that was intended to transform a group of civilian craftsmen and apprentices into soldiers. Initial basic military training included such essential skills as saluting, standing to attention, forming a straight line on parade, turning by numbers, and wheeling from line into a column of fours for route marching: skills to which many members of the company who had been Boy Scouts (e.g. Frank Adams and Frank Hextall), or members of the Church Lads' Brigade (e.g. Addison, Daulman, Wilf Cox, and the two Fenn brothers) or the Junior Citizens' Training Corps (which Charles Streather helped to set up in Nuneaton) were no strangers. Men with experience of such typical Edwardian embodiments of smartness, good order, discipline, patriotism, and respect for the established social order were put in key positions on the flanks during squad and company drill, which was carried out (or, as my father preferred to say, 'muddled through') on the recreation ground beside the Drill Hall. Arthur Daulman was struck by the fact that 'much of the drill came from the Boer War experience'.

The local newspapers never tired of praising the smartness of the company in the hands of their 'popular' sergeant-major, but my father was not so sure that his comrades came up to scratch. He recalls that C.S.M. Mitchinson 'presided over all these outdoor shows with the idea in his head that we could equal the Guards in smartness and precision, but we never did, no one else wanted to. After six weeks our square bashing was over. We had passed out after a brilliant display and an inspection. I think it was more likely John and the two other N.C.O.s were weary of shouting and having to watch our performance. We ourselves were weary of going through such silly evolutions as "At the halt on the left form platoon", carried out from columns of fours. This particularly out-of-date movement was satirized in a part-song popular in canteens and places where they sing. Sung to the tune of "Three Cheers for the Red White and Blue", it went: "At the halt on the left form platoon, At the halt, etc. If the odd numbers don't mark time two paces, How the hell can the rest form platoon." In our case, if the even numbers and the right flank came round running we made some sort of a show. Actually, apart from forming fours, about turning, turning right and left, this platoon business was our best performance; the other evolutions in Caesar's drill manual had to be seen to be believed, and even John could not believe while he was watching them.' So much for squad and company drill.

My father also recalls: 'Sometimes we were lectured by Mitch on the behaviour and smartness expected from a crack corps, but on looking round on the ill-fitting khaki uniforms we wore his exhortation did not carry much weight. As these lectures went on we began to wonder if we were in the Household Cavalry instead of the Royal Engineers. The only degree of smartness we could practise was brought about by the use of a button stick and polish on buttons and cap badge.' In the matter of personal smartness the veterans of the Church Lads' Brigade had an advantage of course. Pioneer Daulman 'never had any trouble, for example, putting on puttees and arranging them smartly, as some did'. He 'had done it so often before. The trick was to put a half twist in the puttee which prevented a loop in the back. To pull them tight was to invite varicose veins,' he recalled.

Physical training, including exercises on the vaulting horse and varied sometimes by a three-mile run, was supervised by C.S.M. Mitchinson. There were regular bathing parades to the Corporation swimming baths. The War Office manual of Royal Engineer training stipulated that 'manly games are of value', especially if 'so arranged that all, and not only selected teams, take their part'[11]. This was the principle enshrined in C.S.M.Mitchinson's speciality, the boxing parade. My father recalls that 'the company was formed up in two equal ranks, facing inwards. "John" produced two pairs of boxing gloves, which were donned by the first opposite chaps and then they sparred and punched for three minutes, and so on until everyone had taken his turn. Any man who in John's opinion was not making a proper effort, he took on himself for three minutes. Such a case occurred in the match Dodds v "Cubby" Marston. Dodds was an amateur middleweight of some local renown, about 25 years of age. Cubby was 48 years old and had no idea of punching anyone. Dodds just sparred round and contented himself with tapping Cubby's gloves. Cubby thought that was real boxing and did the same until John in disgust bellowed out "Get stuck into each other you pair of cripples" and stopped the round, saying "I'll show you what boxing is, Dodds". When John put on Cubby's gloves the rest of us began to take some interest. The round started by John putting his face forward, dancing about from side to side, and saying "See if you can hit that Dodds". This was John's usual technique, moving his head out of the way, and evading his opponent's blows. "Easy", replied Dodds: "How's that?", delivering a punch which made the sergeant-major wipe his nose. "That's luck", said John and held his face out again. "That's asking for it", replied Dodds, connecting with another hefty punch, and then they both set to in earnest. John got a good dusting. When the bout was ended Mitch said "I see what you mean Dodds". Thereafter the boxing gloves seem to have been mislaid and we had no more boxing sessions.'

The sergeant-major also sportingly turned out for the cricket eleven captained by Sapper Streather. One day, combining business with pleasure, the company route-marched to the Butts ground in Coventry for the cricket team to play the local Coventry Royal Engineers company, and then marched back. The 216th R.E. cricketers were good enough to defeat all local Nuneaton competition and win the F.C.Payne cup, but met more than their match when Gilbert Jessop, the England and Gloucestershire player (famed for scoring the fastest ever first-class century), brought to Nuneaton a side drawn from his battalion of the Manchester Regiment, then stationed at Lichfield. The Nuneaton company were all out for 44 (Jessop 7 for 23); the Manchesters passed this total for the loss of one wicket and then went on to make 215 for 8. Jessop scored 68 in next to no time before being caught at deep cover by Charlie Streather: 'the old Grammar School boy doing a little somersault, evidently proud of the honour in bringing about the downfall of one of England's greatest cricketers'[12]. Jessop's side consisted almost entirely of officers, including a lieutenant-colonel; there were no officers in the 216 R.E.'s eleven. The Gentlemen beat the (sort of) Players.

All through their initial training in Nuneaton the local men lived each day partly under military discipline and partly at home, as if civilians. This was the general case with locally raised units: it was an expedient forced upon a War Office which did not have enough camps to cope with the flood of volunteers to an unprecedentedly large army, but it had the valuable side effect of giving the local community a visible share in a common patriotic duty. On a typical day the newly-enlisted sapper might report to the Drill Hall at 0700 hours in canvas shoes for P.T. until 0830, go home for breakfast, come back on parade to spend the rest of the morning on squad and company drill and general infantry training, go home for dinner, come back for afternoon exercises in a range of skills from the judging of distances outdoors, when dry, to the tying of knots indoors, when wet, then home for tea. For meals at home there was a ration allowance of 1s.2d. a day. In the later stages of training there were route marches, progressively increasing from five or six miles to twelve or thirteen, and eventually more than twenty. The company also learned the all-important skill of trench-digging, though not in quite the conditions they were to experience in France. My father recalls: 'We spent hours in front of the parapets, lifting turfs from the ground in front to mask the earth dug and thrown out of the trench. Cook, Knox, and Smith went up the slope facing to see if these defences were concealed.' The *Nuneaton Chronicle* of 6 August tells us more of these earthworks, which were laid out on five acres in the Slang, near Haunchwood Brick Works, made available by Lieutenant Knox's father and 'supposed to be dominated by an enemy advancing from Camp Hill'. The trenches, *Chronicle* readers were told, 'were planned on the actual models used at the memorable Battle of the Aisne, and constituted splendid examples of skill, the works including a redoubt, machine-gun emplacements, and every detail made familiar to present-day readers of newspapers.' We can be sure they were full-sized too, because the Engineer Training manual declared sternly: 'The making of works on reduced scales is forbidden'[13].

In all these activities the civilian world was very close. Nuneaton townsfolk turned out to watch their sons, husbands, and fathers carrying out their drill and physical jerks on the recreation ground, and on fine Sunday evenings inspected and admired the trenches at Haunchwood. When the Company was fallen out for a breather during drill the older men would go to the Nag's Head, the nearest pub to the recreation ground, for a pint, while the youngsters (such as Pioneers Daulman, Hextall, and Sambrook) would repair to a cafe on the corner of Queen's Road (where Clarke's the greengrocer stood later) for a glass of pop with a dollop of ice-cream in it.

The proximity of public houses imposed problems of discipline. Arthur Daulman recalled an episode very early in the Company's history, when C.S.M. Mitchinson was their only N.C.O.: 'It was Saturday morning and we were on parade on the rec. when Joe Webster, bricklayer, and George Harris, plasterer, appeared in a very merry state. They had been detailed to squeezee the Drill Hall but had gone off leaving their tunics and caps behind. At this time public houses were open all day and they found their way to the Coach and Horses. In this dishevelled state they appeared to the amusement and anticipation of most of us. "Fall in two men" was the order and the culprits were marched to the clink. The clink was alongside the Drill Hall. The billiard room was the Orderly Room, another room was the Q.M. stores, and the third, where the culprits were locked, contained miscellaneous items including pancheons[14]. Harry Ashley, no stripes, was in charge, probably because he had had service in the Volunteers. It was not long before the culprits needed to go to the toilet and the conversation went like this. "Let us aht, 'arry." "I daren't." A little while and the pathetic request came once more with the same reply. This time some extra information was added, namely: "If you don't let us 'aht I'll piss in the pancheons." What happened then I never found out, but the pancheons were used for oatmeal water which was the drink after route marches.'

The shortage of stripes in the Company was soon remedied, for during the training period in Nuneaton seventeen sappers were promoted. They were Corporal Albert John Taylor, 2nd Corporals Ashley, Barker, Duckering, Marriott, Mobbs, and Streather, and Lance Corporals Berry, Copson, Frank Cox, Charles Harris, William Keen, Shade, Shelmerdine, Stone, William Toogood, and Wiggins. Not all of them were to keep their stripes.

Route marches in full equipment took the Company over every road within a twenty mile radius at one time or another, always accompanied by a band playing instruments on loan from the Chilvers Coton Company of the Church Lads' Brigade. The bandsmen were Frank Hextall, big drum, Ernie Fenn, Sim Fenn, Wilf Cox, and Edwin Pullen, side drums, Frank Adams, Arthur Daulman, Fred Mobbs, and Bill Ross, bugles. Pullen had been a Salvation Army bandsman and Mobbs had played in a brass band; the others had played in the bands of the Boy Scouts or the Church Lads' Brigade. They were paid two shillings a week for this extra duty.

Daulman recalled that they led the Company every Sunday to Nuneaton Parish Church for church parade: 'L/Cpl. Mobbs gallantly volunteered to look after the drums stacked outside, although the drums had never been known to run away. We others trooped in.' Also: 'We headed the company on route marches and coming back under Coton Arches we really let it rip, as the sound was magnified and really impressive. But Nuneaton horses, and there was plenty about in those days, didn't think much of it and showed signs of hurrying away, so we and the horses had to be restrained. At the end Capt. Cook would say "Well done the band".'

'On one occasion', says Daulman, 'our route march took us well beyond Atherstone, where we fell out for our mid-day break. . . . we came back with Frank Hextall, the big drummer, leaving the straps behind on the road side, nowhere in particular, in no-man's-land sort of style. He must have carried the drum on his own for he said nothing to anyone. From time to time the sergeant-major would say two more for the drum, thus allowing relief for the big drummer. Frank, when he got home, mounted his bike, rode back, and found the straps; otherwise there would have been quite a rumpus, with Frank looking quite a bit foolish.'

The buglers were occasionally detailed off to play at military funerals and memorial services in and around Nuneaton; so, with plenty of practice, they perfected their rendering of 'The Last Post'. There were incidental benefits from this duty. Daulman recalls that, after one funeral that Adams, Mobbs, and he were ordered to attend, they found themselves in an Atherstone pub, and Fred Mobbs 'sat down at the piano and in five minutes the top of the piano was covered in half pints. Frank and I, being youngsters, only drank lemonade. At last, back home by train, helping the L/Cpl. who had imbibed too freely. The following day L/Cpl. Mobbs remarked "I could do with a funeral like that every day".'

The *Nuneaton Observer* of 9 July paid tribute to Lance-Corporal Mobbs's talent as a comedian when, in the report of smoking concert at Nuneaton Liberal Club, it called him 'the "K'nut" of the company'. This concert, its programme arranged by Corporal Wheway and the room 'tastefully decorated by a fatigue party of the company', was a farewell celebration. Another was a tea party at the palatial house and gardens of Councillor Grant on the Foleshill Road. The company marched there and back, singing, the *Observer* would have us believe, 'When Irish eyes are smiling' and 'It's a long way to Tipperary'. As it was raining, the men had tea in the nearby public hall and 'various arbours in the gardens, while the officers assembled in the house'. 'Every visitor was presented with a packet of cigarettes, containing a silk flag and also a picture card. The latter contained either the figure of Lord Kitchener or Sir John French, woven in silk. The cards and badges were all made at Councillor Grant's factory.'[15]

The last Nuneaton church parade was on 8 August, the sermon being fully reported in the *Nuneaton Chronicle* on the following Friday (the 13th). On the morning of 9 August the company marched from the Drill Hall to Trent Valley L.N.W.R. station, where they were seen off by the Mayor, other prominent citizens, cheering crowds, and the strains of 'Auld Land Syne' played by the Borough band. One small sourness was that the L.N.W.R. authorities compelled those members of the crowd who went onto the station platforms for the farewells to buy platform tickets.[16] Another sour note was recalled by Arthur Daulman, who writes that Major McMullen, the recruiting officer, 'came to see us off from the rec., where we were drawn up, column of route, for the station. He came, he said, to wish us "Bon Voyage" and added "Some of you will come back and some of you will not come back. I know some of you will not come back." We felt that he was speaking the truth at the wrong moment.' On the station platform the Commandant of the Nuneaton Junior Citizens' training Corps (Mr W.W.Day, science master at the Grammar School) presented a wristlet watch to Lance Corporal Streather in recognition of his part in founding the Corps. 'In the train', says Daulman, 'Hextall and Adams, ex-scouts and Vicarage Street pupils, were singing "To Portsmouth To Portsmouth It is a gallant town..." and so on. But I didn't join in. I just didn't feel like it.'

We learn from newspaper reports of the farewell celebrations that Major McMullen gave every man a packet of cigarettes and that further supplies were handed round by the Mayoress and other important ladies 'so that none of the men would be without the wherewithal to indulge in the soothing weed during their lengthy journey'. The same report also tells us that the 216th R.E. now had a mascot, in the shape of 'a handsome Dalmatian dog' that had once followed the Dublin Fusiliers around Nuneaton when they were billeted in the town the year before.[17] The Fusiliers themselves were still pinned down at Gallipoli no more than four miles from their April landing places; on the night of 6-7 August the Dublins and Lancashires suffered a further 240 casualties between them. By this time the accumulated casualties on both sides at Gallipoli amounted to well over half a million, or more than fifty percent of the forces engaged. In France, where the fighting had been less severe over the previous few months, casualties amounted to about half that figure for a shift of nowhere more than three miles in the front lines.

All the Nuneaton newspapers reported the departure of the 216th Company as a scene of great rejoicing, but the *Observer* (13 August), unsettlingly reminded its readers of the slaughter, while simultaneously expressing an optimism that seems fatuous only in hindsight: 'the Royal Engineers left the town amidst general enthusiasm. The "Blue Sky School"[18] were in the ascendancy. The people had lived through twelve months of war, had learned of its worst and most diabolical features, and had fortified themselves against every conceivable phase. Even the awful stupendity of death had been almost swallowed up in the enormity of numbers. Only the closely related felt the sorrow of a loved one's passage into the unknown. The aggregate of killed only feebly impressed the mass of the population. A host of maimed soldiers, an unlimited amount of pain and suffering — these things were regarded with a sort of complacency as the inevitable result of the struggle! Therefore, why be sad when more khaki-clad boys were going into the fray. The contest was a righteous and honourable one, and there was joy in righteousness and honour! Besides, the British nation had seen the worst of the war, the turning point had been reached. Those inhuman Germans were going to be smashed up by "Kitchener's surprise".'

Chapter Two:
Cosham and Buxton, August 1915 to January 1916

The Company's destination on 9 August was Cosham, near Portsmouth. They arrived there a little after 5 p.m. and marched two miles uphill to Farlington Redoubt on the heights overlooking Portsmouth and Langstone Harbours. An advance party, consisting of Quartermaster-Sergeant Wheway and eight men, had preceded them by two days to prepare for their reception and accommodation in bell tents on the hill where the redoubt stood. Their tents were a few yards from a deep dry ditch, thirty feet wide and thirty feet deep, with barricaded blockhouses (casemates) sited at the bottom where they could enfilade the ditch: an impressive example of military engineering from the early Victorian era.

Here the Nuneaton men were introduced to Army food. Arthur Daulman remembers his first meal: 'At the head of the table was a large enamel bowl and a piece of fatty meat was put on my plate by someone using his fingers. Down came the plate, but as I had never been given fatty meat to eat I couldn't eat anything. Then followed the tea in a greasy bowl drawn from a greasy dixie. I got up, walked out into the canteen, where I bought biscuits, Fry's chocolate, of which I was very fond, and tea. My first meal away from home. Not really a meal for a warrior.' Accommodation was no more satisfactory. There were only five tents for the 105-strong company, making 21 men per tent, and the tents were designed to accommodate only 8, so the men slept like sardines, unable to turn once they had got down.

A Territorial company, the Hampshire Mounted Company of Royal Engineers was also camped at Farlington Redoubt. Their food seemed more attractive in Pioneer Daulman's eyes, though evidently they did not care for it: 'They were throwing whole trays of cottage pies away when we had our tongues hanging out'. They were objects of envy to the Nuneaton buglers also, as my father remembers, because their various calls were sounded on trumpets, not bugles. They also indirectly contributed to the excitement of Daulman's first guard-duty: 'I was on from midnight to two o'clock and after a period of time there was a noise of chains rattling through the silence and loneliness of the night. I was at first perturbed, then I got the wind up, but there was nothing I could do in the dark but warn my relief of the incident. It turned out at daybreak to be the goat mascot of the Hampshire Terriers R.E.s, fastened by a chain to a stake.'

On other nights the Nuneaton men's rest was disturbed by aeroplanes and searchlights, according to a letter home from Sapper Frank Arnold, printed in the *Midland Counties Tribune* on 13 August; Arnold, evidently a less picky eater than Daulman, also noted that the food was good. Probably only morale-boosting letters found their way into print: an impression confirmed by Sapper Joe Smith, former employee of the *Nuneaton Observer*, whose rosy 'pen picture' of army food and service life in general, printed in that newspaper on 20 August, would have done credit to any conventional war correspondent of the day: 'If ever a man had any qualms of joining the British Army surely they would be dispelled by the treatment meted out to the men of the local R.E. Co. . . . Certainly men were never fed better. . . . Some of the men of the local Co. complained of their loss of weight and how their waist lines had diminished during the preliminary training at Nuneaton, but since we left there the complaint has chiefly been of the waist line growing too big and the clothing too small. . . . Reveille is generally at 5.30, but before that hour many of the men are astir and starting on their daily round of work. The early morning cup of coffee is always welcome, and after the physical drill the men wait anxiously for breakfast. . . . Breakfast over, drills are tackled with renewed vigour, and again at dinner time the men flock round eagerly for the good things provided. Afternoon drills are a pleasure when one has such a feeling round the belt, and tea comes with a sort of gladness. . . . Drills are now undertaken that were not possible at Nuneaton, and the progress made has been a source of delight both to the Co. officers and men. . . . One little item is the humour of the men in the names they have given to their tents, a sample being as follows :— "The Plasterer's Rest and Bricklayer's Arms", "The Ritz", "Watford Abbey Street Hotel", "The Home of Contentment", "The Abode of Love", "The Knuts' Home". Those at home who are anxious about the welfare of sons, husbands, fathers, or brothers need have no fear, for never were men being better treated. The menus are something like this:— Breakfast: Tea, bread, butter, bacon and tomatoes. Dinner: Roast beef or meat pie, potatoes, cabbage or butter beans. Tea: Bread and butter, jam or marmalade, and tea. Certainly this would whet the appetite of any man, and if one could see the looks of the men after every meal there would be no need for any apprehension.'

The 216th Company drivers were issued with spurs on arrival in Cosham; the horses and mules appeared later; so, until they did, C.S.M. Mitchinson, coming into his own as an ex-cavalryman, trained them in the horse lines of the Hampshire Company. Other training was in fieldworks, trenching, and wiring. A notebook kept by 2nd Cpl Streather at this time survives (see illustration 5). It contains many pages of notes on such matters as the siting of trenches, the construction of revetments (i.e. retaining walls for earthworks, especially for the sides of trenches), the making of head cover, overhead cover, and loopholes, and the cutting of brushwood. Brushwood is evidently a staple material. It is tied into long, tight bundles to make fascines (used in road-making, the draining of trenches, and revetments); and it is woven into hurdles (for temporary roadways, hutting, and revetments) and into gabions (cylinders open at both ends, to be filled with earth and used in revetments). Detailed notes on the making of these devices suggest that military engineering still drew to some extent upon peaceful traditional rural crafts, albeit for unpeaceful purposes. For instance there are instructions for felling trees, but here the felled trees are to be formed into an abatis (i.e. an obstacle of felled trees and branches picketed to the ground, with their points towards the enemy, and festooned with barbed wire) upon which Streather notes that it 'is a very useful obstacle in savage warfare but is liable to be set on fire by artillery fire'. We do not hear of the 216th Company making an abatis in France, but Streather, as a N.C.O., would have made considerable use of his far more copious notes on the drill for making barbed-wire entanglements of various patterns.

If one was not on guard duty, the evenings were passed at Cosham or Havant nearby, or scrumping in the spinneys and hedges around Waterlooville to supplement an Army diet that did not please everyone as much as it pleased Sapper Joe Smith. Rations and candles and fodder for the animals were drawn from Portsmouth, six miles away, making a pleasant day's break from routine for a ration party consisting of a lance-corporal and two pioneers with a G.S. (General Service) wagon, drawn by two horses or two mules: never horse and mule together. On Saturday afternoons and Sundays it was possible to walk into Portsmouth and Southsea for tea and other amusements. Washing was taken to civilians in Bedhampton. Everyone was inoculated against typhoid. For haircuts the men went to the company drivers, with their horse-clippers. The weather was sunny and hot, with a few thunderstorms. Back in Nuneaton the Borough Council, which had met the initial costs of raising the Company, was reimbursed and thanked by the War Office on 8 September.

On 9 September the Company left Cosham for Buxton, travelling by train of course, and passing close to home on the Midland line from Leicester. They arrived very late; policemen with oil lamps conducted them through dark streets to their billets. Arthur Daulman said of his arrival: 'Standing on the dark platform it seemed like fairy land with the glittering lights up in the air from a large hotel. I found out later it was the Palace Hotel.' Though zeppelins had carried out raids over the Midlands as early as January 1915, it would seem that Buxton hoteliers did not observe a blackout.

Since November 1914 Buxton had been one of the main training depots for the Royal Engineers; it catered for a shifting population of about 1,400 trainees. The provision of billets for so many men was welcomed as 'a boom and a boon' to the lodging-house keepers. How much of a boon is shown by the published billeting allowances, per man, per diem: 'Lodging and attendance, ninepence; Breakfast (6 oz. bread, 1 pint tea, milk, and sugar, 4 oz. bacon) sevenpence halfpenny; Hot dinner (1 lb. meat previous to being dressed, 8 oz. bread, 8 oz. potatoes, 1 pint beer or mineral water) one shilling and sevenpence halfpenny; Supper (6 oz. bread, 1 pint tea, milk, and sugar, 2 oz. cheese)'.[1] The total allowance was nearly three times what was paid when the men were eating and sleeping at home in Nuneaton, but this was Buxton, and the diet actually provided was mercifully more varied than the official scale demanded.

The 216th Company was at first billeted in private houses in the Higher Buxton and Fairfield part of the town. The two youngsters, Daulman and Sambrook, were with a Mr & Mrs Morris, their two daughters and a son-in-law, at Nunfield Road, Higher Buxton. Arthur Daulman says that they lived like lords: 'The old lady who looked after us was a good cook and I still remember her lovely jam and apple tarts'. My father writes of Mr Morris: 'He was a costermonger[2] and went to Sheffield for his stock every Wednesday and invariably arrived back drunk, and Wednesday evening he spent sleeping off the effects. Mrs M. was out every night and usually returned home merry. They both patronized different "locals". It was comfortable, and a cheerful atmosphere most of the time, and the food was good and plentiful.' Daulman was moved elsewhere after three weeks, to the disappointment of the younger daughter, about twenty years old, who wanted to be taken out every evening: he says that she was 'nice looking' and that my father 'took her to the opera house one night where they were performing an opera but she ditched him for someone else, though Arthur had paid'. However, it was more probably the requirements of the army than a broken heart, which made my father move to a billet in Highfield Road, where he shared first with Sherriff; then after a fortnight of being on his own was joined by a new member of the company, named C.H.Douglas, who, says my father 'had returned to England after some years in Canada. He was a surveyor by profession and had been working with the Canadian Pacific Railway on a track through the Rocky Mountains and British Columbia. We got on very well together and were friends throughout the war.'

After a month all the men, except the drivers, who had to be close to their animals, were found billets together in the Grosvenor and Kensington hotels on Broad Walk. The sergeants' mess was in a ground-floor front room of the Grosvenor, the kitchens were at the back of the hotel at the end of a long corridor. The mess servant was a fat man named Harry Holt. The room opposite the sergeants' mess was occupied by some of the rank and file as a billet. My father tells that the occupants of this billet 'picked up a bell similar to the one used by the sergeants when they wanted to summon Holt, and between the two bell-ringers Holt was running backwards and forwards quite a lot. When he entered the mess in answer to a false call the Sergt Major cursed him and told him to keep out until he was wanted. Holt's assertions that the bell had been rung were disbelieved at first, but after some time Holt's frequent appearances and his annoyance at his reception on his unauthorized entries, convinced the mess that someone was playing a game. The bell was hidden behind the soot plate in the chimney of the room. Despite searches of the opposite billet and adjacent rooms, neither Mitch nor Holt found out who was working the ghost bell until we were in the train from Le Havre to Rouen, when we were seen ringing for Holt from our Hommes 40'[3].

Another of my father's stories concerns a group of sappers coming home one night to the Grosvenor. Passing through the back yard, 'we found the kitchen window was open and a large freshly cooked ham was placed to cool on the window sill. The passage was scouted and the kitchen was deserted, so the ham was lifted from the dish and safely bestowed at the back of the soot plate, wrapped in the News of the World. Soon after, Alfred Wiggins, the cook, came round the various rooms enquiring if anyone had seen a ham. He said it was [Quartermaster-Sergeant] Wheway's birthday, and he had acquired the ham for a party in the sergeants' mess. Wiggins said he had been boiling the ham all afternoon, and when it was cooked had put it in the open window to cool. He had gone away for a short time and when he got back "There it was: gone". Our beds and other kit were ransacked during our absence on duty for weeks afterwards, but no one ever found out what happened except the persons who took it.'

The *Buxton Advertiser* noted that 'the fine fellows upon whose shoulders are the letters R.E.', when not on duty, 'have plenty of places open for their use: the churches and chapels having placed reading and recreation rooms at their disposal' (28 November 1914). Such places do not figure in the recollections of the 216th Company, but my father remembers that they were given free admission to the thermal baths under St.Ann's Hotel, where sufferers from rheumatism went for relief: 'one was big enough for a swimming bath and was pleasant on a snowy and frosty afternoon'.

At some distance from these comforts, 800,000 Allied troops went into action on 25 September, the British on the left attacking Loos, the French on the right attempting to storm Vimy Ridge. When the great autumn offensive duly ran out of steam and blood there was little to show for half a million Allied and German casualties apart from the writing on the wall for Sir John French, the British Commander in Chief. At the end of the year he was replaced by Sir Douglas Haig in a kind of palace revolution: Haig having repeatedly expressed well-justified doubts about French's competence in private letters to King George V.

The 216th Company learned how to erect barrel-pier bridges (resting on barrels which floated upon the water) and pontoon bridges on the calm ornamental waters of a lake in Buxton Pavilion Gardens. From photographs reproduced in the Appendix of the present volume it appears that the shore end (i.e. starting point) of a composite bridge that they built, using both those methods, was virtually on the doorstep of the Grosvenor Hotel. In illustration 30 the shore end of this bridge is in the foreground; in the background are some of the ladies of Buxton who perhaps looked on pontooning as another entertainment in the park. Illustration 31 is a view from the far bank of presumably the same bridge under construction, with the houses and hotels of Broad Walk in the background. Broad Walk is also the background to illustration 29: the inscription on this photograph reads: 'Rowing drill on lake in park, Buxton, October 1915: from bows Spr Trevis, 2nd Cpl Toogood, Sprs Phillips, Douglas, Gibberd, Dyer; Lieutenant Smith steering'.[4]

The Company learned about heavy bridging at Lightwood Road, off the Manchester Road, where they practised building timber trestle bridges over a deep gully: see illustration 34. Their instructor sergeant-major for heavy bridging was nicknamed 'Detail'. 'What his name was nobody knew or bothered to find out', says my father. 'He would look at the work in hand and say "Let's see: so many feet of so and so, a detail of so many is required". That was not the end of the matter: everything had to be done by numbers "at a word of command". On one day a party of four of us was "detailed off" to fetch a tool chest from the bridging stores. "Detail" followed us and pointed out a box with handles projecting from each end, like a stretcher, containing the tools we needed. We just casually picked the box up and were walking away with it when "Detail" ordered us back. "That ain't the way Royal Engineers do it. Put it down here and stand to attention round it. Right. On the command prepare to lift box, each man bend forward and grasp a handle." We did as ordered and then the command "Lift box" came, which we carried out. As we stood erect with the box "Detail" said "Wait for it", so we waited; after a moment we were ordered "By the left, walk march". This ceremonial drill delayed us somewhat, and when we reached the job Seymour wanted to know "Where the hell have you lot been hiding?" We explained that we had been learning from "Detail" how the Royal Engineers lifted and carried toolboxes. The sergeant's comment was "Pity that old sod ain't got something better to do".'

'Detail' may have been unduly scrupulous in this case, but perhaps he was right to order these trainees to do everything by the book. The War Office manual, *Military Bridging* (1914), goes into minute detail on what a layman might think are simple matters: for instance the unloading of bridging stores from a pontoon wagon. It stipulated that each man in the unloading party had to be sized and numbered, then it detailed the positioning, actions, and movements of each man in a drill that fills several pages of explanation and a long string of orders.[5] If a pontoon bridge was to be built quickly and efficiently in the field, perhaps in darkness, it was vital that every man knew exactly what he had to do and did not impede anyone else.

The retired R.E. sergeant in charge of pontoon and light trestle bridging and trenching and other field works was nicknamed 'Swing Derrick' because his speciality was the erection of swinging derricks, but his name — Luxton — was also remembered. My father recalls: 'Once when the section was digging trenches on the moor at Axe Edge, a few miles outside Buxton, I was requested by some of my comrades to "Get out of the way, you young sod". Luxton stood near, and, hearing the request, asked "Do any of you men know the dimensions of an R.E. sod?" Sapper Tom Norman replied "Yes Sergeant, one about his size", indicating me. "You're wrong, Sapper, an R.E. sod, as used in revetments, and to cover and hide the loose earth thrown out onto the parapet and parados of a slit trench,

4. *'Hasty entrenchments on Axe Edge, near Buxton: one and a half hours' work; traverses revetted with turf': (note by Arthur Sambrook).*

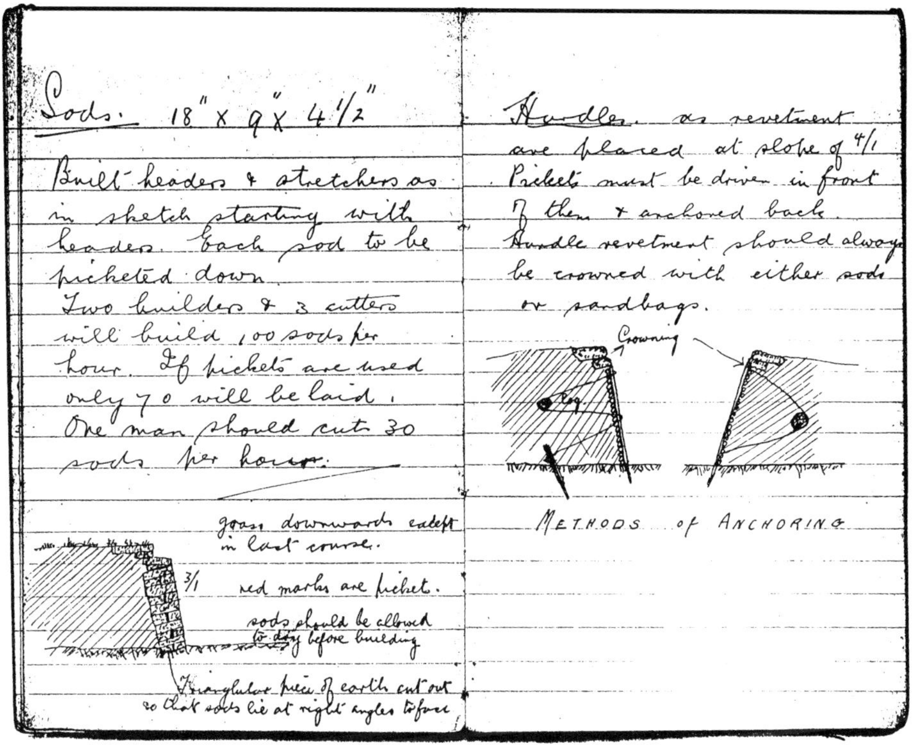

5. Corporal Streather's notebook, with instructions on entrenchments.

measures 18 inches long, 9 inches wide, and 3 inches thick. Don't forget that you men."' My father admired Sergeant Luxton; Arthur Daulman remembered him as 'a gentleman in his dealings with us: tolerant, kindly and efficient, without being too regimental' He was 'an excellent instructor who knew what he was talking about as he had done it all before. Another of his phrases was "just one more thing not laid down in the book but from my own practical experience, it's well for you to know it, it's well for you to know it".' Strictly speaking, the Sergeant's sod was not in the book (or my father's recollection is slightly inaccurate), for 2nd Cpl Streather's notebook, quoting *The Manual of Field Engineering*, 1911, Section 7, 'Sods', says that they should be 4½ inches thick. They were to be cut at a rate of thirty sods per hour by one man in four hours, and, when built into a correctly sloping revetement (at a gradient of three in seven), five sods were required for each square foot of surface revetted.

It was generally wet and cold at Buxton. On particularly wet days the men practised knotting and lashing in the ballroom of the Pavilion Gardens. Much engineering involved rope and timber, so it was essential that knots and lashings should be made with rapidity and sureness that came only with long practice. The Company undertook the inevitable long route marches with full pack, rifle, and bayonet over the pretty hills surrounding the town. They had target practice with their Lee Enfield rifles at the Cheshire Regiment's range on Coombs Moss.

Sappers Simmonds and Albert Thomas and Pioneer Daulman learned to ride motor cycles. An incidental benefit of acquiring this skill was that motor cyclists were issued with shorter greatcoats, generally agreed to be smarter than the ordinary longer type, and consequently much sought after. The *Buxton Advertiser* thought the R.E. motor cycles were 'fine machines' and their riders 'fine chaps', and noted that the Derbyshire hills would provide an ideal training ground for them, because 'the High Peak country was, in the Boer War, compared to many South African regions in which our Armies had to ferret out, and blow out, the wily Boers'. This newspaper was even more impressed by the Engineers' route marching: 'They swing along, sing along, as merrily as sand-boys ever did'.[6]

Periodically the officers and N.C.O.s were sent away on training courses. The letters of Charles Streather, newly promoted to full corporal, give lively impressions of a bridging course at Newark-upon-Trent. 'We fall in at 6.45 and have to be as clean as a new pin from head to foot. The first day I got into hot water for having long hair and nearly every N.C.O. in the class had something wrong with him. The parade only lasts $3/4$ hr but it's very stiff while it lasts; you have to be absolutely perfect in every detail. The C.S.M.'s tuition comes in useful to me now; I find I can get on much better than some of the Sgts and better than any other Cpl. After breakfast we have a lecture for $1\frac{1}{2}$ hrs and then go to work till 5 o'clock. We have to march 3 miles, so we take dinner. I get plenty of dinner put up [by his landlady, Mrs Williams of 19 Jubilee Street] and then a proper hot dinner at night, just as if I were at home. The course I am going through is very instructive and there is plenty of work to do especially writing notes at home at night. . . . Have started pontooning this week. I thought I had done some work before but found what we had done was child's play. We bridged the river 100 yds wide in 23 mins: 42 of us — and a bridge to carry Artillery.'

Some of the training at Newark was done at night. 'Last Wednesday it was pitch dark when we started and then a thick fog came over. You could not see your hand in front of you. I had to go out on top of the trestles in the middle of the river and climb along a guy rope 15 ft from the water and about 50 ft out. Having

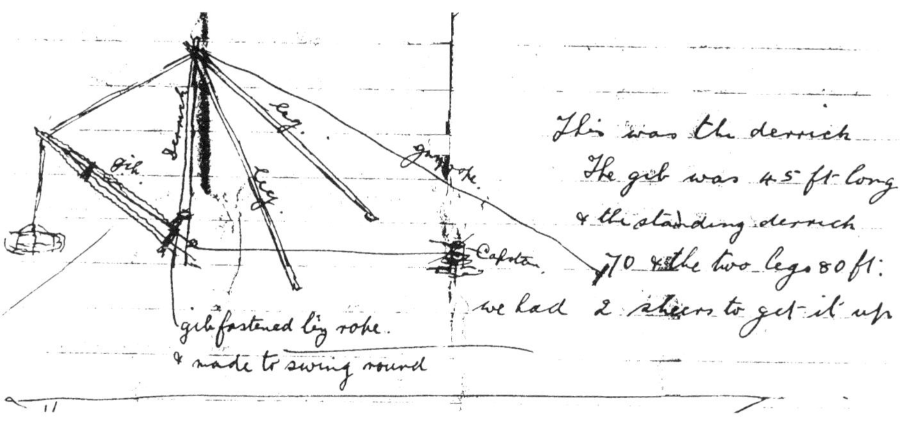

6. Letter by Corporal Streather to his parents in 1915, describing a training course at Newark.

perched myself in a more or less comfortable attitude I had to haul over a cable and make it fast to some tackles and then get back. We bridged the river twice that night before 1 o'clock. One was a trestle bridge to carry infantry in fours and field artillery and the other was a barrel pier to carry infantry in file.[7] On Saturday we put up a swinging derrick to lift 2 tons. We made a raft and lifted it on to the river the raft weighed about 30 cwts and the whole lot was built and demolished again by 25 men in 2 hrs and a half.'

At Buxton the Nuneaton Company's title was changed from 216th Fortress Company to 216th Army Troops Company. The change, which was made with few exceptions to Fortress Companies throughout the Corps, reflected the new functions of a body that would operate in the field, rather than build and maintain garrison fortresses in various parts of the British Empire. A company of Army Troops engineers was not allocated to any particular Division, in the way that Field Companies, R.E., were, but came directly under the orders of a higher echelon (i.e. the headquarters of either a Corps or an Army), to be distributed among fighting formations according to the needs of the situation in the field. According to an historian of the Royal Engineers, they were intended mainly 'for rear area work such as water supply, work on corps defence lines, observation posts for artillery, gun positions for heavy artillery, trench tramways, road-screening, corps engineer dumps and workshops, and erection of hangars for the Royal Flying Corps – in fact, a very varied programme. . . . Their establishment was three officers and 139 other ranks, but they were provided with mechanical transport'.[8] 'Sappers' were traditionally versatile: Kipling wrote of them, '*we* are the men that do something all round'.[9] The Army Troops, R.E., programme is indeed varied, but it omits what would eventually become the 216th Company's special skill in a war where technology tended to advance more rapidly than troops did: the erection of heavy steel bridges.

Army Troops companies required longer training than the old Fortress companies, to judge by a letter from a sapper in the 230th (Tottenham) Company at Buxton on 20 September: 'Some disappointment is felt owing to the six companies who were on the top line for the Front being turned into Army Troops Companies, which will mean some further time before we "get at em"'.[10] The 216th was one of those six companies; it went to France to 'get at' the Germans just a week after the 230th. The immediate effect of the Company's change in name and function was that Captain Cook now made his last appeal for recruits in the Nuneaton newspapers. He called for thirty more men, including 'three draughtsmen, three traction engine drivers, four fitters, one harness maker, five masons, five plumbers, two blacksmiths, three surveyors, and five miscellaneous'. Intending recruits were asked to apply to Major McMullen, as usual. At the same time it was reported that Captain Cook's wife was arranging a recruiting concert by the Royal Warwickshire Regimental Band in Nuneaton.[11] A few Nuneaton men were recruited but most of the additions to the 216th came from other Midland towns, including Buxton. One of the newcomers was Sapper Leishman, from London, who played the hotel piano to accompany ballad-singing sessions: the last of these would be in an estaminet at Demuin, east of Amiens, at a dark time in the great retreat of the British Fifth Army in March 1918.[12]

At last, on 11 November, Captain Cook was able to announce (in the *Nuneaton Chronicle*) that his Company was over full strength, with all its transport complete. He thanked Nuneaton folk for their gift of cigarettes, collected by Boy Scouts on a recent 'Tobacco Day', and concluded: 'I often wish we could include Nuneaton within the compass of a route march. But we shall get there some day, by however circuitous a route, and in the meantime it is nice to feel (in common with all other locally-raised units) that there is a town taking special interest in the welfare of its own Company'. Doubtless his men were relieved to know there were limits to their route marches, but, equally doubtless, they would have felt the bond with their home town of which he writes. The complete transport he refers to provided for each half-company a G.S. (General Service) wagon, limber wagon, and tool cart, drawn by horses or mules, and a lorry — in this case a 'Berna' lorry, captured from the Germans. The horse and mule transport was handled by the Company's own drivers, but each lorry was the responsibility of a driver and mate attached to the company from the A.S.C. (Army Service Corps); according to my father, the driver of the left half-company lorry was a London bus driver. Though Captain Cook's last recruiting appeal called for traction-engine drivers, I have found no reference to traction engines in records of the 216th Company.

The only surviving photographs of the Nuneaton Company engaged in engineering work are from Buxton: the side-effect of training in a spa town where there were many pre-war professional photographers and a wartime shortage of holiday-makers. Though the Buxton photographers did go with their cameras up to the sods in and on the Axe Edge entrenchments (illustration 4), their favourite haunt was evidently the Pavilion Gardens. Thanks to them we have a visual record of light and heavy trestle, pontoon, and barrel-pier bridging (illustrations 29-36). Also, several surviving photographic portraits of Nuneaton sappers

7. Tea break at Buxton: on left Sapper Higham, on right Sapper Pullen (killed in France, March 1916), third from right Sergeant Seymour.

8. Arthur Sambrook: studio portrait at Buxton.

(swagger stick and all) were manifestly snapped against the same Arcadian backcloth in the same Buxton studio (e.g. illustration 8). No doubt the photographers did as well from the dozen other R.E. Army Troops companies being trained in the town when the Nuneaton men were there. All were locally raised; they came variously from Coventry, Rugby, Leamington, the Isle of Wight, Monmouth, Abergavenny, Tottenham, Ripon, Middlesbrough, Glasgow, Dundee, and Buxton itself. Occasionally, on a Saturday afternoon, the companies played one another at football. The Nuneaton company, captained by the famous Billy Barratt and playing in Nuneaton Town colours, were particularly pleased by their two victories over the 214th (Coventry) Army Troops Company.[13] Corporal Streather described the first game as 'the most exciting time I have had since being in the army'. It must, indeed, have been something if it eclipsed his catching out the great Gilbert Jessop.

My father recalls a less sporting contest with the 220th (Rugby) Company during infantry manoeuvres near Harpurhill when the 216th were defending a hill which the Rugby men tried to capture. 'We had a strong position behind one of the stone walls, and, as the attackers puffed their way in extended order up the steep slope we clicked the bolts of our empty rifles with no effect on the enemy, one of our chaps said, "This is only playing silly buggers. I'll show you how to stop that lot", and he shoved a piece of the wall over. His example was followed with enthusiasm by the rest of us, and the lumps of stone bounding down the slope caused the enemy to scatter and retire, luckily without any casualties. This was against the rules of this sort of warfare: next day the victorious defenders were detailed off to collect the expended ammunition and rebuild the wall.'

Hostilities between the Nuneaton and the Rugby men were continued in the streets of Buxton, for my father writes that 'things were a bit lively in the evenings in the pubs and after closing time. Both Companies took turns to have piquets patrolling the streets, which patrolling avoided the known locals of each Company. In the event of a street disturbance the piquet was usually investigating a supposed disturbance in another part of Buxton. The people were not molested at all, and as there was no instance of kicking or throwing things, but just normal punching, the damage to the combatants did not interfere with their military duties. I was on this duty twice: ordinary walking-out uniform with bayonets. In the early, quieter parts of the evening we were conspicuous everywhere in our patrolling, but when it got dark, our bayonets went under our tunics, up a pub yard to investigate something and in at the back door till our tour was up.'

Daulman seems to claim a greater seriousness for his spells of duty as town piquet when he says that 'We were especially regimental in dealing with other companies, and many a sharp rebuke such as "Take your hands out of your pockets" could be heard'; but he spoils the effect by adding: 'We were generally marched to the outskirts of Higher Buxton beyond the Town Hall, where our lance-corporal would say "Fall out" before he disappeared into the Cheshire Cheese for his drink'. Of the magazine guard, two miles from Buxton, up in the hills at Burbage, he recalls that a bucket was placed behind the gate to the magazine compound 'so that when the orderly officer opened the gate, down fell the bucket, startled the officer, alerted the guard'. There was no shortage of guard duty: guards were mounted also at the heavy bridging and light bridging grounds and the tailor's shop, as well as the main barrack guard along a raised path in front of the hotels on Broad Walk (but evidently not at the back where Sergeant Wheway's birthday ham became a casualty). My father recalls a sentry in the bushes with his girl-friend on the pontoon bridging ground in the Pavilion Gardens.

The stable piquet on the football field posed problems of its own. Daulman recalls that it 'was quite hair raising at times when the mules broke loose. Then they had to be driven into the lines where they were tethered and grabbed by the halter from the front. To approach from behind was suicide. The mules could untie every knot known to man and untie the best we could do, and as R.E.s we prided ourselves on our expertise.' My father recalled the arrival of the mules and horses at Buxton, when 'everybody was required at the Station to unload them. The mules were hardly broken in and were kicking and biting everything on two legs who went near, but I must say we treated them equally roughly, and got them out and tied to picket lines to cool off. Most of them were fitted for their new shoes lying down tied with head to tail or in a shoeing frame.' (The shoeing-frame or travis was a strong portable framework of posts and bars in which a horse could be confined for shoeing or veterinary work.) Evidently there was enough livestock here to keep the Company's hands full. The dalmatian was still on the strength, for it appears in a group photograph of the N.C.O.s; also my father mentions Sapper Sol Walker's pet cockerel at Buxton: 'an aggressive Rhode Island Red'.

It was not the only aggressive creature. Arthur Daulman recalls: 'One night Spr Jack Williams had been on the beer and came in very noisy indeed. Sgt-Major Mitchinson tried to get him quietly up to his bedroom. On the landing there was a bit of a skirmish and they came through the banisters with Williams on top and his hands around Mitchinson's throat. Well, the guard had to intervene and Williams was given ninety days in Knutsford, a military prison, and transferred to another company. I was to see him about three years later in France on Armistice Day.'

Sapper Williams was the most conspicuous case of indiscipline, but there were mutinous mutterings elsewhere in the lower ranks. Arthur Daulman recalls: 'For the last two months of 1915 we were under orders to overseas so consequently there was no leave, although our C.O. did try to get some for us, and Lieutenant Knox had tried his luck with Colonel Carnegie, Royal Engineers, only to be ordered out in no uncertain terms. This meant there was a good deal of dissatisfaction, which resulted in a meeting in the dining room of the Coventry Company to which we were all invited. All other ranks of course. It was decided that no one would go on parade until leave was granted, and a spokesman was appointed. Word must have been carried to Sergeant-Major Mitchinson, for in he came with his cane under his arm and this is what he said: "I feel sorry for you, my lads. I'll send this telegram off and in no time there'll be a battalion of infantry here with ball ammunition and fixed bayonets". He did not need to explain further. We dispersed, tails between legs. We said no more. He said no more.'

Lack of leave, though, did not interfere with high spirits at Christmas. An anonymous contributor to the *Nuneaton Observer* on 31 December (undoubtedly Sapper Joe Smith, for his style is inimitable) told Nuneaton how the local company had celebrated: 'The Company, along with all the other Companies in training at this centre, were entertained to tea on Friday night in the Pavilion by the ladies of the town, and with a concert following, the eve of Christmas was spent in right good style. . . it was a fine sight to see so many men banded together for the tea, men who are the pick of the country's skilled trades all joined together with one common cause, the bringing to the dust of the world's greatest tyrant. . . . There was a strong muster for the Church Parade on Xmas Day, and the service was characterised by the hearty singing of the Christmas hymns. The 216th men adjourned to their own billets for the dinner, and the dining room of the hotel was crowded before the good things were brought in. To give an additional amount of good feeling to the gathering, Sergt-Major C.J. Mitchinson enrolled the whole of the N.C.O.s to carve and wait upon the men. Capt. Cook, Lieut. Knox and Lieut. Jones were in attendance. . . . Turkey was the principal item of the feast, and vegetables helped the bird on its way to its future "home", not to mention the allowance of a pint of beer to each man. Plum pudding was also served, and everyone had their fill. At four o'clock a ham tea was served, and greatly enjoyed. The rest of the evening was spent as only Nuneaton men know how to spend it.' Corporal Streather, one of the N.C.O.s who waited upon the sappers, notes that there were eight turkeys for a hundred men. 'Jones' in the newspaper report is surely a misprint for 'Smith': a mistake perhaps made by an *Observer* compositor who had spent the evening as only Nuneaton men know how to spend it.

For what exactly is meant by spending the evening as only Nuneaton men know how to spend it we must turn to my father's recollections: 'I was on guard that night and after a visit by the Orderly Officer about 10 o'clock went in search of the Corporal (Shelmerdine) and the relief sentry. No one was in the guardroom except two drunken sappers who had given themselves up as they said, and were lying down very comfortably in the only quiet and peaceful place in the billet. Shelley was on the stairs giving his rendering of "I've come from the country, my name it is Giles". Sgt Seymour was threatening to push a bayonet into Wiggins to persuade him to hand over his cask. Seymour's companion, Cpl Rogers, was keeping a look out, and every now and then telling Seymour not to delay in doing Wiggins. As they were both very drunk Wiggins began to take a serious view of his situation and was begging every passing sapper to help him, but every sapper in a callous manner told Seymour to do him and then we would stand a chance of getting a better cook. In the end Wiggins parted with *[at which point, appropriately, there is a page missing from the Memoir]* retire to bed. Next day the fall-in for work was a spectacle of slovenly dress and equipment, gaps in the ranks, N.C.O.s and sappers very unsteady, most unshaved and half the company still sleeping peacefully amidst the ruins of their beds. Some of us were detailed off to mend the doors smashed in the night's celebrations, and the whole episode was closed by the worst evening meal that Wiggins ever spoilt in the cooking.' Corporal Streather, more circumspectly, told his parents: 'We have got over Xmas here. . . We all enjoyed ourselves pretty well but it was rotten to have to go to work.' Part of his own current work was 'attending a course of lectures on bombs and grenades under an officer from the front'. Even the best of sons does not tell his parents everything. My father's list of men who left the 216th at Buxton includes 'Corporal Marriott discharged with a broken ankle, incurred while wrestling with Corporal Streather one night after a wet evening in the N.C.O.s' mess'.[14]

In the last days of December there was a full parade of the Royal Engineers in Buxton. It was rumoured that the 220th Rugby Company would go to France and the 216th to the Middle East; the rumour was confirmed when the Nuneaton men were ordered to draw tropical kit, only to be contradicted when they were ordered to return the kit almost immediately. In the event, as my father says, 'The Rugby

Company got the Egypt ticket and our Company the French one, and a last battle was fought after closing time, when a lot of the new khaki topees the Rugby chaps were swanking about in got damaged and dirty: the piquet watching from a safe distance and not interfering'. Meanwhile in the real war the British army in France now numbered one million men and the evacuation of Allied troops from the disaster called Gallipoli was under way.

The Nuneaton men were still without the prospect of any leave, but on New Year's Eve, recalls Daulman: 'there was a special parade and roll call under Sergeant-Major Mitchinson. He said there was no leave but he gave us, as he said, a tip, and it was that there would be NO PARADE ON NEW YEAR'S DAY. He also added that a train went at such and such a time. He wound up saying we were to be back by Jan 2nd and heaven help us if we weren't.' The men who chose to go reached Leicester by midnight on New Year's Eve, but had to wait till 7 a.m. for a train to Nuneaton, so no one could have had more than a few hours at home if he was to return to Buxton on time.

New Year's Day was a Saturday when the 216th were due to play football against another company, the 235th (Middlesbrough), but as so many men were away on unofficial leave there had to be drastic team changes. So the elderly Sergeant Lee replaced the great Nuneaton Town player, Billy Barratt, at left back, and both wingers were new caps, in the shape of Sapper Joe Smith and the ever-sporting Sergeant Major Mitchinson. Smith himself may have prepared the way for his own selection by rubbishing the wingers in his otherwise laudatory assessment of the team after its second victory over the Coventry company. In the event, the New Year's Day game was rained off early in the second half, with the Nuneaton men a goal down, but having so great a territorial advantage that their goalkeeper, Corporal Shelmerdine was taking corner kicks.[15] Evidently it was "that sort of game" and "Shelley", as we have heard, was "that sort of man". Joe Smith did not report what Charles Streather mentions in a letter home: 'We lost the ball and it took half an hour to find it: it was nearly three quarters of a mile from the field, so you can tell what the wind was like. It carried right from the top of the hill into the valley below.' The day ended for the 216th with a "smoker" in the White Lion Hotel.

About forty men went home on New Year's Day. Some did not return by Sunday evening and were duly punished: Lance Corporal Copson was reduced to the ranks; delinquent sappers and pioneers were given seven or five days' Confined to Barracks. Streather reported to his parents: 'things are very quiet after a rowdy weekend caused by the absentees. I don't think the weekend passes will be stopped altogether but only 10% of the men will be allowed away and we shall be forced to draw for it.' A little later, on 13 January, he describes his work-in-hand: 'For some time we have been putting up a heavy bridge. We have made a big girder to carry a 22 ton locomotive and today we got it up. It was 28 ft high from the foot of the trestle to the bottom of the girder. The girder was 70ft long, 6ft deep, 18" boom, and weighed over three tons. It is put up over a gap very much like one of those ironstone pits at Corby. Yesterday I was muck carting from the stables to a farm 2½ miles from Buxton.'

A peace-time sapper's training was officially reckoned to take 29 weeks.[16] The 216th Company's training was now virtually complete, so, writes Arthur Daulman, 'there was plenty of route marches to keep us occupied and fit I suppose. On one occasion we marched, perhaps climbed would be the better word, to the Cat and Fiddle, the highest fully licensed public house in England at that time. It was a wild lonely place set in moorland especially bleak on that January day. A route march that brought us close to Miller's Dale provided us with a surprise. It was a long march and at mid-day we fell out and opened our haversack rations. Captain Cook then produced sealed orders which he opened in dead silence. He then read out the date for our going overseas. Some of the young bloods went berserk, hooraying and shouting. To go overseas we were allowed just one suit. We were allowed a hairbrush or comb, not both; a clothesbrush or bootbrush, not both. We had to black out our buttons and cap badge over a candle flame, only to be told to clean them fourteen days later. We had to leave button-stick and other cleaning apparatus behind, and when we asked how we were to clean them we were told to tear a bit off one's shirt.' Corporal Streather wrote comfortingly but inaccurately to his parents: 'We are the head quarters staff Army Troops Company of the 4th Army so I suppose we shall not see any fighting.'

On Thursday, 27 January 1916, after a week or so marking up equipment, the Company paraded on Broad Walk in full marching order with two days' haversack rations and full water bottles. They marched to the railway station at 5 a.m. on a cold raw morning; the drivers had already collected their horses and mules from the stables in the rear of the White Lion in Spring Gardens, together with the transport vehicles, and were loading them onto a train standing in the goods siding when the rest of the company arrived. While the drivers and a few of the railway staff were occupied with this business the rest of the company stood about in groups on the station platform, speculating about their destination or singing to keep warm. Some Nuneaton people had gone to Buxton on the Wednesday evening; they 'saw their soldier friends on parade to the station, but they were not permitted on the platform',[17] with or without platform tickets.

When the train was loaded it drew into the platform where the men waited; they crowded on and settled themselves. After another delay they left Buxton about 6.30 a.m. and travelled south in a leisurely fashion; they were shunted around the edge of London, without changing trains, and found themselves at Clapham Junction about 11 a.m. 'Here', recalls my father, 'for nearly three hours the train stood in a siding and we started our rations and lunched on very appetising tinned mutton and not so appetising biscuit. The only other diversion available was provided by a few advertisement hoardings, partially concealing a view of drab, congested roofs and chimneys, which soon palled'.

Eventually the train moved on, and finally, at about 4.30 p.m., arrived beside the Ocean Dock Quay in Southampton, where the men thankfully left the cramped compartments in which they had spent all day, and fell in at ease on the dock opposite a large ship called *North Western Miller*, which was being loaded with horses, mules, field guns, limbers, and transports. Other units were waiting to embark on this ship: Royal Engineers, Royal Artillery, and Royal Army Medical

Corps. 'Not a soldier amongst the lot of us', someone remarked to my father. My father recalls that it was 'a grey, mizzling, cheerless afternoon, with night coming on soon. I felt lost. I was depressed and no doubt many others were also as we stood silently looking about us. The trees on the other side of the water looked dismal, half obscured by the mist. There was a lot of shouting and scuffling going on where the dock workers were hoisting the animals on board; after the animals the guns and various vehicles were shipped, and then the troops embarked. The evening was drawing in, cold and misty, with a persistent drizzle which damped our uniforms and our spirits, and we were a gloomy, homesick lot of heroes when we eventually filed up the gangways.'

Once on board, the men were detailed off to their quarters below. As this was a cattle-boat they occupied freshly whitewashed cattle pens. They learned that after they had been taken to France the ship would whip over to Canada for horses and mules. 'Here', says my father, 'it was warm and dry, and the novelty of our situation was too intriguing for any despondency to last very long, and apart from a few remarks about the difference between a feather bed and the deck, there was no grousing. After shedding our equipment, a few of the younger members in the company went back on deck to see the ship cast off and to have a look round. Apart from a couple of tugs loitering near the ship, Southampton Water was practically deserted, and the trees on the opposite shore were obscured by a thick wet mist. We stayed on deck while the ship cast off and the tugs pulled us into the fairway; here they cast off and we went on in darkness towards Calshot and the Needles. Presently we noticed a glowing red and white light approaching, which turned out to be a large four-funnelled liner coming in and lit up just like a Chinese lantern; her deck lights were glowing and a brilliantly illuminated red cross on each side amidships made a strong contrast to our darkened progress to sea. We were sitting in the bows of the ship near the look-out man, and he told us it was the *Mauretania*,[18] which was then serving as a hospital ship. "They come back in style anyway", someone in the group said. "Some on 'em don't come back at all", replied the look-out moodily.' *Mauretania* was returning from the eastern Mediterranean with wounded Gallipoli evacuees.

When *North Western Mille*r reached the English Channel an escort of two destroyers circled round and led the way. Soon afterwards the troops on deck were ordered below because they were making too much noise: descending to their cattle pens, they turned in and were soon asleep. Apart from a few veterans of the South African War and Sergeant Seymour, who had been shell-shocked in France once already, the men of the 216th had little notion of what they were going into. They were all Kitchener's volunteers, as were the majority of British soldiers in January 1916. The British government had only just enacted conscription for unmarried men between the ages of 18 and 41, with the proviso that no man would be sent overseas until he was over 19; but several of the 216th were still under 18. Over the eight months or so that they had been in the army there had been a change in public perception of the war: after Gallipoli and Loos there was less faith in the promise of quick victory and the dream of easy martial glory. The mood was rather of sombre, anxious realism.

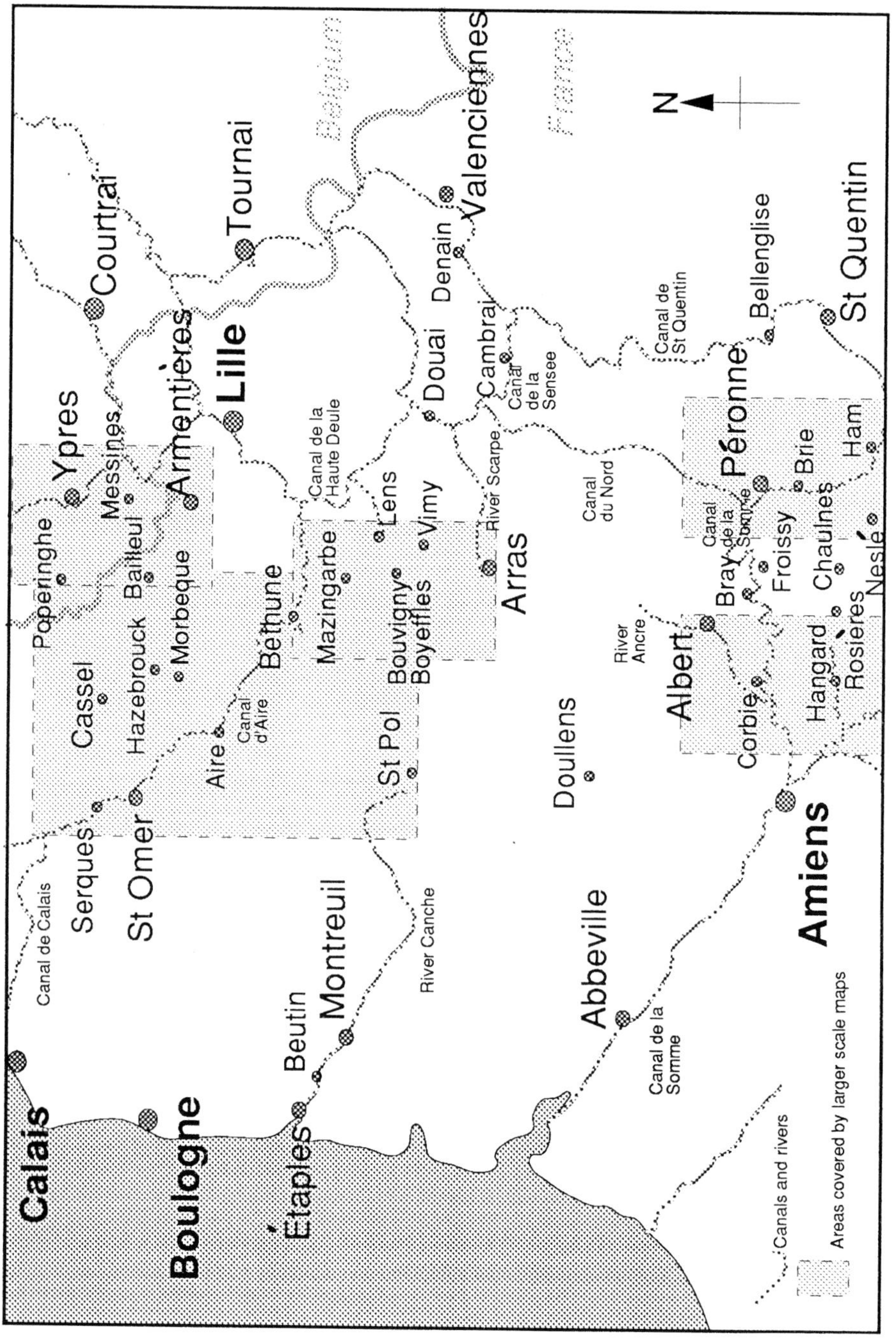

Map 2: Northern France and Southern Belgium

Chapter Three: Mazingarbe, January and February 1916

On the morning of 28 January the *North Western Miller* was tied up to a quay at Le Havre. Arthur Daulman recalls 'seeing a sign which read "Defense de fumer" on the docks. It was the first bit of French I had seen and it was unintelligible to me at the time. A doctor inspected us. That is he walked quickly along the ranks to see, I think, if we were able to stand without assistance.' After breakfast the Company disembarked, collected their animals and transport, and marched along the docks and through the streets of the city up to a camp on the cliffs at Harfleur. Here they spent a cold, very uncomfortable night, ten men to a bell tent. Next morning they marched back down to Le Havre railway station. Here, writes my father, 'we boarded a train composed of 1st class carriages for the officers, 2nd class for N.C.O.s, and box wagons, with the inscription in large white letters on the sides, "Hommes 40, Chevaux 8", for the lower ranks; the lower ranks found them very roomy and comfortable, as there were enough wagons to enable twenty hommes to spread themselves out in, instead of the specified forty.' Forty men with forty rifles, packs, and other equipment would, indeed, have been a crowd. Daulman seems to have obtained a better class than my father because he travelled in a compartment with 'wooden seats which were condemned whole-heartedly'. Perhaps he did not have the benefit of the straw that was normally provided in the "Hommes 40, Chevaux 8" wagons. Also, if there was no glass in his carriage windows (which was generally the case in trains going anywhere near the front line), he would have had a colder journey than the men in the wagons.

After some delay the train moved off into France, and after a slow journey, with frequent halts, crawled into Rouen station. My father observes: 'For most of us France was a new and interesting country, and we half expected our entry to attract some attention, but nobody seemed to notice anything special about us: one chap remarked "They've seen things like us before". What little we saw of the city was interesting, but the large base camp established here and the swarms of "red caps" infesting the station and streets put us off the place. The prices and quality of the goods sold at the Expeditionary Forces Canteen were cheap and excellent, enabling us to stock up with tobacco, chocolate, and tinned food. Some of us bought French-English phrase books and practised on any fellow student patient enough to listen, but none of us shone at this exercise: even the French people we spoke to did not recognise their own language. These phrase books were soon discarded in favour of "Soldiers' French"; the French people replied in "Soldiers' English", so we got about well enough. The French beer was disappointing: very weak stuff. "Just about fit to mix with the milk in babies' bottles" was the verdict of our beer connoisseurs. "At ten centimes a glass, a franc's worth would bust us".' In 1916 a franc was worth 9½d (about 4p in modern money), or just under a third of a day's pay for a sapper. Oeufs et pommes de terre frites could be had for 50 centimes; the same sum would buy a litre of wine. Army rations were rarely sufficient; any spare cash the soldiers had was spent on food and drink.

'Leaving Rouen', says my father, 'the train went on in slow motion; the usual short crawls and long halts. During these stops we walked along the track to the

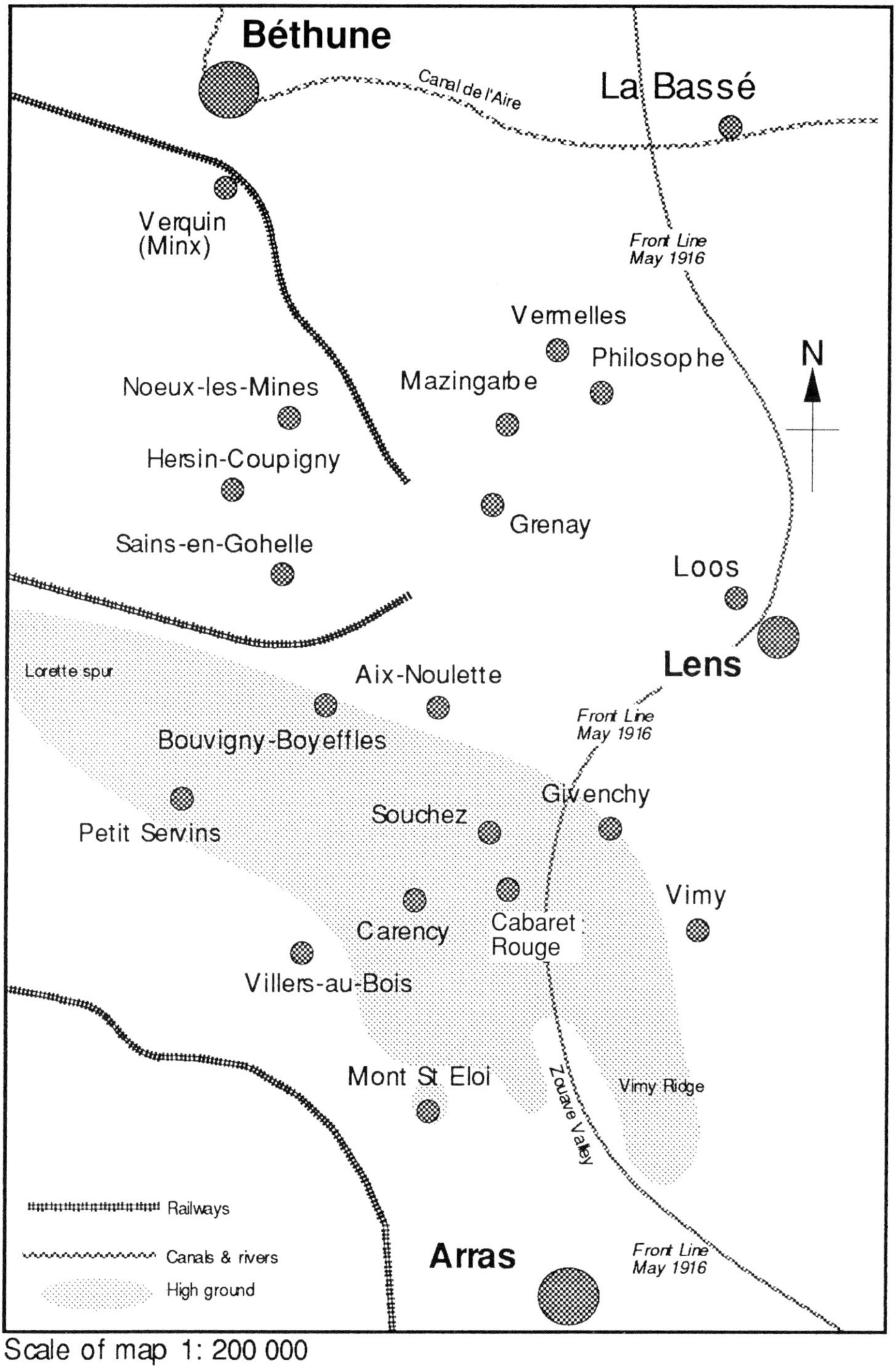

Map 3: Mazingarbe, Bouvigny-Boyeffles, Villers-au-Bois, January 1916–May 1916

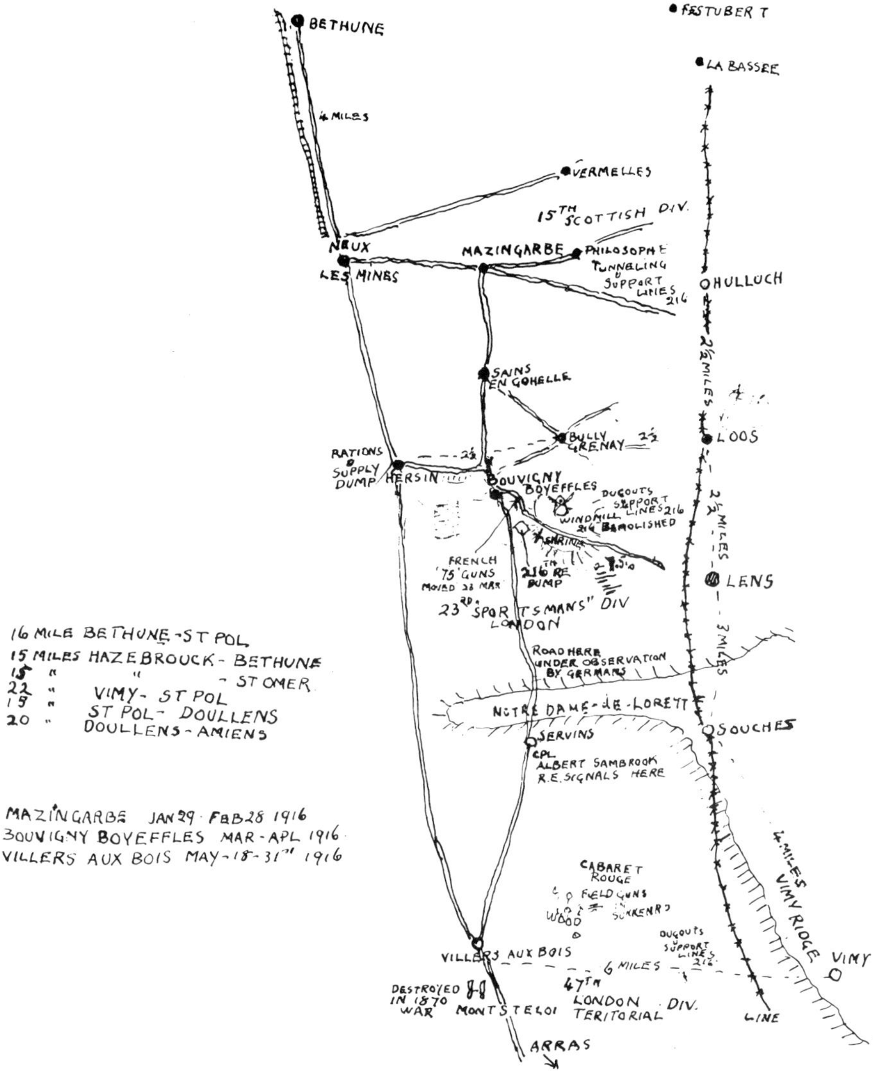

Map 3A: Mazingarbe area as in Map 3 – Arthur Sambrook's sketch map of 216 Company billets and works

engine to get hot water for "brewing up". Our phrase books were not needed for this business: the proffered mess tin, and the long acquaintance of French train crews with the habits of British Hommes 40 passengers, made language superfluous, and as the train crews did very well for biscuits and bully they always obliged us. There were times when we wondered if this frequent dispensing of hot water was one of the causes of the long delays, but the train crews did not seem to mind and we were in no hurry to reach our destination.'

That evening the train was shunted into sidings at Abbeville and a meal was served. The night was spent comfortably by my father's comrades, 'relaxed in our Hommes 40 billets until we were jolted awake at daybreak by the train resuming its leisurely progress, soon afterwards stopping at Béthune station. During a short stay here the cooks dished up some breakfast, and later that morning we finished our journey at a quick pace, finally arriving at a small village called Noeux-les-Mines: beyond this place the railway was destroyed.' The station itself had been shelled the day before and was now half ruined. The explanation of the 'quick pace' near the end of the journey is given by Arthur Daulman: 'we were under observation from the craters [held by the Germans on higher ground] at Givenchy. This I realized on August 20th 1918, when we captured the craters and I was able to stand there and look back.'

While Captain Cook, the C.O., was busy with the local Railway Transport Officer at Noeux-les-Mines the Company unloaded their animals and transport and then fell in outside the station. My father recalls: 'When the C.O. rejoined us we moved off along a muddy road which had more pot-holes in it than paving stones. This was a mining district, and Noeux-les-Mines and its surroundings did not look very inviting on a dull, rainy day. Our comments on the scenery were loud and uncomplimentary. Sergeant Seymour told us to shut up moaning, adding: "We shall soon be in a worse place than this; listen to that lot". "That lot" referred to was an intermittent thudding noise which we had been hearing for some time past and had been wondering about. In reply to someone's question, "What's that noise Sergeant?", he answered, "That's shelling and that's where we'm going to: it won't be a Sunday School picnic from now on". After marching for some hours, past clod tips and pit-head buildings, with a few scruffy hamlets in between, adding a bit of variety, we eventually approached a small town. As the company drew near, we heard a peculiar high-pitched whistle, followed by a loud crash, and a cloud of smoke and brickdust billowed up and drifted away over the houses. We were halted on the road and uneasily watched while a few more shells fell in the town. The last shell of that 'strafe' overshot the town and fell very close to us, luckily burying itself deep in the soft ground near the road where we stood. The explosion smothered us with mud and earth, but no shell splinters came our way. A few chaps dived into the ditches bordering the road, emerging afterwards dripping with mud and water; their rifles and equipment had to be washed under a pump before being fit to use, but the majority of us stood gaping on the road, too startled even to duck our heads under the shower of debris falling amongst us. This was our welcome to Mazingarbe, and a foretaste of the entertainment we received during our stay in this place.' This indeed was the place where the 216th Company would soon learn that artillery was the big killer in the Great War.

Corporal Streather reflected the common experience when he wrote three months later to a younger brother also in the Royal Engineers: 'Strange to say, the first time shells dropped round me I was not in the least afraid: rather curious in fact. It's not until after you have come through that you feel nervy. While they whistle and bang you are thinking how to dodge them, where to get, and what to do, but when it's quiet again often you feel quite weak and shaken.' My father's description of the sound of a shell in flight is as low-key as the rest of his or Streather's narratives. For something more graphic we must turn to the novelists: R.H. Mottram — 'an unforgettable sound, as though the heavens, made of cheap calico, were being torn to lengths by some demoniac draper' —; or Henry Williamson – 'a noise filling the air as though the sky were a dome of solid glass, and an immense diamond were cutting a slow curve down it. A hard noise, as of gem-hard dust being ground away. As it drew nearer it changed to a coarse vibration of steel, opening a furrow in the very heavens, droning, buzzing, hissing, dropping in scale to a deep bass and growing louder and louder, a noise enormous and terrifying'[1].

The Company re-formed and marched into the village in some sort of order. Here the men were allotted to their billets: 1 and 2 Sections sharing a large barn, and 3 and 4 Sections each having a dug-out in the garden at the rear of the barn. The first thing the men of No 3 Section had to do, as my father recalls, 'was to clear our billets of the soiled straw, acting as both carpet and bedding. Here we came under fire for the second time that day, from the carelessly dropped ammunition mixed with the rubbish exploding when we burned it. There was no danger provided one kept well back from the blazing fire, as the bullets just jumped out like roasted chestnuts bursting. After remaking our beds and relaying the carpet with some clean straw, we had a meal and settled in. Afterwards most of us ventured out into the dark streets to sample the night life of Mazingarbe in the estaminets, which were plentiful. Groping our way into the bar of the first one we came to, which was crowded with kilted units of the 15th (Scottish) Division, Douglas, Chamberlain, and myself tried to ignore the ragged holes in the ceiling and the shrapnel-scarred walls, dimly visible in the faint light of a couple of small oil lamps, glimmering through a pungent fog of tobacco smoke. We joined two or three Jocks at a table in a comparatively quiet corner, where the draught from a broken window enabled us to breathe. During the ensuing conversation one of us remarked on the amount of damage done to the town. "Ay, it's the pipes. Jerry doesn't care for the pipe music", replied one of our new companions: "At sunrise, noon, and sunset the Division pipes and drums parade round the town, and Jerry always sends a few whizz-bangs over tae quieten them".' The Scotsmen also gave the usual old soldiers' advice that the shell you hear whistling has already missed you: 'it's the one ye don't hear to watch oot for'. The estaminets closed at 8 p.m., after which all troops returned to their billets.

Mazingarbe was a place from which many British troops had advanced for the battle of Loos; it was about three miles from the present front line. The village lay in a mining area, a flat plain, dominated by pithead gear, now smashed and twisted by gunfire, and black slag heaps which provided observation and machine-gun posts for both Germans and British. Around each pithead, or 'fosse', there were rows ('corons') of small red-brick miners' cottages, many of them now destroyed, but with habitable cellars beneath the ruins. At the village of Loos the twin mine-shaft towers, one with the top blown off, joined by a gantry, made a prominent landmark, inevitably nicknamed 'Tower Bridge'. In peacetime the mixture of mining and farming would have presented a scene not so very different from the villages around Nuneaton. French people were living and farming thereabouts despite all the shelling. The weather was atrocious; there was plenty of snow, rain, and knee-deep mud.

The Company were here to dig reserve trenches and make strong points on a defensive line between Vermelles and Grenay, taking over from another Buxton-trained Army Troops company, the 138th, which had been at Mazingarbe for four months. The 216th started work on 2 February; Sapper Fred Moore was of the opinion that 'that the job we are on now will last till the war is over, if ever it is'. As with everyone else at this stage, his mind was much exercised with shell fire: 'We had a couple of shells come over our billet the other night, but no damage was done. Yesterday, when we were at work, about a dozen shells burst 400 yards in front of us, but I don't think anyone was working there at the time. . . . There have been several aeroplanes up each day, both ours and Germans, and we can see the [anti-] aircraft shells bursting all round them'[2].

Arthur Daulman has a more circumstantial account of his experience of shell-fire that week. 'On the third day, a Wednesday, I was detailed to look after Lieut Smith's mid-day meal, so I set off back from the trenching to Mazingarbe. On the way I heard a big shell coming, so I dropped down on one knee, kettle in one hand and sandbag with the utensils in the other. The shell burst to the right-hand side about a couple of hundred yards away, so I got a move on until I found I had lost the kettle lid. I started back for the lid when a shell burst on the road about where I would have been if it hadn't been for that kettle lid. I reckon going back saved my bacon. I just didn't know what to do. Go on? Go back? So I stood well on the left hand of the road by a wall and the next shell dropped over the wall, so I decided to run the gauntlet and carry on. I made my way back to the village complete with lid. It had been just as though the German gunners were after me. But in fact they were after a more important target, for behind the wall, as I later found out, was a battery of 9.2s, really heavy guns. At that time those particular German shells that so alarmed me were nicknamed "coal box" or "Jack Johnson" because they buried themselves before exploding and threw clouds of black smoke and earth. Later they became even more lethal as they exploded on impact, and shrapnel flew low over a wide area'.

The 'Jack Johnson', named after the black American boxer who was world heavyweight champion, 1908-15, was the heavy shell fired over a very long range by the German 150 mm. howitzer, called by the English a 'five-nine' (150 mm. = 5.9"). It was not too difficult to detect *en route* because the roar of its passage preceded it, giving a few seconds' notice for men to dive for cover: one was safe if the roar continued. The black smoke came from the T.N.T. with which German high-explosive shells were charged. English shells were charged with lyddite, which burst with yellowish-white smoke, but my father remarks that the English heavy guns fired very rarely at this time on this sector of the front. 'Coal box' was also a nickname for the German 'minnie', the huge, devastating bomb lobbed by a heavy trench mortar ('minenwerfer').

Sapper Moore adds a couple of domestic details: 'Fred Sherriff has been making frying pans and tins the last two days. We have to be in billet at 8.30 and all lights out'.[3] It was presumably about this time that the men were ordered to polish the buttons and badges they had been ordered to blacken before leaving Buxton. What the 216th R.E. thought of the new order is not more fully recorded than in Pioneer Daulman's bemused comment quoted in the previous chapter, but the words of George Coppard, a private in the Machine Gun Corps, may well reflect their feeling: 'the luxury of not having to waste time and energy in senseless drudgery was to end. Could it be that the Top Brass feared that they might lose proper control of the troops unless they re-imposed the iron hand of "Bull"? The polishing of brass gear in the trenches was the very negation of the superb camouflage of the khaki uniform'[4].

A letter by Sapper Joe Smith to the *Nuneaton Observer*, printed on the same day as Fred Moore's in the *Chronicle*, considerately avoids direct mention of shelling: 'We are now settled down as comfortably as can be expected under the circumstances, and things are, of course, vastly different to what they were in training. I am taking advantage of this opportunity of writing to you to ask Nuneaton people if they can send us a melodion and a concertina to while away a few of our lonely hours out here. We do our best to amuse ourselves, trust us for that, but when the day's work is over night life in a French village is not very inspiring. Some people were inclined to laugh at us during our initial training at Nuneaton, but did they know the nature of our work now they would cease their carping criticisms and be inclined to praise us. We have experienced all the "joys" of French railway travelling, and the road marching is glorious, but we do our best to "keep smiling". When we think of the issue at stake, and what we are helping to bring about, any little inconvenience is cheerily passed over and we are eagerly awaiting more strenuous work to do. From training centre to firing-line in three days was a record for a company like ours just now, and we appreciate it.'

Neither Moore nor Smith mentions their need to while away part of the time in that highly necessary piece of domestic routine: personal delousing. Every front-line soldier was infested by lice, or 'chats' as the soldiers (adopting a very old term of thieves' cant) called them. They were a constant irritation, leaving blotchy red bite-marks all over the body and producing a distinctive sour, stale smell. My father recalls: 'We had not been in Mazingarbe above a day or two when we became acquainted with some very intimate companions, who travelled with us and on us, wherever we went. During our time in France we provided board and lodging for them, their descendants, and visiting relatives. In return for our hospitality they provided a relaxing indoor sport, we called "chatting". The hunt started by passing a candle flame along the seams of our clothes, which exploded the tiny white nits deposited there by the adults for us to hatch out and rear. Then the slothful adult population was dealt with, all captures being executed between our thumbs. One lot cleared away only made room for a fresh lot of immigrants, attracted by the various evil-smelling ointments sent by relatives at home which were guaranteed to eliminate them.'

Lice could carry disease as well as cause acute discomfort, so the military authorities attempted to combat them by providing the men with baths. During their three weeks at Mazingarbe the 216th Company had one bath, taken in a nearby disused brewery. My father recalls: 'Here we first deposited our clothes, and then went into a large brick-floored room, with bath tubs cut from beer barrels scattered about thereon. In these we squatted, and were then issued with one bucketful of hot water per man; the first served had hot water, the next lot found the water lukewarm, while the last served unfortunately usually scrambled from their tubs cursing and shivering after a douche of cold water down their backs. We took our own soap and towels. On our way back to our uniforms, we filed past a table piled with underclothes which had been fumigated; these were the discarded garments of previous units who had bathed and swapped their lingerie here. Despite the fumigation, they still sheltered a number of lice, which had survived this operation, and they were revived by their new landlords during the march back to billets. This annoyed us. "I don't mind my own lot so much, but damn anybody else's; the breed gets mixed up too much", complained several of us.'

No doubt they also retained some of their own personal lice in their own uniforms, which had been sulphured and ironed during the bathing session, to the same effect as the underwear. That is, some eggs remained, which within two or three hours were hatched by the wearer's body heat, so that the maddening itching and scratching began again. Lice were everywhere in the front line, so there is no reason to suspect that it was the Highlanders of 15th Division who infected the 216th R.E., but the Scots were notoriously lousy because their kilts had numerous pleats, which provided a perfect home for chats.

My father was well disposed towards these Scotsmen, who had been holding this part of the line since the previous summer. He writes: 'These chaps provided our working parties here, and we also mixed together in the evenings in the estaminets: in their company we soon passed through the "windy" period and began to take things as they came.' The 15th Division had certainly taken a great deal: by the end of the battle of Loos in the previous October it had taken nearly seven thousand casualties — a greater loss than any other British division involved in that bloody, indecisive action. At Mazingarbe now, with their numbers made up by new drafts, they were 'resting' behind other units of the First Army, billeted at roughly the same place from which they had advanced on the first morning of the battle. Their divisional headquarters were at Chateau Mazingarbe.

My father implies that the 216th and the Jocks at Mazingarbe enjoyed more harmonious relations than were traditionally thought to be normal between infantry and engineers. Royal Engineers, as skilled men, were much more highly paid than the infantry: a trained sapper for instance received half a crown a day, a private only a shilling. So, as much of the unskilled labouring and most of the fetching and carrying for field engineering work was done by gangs of infantrymen supervised by sappers, there was a rhyme, one version of which reads:

9. Chateau at Mazingarbe, pre-war: postcard sent by Sapper Thomas Wright to his parents, with the message: 'How should you like to live in a place such as this, rather a fine looking shanty. Not so nice as it looks though at present.'

'The Lord made men, bees make honey;
The infantry do the work, the R.E.s get the money.'

However, an infantry subaltern explained the relationship between infantryman and engineer in a way that reflects credit on both kinds of soldier: 'The infantry soldier regarded himself as a fighting man and could not be persuaded to take kindly to the role of pack animal. Soldiers who could be relied on to remain cheerful in the most exposed trenches on the front line became unwilling and resentful on fatigue... In public the infantry reviled the sappers day and night; in private they extended an admiration, no greater than was due, to a body of men who never enjoyed a period of even nominal "rest" out of the line, who endured many of the dangers and discomforts of the infantryman's life, yet were denied the occasional moment of exultation which was his compensation and reward'[5].

A letter by Corporal Streather on 20 February notes 'eleven French civvies have been working with us but they are not much good' and adds 'Everybody out here seems to be very confident that we can advance when we like, so we hope it will be over soon'. For some tasks the 216th R.E. chose not to avail themselves of the services of French civilians or Jocks — whether resentful or admiring. My father recalls: 'In this part of the line we were engaged in constructing strong points, improving the support lines and communication trenches. In some parts of the communication trenches tunnels were driven underneath the clod tips [slag heaps]; this work was done by small parties of the company without the assistance of infantry working parties. One of these gangs of four men consisted of Sappers Higham, Leishman, Chamberlain, and myself. Higham did the tunnelling, the rest

Army Form B. 218.

G. R.

HIS MAJESTY'S ARMY.

10th November, 1914.

This Leaflet is intended to take the place of any issued before this date.

WEEKLY RATES OF PAY OF PRIVATE SOLDIERS IN THE REGULAR ARMY AND SPECIAL RESERVE.

ARMS DRAWING PROFICIENCY PAY.	On Enlistment.	After two years' service.	PERIODS OF SERVICE. For the War only, or With Colours.	With Reserve.
Household Cavalry	12/3	14/- to 15/9	8 yrs.	4 yrs.
Cavalry of the Line	8/2	9/11 „ 11/8	7 „	5 „
Horse Artillery—				
Gunner	9/4	11/1 „ 12/10	6 „	6 „
Driver	8/9	10/6 „ 12/3	6 „	6 „
Royal Field Artillery	8/5½	10/2½ „ 11/11½	3 „	9 „
Royal Garrison Artillery	8/5½	10/2½ „ 11/11½	8 „	4 „
Foot Guards	7/7	9/4 „ 11/1	3 „	9 „
Infantry of the Line	7/-	8/9 „ 10/6	7 „	5 „

ARMS DRAWING ENGINEER OR CORPS PAY.	On Enlistment.	On completion of recruit training if qualified for corps duties.	Thereafter according to qualifications.	With Colours.	With Reserve.
Royal Engineers				3 yrs.	9 yrs.
Sapper	11/8	15/2	17/6 to 22/2	6 „	6 „
Pioneer	8/2	11/8	11/8	6 „	6 „
Driver	8/2	10/6	10/6 to 11/8	2 „	10 „
Royal Flying Corps	Special Rates.			4 „	4 „
Army Service Corps— Supply Branch, Private	8/2	9/11	11/8 „ 16/4	3 „	9 „
Horse Transport Driver	8/2	9/11	11/8	2 „	10 „
Mechanical Transport Section Artificer	8/2	9/11	11/8 to 17/6	7 „	5 „
Driver	8/2	9/11	11/8 „ 16/4		
Royal Army Med.	8/2	10/6	11/8 „ 12/10	3 „	9 „
Army Ordnance Corps	8/2	9/11	11/8 „ 16/4	6 „	6 „

Pay increases considerably on promotion.

10. Army rates of pay (Sappers were more highly paid than almost all soldiers of equivalent rank).

of us removed the loose earth and timbered the sides and roof of the tunnel as the heading was driven. A similar gang started from the other side of the tip to meet us; the directions and levels were checked daily by section officers or the company surveyors. The work went on normally for a day or two, and then we in our heading ran into trouble: nobody knew that the ground underneath this tip was intersected by deep ditches, and Higham was the first one to find out. While we three labourers were outside we heard a shout from Higham and a loud rumbling noise; then a cloud of dust slowly drifted out of the tunnel entrance. "That's it", said Chamberlain, "Let's go and see if Bill's all right". We found him partially buried, at the edge of a large mound of rubble and ashes raining down from a dome-like cavity in the underside of the tip. Higham was quickly excavated and taken outside, where we met Corporal Douglas, who had come to check our directions and levels. Finding all of us spitting ashes and dusting ourselves, he asked "What's the matter?" "The bloody tip's fell in, that's what's the matter", replied Higham. "How has that come about?" said Douglas. We indicated the last lot of debris brought out, which consisted mostly of topsoil and decayed vegetable matter. "When the dust has settled we'll go and have a look, then I'll go round and report to Lieutenant Smith; he's in the other heading." On inspection it was found that we had broken into a wide and deep ditch, but with a plentiful supply of sandbags, which we filled inside the tunnel with the fallen rubble and stacked behind the timbering, the sides and roof of the tunnel were made safe and the work was finished without any further setback. After three tunnels were finished, we joined the rest of the Company, who were at a small partly-obliterated hamlet called Philosophe, near to the remains of the chateau of Vermelles, where they were remaking communication trenches to the front line, about a mile away.'

During the battle of Loos, Philosophe, a derelict coal-mining village, had been the headquarters of an ill-fated New Army formation, the 21st Division, thrown into action within sixteen days of landing in France, thrown back by the Germans, and somewhat unfairly blamed for the lack of British success. One result of the battle was the replacement of Sir John French by Sir Douglas Haig as Commander in Chief. Haig was now meditating his 'Big Push' for 1916, but first it was necessary to establish a satisfactory defensive line in case the enemy should attempt to forestall his long-heralded Big Push by attacking first. The Nuneaton Company was helping to build this line. They worked southwards from Vermelles and Philosophe and, with the assistance of working parties provided by infantry units 'resting' out of the front line, they repaired and improved support lines and strong points. My father writes: 'Some rising ground in front of this place screened our work from Jerry, but there were plenty of whizz-bangs and shrapnel shells coming over, which hindered the work, but fortunately caused no casualties

11. Chateau at Vermelles after bombardment: 216 Company dug support trenches here in February 1916.

in the Company or the working parties.' The 'whizz-bangs' referred to were the high-explosive shells, fired with a flat trajectory by light artillery. They travelled faster than sound, so that anyone near the receiving end first heard the thing burst, then the whizz of its approach, and lastly the boom of the gun that fired it. There was no split-second warning, as was the case with howitzer shells, which had higher trajectories and less speed. Shrapnel shells were packed with small projectiles (usually metal balls) with a time-fused charge, so that they burst overhead and hurled down lethal rain.

The first casualties in the Company were received at ten minutes to nine o'clock on Sunday night, 6 February, a week after their arrival in Mazingarbe, when two shells fell on the barn where the right half-company and a few men from Section 3 of the left half were billeted, instantly killing five men and wounding twenty-one others, five of them seriously. Two Nuneaton men, Sappers "Dick" Harvey and "Cubby" Marston, were killed, and Sapper George Copson died of his wounds the following day. Harvey had been the articled pupil of an architect before enlistment, he would have been 21 had he lived another day. Copson, a bricklayer, was 36 with a wife and five young children. Marston was also married, with three children; he was recorded as being 41 but he was probably older; he was a wheelwright by trade, but had a wider expertise in country crafts because Arthur Daulman remembered that he was 'very good at making gabions and hurdles'. The other three killed on Sunday night, Sappers Barrier and Kerwood and Pioneer Ward were members of the Buxton draft, as also were Sappers Jacobs and Heath, who died of their wounds. Heath had married a fortnight before leaving Buxton. Among the seriously wounded were five Nuneaton men: 2nd Cpl Ernest Shade, the only N.C.O. among the twenty-six casualties, and Sappers Simmonds, Thomas, Warner, and Dennis Douglas. A French diary of this period records the number and calibre of German shells falling on Mazingarbe each day, together with the damage, injury, and death they caused.[6] From it we learn that the village was shelled on most days the 216th Company were there. On average, about half a dozen English soldiers were being killed and about twenty wounded every week, so the Nuneaton company's losses were normal for a very quiet week in a very unimportant place. Compared with a set-piece battle, this was indeed chicken feed.

The deaths and injuries on that Sunday night were caused not only by shells but also by heavy pantiles crashing down from the roof from the force of the explosions. Some men were lying on their beds, including Sapper Kerwood, who was reading his Bible. Four were playing nap, one of whom, 2nd Corporal Frank Cox, was badly shocked by seeing two of the players killed and having one of his tunic buttons cut off by a shell splinter. My father recalls: 'He was walking about during the clearing-up business, carrying his last cards, showing everyone, and complaining : "the best hand I've had all night, then Jerry stopped the game". Captain Cook took the cards from him and said "Yes, Corporal, I'll hold these while you help these other fellows", and in time Cox was calmed down.' The dead were each covered with a blanket, and the wounded were taken to a casualty clearing station; Copson, Jacobs, and Heath were moved to a field hospital, but the first two died the following day and Heath a short while afterwards.

On Monday the seven dead were buried among the local people in a communal cemetery outside Mazingarbe, with due military honours. The morning was spent rehearsing the funeral drill; in the afternoon the company paraded in strength on the road, ankle deep in sludge; my father was one of the party who fired the farewell salute; Frank Adams and Arthur Daulman blew the Last Post, the latter recalling that they 'had to take the bugles to the farm before the funeral to wash out the accumulated dust of weeks without use'. 'During the march back to billets after the ceremony', writes my father, 'a few whizz-bangs fell close to us, which caused a lot of dodging about and flopping down on the muddy road, the prone men usually causing the following files to trip over them. A few bruises and cuts from rifles swinging about were the only casualties.'

Captain Cook and Lieutenant Knox, whose half-company had sustained the casualties, wrote letters of condolence to widows and parents, some of which, along with letters from wounded survivors, were printed in the Nuneaton newspapers, not without an awareness of their possible effect upon recruitment. Thus Captain Cook told Mr Harvey that his boy, shortly before his death, attended a voluntary service 'at which a large number of men were present' and 'a hymn which was sung very heartily by everybody was, "The day Thou gavest, Lord, is ended".' Thus Lieutenant Knox, offering sympathy to Mrs Marston: 'The way your husband came forward at a time when his services were urgently needed set an example which many younger men might well follow'. Thus 2nd Corporal Ernest Shade, in hospital and lucky to have kept his leg, praising the officers and N.C.O.s of the 'happy family', the 'tip-top Company, and adding: 'I firmly believe that, if ever they do get a chance to have a real go at the Germans, they will give them one for themselves and another for their pals who have suffered'.[7]

As the barns were a total loss, the men formerly billeted in them removed to cellars in deserted houses near the church in the middle of the village. Corporal Toogood, Sapper Shelmerdine and one other man made a memorial cross in oak which was placed in Mazingarbe cemetery; later a brass plate, inscribed with numbers, ranks, and names was added to the cross. According to my father: 'For the next month or so Cox was very religious, and during his leisure hours in the cellar studied his pocket New Testament, quoting the "Good Book" at one moment, and the next swearing at any jester who requested him to read a chapter out loud, "for the good of us all". His chief tormentor was Sapper Salmon, and his request always brought a tirade from Cox. Looking over the top of his spectacles, he would ask in an aggrieved tone to the billet in general: "What's that bugger Salmon on about: can't a fellow read the bloody Bible without that bugger Salmon opening his bloody big mouth". Cox seemed surprised when the other chaps burst out laughing, but after a while his religious fervour abated and he returned to his normal sinful ways.'

'These New Testaments were presented to all of us on leaving England, and were usually carried in one of the top tunic pockets, along with our cigarettes and matches. Most of these books returned to the ladies in England who made the millions of sandbags sent to us for filling. Some of these women stitched a card inside a sandbag, giving their name and address, with an invitation to the "lonely soldier" finding it to correspond with them. We had a lot of lonely soldiers amongst us who were only too pleased to have an opportunity to "tell the tale" to a sympathetic lady friend. Our officers, when they censored some of these soldiers' tales must have been amused when they learned of the heroic feats some of their charges were performing, and wondering if they really knew their men. Anyway it was what the ladies wanted to read about, and the return parcel of comforts was always welcome. When the time came for breaking off these affairs, the pocket Testaments came in very handy; a neat bullet hole was punched through them with a hammer and a six-inch nail, and despatched with a covering note giving the fatal details to the lady. Quite a lot of these Testaments returned to England in this manner. If a photograph of the fair correspondent happened to be in the "dead" man's wallet, it went into the book before the fatal "bullet" struck. With the assurance that the end was quick and painless; this statement was quite true; the only thing the lady could do then was to stitch another card into a sandbag, and hope for better luck with her next lonely soldier.' One way to cope with the possibility of one's own sudden death is to make a joke about it. So these men devised their blackly-humorous reversal of the familiar 'pocket-book-that-stopped-the-bullet' story that they had read time and time again in the newspapers. This was comedy in 'the theatre of war'[8].

After the deaths at Mazingarbe the Sergeant-Major insisted that the survivors should immediately send field cards, reading either 'I am quite well' or 'I have been admitted into hospital wounded and hope to be discharged soon'; Arthur Daulman notes that 'later casualties were not accorded the same treatment'. The field card was one of three different ways of sending letters. First, a green envelope which was issued once a month, the contents of which were liable to be censored at the base. Second, a plain envelope which could be posted at the company orderly room unsealed, the contents of which were censored by the company officers. Third, the quick and easy, buff-coloured, uncensored field card, with printed phrases, the irrelevant ones of which were to be crossed out by the sender. The cards my father sent read: 'I am quite well and hope to be discharged soon. I have received your letter, etc. Letter follows at first opportunity.' He notes that 'the "discharged soon" bit was just wishful thinking, and the "letter follows soon" never materialized: we always seemed to be too busy.'

Some of his comrades found time for longer letters, though. Charles Streather's letters to his parents are full and, considering the fact of censorship, remarkably informative. On 22 February, for instance: 'We have had a rough day here today: about three inches of snow on the ground now. However the wind has changed and it is warmer and the snow is going fast. Yesterday was a beautiful day as far as the weather went. We got on the works, Douglas and I and the Royal Scots, and two German aeroplanes were over. They flew over our lines twice then were driven back; this was about 8.30. At 9.30 they began to shell the trenches and the batteries in front of us quietly at first but heavily afterwards. As the day wore on the bombardment grew more intense and at times we could see as many as 30 shells bursting all at once. The din was deafening as they were using some very big guns and of course our own guns replied. I think I told you that the front where we are is in the form of a horseshoe and we are in the centre of it. So we

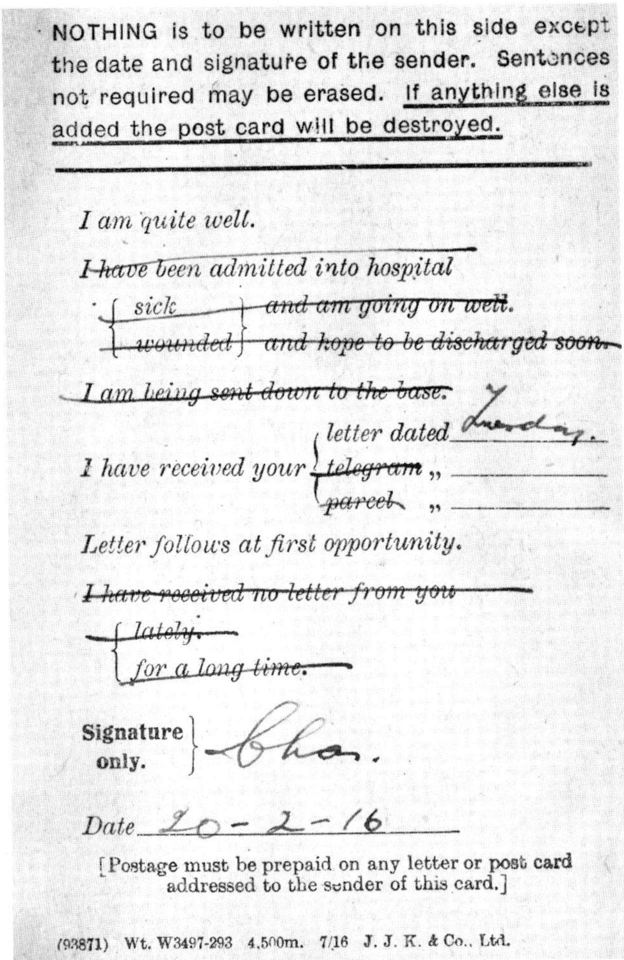

NOTHING is to be written on this side except the date and signature of the sender. Sentences not required may be erased. If anything else is added the post card will be destroyed.

I am quite well.

~~*I have been admitted into hospital*~~

~~*sick*~~ ~~*and am going on well.*~~
~~*wounded*~~ ~~*and hope to be discharged soon.*~~

~~*I am being sent down to the base.*~~

I have received your *letter dated* Tuesday.
~~*telegram*~~ ,,
~~*parcel*~~ ,,

Letter follows at first opportunity.

~~*I have received no letter from you*~~
~~*lately.*~~
~~*for a long time.*~~

Signature only. Chas.

Date 20 - 2 - 16

[Postage must be prepaid on any letter or post card addressed to the sender of this card.]

(93871) Wt. W3497-293 4,500m. 7/16 J. J. K. & Co., Ltd.

12. Army Field Card.

had shells bursting all round: most of them were between half a mile and a mile off but two or three came within 120 yds of our work. On one patch of land about as big as our garden they dropped 50, if not more, and there was absolutely nothing on it. This was about 300 yds from our work so we could see the effect. The shell holes are about 4ft 6ins or 5ft deep and about 16 or 17ft across. They fell close together and the ground was simply ploughed up all over and not one bit of damage done. The country here is perfectly flat and is not enclosed in any way: no hedges or fences of any kind, not even at the road side. This makes it possible to see right on to the horizon just like you can at sea. The only landmarks are buildings and big clod banks just like you get at the pits in Nuneaton. These banks provide good marks and they get pounded terribly but we have nothing in them or on them. In fact although thousands of shells dropped within sight and hearing I only heard of 3 casualties all only slightly wounded. The 3 men were in the R.G.A. [Royal Garrison Artillery]. An English airman was brought down; he landed well to start with but rose again and then turned turtle. Straight away 50 shells were sent round [the plane] but it was not hit nor were the men nor the rescue party. While this was going on we captured 2 lines of trenches to our front so we came off pretty well yesterday. I shall never forget the row, though of course we were never in danger. . . The Northamptons are billeted close to us now; they have just come out for a six day rest. We go down 5 miles on Thursday and shall then get no shells near at all. None came into the village yesterday. . . Have only seen two or three battalions that have not been Scots yet.'

This, as it happens, was sent in a green envelope, to be censored, if at all, at base. It appears that the second kind of letter, censored in the Company, was favoured by Sapper West. My father recalls that he 'made good use of the second method to air any grievance relating to the officers' conduct, the quality and quantity of the rations, or billets, etc. He would announce that it was time he sent a letter to the Captain; he would ask of the billet in general for any current grouses, and include them in a letter to his "Aunt Fanny". When the letter was censored and prolifically blue pencilled, West was ordered to the orderly room, where Captain Cook handed to him the blue-pencilled script with the remark, "I don't like the tone of that letter, West, I advise you to stop writing that kind of letter to your aunt". When Capt Cook left us at Morbecque, and Capt MacDougall took command, West had no further use for any fictitious relatives.'

The memoirs of officers in other units sometimes refer to the tiresome duty of reading and censoring men's letters. Charles Carrington, Royal Warwickshire Regiment, writes: 'in retrospect, this seems one of the most intolerable intrusions into privacy that the military life demanded. It was also a great burden to the company officers to read a hundred ill-written letters every evening'. We may assume that letters from the skilled, and in several cases grammar-school educated, men of the 216th R.E. were more literate than the average, and Carrington himself goes on to concede that the letters of his men were not so very ill-written. He reflects: 'As we sat round the dug-out table, reading piles of letters by the light of one candle-end, we got to know our men with a new intimacy, not because they opened their hearts in letters which would be so public, but because they revealed their characters. Whatever else, this sharing of privacy tightened the bond between officers and men'[9]. Even so, one imagines that Captain Cook did not care for Sapper West's effort to tighten the bond of this intimacy.

There was an Army Post Office at Mazingarbe, managed by a Royal Engineer sapper named David Edge, a Stockingford man, who knew a lot of the men in the Nuneaton company. The postal connection between home and the front was very rapid and efficient: bringing two utterly different worlds into a proximity the absurdity of which was not lost on the men at Mazingarbe. My father recalls; 'Some of the chaps in the Company received the "Nuneaton Observer" regularly; one copy received at this time contained an advertisement by a local bricklayer, who had several former workmates amongst our number, stating his ability and willingness to carry out all repairs to roofs and chimneys (estimates free). A very enjoyable evening was spent in our local estaminet replying to this advertisement, inviting him to join the company, and assuring him that there were enough damaged roofs and chimneys in Mazingarbe to keep him busy for the duration of the war. Everyone who knew him signed this letter, but we got no reply.'

To judge by the reminiscences of other British soldiers in France, Sapper West would have found much to tell his Aunt Fanny about Army rations. Other Great-War memoirs tell of the unvaried diet of plum and apple jam, corned beef ('bully') and Army biscuit, indistinguishable from dog biscuit. A Royal Artillery private claimed that the biscuits were 'so hard that you had to put them on a firm surface and smash them with a stone or something. I've held one in my hand and hit the sharp corner of a brick wall and only hurt my hand. Sometimes we soaked the smashed fragments in water for several days. Then we would heat and drain, pour condensed milk over a dishful of the stuff and get it down'[10]. Royal Engineers, though, could afford, and the Nuneaton men at Mazingarbe had the opportunity, to buy food locally. My father recalls that, whenever they could, they bought French bread as a relief from Army biscuit. He also recalls Pioneer Hallsworth bringing a Camembert cheese he had bought into number 3 Section dug-out and proclaiming that it was an 'epicure's dream'; but his comrades did not agree, so it was decided to drop the delicacy into the stove-pipe sticking through the roof of Section 4's dug-out. He writes: 'Our stoves were home-made affairs, consisting of a large paint drum, with a pipe (made of biscuit tins hammered round a pole) let into the top, and leading straight up through the surface of the ground. Anything dropped down this pipe dropped into the fire below. After dark we scouted the position, and finding no one about, the cheese was dropped down the pipe, with a turf put over the chimney top so that the inmates below would get the full benefit of the aroma.' The resulting stench and smoke compelled the Section 4 men to put their gas helmets on. 'The cheese party came in for some suspicious glances, but nothing could be proved against us, and after a few remarks about childish behaviour the incident was closed.'

The fear of genuine poison gas was real and justified. It was, after all, in this very sector of the front, four months earlier, that the British had first used poison gas against the Germans, and, incidentally, experienced the unpredictability of that weapon. The *Official History* dryly records that, on that occasion, the gas discharge floated back towards the British trenches, 'causing great inconvenience and some loss'[11]. Gas would be used by both sides with increasing frequency through 1916. German gas shells fell on Mazingarbe on 8 and 21 February. At the end of April the Germans made two more sustained gas attacks on the front just north of Loos, necessitating the use of gas hoods three miles behind the front line; the smell of gas was noticed fifteen miles away. The 216th R.E. would come under gas attack at Cabaret Rouge in May. The gas helmet referred to in my father's tale was a large bag consisting of two thicknesses of flannelette, made to cover the head, with goggles sewn in, and a clip which was placed in the mouth; this enabled the wearer to breathe out normally, but breathe in through the material of the hood which was impregnated with a solution of protective chemicals (sodium hyposulphite and phenate); the opening of the bag had to be tucked tightly into the neck of the wearer's buttoned tunic.[12] My father described the chemical as 'foul' and said: 'Wearing one of these masks was worse than being gassed'.

Apart from such escapades and alarms, the work of the Company and their working parties in tunnelling, digging trenches, and constructing strong points continued as normal. Their main task was to build a support line to the immediate rear of the front line north of Loos in the strip of land captured so bloodily during the previous autumn. They were also creating defences in depth, for, when some of the Company were digging and tunnelling near the oddly-named village of Philosophe, a mile from the front, a detachment of bricklayers and carpenters, including my father, was to the south, further in the rear, constructing brick and concrete machine-gun emplacements in a field bordering the road from Mazingarbe to Hersin Coupigny.

My father recalls: 'Opposite this field on the other side of the road was a large colliery, the dominant feature of which was a tall chimney. Some of the buildings in the yard were used as the divisional ration dump, and the yard was extensive enough to accommodate the swarm of mules and G.S. wagons sent here to collect the rations of the various units in the division. We had not been many days on this work before Jerry tried to knock this chimney down and at the same time to scatter the ration parties. These shells were long-range stuff, and came over at intervals, so the ration distribution was speeded up, and the wagons were leaving at a faster rate than usual. The first one or two fell wide, and there were very few wagons left in the yard when one of the shells scored a direct hit on the base of the chimney, which broke half way up, and the lot collapsed in a cloud of soot and flying bricks. The animals stampeded through the gates and away along the roads, with their drivers running after, trying to catch up with them. Although there were some injuries to man and beast, there were no fatal casualties. When we went across afterwards we found no one lying about.'

Shelling, food, and drink were the major concerns of soldiers in the Great War, so my father's recollection continues unsurprisingly: 'There was an estaminet opposite the colliery gates, where we were in the habit of spending our mid-day break, and having vin blanc to help our biscuits and bully down. On this morning a wedding party was having a reception in the estaminet, and when the shelling started had taken refuge in the cellar with the patron and his family, leaving plenty of wine and most of the wedding breakfast on the table. Corporal Keen, who was in charge, said, "If this place gets hit, that lot will get smashed; we'll see it off". So we kept the festivities going and drank the healths of the bride and groom. It was while we were here that the chimney was struck, and we had a good view of the collapse and the ensuing commotion. After leaving our bully and biscuits on the table in payment for a very excellent time, we went over to the colliery to see if anyone was about, but found no one, so we returned to our work. Next day we called at the estaminet at our usual time and sympathised with the patron's complaints about the "brigands" who had made such havoc with the wedding breakfast.'

Chapter Four: Bouvigny-Boyeffles, March to May 1916

On 14 February 1916 the Company left Mazingarbe, and, with all its equipment, marched north-west towards Béthune. The march was very disagreeable, for the start was long delayed, a bitterly cold blustery wind and snow showers continued throughout the day, and snow and ice made a thin crust on the ever-present mud. After dark the men arrived at a large isolated farm. My father recalls: 'The transport pulled into the farmyard, where the four leading mules got bogged down in the midden which filled up the centre of the yard. In the ensuing struggling and swearing to extricate them and the G.S. wagon, everyone engaged was liberally spattered with liquid manure. When everything was finally sorted out and men and mules had been rubbed down, we were allotted our billets in the barns and sheds on each side of the yard. The cooks got busy making tea, and we supped on the usual bully and biscuits we carried in our haversacks, and then got down to get some rest, fully dressed, except for our boots, with our overcoats on. There was a sharp frost during the night, but we slept well enough, and woke at dawn to find we had been provided with a blanket composed of a thick layer of snow over us. When we scrambled out we found we had a billet without any roof and the snow was still falling onto us.' However, he continues, 'There was no lack of broken rafters and tiling laths lying about, so we soon got a large fire going to dry ourselves out and to air the shed. The smoke had plenty of room to escape, and did not bother us. The cooks had a fire going outside, and made a dixie of tea for each section, and we had the similar breakfast as we had at supper. Whilst drying out and getting warm, we used the tepid tea left in our mess tins for shaving, afterwards washing our faces with a tea-soaked shaving brush. When we fell in ready to move off, Captain Cook and the Sergt Major inspected us, duly noticing the many razor nicks which proved that the bearers thereof had at least gone through the motions of shaving. When they were satisfied that everything about us was more or less in order, we went on our way in the direction of Béthune.'

At last in the afternoon they reached Minx, or Verquin, in the rear of the 15th Division's sector. This was a small village with a large colliery (Leon Renaud, Fosse No 2), in the empty store rooms of which the men were billeted. Their duty here was to acquire skill and speed in putting together and taking apart steel girder bridges, the parts of which lay in a corner of the colliery yard. While most of the Company trained at Minx, Lieutenant Knox and half a dozen men and N.C.O.s, including Corporal Streather, went to the R.E. depot at Le Havre for a more advanced course in heavy steel bridging. Charles Streather wrote to his parents from the Le Havre Y.M.C.A. on Wednesday, 1 March: 'I am pleased to say I am quite well and down at the base camp where we landed. Mr. Knox, Stone, Douglas, Loam, Moore, and Keen are with me: we are on a course of heavy steel girder bridging. We are working by the sea side actually on the beach at times. We left M— at 8.0 a.m. on Monday and were travelling for 36 hours. We had plenty of grub and got a lot of sleep but it was cold and we had to carry all our kit, so it was a rotten journey. The last 100 miles we were in trucks. I was asleep all the time pretty well so I was not tired, which was a good thing for we had about 4 miles to march and the kit weighs about 120 lbs now, all told. The work we are doing here is quite interesting and wonderfully good training. Today we launched a 17 ton steel girder 90 ft long; tomorrow we shall complete the bridge which will carry 33 tons, that is anything, you may say. There are all sorts of tackle here: factories with all kinds of machinery, and material and men without end. The camping arrangements are very good but as we are only here for 5 days we are under canvas. . . I never felt better, the open air seems to suit me. I am as strong as any one and can work as hard as the next when it is required. Knox is a good chap to be with on a job like the present. He gave us some money to get a good feed at the Y.M.C.A. and a pass to get in there in working hours. These Y.M.C.A.s are good places and they are all over the place anywhere where numbers of soldiers are likely to congregate. . . Stone and I have our meals in the N.C.O.s' mess and live like human beings once more. I had almost forgotten how to eat from a plate and the knife and fork seemed quite strange weapons. I expect to get back to M— about Monday or Tuesday.' Corporal Streather thought that Le Havre was, 'like all French towns, very dirty', though he was impressed by the brightness of its lights. My father writes of the Le Havre party: 'judging from their conversation when they rejoined us, night life was more advanced than night life at Minx'.

The Company had built heavy wooden girders at Buxton in January: six weeks later they were assembling girders of steel. Their new training was evidence of forward thinking by High Command: (very far forward in the case of the Nuneaton men, who would not put their newly-developed skills into practice until 1918). From the beginning of the war the British, unlike the Germans, had understood the value of motor transport.[1] The historian of R.E. bridging in the Great War observes: 'the rate of advance of an army fed and supplied mainly by motor transport, and with a very large proportion of heavy artillery, would depend in a measure on the rapidity with which heavy bridges could be constructed. The width of the front demanded a large number of bridges to be constructed simultaneously, with labour which could only be partly skilled, consequently the organisation of supply of materials, namely — storage, sorting, loading and despatch, reception near site, and transport, had to be perfected, and full instructions for erection had to be formulated, based on local conditions. Types of bridges had to be standardised after experiment, and also methods of erection to compensate for the lack of fully skilled labour and superintendence. . . . The appointment of field engineers (civil engineers of good technical experience) made early in 1915 was partly designed with a view to the superintendence of heavy bridging work . . . as demands for bridges increased, the field engineers were gradually taken on to the staff of Chief Engineers of corps and armies as bridging officers.'[2]

Specifications were approved for steel girder bridges in a range of standard lengths (16', 21'6", 30', 60', and 85') to carry a 13 ton axle load ('B type' bridge) or 17 tons ('A type'). As the war had become static by 1915 there was little demand for spans when first ordered, so they were held at the R.E. Base Park, Le Havre, which thereupon developed as a Heavy Bridging School until a Bridging School was established at Aire. Nevertheless, in October 1915, the Engineer-in-Chief, Brig-Gen G.H.Fowke, sought and obtained authority from Sir John French, the Commander-in-Chief, to order a 10,000 ft run of additional steel bridging: his object was to allow for ten bridges per army corps (British and French), assuming twenty corps (British and French) in the line.[3]

Meanwhile, training in steel-bridge assembly continued: one of its incidental benefits being an interesting break from field fortifications for the 216th Company. Notwithstanding its lack of night life Minx was an agreeable posting. My father recalls: 'The billets here were comfortable and weatherproof, the main feature of each one being a large cast-iron stove standing in the centre. Trestle tables and benches completed the furnishing, and hurricane lamps suspended from the ceiling provided light: we bought the oil with our usual bully beef currency from the colliery lamp man. Occasionally we bought some coal from the office just to keep near the stove as proof that we were not thieving coal all the time.' There were no rats and the village had never been shelled.

During the time they were at Minx, the Company was brought up to strength by a draft from the base at Rouen. Most of the new men were Northerners, but Sapper Thomas came from Nuneaton to join his brother who was already in the Company. They were all sappers, except Corporal Henley, soon to be promoted Sergeant of No 1 Section after Sergeant Lee went home. My father writes of two of the new sappers, James Crawford and James Mitchel,[4] that they 'were lively lads and Crawford could always tell the tale. They had enlisted together at Glasgow and were sent from there to the R.E. barracks at Chatham. Leaving Scotland with plenty of whisky inside them and a sufficient stock to last out the journey, they arrived at Euston in a somnolent state, and spent some time there, enquiring for the Chatham train. Getting the answer "Victoria, mate" from every ticket-inspector or porter they accosted, they were eventually handed over to the care of one of the Civil Defence Volunteers, who haunted the stations, directing and assisting any servicemen who found London confusing. This chap took them to Victoria and put them on the right train. They arrived at Chatham after dark and finished their remaining whisky, and then decided to telephone to the barracks. Inside the telephone booth, whilst looking for the number in the directory, Mitchel sat on the floor and went to sleep, and Crawford, after vainly trying to find the number, sat on Mitchel and also dropped off, and they both had a "cat nap", as Crawford said, for about an hour. They were jolted awake by the door being forcibly opened, and became aware of a crowd of excited people who wished to use the telephone, behind a couple of Military Policemen trying to get in to arrest them. They were taken to the R.E. barracks in a police van and spent their first night of service in the guard room. The following morning they were both awarded fourteen days' confined to barracks (C.B.), and "thus", concluded Crawford, "we made our debut in the Corps of Royal Engineers".'

Minx was a quiet place. My father writes: 'The only shells we heard here were the occasional heavy long-distance stuff droning over in the distance towards Béthune, which did not disturb us in any way, and we got on with our course for eight hours every day, except Sunday, which was a holiday. Our evenings were spent until eight o'clock in the estaminets. After nearly three weeks of this nut and bolt work, the detached N.C.O.s rejoined us, and a day or two afterwards we cleared everything away and left Minx. Before we left, we spent a last evening with the friends we had made in the 15th Division, who were out on rest in the neighbourhood, and listened to the pipes unmolested by Jerry.'

While the 216th were at peace in Minx the Germans began a massive assault upon the important French stronghold of Verdun, the immediate result of which was that between 2 and 14 March the French Tenth Army had to be transferred from its section of the front near Arras to a section of the River Somme front, so that other French units could join in the defence of Verdun and play their part in a battle of attrition that became the 'mincing machine', which for eleven months drew in and destroyed more and more units on both sides, until, by December, the total casualties were over 700,000 men. As the French moved their troops away from the Arras front, the British First Army gradually extended its right flank southwards to take over the French positions. Among the British units involved in this movement was the 23rd Division, to whose area the 216th Company was now posted. This division consisted mostly of battalions drawn from the county regiments of north-east England. Not surprisingly, in view of their recruiting area, these battalions were rich in miners; the division was therefore able to form its own tunnelling company for offensive and defensive mining; so we do not hear of the Nuneaton Company tunnelling in this divisional area.

On 6 March the 216th Company marched south along the main Béthune-Arras road in the ever-present snow and slush, through the village of Sains-en-Gohelle, arriving at Bouvigny-Boyeffles that evening. This village straggled for about a mile on either side of the road, which then continued up to the wooded crest of Notre Dame de Lorette, which was an outlying spur of Vimy Ridge held by the British, though the Germans still held the main part of the ridge. My father noted of their march that day: 'Close to Bouvigny the road came under observation from the German lines and we on our side had a good view of their territory, but did not linger to admire it'. The Nuneaton men would become accustomed to this view, however, because much of their work was to be carried out between Bouvigny-Boyeffles and the town of Lens, which was in German hands. This terrain was chalk downland, rather like Wiltshire but more steeply scarped; much of it was overlooked by the Germans on Vimy Ridge to the south-east.

My father writes: 'The French Army had moved away further south to the Somme area, but a battery of their 75 mm. guns were still emplaced in the bank of a sunken road. We passed this way to our work on the ridge, going to and from Bouvigny. They were here for a fortnight after the 23rd Division took over, but they kept close to their dug-outs, and very rarely replied when we wished them "bon jour", and did not mix with our chaps in any way.' The British brought some heavier guns to this area when the 24th Siege Battery, Royal Garrison Artillery, moved in. My father mentions two 9.5 howitzers at Maroc, in the hollow below Notre Dame de Lorette, and notes that one burst while firing on Lens. He also observes 'At that time the English were very short of shells, so that the guns fired hardly at all': stocks of ammunition were being conserved for the Big Push to come. The artillery headquarters for the 23rd Division was in Bouvigny, but, apart from artillerymen, the 216th Company had the village to themselves as far as troops were concerned. 'Resting' infantrymen of the division provided working parties when required. 'There were plenty of French civilians still living here', says my father: 'a few farmers and labourers, some miners who worked in the collieries of the pits still in production between Bouvigny and Hersin, and the village was comfortably off for estaminets'.

13. Arthur Sambrook's sketch of his billet at Bouvigny.

Corporal Streather's first letters from Bouvigny mention French civilians and the terrain, but, like most letters from the front, are concerned mostly with the weather and physical comforts (or the lack of them): 'We had a very heavy fall of snow again yesterday and last night, and it was cold out on the works today. I have never had dry feet since leaving England till today, and I have got a pair of India Rubber waders so I shall be alright now. . . . I should like a pair of socks please; my others are pretty well done for now. You see we get very little chance to wash them' (10 March). 'Today it was quite hot and yet the snow is still on the ground in one or two places. . . . The country we are working in now is rather hilly: quite a change for us. From the works we get a splendid view of the line: it is almost like looking down on a big map, but of course I must not tell you about that. The people here know very little English; I have found my French very useful and shall soon be quite expert' (13 March).

It was in the woods around Bouvigny that the German advance had been halted in October 1914, but in the later months of the French occupation of this part of the front it was very quiet. According to Arthur Daulman, 'it was said that the French had been playing cards with the Germans'. It was the policy of the British High Command, though, to cultivate the 'offensive spirit', so the 23rd Division was ordered to make the Germans feel its presence by way of artillery fire and trench raids. This provoked retaliatory shelling, on which account, and in the light of their experience at Mazingarbe, the various sections of the 216th Company were billeted as far apart as possible in sheds, barns, and the cellars of partly-demolished houses. Company headquarters, quartermaster's stores, and officers' billets were scattered about the lower end of the village; Section 3 of the left half-company thought itself fortunate in being nearly a mile away at the top end of the village, albeit nearer to the front line by that distance.

Allocation of billets seems to have involved a certain degree of self help. My father writes: 'A few of us, including Corporal Streather, took over a small hovel at the entrance to a farmyard; there were no windows and the place was dark and damp, having a well underneath. We were frequently disturbed by the farmer's wife coming in to draw water, so we did not stay here above a day or two.' Corporal Streather luckily found a place with 'no rats, on a ground floor in a barn with plenty of straw and a good door so we can keep free from wind and snow' (letter of 8 March). My father recalls: 'After looking over the various vacant properties available, Douglas, Chamberlain, Leishman, and myself took over the only habitable room in a wrecked farmhouse on the other side of the road. The only entrance to this room was by a small casement window, where our first job was to nail sandbags over the frame to exclude the weather. The usual entrance by the door from the house was blocked up on the other side by rubble and beams, rafters, etc., from the rest of the place. The stables and barns on each side of the yard fronting onto the road were used to stable the horses and mules of the left half-company. Our tool carts and other vehicles were parked in the centre of the yard. The section cookhouse was established in one of the larger barns. Occupying as we did the last room in the village, from our window we had an extended view of the road continuing up to the wooded crest of Notre Dame de Lorette, an outlying spur of Vimy ridge and the undulating fields on either side of the road between the ridge and the village. Some of these fields were still cultivated by a farmer who lived near to our billet in a farm which had only suffered slight damage, together with his very fat madame and three attractive teen-age daughters named Stephanie, Sophie, and Marie.'

It seems that the village housed, or was intended to house, a far grander military formation than a company of Royal Engineers because at one stage the 216th were ordered to fit out an empty chateau which had been requisitioned for a Brigade Headquarters. However, writes Arthur Daulman, 'Before we had time to take it over it was destroyed by German gunners: six salvos, eight shells at a time of 5.9s, a real forerunner of blitzkrieg, left the chateau in ruins'. Daulman wonders if the Germans knew that the building was to be a headquarters, and adds a spy story: 'At that time we were very spy conscious. Anyone catching a spy was rewarded with a sum of money and a month's leave. Well worth having. At this time one Sunday night an officer inquired the way to Bouvigny Church of someone standing outside our billet. He, the soldier, went inside to say what had been asked. Sapper Reynolds, a policeman from Leamington, growled, "Tell him to come inside. Let's have a look at him." The officer probably guessed that suspicions had been aroused, for he volunteered, "I'm an officer of the 23rd Fusiliers, I'm not a Bosche". Pre-war shafts and galleries of coal mines extended from Mazingarbe and Philosophe to places behind the German front. 'That the French used the galleries for the purpose of passing agents behind the German lines is now certain, and that the Germans used them for the same purpose is at least highly probable'[5].

Even so, there were far more real dangers than spies here. As at Mazingarbe, shell fire was the killer. On 16 March, a sunny, warm day, Sapper Pullen of No.3 Section was killed when, writes my father, 'he went out of the village up the road to look for two artillery men who had gone there some time previously.' Arthur

Daulman adds that he 'was killed here by a shell which landed between two farm buildings, killing him but harming no one else. We were getting hardened to casualties but we missed him for, when all was quiet, many a time he gave us a service; he being a Salvation Army man (and the company very rarely saw a padre). Once, when someone not in our company got hit on the road to the Observation Post and lay there, Pullen went straight away to see what he could do, much to the anger of the Sergeant-Major for risking himself. It seemed a bit uncharitable, but I think our Sergeant-Major was really expressing his concern for us all. Harry Trevis waited by Pullen's side all night until the R.A.M.C. came to take the body away.' Photographs of the company at Buxton show Sapper Pullen as a dapper, kindly-looking, small man. His death was reported in the *Nuneaton Tribune* on 7 April, together with the unlikely information that he 'was serving at the front with a bombing party of the Royal Engineers'. A memorial service was held in Nuneaton Salvation Army Citadel. On the day Pullen was killed Sapper Dodds the boxer was seriously wounded, Sappers Baxter and Croft were slightly wounded, and Corporal Wiggins' leg was fractured by falling masonry. My father writes ungenerously of the Corporal: 'so we lost a bad cook and got a worse one when "Monkey" Williams was promoted into that job. We went across to the house and took Wiggins to the dressing station, which was at the bottom end of the village, near to our headquarters, and that was the last the company saw of him.'

On the following day my father had a visit from his older brother Albert, a corporal in a Royal Engineer Signals company at Petit Servins, on the far side of the Lorette ridge; he had heard about the Mazingarbe casualties and had come to

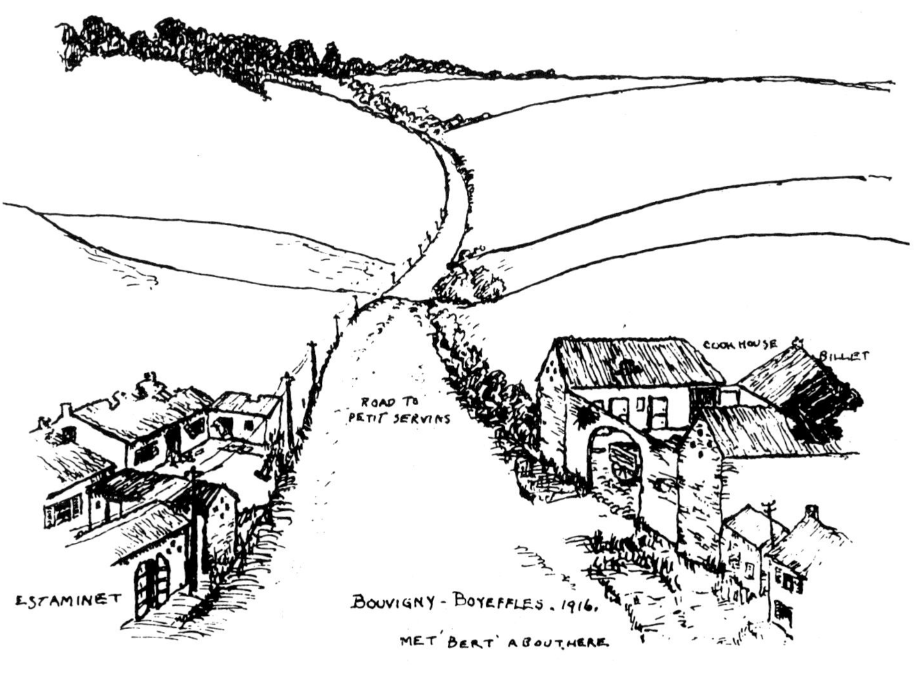

14. Bouvigny, looking south (sketch by Arthur Sambrook).

see if his kid brother was O.K. Sergeant-Major Mitchinson showed his humanity again by allowing my father, who was on cookhouse fatigues that day, to spend an hour drinking and yarning with his brother. On the following Sunday the Company was to have one of its rare holidays. Corporal Streather wrote, 'there is a service in the billet at 10 and after that we get a pass to go and have a look round the next village, though I don't suppose it is much better than the one we are in. All the French villages and the people seem to be about alike: "dirty".' Pioneers Sambrook and Daulman, however, did use their pass because my father wanted to make a return call on brother Bert. After returning from the Saturday night's work, he writes, 'we had breakfast, cleaned ourselves up a bit, and set off up the road and over the ridge. When we got to the trees on the crest of the hill we sat on the roadside and ate a large tin of pears between us before we went on to Servins. We found Bert playing nap with a few others, so we sat in with them until the estaminet opened.' The two youngsters stayed for lunch, which Daulman remembers as 'Maconochies tinned meat and vegetables, a good meal for two', though not every soldier would agree with this verdict on the famous or infamous tinned meat and vegetables named after the manufacturer, Maconochie.[6] Daulman and Sambrook then walked back the three miles or so to Bouvigny in the afternoon, 'resting on the top again' says my father 'to enjoy the extensive view over the German-held territory, and the bare slope of Vimy ridge away to our right hand'. Though this was part of the same landscape as theirs, it was a sealed-off, foreign world, full of the invisible enemy. Daulman remarked that 'the trees showed little sign of shell fire damage and everything looked very peaceful, considering the road was open to hostile observation.'

An officer of the 23rd Division wrote of this view one morning in the early summer of 1916: 'as I came down the wooded slope on the north side of the Notre Dame de Lorette Spur I could see the whole plain as far as La Bassée. Lens was quite distinct, and the flash of a gun firing near Loos was visible, though the report could not be heard. Birds all round were singing, and but for that one gun, the only sign of war, all seemed perfect peace. Very pleasant it was, too, to reach the village as the men's breakfast was being cooked. The whole village was fragrant with the aroma of frying bacon, and I reflected that at that hour a similar fragrance must exhale from the whole British line'.[7] Perhaps the 216th Company was a culinary exception, because Frank Hextall thought that their food at Bouvigny was poor: 'bully beef and biscuits all Easter week'. Army biscuits were described as 'not McVitie's: definitely Spratt's'. A letter written by Corporal Streather on Easter Sunday gives more detail about food: 'we did not do so bad for some time but it's pretty rotten now. However we get plenty of money and can buy, though the price is tremendous. Eggs are fairly cheap and plentiful so is milk. Meat to the French is almost unknown so we can't buy that, but we sometimes get bacon which is pretty good. We get plenty of biscuits and the eternal army marmalade (I think the jam has all gone) and plenty of bacca and fags dished out.' Even so, 'What strikes me most in France is the spirit of our troops, though they grumble night and day of course. It's wonderful. No matter where or when, in danger, privation, or what, they always manage to keep a smile on and are ready to turn anything to ridicule.' There were exceptions of course. It was about this time that the Company lost Sergeant Lee. My father says: 'Cook did not like it, as Lee had promised him he would stay with the company. Lee said he had had enough of this silly game and was time expired and was going home.'

My father describes their work at Bouvigny: 'we laid out and constructed a system of trenches and dug-outs in the rear of the front line on a ridge which overlooked the town of Lens, in the German lines, on one side, and Bouvigny on the other side. From this ridge we had an extensive view of the front in every direction, which we found very interesting. Jerry evidently found our activities equally interesting and soon treated us to a few "whizz-bangs" and crumps of heavy shrapnel, which made us get out of sight quickly. During this excitement I came by a piece of shrapnel on my right knee, resulting in torn trousers and a bruise which made walking difficult for over a week. Luckily it was a glancing blow, which broke neither bone nor skin. Afterwards we always worked here during the darkness', and, says Arthur Daulman, 'we developed cats' eyes'. One reason for not working on the ridge in daylight is given in a letter of Corporal Streather's on 20 March: 'The mud along the roads has all dried up now and there are clouds of dust about: of course the amount of traffic on the roads round us is abnormal.' (Dust raised by traffic attracted shell fire.)

The Company occasionally raised dust, as my father recalls: 'On the highest part of the ridge, and in the centre of our layout, stood a windmill, together with a farm house and barns. The miller and his wife lived in the mill, as the house and barns were considerably damaged. The mill, having walls about two feet thick, had resisted the light shells, and apart from the loss of the sails and a chip or two of stone knocked off, there was nothing much wrong with it. As this prominent landmark was useful to the German artillery as a range marker, it was decided it should be demolished, so the family were evicted by the French authorities, and

15. The windmill at Bouvigny before it was demolished by 216 Company in April 1916.

our demolition squad moved in the same night. After spending most of the night knocking holes all round the building to receive the gun-cotton slabs, one pound with the primer each, the following night the charges were put in position and then connected up to an electric exploder, placed in the nearby half constructed trench. The front-line troops were being relieved this night and in consequence, owing to the proximity of the road, we had to wait until the change-over was finished, in case the flying debris from the demolition should cause casualties amongst the passing troops, and was almost sure to bring some German artillery fire on this area. These troops marched along the road in open formation, as was the usual practice near the line, with wide gaps between each company, to minimise casualties in the event of enemy shell fire, and it was nearly dawn before the last lot passed us on their way out for a spell of rest. When they had all got safely over the brow of the ridge, Lieutenant Smith pressed the plunger of the exploder, and the mill collapsed in a cloud of white flour dust and flying chunks of stone. We got out of that area quickly.' (Presumably Lieutenant Smith had been trained in explosives.)

My father continues: 'It was an order that everyone should be away from the ridge before daylight and back in billets. After breakfast we "kipped down" for an hour or two and spent the day, if free from any fatigues, as we pleased, until we "fell in" for work at 8 p.m. Sometimes I was sent to our stores dump to wait for any working party sent to us, where I sorted out the tools and materials required for the night's work, and then I conducted the party to their job. Our dump was at the roadside, halfway up the ridge, in the cellar of a demolished house; the only serviceable part of this building was a red brick and tile floor, which covered a large cellar and also harboured a large colony of rats. However, there was still room enough for a sufficient stock of wire, picks, shovels, and sandbags to be stored, to equip any of our working parties. As the place was sheltered by the ridge during daylight, the transport wagons were able to get to it when more stores were required. I was lucky if my vigil in the cellar was a short one; more often I waited one or two hours, sometimes I was there all night, and then rejoined the returning sections at dawn on their way back to Bouvigny. To make the waiting time more interesting I sat with only one candle alight, and then scattered some bits of bully around within easy striking distance, then made myself comfortable on a pile of sandbags, with a pick helve, until the rats came to supper. There was no shifting of bundles of wire or anything else in this operation, the rats came out to be clouted as long as the supply of bully lasted.'

Arthur Daulman writes of the rats in his billet, which was on the second floor, with a Jacob's ladder up to the top deck: 'We kept candles burning to deter them, but when we had settled down we would watch them appear. The saying was "Here comes Number One Section" as they made their way quite openly down and along the rafters. I slept on half a blanket with the other half pulled over me. I woke one night aware of something fidgeting inside the fold and when I threw off the blanket a rat scurried away. I have known them run over my face'. Corporal Streather gives a sunny account of ratting and other sports in a letter of 13 March: 'last night we had a great rat hunt: we caught about a dozen. The barns we live in are simply alive: they run along the ridges and the spouts on the wall plates and the rafters and everywhere. They are quite tame and if one lies still for a few minutes they are running all over one. Of course we get fun out of all these little troubles: men walk in and say that they have heard the Colonel of the rats telling his battalion to fall in. Others saw them play football and say that a team had come over from M————-. It is always the way with the troops out here: no matter what the conditions they always manage to keep happy. I saw about 100 one day having a snowball fight and they reminded me of boys at school. No one would have thought they had ever been near the trenches.'

Ratting was an operation conducted right round the clock. My father recalls that the entrance window to his billet 'overlooked what was once a garden, but it was now cut up by old, waterlogged trenches which the French had occupied during the fighting here in 1915. At this time these trenches sheltered a numerous population of rats, which in our leisure time we harried in various ways, assisted by a small smooth-haired terrier bitch who had adopted us. Sometimes we crammed most of the holes with cordite sticks taken from the 18-pounder gun charges and smoked them out to meet our pick helves and Taffy's teeth, and sometimes we blocked the lower holes and ladled water from the trench to fill up the burrow and drive them out that way. Being so close to the line we mounted a guard every night to keep an eye on any untoward occurrences, and Taffy always accompanied the sentry during his patrolling of the village, and spent her tour of duty exterminating any rats abroad in the dark hours which crossed her path. When she had a rat cornered behind some obstacle the officiating sentry with her was expected to dislodge the rat, and enable Taffy to do her duty. She seemed to consider killing rats was the sole purpose of our nightly promenades, and insisted on our full co-operation in the business.' Arthur Daulman also testifies to Taffy's skill: 'one shake and they'd had it'.

My father writes of another good ratter: 'Joe Webster of No 3 Section also thinned the rat population by his unerring skill with his catapult, and on a warm evening would sit outside the estaminet he patronised, with a bottle of vin blanc and a pocketful of pebbles. There were always plenty of rats at this time of day scurrying about, and he killed every one he shot at.' Joe Webster regularly fell in and marched with my father, who recalls that, as they were marching, Joe would take out and load his catapult, and, without checking his step, fire it unobtrusively from low down in front of his body to knock down any bird sitting on the telegraph wires they happened to be passing at the time.

Presumably my father also fell in alongside Joe Webster for what he describes as 'the most unpleasant parade'. This was the scabies, crab lice, and venereal disease inspection, also irreverently known as the 'short-arm inspection', which was conducted out in the village street by the Divisional Medical Officer. My father writes: 'We lined up with our tunics off and our trousers unbuttoned; the doctor examined every man's outstretched hands for signs of scabies, then our shirts were pulled up and our trousers lowered for the doctor to examine our abdomen for signs of crab lice. The normal population of "chats" we carried about were expected to be kept under control by their owners. Apart from a few remarks from rude little boys, the local adults of both sexes ignored the whole business; our own reactions depended on the weather conditions, whether they were dry and warm or wet and cold. Sapper Holt was the only one who publicly voiced his disapproval. "I ain't letting my trousers down for nobody, not with all them women about; it ain't decent." Holt's complaints died away into silence as the doctor approached him, and when his turn came he went through the drill like everyone else.' Arthur Daulman's recollection is that madame, standing in the doorway, was quite interested in the sappers' equipment, but my father reiterates that the village women didn't mind. 'After all, he adds, 'when they were out walking with their own menfolk the men would stop and turn and piss up against the wall with the women still hanging onto their arms and talking to them all the while. The old village priest would come out after service and stand up at the top of the church steps and piss up against the church wall.'

The draughty, public medical examination was a trial, but my father did have a happier encounter with the R.A.M.C. during the time at Bouvigny. He writes: 'One night when we went to work after a day of snow and cold winds the storm increased to a blizzard, making any kind of work impossible, so the night was spent sheltering in the half-completed dug-outs. None of us had expected to turn out for work at all, but we went off as usual at 8 p.m. and I was "detailed off" at the stores dump in case the expected working party turned up. I was suffering with a bad toothache, which got worse as the night passed, and the rats also had a bad night in consequence, until the return of the company relieved them of my attentions. At sick parade I was sent to the dressing station to have the tooth out, and there reported to the medical orderly. His answer, "You'll be welcome, sit down till the quack comes in", puzzled me, and the doctor also seemed very pleased when he heard what my trouble was. Indicating another box near his table, he told me to sit down facing the window and show him the tooth; after inspecting it he decided to remove it, and unrolled a holdall containing a small set of forceps and other dental instruments. Summoning two orderlies in to hold me securely, he selected one of the forceps and set to work. The instrument being on the small side and the doctor's hand rather large, my protests during the struggling and wrenching which ensued were limited to grunts. Something gave way at last, and the doctor removed his hand and implement from my mouth, and displayed the offending tooth in one piece. "Clean as a whistle", he said. "Sit where you are and wash your mouth out with this", and handed me half a mug full of rum. After he went out the orderlies told me that I was the doctor's first dental patient, and we all had some more mouthwash to celebrate the occasion. On the way back to the company I had a few more mouthwashes in various estaminets, and got back to the billet a lot happier than I had been for the last few days.'

Rum was the universal sedative: even more so in the front line than in casualty clearing stations. For many soldiers life was made bearable only by the daily tot. One of the medical officers who testified before the War Office's 1922 Shell Shock Committee said 'had it not been for the rum ration I do not think we should have won the war'.[8] As with most ex-soldiers, my father's recollections are more of food and drink than of fighting. A post card showing the main street of Hersin-Coupigny (four miles from Bouvigny) is annotated: 'In this village there was an Expeditionary Force Canteen. We walked here from Bouvigny to stock up with

16. Hersin-Coupigny: postcard on which Arthur Sambrook noted: 'In this village there was an Expeditionary Force canteen. We walked here from Bouvigny to stock up with tobacco and tinned stuff at every opportunity.'

tobacco and tinned stuff at every opportunity.' He recalls: 'At Boyeffles our usual midday snack was omelette and chips in an estaminet. The first time, some of us tried a sickly sweet called grenadine and custard, afterwards we found coffee and Benedictine more palatable. Higham came with us one day, and asked us what we were having. Chamberlain replied shortly, "egg and chips", so Higham ordered some. When his order was set before him, he was very annoyed because the cook had broken the egg yolks and he created quite a scene. His plate was taken away and he was told to leave.' Other members of the company seemed to have practised self-service, because Driver Frank Hextall recalled that 'we often "found" a few eggs' and my father celebrated his 18th birthday (28 March) by stealing a pudding made with rhubarb stolen from a cottage garden by Sapper Colenso.

Corporal Streather, coming from a more comfortable background, had weekly food parcels from home, though they did not always arrive safely. Thus on 3 April he wrote to his parents: 'Unfortunately the pastry was rather badly crushed: in fact it has been in the last two or three parcels... I like the cake very much and the chocolate; you need not send any more Oxo now, thank you, but I should like some of those powders for making lemon water.' His next letter, 9 April, reports that his latest food parcel was happily unbroken and that the cake, sardines, and cocoa were particularly welcome. His great news, though, is of working parties recently in his charge: 'Did I tell you we had the football battalion at work for us Sunday: Sheldon and lots of other cracks, in fact there was an international team on our job. They all are just as dirty and fed up and yet just as cheerful as all the other troops. We have also had the U. & P. S. corps with us one day. I had two M.A.s from

Oxford at work for me, both privates, at work with pick and shovel: one of them the Sgt told me was a Civil Servant in Egypt and had been earning £1,500 a year.' As for the war, he mentions 'heavy fighting' in passing and asks 'I wonder if it will be all over for next year?' The 'football battalion' was the 17th Middlesex, serving in 2nd Division, which had recently replaced 23rd Division in the line. Jack Sheldon ('Sandy') played for Nuneaton Town, subsequently for Manchester United, and was outside-right for Liverpool in the 1914 F.A. Cup Final.[9] The other working party's unit (University and Public School *Corps*?) is less certain. It might be another from the Middlesex Regiment, the 16th (Public Schools) Battalion, which had been transferred to G.H.Q. Reserve in February for the purpose of withdrawing men for temporary commissions and did not rejoin its Division (the 29th) until 24 April.[10]

Easter Sunday, 23 April, seems to have passed without religious observance. Corporal Streather wrote that day to his parents: 'we have had some very rotten weather lately: the only nice day we have had was last Sunday and then it rained at night. I was very wet yesterday and simply covered in mud from head to foot.... Most of the work is in red clay and as we have had nearly a fortnight's rain you can guess what it's like. I am using a lot of concrete just now but of course I must not tell you about that. . . We had a soaking in bed one night but I got up and put some tiles on the roof so it's alright now. You ought to see some of us when we come off the works now mud from head to foot. It takes hours to clean your tackle especially the rifle. . . . Thank you for the parcel . . . I liked the cucumber and the sardines very much. Leave has been stopped for all H.M. forces in France. . . . We have had some conscientious objectors at work with us this week. They had been called up about a fortnight ago and some are back in England now wounded. They were working on a road when a shell dropped among them.'

On Easter Sunday night my father was enjoying one of his solitary vigils in the cellar of the R.E. dump, waiting, watching, and killing rats with his pick helve. It was a long night, as the working party went astray and did not arrive until dawn. He was back in his billet, resting at nine o'clock on Easter Monday, when Alf Chamberlain roused him and his mates, 'saying Jerry was sending some shrapnel over the fields near the road. We all got up and watched from our window; a few more shells burst over the undulating fields rising up to the Lorette spur. Chamberlain remarked "Jerry's spotted something there: must be over that rise, whatever it is". As we looked, Stephanie and Sophie came round to us, looking apprehensive and very excited; they were talking to us both together and pointing up the slope. We understood the "mon Père" bit, but the rest of the chatter was beyond us. Douglas understood a smattering of French, and when they said something about a vache, he said "I think they are telling us that the old man's gone up there: something to do with a cow". As they were talking, another shell burst over the rise, and a mule and a cow came charging over the crest, followed by "mon Père", with the plough-stilts held up under his arms.'

'As we watched he stumbled and fell, the plough plunged into the ground, breaking the traces, and the mule and the cow came belting along for home. As Stephanie and Sophie were having hysterics by this time, we went up to fetch the farmer, who was still lying where he had fallen. When we picked him up, we found that he was only winded, so we brought him in. The only thing we could get out of him when he got his breath back was "Allemand bombard, him no bloody bon"; in case we were not aware of that fact, he repeated it all the way home. We sat "mon Père" in his armchair, and he desired us to serve out some cognac, telling Douglas where to find the bottle and glasses, and during this time we became aware of someone babbling away in one of the bedrooms. The old man remarked, "Ah Madame", and told us to go and see if she was all right: as Douglas was busy serving out "encore cognac", Chamberlain, Leishman, and I went. We discovered Madame on her elbows and knees, with her head under the bed and her bulky posterior stuck up into the air, "like an elephant's arse", Chamberlain remarked. She was rattling her beads and praying volubly for Monsieur, who she imagined was a corpse on the hillside. Our laughter at this spectacle put a stop to her prayers, so we helped her up and told her that "Monsieur was tres bon and supping cognac in the kitchen". Madame flung her rosary on the bed and hurried into the kitchen to make sure that the old man was uninjured, and, after a final cognac all round, we left them to their reunion, and went out to look at the animals. The cow and the mule had arrived and were wandering about in the yard; the mule was undamaged but the cow had a hole in her rump. Leishman went to the artillery headquarters to find a veterinary officer to attend to her.'

'The vet diagnosed shrapnel, and after consulting Monsieur, who had in the meantime joined us, told us to hold the cow while he operated. Chamberlain held the cow's tail out of the way, Douglas held on to the horns, and I was told to put my fingers and thumb up the cow's nostrils and pinch them. When we were all in position, the vet probed into the hole with some long, slim tongs, located and extracted the splinter. The cow bore the operation patiently, mooing softly, and at the same time filling my hand and tunic sleeve with a copious discharge of mucus. At his end, Chamberlain got a few splashes; Douglas and Leishman were unmarked. After the operation the cow was bedded down comfortably, and everybody was invited into the kitchen for a drink. For the remainder of our stay in Bouvigny the four of us were adopted members of the family.'

On the following Thursday, 27 April, the men detailed for the daily water-cart fatigue were my father, Joe Webster, "Monkey" Williams, the cook's mate, and Driver Smith. They took the limber cart, pulled by two horses, attached to which was a trailer fitted with a galvanized tank and a dicky seat. They set off in the early afternoon for the well in the long main street of Sains-en-Gohelle, about two and a half miles from Bouvigny-Boyeffles. 'A circular stone wall about three feet high surrounded it, which was crowned by a roof resembling a lych gate, under which was a strong wooden windlass', writes my father, 'the iron-bound wooden bucket held two gallons and seemed to weigh two tons as we wound it up from the well bottom'. Access to civilian supplies of drinking water was always a matter of delicacy for the British army, but the 216th Company seems to have learned a diplomacy adequate for the matter. My father writes 'As usual, filling our tank was a long and tiring business, the arrival of our cart being the signal for all the women in the village to come and have their water supply without the trouble to wind up the bucket. For every bucketful we managed to put into our tank, we filled several of the villagers' buckets, so this fatigue was generally referred to as the "beaucoup fatigué". When the locals had been supplied, we made haste to fill our tank and get away.'

Their journey lay along the direct road between Sains and Bouvigny, a road which had not been used in day-time when the French army held this part of the line, and had therefore been left alone by German artillery, except for a few shrapnel shells during the dark hours. Things changed when the 23rd Division took over in this area: this road leading directly south was thought conveniently situated for easy contact with the Vimy sector and further south and was used all day for any necessary transport and troop movements; these movements inevitably attracted the attention of German gunners. Thus there was some artillery activity as the water-fatigue party made its way home, this was at first directed elsewhere, so that, as they reached Bouvigny, they enjoyed a grandstand view of a famous direct hit when German shell fire brought down the twinned pit-head gear, known to the British as 'Tower Bridge', in the village of Loos.

This prominent landmark had provided the Germans with perfect artillery observation for two or three miles during the first year of the war, in which time the Allied gunners had enjoyed no success in their repeated efforts to demolish it. It was captured by infantry of the 47th (London Territorial) Division on 25 September 1915, the leading assault troops dribbling a football in the approved (though rarely practised) morale-boosting manner[11], and held despite heavy casualties. Thereafter it became a target for German guns. Even so, it was not until the afternoon of 27 April that it was knocked down. My father recalls, 'As this occurred when we were passing the open space at the entrance into Bouvigny, we had a good view of the explosion and collapse, but hurried on out of observation'.

He continues: 'When we got into the village we found that Jerry was also paying some attention to the top end and the road going up to the ridge, but we went on leisurely up the road. Halfway along the road Smith pulled his horses with a violent jerk when a shell screamed over and exploded on our cookhouse, and the resulting smoke swirled out under the yard entrance and across the road. The sudden stop caused the back part of the cart to break loose, and, overbalanced by the weight of the tank full of water and Williams, who sat on the dicky seat beside it, we lost our water, and Williams had a long-overdue bath at the roadside. We picked Williams up and rubbed him down, Joe Webster remarking "That's freshened you up Monkey, how do you feel?", then we righted the cart, and tied the horses up, sheltered by a barn. Williams and the driver, Smith, stayed with the animals, so Webster and myself went on up the street to find out what was happening to the rest of the section billeted there.'

'Sergeant Seymour and Corporal Streather, with some of the section chaps, were very cautiously moving about in the street, and from one cellar or billet to another, on the look-out for any casualties, so we joined the party and spent the next hour dodging about, flopping down whenever another shell came over. The last shell that fell in the village cut one of the electric cables, strung on concrete

17. Sergeant C.W.Streather, M.M.: schoolteacher before and after the war, promoted Sergeant in France, May 1916.

poles on one side of the village street. Some of us, including Seymour, had flopped down at the bottom of a wall underneath, and the severed cable gave most of us a violent slap, which set us feeling for our wounds. Seymour was shell-shocked; we took him to the dressing station afterwards and we saw no more of him.' This was Sergeant Seymour's second dose of shell shock: the first had sent him back to England in time for the formation of the 216th Company a year earlier. We are told nothing in detail of his condition, but perhaps it resembled that of a shell-shocked sergeant-major described by the war correspondent Philip Gibbs: 'He was convulsed with a dreadful rigor like a man in epilepsy, and clawed at his mouth, moaning'[12]. In fact, Seymour's case seems to have been more complicated, because Charles Streather noted mysteriously some two months later that Seymour had 'got a Court Martial'. As for the shell which is said to have invalided him, my father writes: 'The shell which was responsible for this mix up landed on a house opposite, killing Sapper Holt'. So that poor fellow's modesty would never be offended again by the scabies inspection parade.

My father's account continues: 'On our way back we heard what sounded like groans coming from the quartermaster's stores, and went in to investigate. The noise was traced to the only occupant of the place, who was lying on the floor full up with the rum issue and singing. This chap was Spr Dan Firbank, an elderly man in No 1 Section, who was on fatigue in the stores, working out the fourteen days' C.B. he had been awarded following a previous binge on rum. As we could not carry him out, we had a drink apiece from the rum jar he had opened and left him. Dan got a court martial, awarded first field punishment, and we saw him no more. As most of the headquarters staff had taken shelter amongst the brick-stacks, Dan's defence was that he had been left to look after the place, and that anybody could have got in and taken the rum. "Over Dan's dead body", we said, and evidently the Captain thought, when he dished out the sentence.' Field Punishment No.1 was a kind of mild crucifixion, by which the victim was tied by the wrists and ankles to the wheel of a stationary G.S. wagon two hours each day for the period of the sentence. It was, of course, not intended to be lethal, though it so happened that a private's death under field punishment in March 1916 became a *cause célèbre* when it was denounced by Horatio Bottomley in his yellow journal *John Bull*.

Meanwhile the relatively sober and relatively undelinquent sappers continued to dig support and communication trenches to strengthen a British defensive position which was badly sited in respect of ground and observation. The official historian, regretting that the British High Command had not drawn a more easily defensible line further back and noting that the Germans held the higher and drier ground, writes that 'it would have seemed appropriate . . . to have kept as quiet as possible and not provoked the enemy to use his advantages'; but 'With a view to cultivating an "aggressive spirit", as it was called, G.H.Q. did not allow this state of affairs to continue. Sniping, fire surprises and raids were ordered and encouraged'[13]. As an Army Troops company, the 216th were not directly involved in such excitements, but my father recalls: 'One night we heard some activity in the line at the front of our trench workings, and work ceased while we watched until the place became quiet again. We heard all about it a day or two afterwards from a working party we had. It was a raid on a German strong point, which miscarried on account of the officer in charge ignoring the order given for strict silence before launching the attack. The party, of company strength, crawled into position near to the German line and waited for the moment of attack in complete silence, near the German wire. The captain in command had a batman named Baker, and, needing him for some reason, began to call softly "Baker, Baker". One of the waiting men nearby called back "Oh Christ, leave two[14] and piss off." A burst of laughter from the men who heard this remark brought a brilliant display of Very lights and a lot of bombs and small-arms fire from Jerry, which caused the raiders to scramble back to their trenches with a few "Blighty" casualties, but with no other loss. Corporal Streather's letters home refer repeatedly but less specifically to 'pretty heavy' fighting near the Nuneaton men at this time. On 8 May he notes: 'I don't think the Germans will get a look in on our front; it is only a matter of time when all will be over and the longer we wait the less costly will be our victory'. Waiting, though, was not the policy of the High Command, who wished to expel the enemy from France and Belgium as soon as possible.

The gap left by the Nuneaton Company's latest Blighty casualty was filled when Corporal Streather, aged 21, was promoted No 3 Section sergeant in Seymour's place. When Sergeant Lee left the Company Captain Cook had written to the R.E. depot at Chatham for a replacement and then promoted Corporal Henley, a newcomer from the Rouen draft. Now, at last, Streather had his well-deserved promotion, confirming the truism that keen team sportsmen generally make good soldiers. My father writes: 'Douglas was promoted to Corporal in Streather's place, but still shared our humble dwelling in spite of his military advancement, and was still addressed by his name when off parade, as also was Streather. Much to the Sergt Major's displeasure, all our N.C.O.s now were called by name, a practice which "Mitch" condemned as unmilitary and lacking the respect due to rank, but we found it hard to break ourselves of the habit, and he could not break us of it.' Such an offence to good order and discipline was treated far more strictly in the Royal Welch Fusiliers, the regiment in which Robert Graves was serving at this time. Graves tells of a colonel who, when he overheard a private soldier addressing an unprotesting lance-corporal by his first name, promptly reduced the lance-corporal to the ranks for 'conduct unbecoming to an N.C.O.' and awarded Field Punishment No.1 to the private for 'using insubordinate language to an N.C.O.'[15].

18. Arthur Daulman, photographed on leave from France, 7 May 1916.

Chapter Five: Villers-au-Bois and Ribemont, May and June 1916

The letters of Sergeant Streather continue to dwell on the all-important topics of food and leave. He thanks his parents for the usual basic foodstuffs, such as cake and cocoa, custard powder and lemon crystals; also for tomatoes ('the best breakfast I've had in France') and cucumbers, also for bananas (though he asks that the next consignment should be less ripe) and salmon (until the weather turns hot). When he hears that leave is to open in May he calculates that he will come home on 6 June, but on 19 May he sadly announces that 'all leave is stopped until the company has been six months in France; that means I shall probably get home in September now which is rather rotten. Those who have been are lucky, but it is hardly fair that they should have been, as there are over 500,000 men who have been here over 9 months without a leave and over 20,000 who have not had one from the start.'

Among the lucky few was Arthur Daulman, now rewarded for being one of the very first to enlist in the Company, but his week's leave was not unalloyed pleasure. He writes: 'Five of us, Wilf Cox, Ernie Addison, Joe Webster, the Sergeant-Major and myself went down to Béthune by lorry where we had a meal at the Sergeant-Major's expense before boarding a train, with the usual wooden seats, at midnight. We pulled out at 2 a.m. and went straight to Boulogne arriving at 7.40. We boarded the ship and sailed at 10.00 hrs to Dover. Then train to London, across to Euston and home. It all went like clockwork. It rained every day of my seven days' leave. On the last day I went to my sister's house at Oaston Crossing where she opened the gates to allow farm animals mostly to cross the Midland Railway. We put on records and for the last one she chose Home Sweet Home. I could have knocked it off the table. All the family came to see me off which I didn't want. I found it most uncomfortable. I travelled back on my 18th birthday.' One senses that he was beginning to experience that feeling of alienation from civilians at home which was experienced by so many soldiers in the Great War. England was very close in time and space but emotionally it was in another world.

The weather in England was only marginally worse than in France. Sergeant Streather noted on 19 May that it had been 'wet and cold one day and boiling hot the next. I think that during the last six weeks we have been wet through two days out of every three.' The campaigning season was well under way. The British First Army continued to extend its front southwards by occupying more formerly French-held sectors while more and more French troops were taken away to be fed into the 'mincing machine' at Verdun, where incessant German assaults were intended to bleed France white. A small consequence of this movement was that the 216th Company, R.E., left Bouvigny Boyeffles on 17 May and marched south (by a roundabout road, because the direct road over the Lorette spur was closed for all army movements) to reach Villers-au-Bois on the following day. This hamlet was some three miles from Vimy Ridge; it was badly damaged and deserted by the inhabitants. The surrounding landscape was of shell-pocked, rolling chalk downs, similar to the area they had just left.

'As there were no billeting facilities here of any kind', writes my father, 'we were issued with small ridge-pole tents holding two men and we camped in a field nearby. The surrounding woods screened us from the prying binoculars of Jerry on the ridge and the weather continued hot and dry during our stay here, so we enjoyed the change from straw beds and rat-infested barns.' In fact not all the company were so pleasantly housed. Frank Hextall 'slept under the hedge the first week, no water, didn't wash for four days', until he and the other drivers 'found an old barn for stables and an old house for ourselves'. Arthur Daulman and some others had 'filthy billets, a stable, until we cleaned them. The walls were fly-covered and black with grime, the floor thickly covered with straw manure, and water carried by hand from a mile away.' The ruins of Villers-au-Bois also accommodated some of the reserve units and wagon lines of the 47th (London) Division, a Territorial formation to which the 216th Company was to be attached. Here the 216th, together with the 138th Company, who had preceded them at Mazingarbe, were placed under the orders of the Officer Commanding the divisional pioneer battalion: not, as it happens, a London unit, but the 1/4th Royal Welch Fusiliers.

The front now held by the 47th Division, along the lower, western slopes of the northern spur of Vimy Ridge, was in a bad state of disrepair, partly as the result of destructive mining over the previous weeks, but mainly because the French who had held this line had placed less reliance on continuous trenches than on their quick-firing 75 mm. field guns. The historian of the 47th Division observes: 'No wire covered the front or support lines; the front line consisted of disconnected posts, isolated by day; there were no shelters of any kind in the front system. Altogether it was a position ill-equipped to counteract the increasingly aggressive efforts of the enemy'. The *Official History* tells the same tale: 'merely shell holes joined up. . . a line of detached posts, accommodated in grouse butts . . . few good communication trenches: most were unfit for use, all were undrained and utterly unsanitary. Dead bodies, months old, still lay unburied, and a vast amount of debris and rubbish covered the whole area. . . the ground offered only precarious tenure as a defensive line'.[1]

It was the job of the 216th to improve these defences, so their work here was much as it had been since their arrival in France. Arthur Daulman writes: 'We were still digging trenches. We had dug trenches from January to May 1916. We had dug trenches at Mazingarbe, Vermelles, right down to Bouvigny, Bully-les-Mines, Aix-Noulette, Souchez, Cabaret Rouge, and so to Vimy Ridge. What we had done is dig one long connected reserve trench.' With its dug outs and other associated works, this was called the 'Village Line'. Though the Allies were preparing a huge offensive for the summer, the British at least were also prudently attending to their system of defence. At Vimy Ridge, recalls my father, 'We were employed in a hollow at the foot of the ridge, improving and strengthening a labyrinth of ditches which passed for trenches when the French occupied them. At the start of the work we were screened by a slight rise between us and the Jerry observation posts on the ridge, and worked during daylight, but later on we came out into the open, so afterwards it was only possible to work at night. This trench system extended to the bottom slope of the ridge, and there we commenced to tunnel down, and continued forward into the slope.'

As it zig-zagged across the low ground towards Vimy Ridge the communication trench was, according to Daulman, about 8 or 9 feet deep. It needed to be because, as my father noted, 'Jerry was on the ridge and could see all over'. Here, as nearly everywhere in France, the position of the Allied front line 'was never deliberately selected on tactical grounds but was always that line to which the exhausted troops happened to be clinging when the last phase of active fighting had come to an end. Any proposal to withdraw from a faulty front line position to another one with better tactical properties a few hundred yards in rear was anathema to the higher command'[2]. So this line was drawn across the lower slopes at the place where the French had been obliged to give up their attempt to take the crest of Vimy Ridge. Had any other course been adopted 'the great efforts of our Allies would have been in vain; it would be revealed that pure defensive was intended on the Vimy front, while it was the special desire of the Commander-in-Chief that the imminence of a spring offensive should be suggested to the enemy — by means of mining and frequent raids — and that the principle of aggression should be instilled into the troops'[3].

'This place', writes my father, 'was officially mapped as Zouave Valley, after the French Zouaves (Moorish) troops[4] who had been there, but was referred to locally as Cabaret Rouge, a reference to French casualties incurred during the attempt to storm the ridge in 1915. That summer the French lost 100,000 men killed and wounded. The decomposing bodies of a lot of these chaps were still lying around in the tattered remnants of the blue coats and red trousers they wore at that time. We came across them hastily buried in the sides of the partly-obliterated trenches, in shell holes, and scattered about generally in bits and pieces. So, if you saw a bit of equipment sticking out and pulled at it, a bit of the bloke would come out with it. There were boots with bits of leg sticking out. The stink in this area, under the hot sun, was, as Sapper West said, "very noticeable". The vulgar expressions used to describe it were as obscene as our surroundings were at the time. We got used to the stink as we carried on with our digging in the new communication trenches, and we buried the bodies we came across under the earth we excavated.'

In fact, Cabaret Rouge (the Red Tavern) was simply a pre-war place name: the bloodshed in 1915 which turned a denotation into a metaphor was a Great War irony. My father's description, written sixty years after the event, is half jocular, but one suspects that these men and boys would have vomited over the chipped bones and putrid grey matter they were reburying. An officer of the 2nd Leinster battalion observed later that year: 'French equipment lay strewn about, with parts of uniform and ammunition clips for the *mitrailleuses*. A rusty and twisted rifle barrel stuck into the ground, surmounted by the familiar *kepi*, indicated the grave of some unknown *poilu*. Skulls and bones bleached white lay strewn throughout the rank grass. Twisted French rifles and equipment lay rotting everywhere. A skull was lying on the top of Uhlan Alley communication trench. Some wag had stuck a derelict *kepi* on it in grim humour. . . As the French had not buried all their dead after their great offensive, they were left to decompose in the sun, and the majority of them provided a feast for the rats.' A British Liaison Officer noted a trench here, 'where the framework of the mud parapet consisted of dead bodies. Equipment and even shelves were laid on feet protruding from the walls.'[5]

During the winter and spring of 1916 this had been a quiet part of the front, where the policy for French and German alike was 'live and let live'; but, as soon as they arrived, the British, 'following their usual policy, after giving due warning by firing a few shells over the enemy's head, at once brought the quietness of the sector to an end'. The Germans responded in kind, so that the sector 'then became a so-called "windy corner of the Western Front".'[6]

Zouave Valley, running north-south just behind the front positions, was frequently blanketed by German artillery, firing from positions hidden on the eastern side of Vimy Ridge. German gunners were unusually busy on 19 and 20 May, and from a very early hour on Sunday the 21st; then, at 3.40 p.m. that day, writes the historian of the 47th Division, 'the bombardment became intense, and a barrage on Zouave Valley – – the first "box barrage" which we had experienced, practically cut all communication with the front. . . . At 7.45 p.m. the shelling was lifted off the front trenches, and fell with increased violence on Zouave Valley and farther back, especially on gun positions. At the same time the German infantry attacked'. After hard fighting the Germans were able in some places to advance as much as a third of a mile, almost as far as the floor of Zouave Valley itself. It is not known whether the 216th Company was directly in action on that Sunday, but we are told that the Divisional Chief Engineer, Lieut-Colonel S. D'A Crookshank, 'who was at advanced Brigade Headquarters at Cabaret Rouge on the same afternoon, organised the R.E., who were in billets thereabouts in an old French line on the forward slope looking across Zouave Valley'. 63 officers of the Division and 2,044 other ranks were killed, wounded, and missing: 'At that price we were taught the necessity to arrange our defences in greater depth to meet new methods of attack with increased weight of artillery'.[7]

Lachrymatory shells made up part of the great German barrage that Sunday. Arthur Daulman writes: 'This is where we first met tear gas. We were making our way through a spinney when we were obviously spotted and down came a salvo of gas shells. At that time we were carrying our gas masks on the side [not at the front]. By the time we realized what had happened we all had had a dose and spent the next hour having a good cry. About a month later we were issued with a new mask with mouthpiece attached and the material still tucked away in our clothing. The tube was to come later.' The 'new mask' referred to was another version of the type of gas helmet worn in the Camembert attack at Mazingarbe (perhaps the P.H.G. helmet, which gave 'better protection against lachrymators' than the P.H. helmet, which was standard issue from January 1916): 'the tube' was a feature of the box respirator, issued from August 1916 onwards.[8] Pioneer Daulman shared the opinion of many British soldiers that German artillerymen were capable of pin-pointing small groups of men: it is more likely that guns were registered upon any spinney likely to shelter troops.

A British counter-attack on 23 and 24 May from Zouave Valley, with the object of recapturing lost ground, was a bloody failure. The Germans were content to hold what they had gained; they quietened down; the line became stable. The 216th Company continued to trench and tunnel, now making their contribution to the earliest stage of a large programme of 'protective tunnelling' on the eastern side of Zouave Valley, under the slopes of Vimy ridge. Subways were dug 25 feet below the ground from the support line to the front line, as well as very deep communication trenches: the work would be continued for nearly a year, mostly by specialist tunnelling companies, until the battles of Arras in April and May 1917. Eventually, in addition to the famous tunnels out of the cellars of Arras, six subways, varying from 300 to 1,537 yards in length were tunnelled into the eastern slope of Zouave Valley, together with four communication trenches, eight to ten feet in depth.[9]

The entrances to these workings were under observation from the Germans on the ridge. My father writes: 'Getting to and from our tunnel was only safe during the dark hours. The most convenient route for us was along a narrow road towards Mont St.Eloi, until opposite the battered twin towers of the church, and then turn left at the side of the splintered remains of a small copse, and then, guided by the Very lights sent up from the front lines, take a chance across the open to our tunnel. When things were quiet we sometimes managed to get a G.S. wagon part of the way, but not often. The usual method was to carry whatever materials and tools we required from a dump established at the roadside at Mont St.Eloi, a mile away from the tunnel. The proper way, through the trenches, was more tiring, and, despite the illumination of the Very flares, it was quite easy to get astray. Numerous ration parties and other working parties were passing up and down most of the night, and during the change-over, when the front line was being relieved, this way was crammed with men and equipment. The various telephone lines between the artillery batteries and their forward observation posts, or between infantry headquarters and units in the line, were laid out on the ground, and where they crossed the communication trenches they sagged down and got entangled in rifles or other equipment, causing, delays, frustration, and a lot of swearing.'

This was a nightly scenario everywhere along the front. An infantry subaltern writes: 'Parties of men in a sequence that needed careful preparation and traffic control came down from the trenches to the dump in the village to collect the night's requirements: dry rations made up in bundles according to the strength of the front-line posts; trench stores — planks, pit-props, duckboards, coils of barbed wire, sand-bags in bales; boxes of rifle ammunition (S.A.A.) and Mills bombs; gallon jars of rum (never let out of sight of a responsible officer); the mail (if there was any) with "comforts" from charitable societies at home and food parcels from their families for the lucky. There was water medicated with chloride of lime and tasting of the petrol cans in which it was carried; there was hot stew in two-gallon "dixies" from the field kitchens. All this was to be sorted in silence and man-handled in the dark. . . Show a light or make too much noise and the enemy would open fire. . . Carrying parties loom up in the memory as the most persistent, fatiguing, hateful chore of the war . . . A roll of barbed wire spitted on a stake and carried by two tired men is at any time an awkward burden. Now manoeuvre it along a deep muddy ditch in the dark. . . you slip in a shell-hole under foot; your helmet is whipped off your head by a trailing wire; you catch your slung rifle on a projecting root; you tear your hand or your sleeve on the damnable wire-coil; you stumble and your mate swears at you; and round the traverse you find yourself face to face with a stretcher-party carrying out a casualty'[10]. No wonder the small (and, they would hope, inconspicuous) parties of men from the 216th Company preferred to chance it in the open.

Their working parties were now drawn from 'resting' battalions of the 47th Division. 'On one occasion', recalls my father, 'we were working as usual; we were tunnelling by the light of several candles, which were frequently shaken to the floor and extinguished by the concussion of every shell nearby, and discovered we had a well-trained butler assisting us, who had, we learned on enquiry, been in service with the "best families", and we were proud to think that he was now serving the "best Engineers in France". Our work was divided between some of us doing the heading, trimming the tunnel sides and floor, some removing the debris, and a party timbering the top and sides, and two tunnel shafts were excavated simultaneously, and were joined underground. The timbering gang had also to take a working party back to the dump for the props and lagging required. The loose earth and chalk was put into sandbags and passed from hand to hand and strewed on the ground outside by the timbering party and their infantry working party. The butler stood at the foot of the steps in a very dignified manner, with his elbows bent and his forearms out, palms uppermost, waiting for the filled sandbags to be placed across his hands. Then he would turn to the next man in line and present his load in the same manner. Apart from a few "What the bloody 'ells" from the recipient, surprised at receiving a sandbag full of chalk in so polite a manner, the work went on well enough. This chap was the only one in the tunnel who kept his tunic on and he did not sweat either.'

Frank Hextall writes in his usual laconic style about the Nuneaton men's time below Vimy Ridge: 'pretty hot show; rotten place to go; last seven days working all day and until 3 next morn; got fairly done up'. He recalled one occasion when he and my father 'got killed' as he said. One night he was driving his G.S. wagon with a load of timber for the support line dug-outs the Company was working on and my father was with him to help unload. They finished unloading and stacking the timber and climbed back into the wagon; Frank began to turn the wagon through a broad half circle (because the front wheels had only a quarter turn on them at most) when a shell hit the pile of timber and scattered it everywhere; the wagon tilted as the mules went off at full gallop. Everyone who saw the shell hit assumed that the two men were dead, but they were unhurt.

Hextall and his comrades endured the shell fire as well as they could probably less by personal courage than by a dogged sense of community —, but the company mascot, the dalmatian, was not able to cope: the creature went mad soon after their arrival at the front and had to be shot by its two-legged comrades. The men of course could be jumpy, especially when they were tired. My father recalls that, on 28 May, towards the end of their stay on this part of the front, 'just before dawn, Sam Hollis, one of the corporals in charge of our transport, came down to tell us that he had brought a G.S. wagon up as far as they could get it, with a load of pit-props and lagging boards, and wanted some of us to go and unload them. It was decided we would all go, as it was nearly time we got out, so the infantry went back along the trenches, and we went with Hollis. As we left the job, our side blew two mines further up on the ridge. After the mines went up, the whole area was illuminated by a "Brocks Benefit" display of Very lights, red, green, and the ordinary white flares, sent up by our chaps and the Germans. The coloured ones were signals requesting artillery support. There was a continuous flash and clatter of machine-gun fire and the bombing sections were busy during the attacks and counter-attacks for the possession of the mine craters, which the 47th Division eventually held. The German support fire, with shrapnel and high-explosive shells, started to come over in the area at the bottom of the ridge, and Sam Hollis was anxious about the drivers and animals waiting near the wood, so we went back as quickly as possible.'

'As we neared the wood, a battery emplaced during the night, started firing, and we made a very hurried detour, but not soon enough to escape the blast and a shower of sparks from the nearest gun; somebody shouted at us, "Get away from our front, you bloody fools"; we thought it a good idea, and did. When we found our wagon, the mules and Sam's horse were getting a bit restive with all the noise and excitement, so some of us helped to control the animals, while the rest of us threw the pit props and lagging timber into a deep shell hole at the side of a track which joined the road. Some got into the empty wagon, and had a rough and bumpy ride, and the rest of us walked towards the dark silhouette of the two ruined towers of St.Eloi and the road. Hollis rode ahead, picking out the best ground near the wood. The shattered tree stumps were useful telegraph-wire poles, and Sam got tangled up in one of them, which pulled him out of the saddle; his fall coincided with a close shell burst, so we thought while we ran to him that he had been hit by a splinter, but he was only winded and shaken up. The horse and the mules bolted and the wagon went on bumping and swaying in the direction of the road; someone shouted "We'll wait for you on the road". The sun was coming up behind the ridge, and the excitement there had died down, except for a few occasional shots, so we lost no more time in getting on to the road, where the wagon was waiting in the shelter of the woods. Here we found that the body of the wagon had been jerked loose from the front-axle forks, and while we were putting the wagon right Driver Toogood found out that his rifle was missing from its straps under the driving seat.'

'This chap was the champion loser and mislayer of Government property in the company. At Bouvigny he went out with the stores cart and two mules, left the equipage unattended for about an hour, returning to his duty to find he had only one mule. The loss of the mule was duly entered in his paybook and was being paid for by small deductions from his modest 1s.8d. a day. When the laughter and joking was finished, we told him not to worry and not to report the loss of the rifle. There were plenty lying about all round the area where we were working and we would get him one the next night. When asked what sort he fancied, English, French, or German, he replied, "I don't care what sort it is, so long as it's English and looks like mine". "Right, we'll bring you the muckiest one we can find, give you a job cleaning it before Mitch sees it." It was no trouble getting him another rifle, but unfortunately the Sergt Major saw it before Toogood cleaned it, and he got seven days C.B. for having a dirty rifle.' We walked or rode back to our camp, which was about two miles away from Mont St.Eloi (it was a mile further on from St.Eloi to the ridge where we worked) and after breakfast we got down in the sun outside our "bivvies" and slept until midday, afterwards spending some time at the local estaminet nearby. The camp fatigues were done by the defaulters and "medicine and duty" men, so the rest of us made the most of our tranquil surroundings until we returned at sunset to the stinking desolation of the ridge.'

The ruined towers of St.Eloi, so prominent in these recollections, were sketched by my father from memory sixty years after he saw them. Their picturesque outline was also etched in the imagination of an A.S.C. officer, who wrote in 1968: 'On a hill nearby was a dramatic ruin. Twin, shattered towers, thrusting their heads towards heaven, joined by a lower architectural link. They were part of the Abbaye of Mont St.Eloi founded in 640 A.D., and, though not necessarily very ancient, or for that matter very picturesque when still intact, the war had turned them into a landmark as distinctive in its way as the church spire in Albert with its leaning Madonna. Their height made them an ideal observation post for the British, after their advance north of Arras, and an essential if not easy target for the German guns. They commanded a superb view, eastward and northward, across a series of terraces, and then over the wide plain, towards the new German lines near Lens. A direct hit at the base might have brought them down; but this was asking rather much of the German gunners. Well over a thousand shells must have fallen around that landmark, but it was still there. One of the towers had been reduced considerably in height, but this only helped to give the structure its present dramatic profile. . . . There were shell-holes all round, shell-holes in the little cemetery about thirty yards away, shell-holes and debris and rubble where the main building of the convent itself had stood. The place had become a text of the incredible extravagance of war.'[11]

19. Arthur Sambrook's sketch of the ruined abbey of Mont St.Eloi, near Vimy Ridge.

When the 216th Company were safely out of it, Sergeant Streather wrote of the ridge: 'I can tell you I am glad to be out of it: the place we left is a perfect inferno and if ever a company was lucky it is ours. The last few days we had in the trenches were awful; we were shelled and sniped at by night and day and the artillery fire at night was murderous beyond all description; the work was heavy, the weather wet and very cold; everything seemed against us but we pulled through, and now I see by the papers that the R.E.s did good work. Well, our company did some of it. . . . I must say that all the officers have been very good to all and have shown great courage and set a fine example when a little nervousness or loss of self control might have led to disaster. The last night up was the worst I have ever known. Mr Smith had gone, I was in charge of the party (30 R.E.s and about 40 infantry) and on the way up we exploded two mines. Immediately the curtain fire opened on us, but by running and ducking and good luck we reached a safe place and lay low for a couple of hours till things grew normal. During this time many of the men were saved by their steel helmets which, although heavy and uncomfortable, are pretty safe' (letter of 6 June).

As Streather said, they were lucky to have no fatal casualties. Soon afterwards, writes my father, 'another company of Royal Engineers came to join us and to take over the work we had been doing, so the last shift was occupied in showing these chaps the way and in clearing away all our company equipment. The 31st May was spent in packing our transport vehicles in readiness for another move.' The 216th Company marched westward to the railway station at Savy-Berlette, loaded themselves and their transport on to a waiting train, and made a leisurely journey through the peaceful countryside of the back areas; a trip which lasted two days, during which time they never heard artillery or saw observation balloons. 'There was', writes my father, 'the usual promenade to the engine and back for our "brewing-up" water. "The more we consumed, the longer the journey lasted, so why worry. We are comfortable, and the rest will do us good". These were the general unheroic opinions of the company. At every small country station we crawled through the local children crowded alongside the track, shouting for bully beef and biscuits, and a scramble ensued to retrieve anything we threw out. There must have been a few cuts and bruises received by some of them, as a tin of bully, however gently thrown, would strike with some force. Some of us preferred to throw our donations well to the side of the crowd, which gave the smaller children a chance to get something without having to join the scramble in the crowd of bigger children.' Their route was by way of St.Pol, Doullens, and Amiens, where they changed trains: Arthur Daulman recalls that they 'marched through Amiens and I remember passing the cathedral. It was not much damaged and we passed a remark "What a gem of a building". I remember this as if it were yesterday'.

The roundabout journey ended on the third morning, when they left the train at Corbie station, on the Somme canal, about half way between Amiens and Albert (see map 7). My father recalls: 'Unloading ourselves and our transport, we marched off in the direction of Albert, seeing on the way plenty of indications that something was "coming off". Everywhere we passed camps and billets crowded with troops and artillery, and the nearer we got to our destination, the congestion of troops and ammunition dumps increased, including to our surprise cavalry horse lines, which was a new sight, so near the front, for us. We stopped finally at a village called Ribemont, where we were billeted in huts in a large camp outside, and welcomed by a few heavy shrapnel shells bursting overhead.'

It was only the left half-company under Lieutenant Smith, together with Captain Cook and the headquarters section, which came to Ribemont. They now found themselves with XV Corps in the Fourth Army, on the right flank of the British front, close to the French. The cavalry that so surprised them belonged to the 2nd Indian Cavalry Division: lances, pennons, and all. What was 'coming off' was the 'Big Push' that would, amongst other benefits, clear a way for the cavalry to break through and manoeuvre in open country. In the nature of things, preparations for the offensive could not be concealed. Charles Carrington writes: 'Every recruit could see new batteries springing up in the night among the woods, violent activity in the skies, for spring brings in war something more than primroses and swallows. Trenches and roads were doubled and redoubled.'[12] The new batteries springing up with the primroses were outrunning available supplies of building material in the R.E. parks and dumps, so the Chief Engineer of XV Corps, Brigadier-General P.G.Grant, reported on 2 June that he had arranged to buy steel girders locally at 75 francs per hundred kilos, 'but declined to pay the exorbitant prices asked for timber' by the local French. He thereupon issued orders to officers commanding Royal Engineer companies limiting their powers of local purchase. It is not known how these orders affected Captain Cook, but we know that Brigadier Grant was not a man to be trifled with. His diary for 12 June records his inspection of roads and water points being constructed by 133rd (Army Troops) Company: 'Found that progress was not satisfactory. Working party had been waiting at Méaulte for 4 to 5 hours with no orders — material for bomb proof over pump not collected — carriage of pipes not arranged — other parties badly organized and loafing — saw Major Muter Commanding 133rd A.T. Company and informed him that I must ask for him to be relieved of his command as inefficient. Saw C.E. 4th Army, reported the case and arranged for another officer.' Within two days the new officer materialized and Major Muter ignominiously lost his command.

One of the tasks of the men at Ribemont was the construction of howitzer pits, dug in and hidden behind houses at Méaulte, south of Albert. In each pit a gun, on its bedplate, would be set upon a heavy wooden baulk platform, with a steel box filled with ten tons of earth mounted on its forward end to balance the force of the recoil. Earth-covered steel and timber shelters were to be built for the gun crews: fourteen men, commanded by a sergeant, for each howitzer. The ammunition was a short distance away; each heavy shell was rolled along a trench dug with a slight incline to the guns, where it could be lifted by two strong artillerymen using twisted sandbags. The firing rate was one shell per minute, to avoid overheating; muzzle velocity was relatively low and trajectory was high. My father writes: 'At one of these emplacements, a bombardier told me it was possible to see the shell in flight after it was fired, and directed me to stand at the back of the gun, and keep my eye fixed at a point over the gable of a ruined barn in front of the gun. I thought he was pulling my leg, but did as I was told, and found it was true. At the highest point of the trajectory it was possible to catch a momentary glimpse of the shell, which resembled a black cricket ball. Everyone in the party stopped work to see this, until we were all reminded by the artillery officer that we were there for something else besides standing at the breech end of his guns and gazing at the sky.'

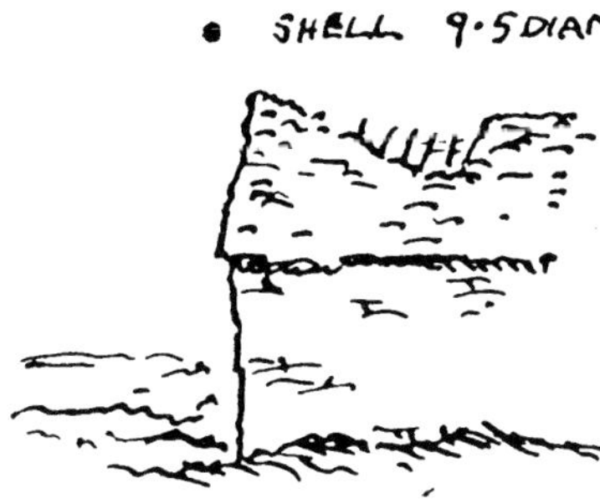

Sergeant Streather and the right half-company remained at Corbie when the rest of the Company went forward, an uncensored fact he was able to communicate to his parents by telling them that 'we have been on the hop again. This time we have made a better move about 30 miles south west to a place of the same name as Dad's birthplace and on the banks of a big river.' Streather's father was born in Corby, Northamptonshire. The letter continues: 'It is a beautiful country round about us and we are at the G.H.Q. of a new army just over 12 miles from the line. Although we have not moved far, we were three days on the way. At one time we could see the English Channel, so you can form some idea of the way trains travel in France. Unfortunately only half the company is here the left half and headquarters remain up in the trenches and will join us later. I hope they will be lucky enough to get away complete. It seems just like being transferred to a new world to get back here; all is quiet and only the ever rolling line of transports tells of the war. I can tell you I am glad to be out of it, the place we left is a perfect inferno. . . The place we have landed at is to us a paradise: we have a good billet, a bedroom and a mess room and a bed — a luxury undreampt of. That is the C.S.M., Sgt Barker, and I. We also have the satisfaction of seeing all the men comfortable: good billet, dry and clean, and the food can be better prepared, and there are ample facilities for keeping clean. . . We work from 7 a.m. to 6 p.m. and then there is a lot of work for the Sgts especially when the Company is split in two as at present. . . We are on a fairly interesting job though I would rather have the work up in the trenches if it were not for the shells etc' (letter of 6 June).

His paradise was not free from Adam's curse. Two weeks' later he wrote: 'Have hardly had time to breathe since I wrote last. We got to headquarters and fitted up a place for the general staff on which we worked overtime every night and as soon as we had finished we had to get a big hospital supplied with water, rig up two pumps and four big tanks, lay half a mile of 3" pipes which crossed a road and make ever so many 1" connections and fit in taps and so on. All this had to be done in two days. Mr Knox was in charge and he put me and 20 men on the job and we did it, but we worked 42 hours out of 48. Got to bed at 3 a.m. after finishing and then had to pack up and move off by 12 noon to do another job similar. We marched 6 miles to a pair of big hospitals stationed opposite one another on either side of a main road and by six at night we were on the works and worked till 10 p.m. Out again at 5.30 and worked till 10 p.m. again. We have done this for a week now and today we were expecting a rest and had to move again and have just arrived at our new place where we are to build a railway bridge in 2 days and dig about half a dozen gun pits all in two days so we shall be hard at it again. The worst of it is that the greater part of the Coy have been resting, only me and 20 men have been on the other jobs. We have lost Seymour who has got a Court Martial and the C.S.M. who is sick and Harris and the Q.M.S. are away so we are pretty well O.C.s, Barker and I. . . . Everybody is working double speed, all is ready, the smash might have taken place before you get this and the war will finish before Xmas if all goes well. In any case the coming battle is sure to sink to insignificance all other battles even of this war.' The headquarters mentioned by Streather was that of the newly created Reserve Army (later the Fifth Army) at Daours; the coming battle was of course the Somme; the C.S.M.'s sickness was occasioned by varicose veins: he was feeling his age as an old campaigner.

Young Pioneer Arthur Daulman recalls being in a party of six detailed to lay distribution water piping for a casualty clearing station at Heilly, on a railway siding between Corbie and Albert (one of many such places being set up in readiness for the coming battle), as a result of which he came by what he called 'a "bobby" job' in the hospital itself. He writes: 'I was given a large tin of biscuits by our Quartermaster as part of our rations and these I presented to the Sergeant-Cook, all dressed up in white hat and jacket, who said, "Take them to the incinerator; we don't want them here". They were hard and disagreeable and who was I to argue, so in they went. My job was to keep a large table clean. We had lovely food there, including fruit and custard instead of the eternal stew. But it only lasted for a week.'

My father was with the left half company: 'in the trenches' according to Streather, but not close to action. He writes that he 'was sent to a Canadian battery of 9.2 howitzers, who were pounding to rubble the village of Contalmaison, behind the German lines, and paying particular attention to an enemy observation post in the village church tower. The battery was emplaced in the high banks of a sunken road, near to the town of Albert, and south of this place, and consisted of four guns in gun pits excavated in the bank of the road. The banks had been scraped clean of grass and bushes liable to catch fire from the blast of the guns during action, and a tarpaulin sheet with a tent peg tied to each corner was pegged over the bank under the muzzle of each gun to blanket the cloud of dust, which otherwise would ensue when the gun fired, and advertise the gun position to the German observation balloons. Every time the guns fired the tarpaulins were whipped up loose from the ground. When I reported to the commanding officer he presented me with a tent-pegging mallet, and told me what he wanted done with it, which was to scramble up the bank when the tarpaulin was dislodged and peg it back in place, then he pointed out some green canvas buckets and told me there was plenty of good water in the well at Méaulte, at the bottom of the hill, away from Albert, and his thirsty gunners liked plenty of water whilst working the guns. It was an active job, but not particularly arduous, and these Canadians were a nice matey crowd with whom I got on very well, and was sorry to leave after about three weeks in their company. Méaulte was considerably damaged by shelling but there were plenty of inhabitants about, and one or two estaminets open for business, which I patronized during my water fatigue. The 9.2 howitzers were manned by personnel of the R.G.A. (Royal Garrison Artillery) and the shell (weighing 290 lb) required two men to put it into the breech of the gun, and a third hefty gunner to ram it from the carrying cradle into the breech. In the prevalent hot, dry weather this was heavy work, and I was kept busy with mallet and water buckets.' Once, in an off-duty period, my father ventured into nearby Albert with some of the Canadians, but the town was 'battered about' and 'it was not much of a night out, so we usually contented ourselves in Méaulte'. Like everybody else who passed through Albert and survived the war, he brought home a postcard portraying the gigantic statue of the Virgin and Child on top of the basilica tower which had been knocked over by a German shell, so that it leaned horizontally over the street, seeming ready to fall at any time.

It was while the 216th were in the Ribemont / Corbie area that news came of the drowning at sea of Lord Kitchener on 5th June. He was the most distinguished Royal Engineer of his generation. As Secretary of State for War, his creation of a national volunteer army vastly larger than any earlier English army out of a horde of unmilitary civilians was an extraordinary achievement. No less extraordinarily, this army was holding its own against the greatest military power the world had ever seen, as well as enduring the worst that the blunders of its own general staff could inflict. My father recalls that the news of Kitchener's death was discussed for some time by his comrades, 'pro and con', (suggesting that ordinary sappers were not of the unanimous opinion that Kitchener's death was a disaster). He recalls some of the conversation: "They will have to get a new recruitment poster up now", said Heston, "Kitchener wants you won't get him many recruits where he's gone". "Well, he fixed England up with a new army." "Yes, and the 216 Company." "He is only one man after all, and we've still got Horatio Bottomley to show us how to win the war. We shall be all right." "As long as he keeps in England we've got a good chance. As the song goes that chap sung in the last concert party: 'Mr Bottomley, good old Horatio! He will see us righted every time. He's the man behind the scenes, the man who gets us pork and beans, Mr Bottomley, John Bull.' Lloyd George got us ammunition, Horatio got us pork and beans, so there's two candidates for Kitchener's job."

I assume that the reference is to a divisional concert party, not one of the 'smoking concerts' or 'smokers' by which the 216th Company occasionally entertained themselves in England and France. The song quoted is, on the face of it, morale-boosting cant, but I think it likely that its singer, like the Nuneaton men, had a sarcastic attitude to his subjects: especially to the well-fed Horatio Bottomley, with his outrageous, profit-taking recruiting rallies.

At the end of June Brigadier-General Charteris wrote of the Somme area: 'It is impossible to describe the scene. We have been bombarding for days, and the Germans replying. The whole area is torn with shells, trees stripped to skeletons, villages just heaps of ruins. The noise is terrific, with the continuous roar of our own guns and the crack of enemy shells. Our observation balloons hang in the sky like great gorged leeches in the air. Our aeroplanes are entirely masters of the air, and are circling like sparrow-hawks over the enemy lines.'[13] Though the Canadian gunners may have reduced Contalmaison to rubble, as my father thought, the bombardment did not destroy German resistance there. Haig's plan was to take this strongpoint on the first day of the Somme battle, but its capture would require ten days and very many deaths among the assaulting infantry. The 216th Company were well out of all this when, on 29th June, numbers 2, 3, and 4 Sections marched back to Corbie station, loaded all their possessions onto a train and, writes my father, 'clambered into our "Hommes 40" billets, wondering at the brevity of our stay in any of the places we had visited, and the frequent train journeys'. Lieutenant Knox, Sergeant Streather, and number 1 Section remained for the time being in the Corbie area.

Chapter Six:
Second Army and Reserve Army, July to October 1916

The sections on the move now had an even longer roundabout ride than the last: via Amiens and Abbeville, then north to the coast at Etaples, then inland to St. Omer, Hazebrouck, and eventually a small military station near Abeele, called Hopoutre, three miles west of Poperinghe. My father observes: 'This was an apt reference to our present situation, which was not lost on some of our N.C.O.s when they came along the platform shouting "Hop out R.E.s with your kit, smartly now".' When all the R.E.s had hopped out and unloaded their animals and transport, they marched eastwards, through Poperinghe towards Ypres, on a road embanked above the low, flat, and usually very wet fields. To each side lay the usual acres of hospitals, hutments, and military cemeteries of a 'back area'; ahead, to the right, could be seen the blue outline of Kemmel Hill, beyond which loomed the Messines-Wytschaete ridge which was held by the Germans. This ridge, about two hundred feet high at its highest point, was at the southern end of a commanding German position on high ground surrounding the battered citadel of Ypres and enjoying perfect observation over the entire British salient. This notorious salient was the result of two years' efforts by the Germans to capture Ypres and by the British not to surrender it; thus it had turned into an obstinately stabilized killing ground.

The area was famous for rain and mud, but when the Nuneaton men arrived it was a hot, dry summer's day. Captain Cook, riding an officer's charger of course, saw that the men were marching badly. Arthur Daulman recalls that he said, "Sergeant-Major, what's the trouble with the men? They're lagging behind. They'll march better if they take their coats off." 'So the greatcoats were stripped off and put on the G.S. wagons and tool carts. He did us a good turn here because the coats were never worn on a route march again.'

The march ended two miles west of Ypres at a hamlet called Brandhoek, near Vlamertinghe; here the company were billeted in a large farm and various huts and barns. The railway from Poperinghe to Ypres ran very close to this farm, but, my father recalls, 'The only traffic this line carried at that time was Commander Samson's armoured train, armed with a six-inch naval gun, and Brandhoek was his only stopping place; beyond the farm the railway was out of action. Nearly every evening, about six o'clock, the train would stop under the cover of the farm buildings, the crew would send Jerry a few rounds, and then pack up and return towards Poperinghe, leaving us to make the best of whatever stuff Jerry sent in retaliation, usually heavy shrapnel, which burst with a loud, vicious crash, and a cloud of thick black smoke. We were not alone in wishing that the commander was back at sea; but apart from this return fire, we were usually unmolested.' The belligerent amphibious Commander Samson did not go back to sea. He had come to France in command of a Royal Naval aeroplane and armoured car detachment; he ended his days as an Air Commodore, his recreations listed in *Who's Who* as hunting and boxing.

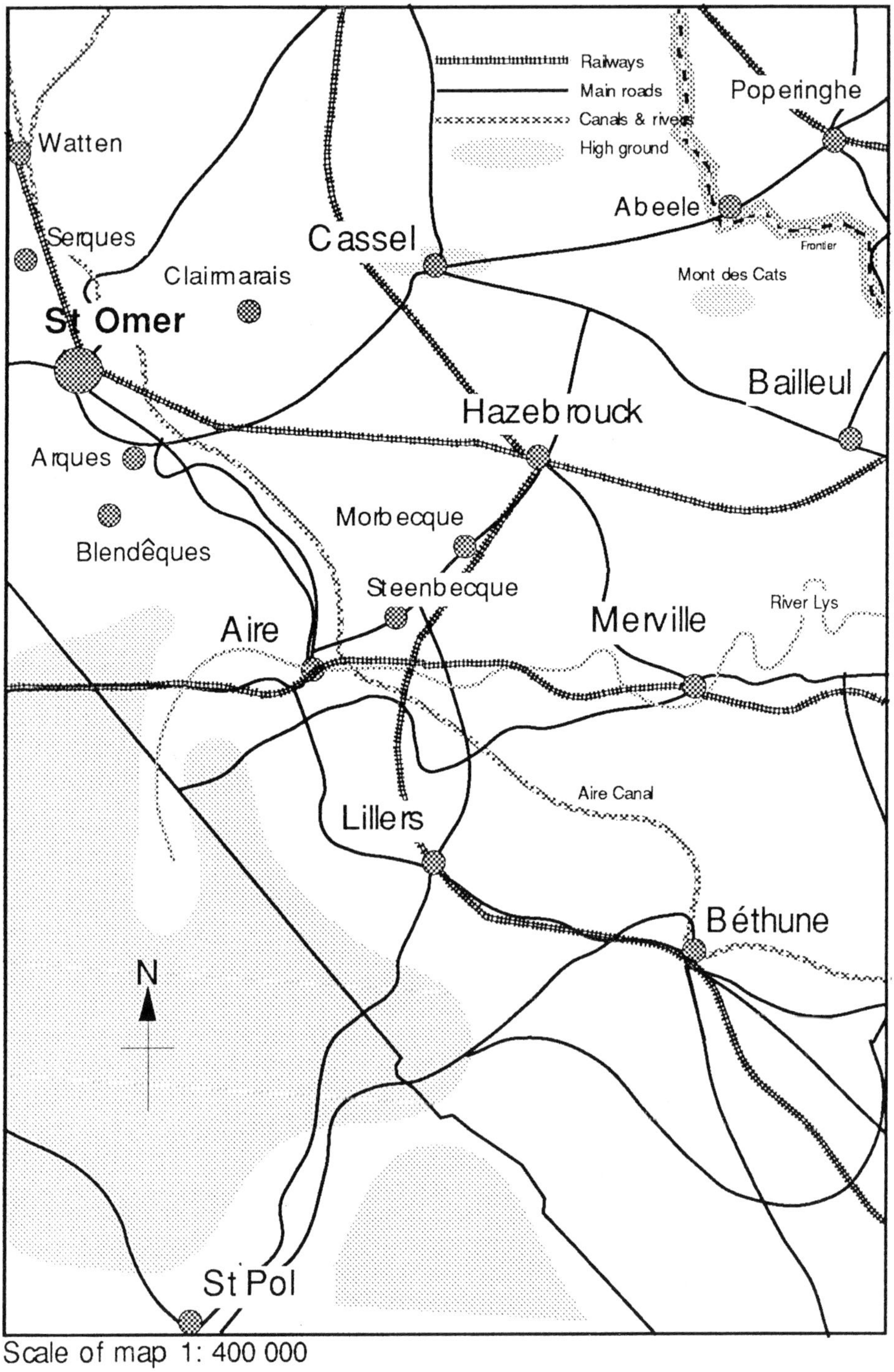

Map 4: Second Army rear area, 1916–18

Though the Ypres salient was a dangerous enough place, it was well away from the bloodbath which began to fill near the Somme on 1 July. Number 1 Section remained with the Reserve (later renamed the Fifth) Army in the Somme area for another three months, and, according to a letter of 6 November by Sergeant Streather, 'worked up the line for some time both before and after the first of July', but much of their work was fortunately a long way from the fighting. On 24 July Streather wrote: 'We have rather an uninteresting job at present. I am generally kept pretty busy doing nothing. Sometimes we get a decent job but generally it's got to be done quick, and somehow I feel as though I am not helping the war much. One thing we are some distance from the line now.' Three days later: 'Still at the same H.Q. . . nice weather here. . . I have lost nearly all my section for the time being: they are away on jobs some few miles distant, but so far there is no sign of joining the company. As far as the work goes this is the most uninteresting job we have had. The chief thing is cleaning up and making other people comfortable and as far as I see we are not helping the war on much. One thing we are quite comfortable in our billet and although the section are comparative strangers to me I get on quite well with all of them, and I must say they are a mixed lot just now. There is a Scotch man and an Irish chap who came in the draft: both are ceaseless yarn spinners and between them they manage to keep us very much alive'. No letters survive from August, but in September Sergeant Streather and his section were again a long way from the Somme battlefield, working in another army headquarters. I do not know what those 'uninteresting' jobs were; I conjecture that some of them were concerned with fixtures and fittings in headquarters buildings.

The three sections which had travelled north were now in the Second Army, in countryside very different from the Somme. During six months they had sampled all three regions of the British front: the grimy mining villages, pitheads and slagheaps near Loos in Artois, the chalk downland near the Somme in Picardy, and now the waterlogged fenlands near Ypres in Flanders. Except for the shell-holes and wreckage, it was like living successively in the Black Country, Wiltshire, and

21. Royal Engineers laying 6 inch water pipe: Royal Engineers Journal.

22. Filling Water Bottles: Royal Engineers Journal.

Cambridgeshire. Their main work during what would prove to be a lengthy stay in the north was to help provide a fresh-water supply for the great battle in Flanders which was always Sir Douglas Haig's pet scheme. The water table here was very high and the old drainage system in this low-lying wet clay had been destroyed by shell fire. 'Rivers and canals were polluted by refuse from the flooded land, and even the artesian wells had become poisoned. The decay and refuse of millions of men, alive and dead, sank into the soil and were carried by the blackened waters throughout the inland plain'.[1] The provision of fresh water for vast numbers of men, horses, and mules at a recommended rate of five gallons per man per day and ten gallons per animal per day (albeit a rate not often achieved in the front line and never in battle) was thus an important logistical matter.

The first work of this kind for the 216th Company was to develop a supply from a large reservoir at Dickebusch, south-west of Ypres. My father writes: 'Here the company commenced laying cast-iron water pipes, four inches in diameter, connected with "screw-on" jointing collars and then buried two feet underground; pumps were put in where necessary and water tanks were installed as far forward as possible for the convenience of the front line and support troops. In some sheltered places in the rear, stand pipes and valves, supplying wooden water troughs were included for the benefit of the transport animals.' There were not too many sheltered places, for the Germans had excellent observation from their high ground.

The Company was, as usual, 'told off' into parties to carry out the varied work that the provision and distribution of water entailed. Arthur Daulman was with the party that laid the pipeline northwards, 'using pumps through the cornfields and into tanks on the side of the N9 between Poperinghe and Ypres. The tanks were set up on stilts so that motor vehicles and horse-drawn carts could draw up underneath to be filled. The pipe then went on to the Guards camp at Elverdinghe. Here on a lovely day we were putting up the tanks on stilts when Lieut. Gordon of No.3 Section came along and said, "C-c-c-come on you ch-ch-chaps. Come and listen to the Guards band and b-b-bugger the work." Who were we to argue, and any way we were only too happy to oblige.' Elverdinghe camp was a relatively safe place, in woods surrounding a remarkably undamaged chateau; Lieutenant Gordon, no doubt, was as pleased as his men that the War Office had long since rescinded its ban, imposed at the beginning of the war, against military bands at the front. This is the earliest reference to Lieutenant Gordon in the surviving records of the 216th R.E.; it appears that he was popular with the men. The Company's complement of officers is uncertain, but it seems that after the middle of 1916 there were sometimes three, even occasionally four, officers in addition to the Officer Commanding. Lieutenant Knox was at this time with number 1 Section in the Somme area, but it seems that he did not return with that section when it rejoined the Company in September: he had been transferred to a Royal Engineer Field Company.

23. Typical Water Point in Flanders: Royal Engineers Journal.

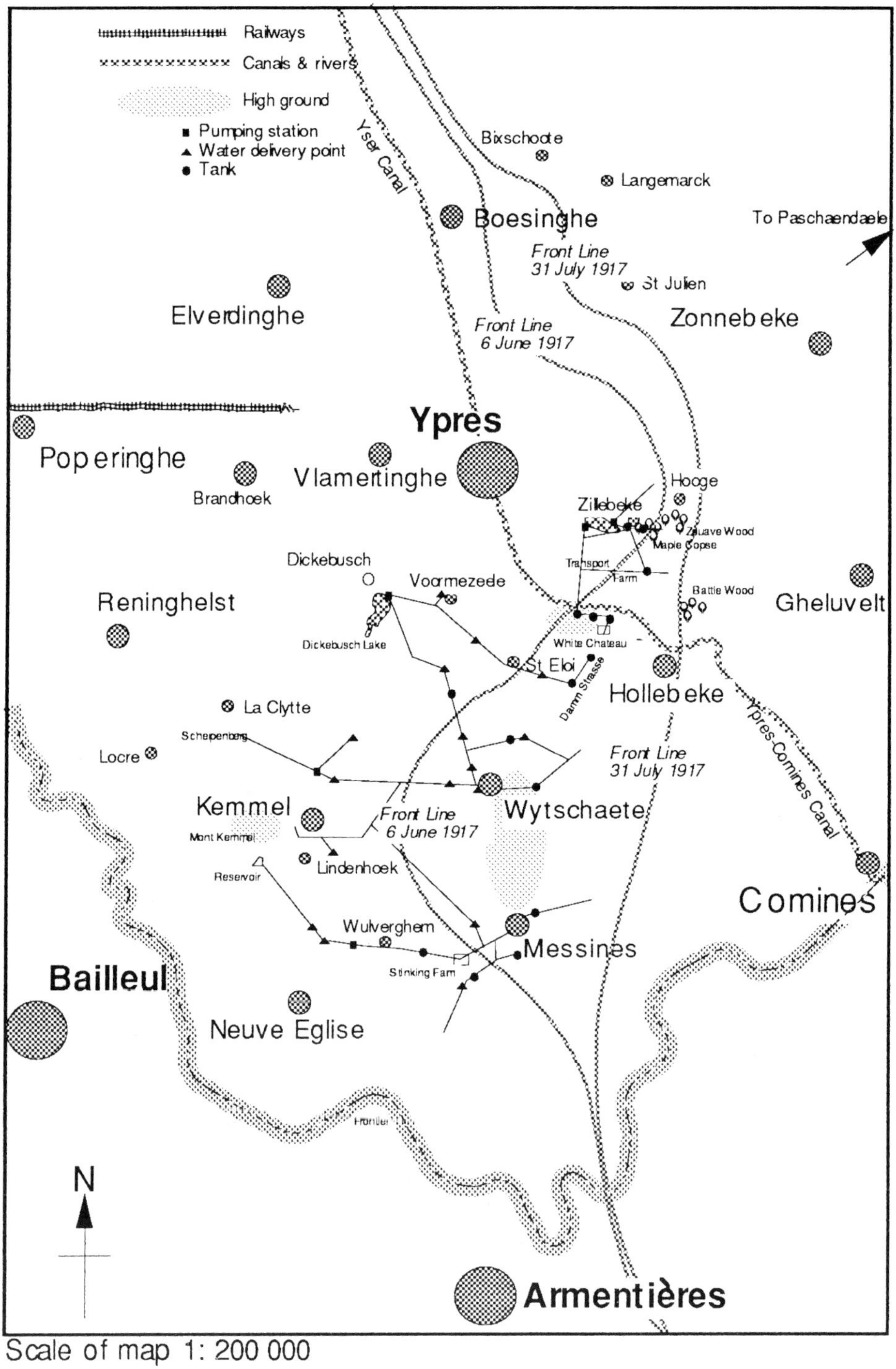

Scale of map 1: 200 000

Map 5: Advance water supply in Ypres salient, July 1916 – January 1918

Another party of the left half-company was sent to build a sandbagged dug-out in the shelter of a dyke bordering Dickebusch reservoir. A pump was installed in this dug-out to supply a pipe line through Ridge Wood to a tank concealed in the ruins of the brasserie at St.Eloi (not the ruined place of that name facing Vimy Ridge and sketched by my father, but a ruined village on the front line south of Ypres, at a crossroads on the Wytschaete-Ypres road). My father recalls: 'We walked to and from Dickebusch, from Brandhoek, through another small hamlet called Busseboon, along a cross-country cart track which came out on to the road at the south end of the village. The street pavé was broken up by shell craters, which were roughly filled in, and the walls of the buildings on each side were shattered and scarred by the exploding missiles. Halfway along the main street a

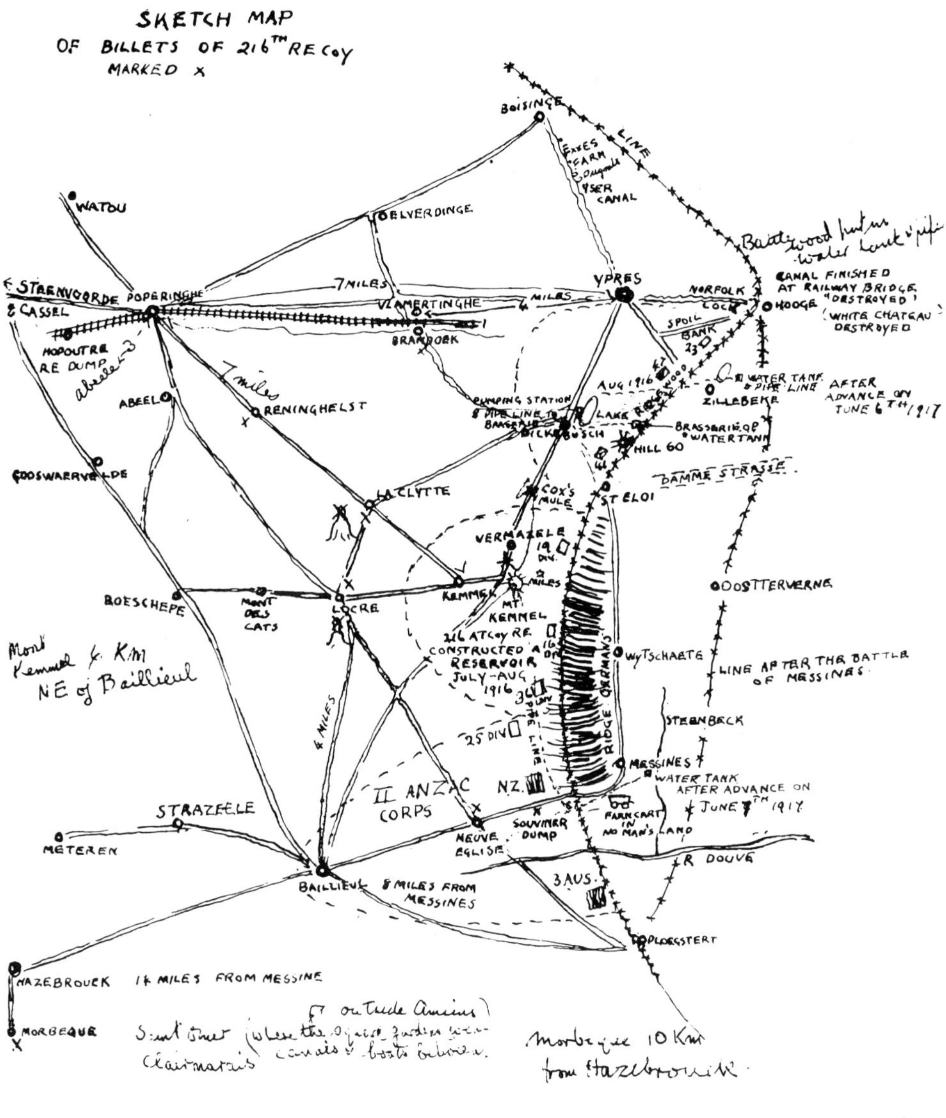

Map 5A: Ypres salient: Arthur Sambrook's sketch map of 216 Company billets and works

narrow lane on the right hand side led past the church and a few small ruined cottages, and ended in a cart track leading to the lake about a quarter of a mile away. The track turned left and continued along the side of the dyke, and a few yards along we constructed the pump house in the rear side of the bank, at the south end of the lake. At the corner a footpath went off to the right over some swampy ground which was flooded in wet weather. A footbridge of duck boards on trestles was put over this swamp by the Royal Engineers and the path continued across some open ground, rising to a ridge crowned by the splintered remains of "Ridge Wood", and eventually came out at the crossroad at the brasserie. There was a Canadian battery of 18-pounder field guns in position on the "dead" ground below the crest of the ridge, which was frequently "strafed" by Jerry's heavy shrapnel, without any apparent damaging result to guns or gunners. When the circles of dust kicked up by the shrapnel bullets, had settled, the gunners usually came out from shelter to send back a few "thank-you" shells to Jerry.'

Dickebusch was deserted by its former inhabitants but the cellars of its ruins housed units of the Canadian Corps, who, says my father, 'added to the general dilapidation by using the woodwork of the upper rooms for firewood'. The Canadian Corps had been in this area for the past nine months: at this time its forces were disposed in great depth from its front line, on a quadrant of the salient south and south-east of Ypres as far back as Poperinghe and Abeele, so it is probable that the dilapidations were widespread and long continued. They remained here, while the men of the 216th Company were pipe laying, until the beginning of September, when they were trundled off to join in the great battle on the Somme and be well and truly dilapidated in their turn.

Local dilapidations by the Nuneaton Company were comparatively trivial: my father writes: 'Our toilet arrangements at Dickebusch, in the earth closet of the nearest cottage to the pump house, were very well ventilated, having neither roof or door, with a very unusual supply of bum fodder, provided by an old edition of Foxe's Book of Martyrs, printed in English, lying on one corner of the worm-eaten box seat. Unfortunately, as this place was well patronized, it was not a complete edition, and it was further depleted during our visits, which combined mental benefit with physical relief. We wondered sometimes where this book had come from, and how it came to be where we found it, but when we left there was plenty of it remaining, to interest any following readers, who would be glad to find it handy, instead of on a library shelf, out of reach.' My father adds: 'I also found an Everyman edition of the Plays of Sophocles in a damaged and deserted house in Kemmel a few weeks later, but I found Greek tragedy a bit flat under our present circumstances, so I gave Sophocles to 2nd Corporal Anderton, who found it very enjoyable, but had a habit of boring any comrades who were near him when he read it out aloud. These two books were the only reading matter I looked at during the two years and three months I spent in France.' Needless to say, bog paper was never issued to the other ranks in the Great War.

The village of Dickebusch itself had more considerable amenities, for, my father writes, 'One of the buildings in the village, well sandbagged and propped, housed a Canadian Expeditionary Force canteen, where we could buy essentials or luxuries at low prices; and one chap remarked, "they sold everything except a Blighty ticket. To get that, one had to stand outside and get one from Jerry." The party working on the pump house did any shopping required by the other chaps in the company who were working elsewhere, and we usually returned to Brandhoek with bulging haversacks.'

'Sapper J.H.Smith and I spent our days filling sandbags for the building gang to cover the pump house, and established ourselves in the field on the right hand side of the track from the village. We chose a place near a thick hedge at the far side from the track, near a deep, dry ditch, which would provide cover in the event of hostile interference, and also to screen us from the enemy observation balloons, which were a prominent daily, ominous feature, silhouetted against the summer sky all round the Ypres salient. Apart from a few occasional shrapnel shells, which damaged neither man nor pump house, Jerry did not bother us overmuch; the only other hostile interference we experienced came from our allies, the Belgians.'

'After we had been at work here for some time, we became aware that someone was interrupting our conversation, and looking round, we saw a sentry on the other side of the hedge, who was ordering us to go away. Then we noticed several grass-covered mounds at intervals along the hedge, with the well-polished barrels of field guns poking through square embrasures in the front. "Look at that lot", remarked Joe, "they've been dug in there so long the buttercups and daisies are growing all over them". We replied to the sentry's repeated order, with the vulgar Army version of "Allez", and went on with our work. "He understood what we said, anyway", said Joe, "he's gone". The sentry soon returned with an officer who also ordered us to go somewhere else, as our activities might bring German shell fire on his battery. "Keep quiet, they don't know you're here", replied Joe, and since we were digging in a nice sandy place, we carried on where we were, replying to any further orders with "Oui, oui, no compree Monsieur". Eventually we were left in peace to fill our sandbags.' However, the Belgian officer telephoned Captain Cook, who sent the sappers to fill their sandbags elsewhere and

24. Joe Smith and Arthur Sambrook filling sandbags for the pump-house (left) near Dickebusch Lake (right), sketched by Sambrook.

ordered Corporal Rogers, in charge of the party, to keep his men under cover. The name 'Belgian Battery Corner', between Dickebusch Lake and Ypres, on a map in the *Official History*[2] suggests that Belgian artillery batteries were fixed features in the landscape of the Ypres Salient. The sandbag affair was one of the 216th Company's very few dealings with 'gallant little Belgium', the protection of which was a principal British war aim.

My father's account continues: 'After inspecting the half-completed pump house, where Rogers was installing the pump, Cook told him to sandbag the corrugated iron roof before doing anything more to the walls, in case the pump got any damage during enemy shelling. Jerry must have heard the word, and responded with a few bursts of shrapnel over the Canadian battery on the slope behind Ridge Wood.' Rogers's party sandbagged the roof, but 'we found that the whole place was top heavy and very shaky, so we hastened to get some bags round the sides to stiffen it, but we were too late, and the pump house slowly heeled over and collapsed, burying the pump under a jumble of pit props, corrugated iron sheets, and sandbags. On receiving the report of the day's work from Corporal Rogers, Cook replied "It can't be helped, it was an act of God". 'After his short and unfortunate visit to us, the captain paid a very brief visit to the party putting the water tank in a brasserie at the crossroads on the Vermezeele-Ypres road, a place known as "Brasserie Corner". This tank was being caulked with lead and the consequent noise was attracting the attention of Jerry, whose lines were in plain view from the opening in the back wall from which the door had been blown out. Cook told the party "to get the job finished quickly, and get out". Afterwards the job was carried on at night.'

As for the party under Corporal Rogers: my father writes: 'We cleared our wreckage up, and finished the pump house in our own fashion, without any further difficulty or interference from God or man, and spent a day or two going to the Divisional R.E. dump at Abeele for material needed by the other parties, some of whom were working at night in Ridge Wood and the Brasserie Corner, so we went up to them with our wagons, to unload their material where needed. There was plenty of traffic on the roads at night, with R.E. materials and infantry rations and ammunition being taken to the various communication trenches, which commenced at certain places on the roadside, where the ration parties from the units in the line waited to collect whatever their transport brought. On some nights there was some shelling and machine-gun fire, which caused a lot of confusion and some casualties, but the only casualty in our company was a mule killed by machine-gun fire one dark night on the road parallel to Wytschaete ridge. The mule was untackled, and left to swell up in the ditch amongst other animals dead and decomposing there, and the wagon completed its deliveries pulled by the remaining three.'

Frank Hextall was one of the mule drivers. Summing up these nights when their pipe-line was advanced to the Brasserie, he writes: 'not many shells but plenty of machine-gun bullets, also snipers; not very pleasant; fairly hot shop'. Henry Williamson, the novelist, gives a far more highly-coloured description of these crowded roads at night: 'Marching men, guns, strings of pack mules, wagons, cars, lorries — all were congested and colliding in the darkness. Shell-holes in the road itself were filled with the ruins of shattered wagons, and perhaps pieces of horse and mule, and hastily covered with earth. Then on again, thousands of tons of material, animate and inanimate, bumping, tramping, jolting forward towards the flare-glimmering Salient. . . The only way over the morass was by the wooden tracks that serpentined over the mud — baulks of teak and beech laid side by side, looking like the sloughs, cast by monsters of the primeval slime. Always at night the tracks glowed and glared with fire and smoke and dreadful crashes; sections would rise splintered into the air, wagons, horses, mules with them; the mud bordering on the tracks was piled with old broken and swelled things. The young German gunner cadets were trained in night-firing on these tracks, which were visible along their ribbed and winding lengths by day.'[3]

In the forward areas the 216th Company were expected to wear steel helmets, which gave rather better protection against shrapnel and shell splinters than the more comfortable regulation soft peaked caps. My father recalls: 'In consequence of a riotous evening in the estaminet at Vlamertinghe and some derogatory remarks made to the Sergeant-Major and Corporal Ashley afterwards, Sapper William Clarkson was awarded seven days field punishment. One evening while spending his two hours' period of relaxation and meditation, tied spreadeagled to one of the rear wheels of a G.S. wagon, Jerry sent a few heavy shrapnel shells over the farm. Corporal Sam Hollis was the orderly corporal on this evening, and was undecided whether to untie Clarkson or not: finally he went out and placed a "tin hat" on the prisoner's head, and returned to the guard room with the remark "I hope he will be all right now, I've done all I can for him". Field punishment was not a rigorous affair, as it was carried out on the two occasions when it was awarded in the company. The prisoner was loosely tied to the wheel spokes, enabling him to ease his backside down on to the hub of the wheel whenever he felt like a rest. Here he would receive visitors, who fed him with a fresh chew of plug tobacco when required and who looked after him in other ways.'

The N.C.O.s were still close enough to their men to play cricket with them. C.S.M. Mitchinson and Sergeant Barker turned out for the eleven that played against a Leicestershire Pioneer battalion about this time. As usual, the Nuneaton team contained no officers, whereas their victorious opponents fielded two captains and two lieutenants. A report in the *Nuneaton Observer* for 28 July (probably contributed by Sapper Joe Smith) blamed loose fielding and lack of practice for his side's defeat, noting that it was their first game for over eleven months. While the game was in progress, 'a visit from three German aeroplanes lent additional excitement to the proceedings. Luckily they did not stop the match, though it must be admitted that their visit aroused more interest than the keenest part of the match.'

The German observation balloons, also much in evidence at Brandhoek, seem to have aroused less interest. My father writes that they 'got on the nerves of a few sappers amongst us, who imagined that every pair of binoculars focussed to the eyes of the two observers suspended therein was concentrated on our activities', but 'the rest of us tried to allay their anxiety by assuring them that Jerry

25. La Clytte church

had got something better to look at than a few shabby R.E.s, and in any case it was better for them to wait and then demolish our work when we had finished it. As Sapper Thomas Norman once told Captain Cook, "If we took any notice of them things, we'd never get nothing done". This was the general opinion, and in time we accepted balloons as a natural feature in the sky hereabouts; as common as clouds elsewhere.' The German balloons were black; the British were grey.

On 23 July the 216th Company moved a mile or two south to La Clytte, a small hamlet on the Reninghelst-Kemmel road, about half way between those two places. There they camped in bell tents in a large field at the back of the church. Arthur Daulman recalls: 'The church of La Clytte was intact at this time, and I have a photo of it prior to it being destroyed by the Germans in their April offensive 1918. My photo shows a typical church of the region with a small central bell tower and blank eastern wall with a Calvary in a recess. The church stood close to the crossroads Ypres-Bailleul-Mont Kemmel and must always have been in danger when within range of the enemy artillery.'

'From La Clytte', my father recalls, 'we went daily to and from Kemmel Hill, about three miles away, where we constructed a reservoir on the west slope of the hill. Here, near the top of a narrow gully, a spring bubbled up, feeding a small stream, which provided ample fresh water for our purpose. After clearing away the undergrowth, we built up a solid dam composed of fascines and puddled clay, enclosing the lower part of the gully. On leaving the dam the water went through two filter beds, each of sand, shingle, and charcoal, which purified and sweetened the flow.'[4] Arthur Daulman 'thought, as a novice, that the trickle would be negligible and the dam totally inadequate. But completion showed that I didn't know what I was talking about', for the Kemmel reservoir supplied water which was afterwards distributed by pipe-lines to many supply places near the front from Hollebeke to Messines. An additional supply was piped to the reservoir from a stream near Locre, soon afterwards, during the time the company was billeted in that village.

Philip Gibbs observed luridly that the German gunners on the Messines-Wytschaete ridge 'looked straight into Kemmel village and turned their guns on to it when our men crouched among its ruins, and opened the graves in the cemetery and laid old bones bare': the village was 'as clear and vivid to them' as were 'the red roofs of Dickebusch village and the gaunt ribs of its broken houses'.[5] The far side of Kemmel hill, three miles from the nearest German, was somewhat safer; my father recalls some pleasant evidence that normal life continued there: 'One hot afternoon I was sent to the reservoir with some nuts and bolts, required for the valves which regulated the water at the dam. Some valves were also placed at intervals along the pipe lines, enabling the water to be cut off while the frequent damage inflicted by enemy shell fire was being repaired. Although the sun was warm, there was a breeze which made my solitary walk very enjoyable, and I took my time. Half way up the track over the Scherpenberg hill, I came to a large brick barn, on the right hand side of the track. A pair of double doors were open to the breeze at the back, and a similar pair of doors were open at the front, opposite. From the front doors a yellow haze of dust and chaff drifted across the track, and inside the barn there was a loud babble of conversation and laughter, accompanied by a regular, continuous, beating noise at intervals. Coming up to the doors, I saw three or four women at work in the clear, sunlit, cleared space between the doors, tossing grain into the air with flat wooden shovels. The breeze coming through the back doorway carried the husks and dust out at the front doorway and across the track. The beating noise was made by a few men spaced out round a heap of sheaves in one end of the barn, threshing out the grain with flails. The resulting heap of grain and husks was then swept into the clear space, where the women winnowed out the chaff and bagged the grain; during these operations the tongues of both men and women were as active as their arms. I stood and watched this primitive husbandry for some time, then, remembering my duty, I went leisurely up the hill and on to the reservoir.'

Another happy chance for my father at Kemmel was that in a wrecked cottage he 'found a very nicely decorated porcelain churchwarden pipe; during our marches to the various places this pipe was carried safely inserted into the barrel of my rifle.' He adds that 'A company of Canadian Engineers came about this time to share our field, establishing themselves in tents at the far side away from us. This company were French Canadians from Quebec, and their language was difficult to understand, but their baseball games were exciting affairs, which always attracted an appreciative audience from our company.' This would have been a memorable encounter not just for the baseball, because there were comparatively few French-speaking 'Canadiens' in the Canadian Corps.

The stay at La Clytte was very brief. Pioneer Daulman remembers it as two weeks; Driver Frank Hextall as one week: perhaps some of the horse transport was moved in advance to the company's new posting, which was in the little village of Locre, less than two miles away. Daulman writes: 'it just didn't seem worthwhile going to the bother of packing up and marching such a short distance'. Locre was due west of Kemmel hill and relatively undamaged; it had estaminets and seems to have been about the most advanced place of civilization relative to the front line.

Overlooking the village on the west was an isolated hill, 'flattered', writes my father, 'by the name of Mont Rouge, though as far as elevation went it was not much of a mont, and the only rouge noticeable among the trees was the red dye on the canvas sails of a tall post windmill on the summit'. It was, however, high enough to provide an excellent view over the front line some four miles away; ten months later it would provide Field Marshal Haig with his grandstand view of the Battle of Messines. My father's account continues: 'There was an estaminet opposite the windmill, and a few cottages were scattered about on both sides of the narrow lane leading from Locre to the buildings on the summit. Bordering this road at the bottom of the hill was a large field, where we established ourselves in tents, each large enough to accommodate a section comfortably, which we erected by fastening tarpaulin sheets over light wooden frames. These huts were lofty and spacious, and rigid enough to cope with the warm settled weather we were then enjoying. The cook-house was built with corrugated iron sheets, and the horses and mules were tethered to picket lines, and we settled down and spent a comfortable month.' Frank Hextall remembered it as a 'jolly nice camp', adding 'could stay here for the duration'.

The company was now closer to Kemmel hill, where work continued on their puddled clay dam. Locre was also convenient for their work on a pipe line from a spring near Westroutre, a small village two miles to the north, which provided an additional water supply for the nearly-completed reservoir at Kemmel. Life was relatively comfortable, because, my father writes, 'The only interference we had from Jerry occurred in the vicinity of the reservoir at Kemmel hill, apart from that our pipe line progressed peacefully from Westoutre, via Sherpenberg to Mont Kemmel'.

As usual, though, my father's recollections are more concerned with off-duty pursuits. He writes: 'At first, some of us spent our evenings at the estaminet on the hilltop, sitting at tables outside, watching the activities of the miller setting the sails, and then being fanned by the evening breeze the circling sails wafted round us. From here we had an extensive view of the surrounding level countryside, with the rounded contours of Mont Kemmel and Sherpenberg to the east, and Mont

Noir and Mont des Cats in the west. The one discordant feature of the landscape was the distant faint smear of smoke, and the glimmering pinpoints of the fires burning in Ypres, becoming visible as the evening light faded. After a few days the Sergeant Major and a few of his cronies among the N.C.O.s started to frequent this estaminet, and their behaviour gave everyone else the impression that they considered this place ought properly to be reserved for the Sergeants' Mess. We equally disliked their company, and afterwards spent our evenings out at the estaminets in the village.'

Arthur Daulman also frequented an estaminet down in the village. He writes in the 1980s: 'On my wall at the time of writing is a picture of silk about two feet square showing the Cloth Hall of Ypres going up in flames. Flanders is famous for its weaving and I bought it about August 1916 for 25 francs in a shop-cum-cafe in Loker [Locre] where we used to consume custard flavoured with grenadine. Quite a few of us were teetotal or nearly so, but we enjoyed this and similar drinks. The old hands preferred vin blanc.' Frank Hextall briefly recalled: 'plenty of fun down the village; had a few blackberry puddings — quite a change'. One can readily see why the estaminet bulks so large in Great War reminiscences. 'Fed on a diet of greasy stew, dry bully beef and hard tack biscuit, men needed fried food and crisp bread rolls to restore both self-respect and digestion. The estaminet where they got all this might be the kitchen of a farmhouse, a village cottage or a tin hut with newspapers lining the walls and selling lace as a sideline at two and half francs the yard, but to the infantryman [or Royal Engineer one might add] it gave pleasure out of proportion to its appearance. . . . Eating in a crowd brought back domestic friendships more strongly than almost any other activity, for a man eating food of his choice at his own time was close to home. . . . The price at the end of the session would probably be about one franc or 10d. for the egg and chips, roll and coffee'. The estaminet was 'truly a little piece of England even down to the opening hours, for no British soldier was served before 1 p.m. and at 8.30 p.m. all estaminets shut down'.[6]

In respect of drinking if not of age my father was among the 'old hands' referred to by Arthur Daulman. One evening he and his delinquent mate Sapper Clarkson were obliged to take cover with their drinks underneath a table in their estaminet during a fight between two parties of Irish infantrymen, one with green shamrock divisional badges sewn on the upper part of their tunic sleeves, the other with red hand of Ulster badges. These quarrelsome troops belonged to the 16th (South Irish) Division and the 36th (Ulster) Division. These men might not have been the best of friends at the best of times, but this was only four months after the Easter Rising. Another factor in their mutual dislike may have been the differing recent battle experience of the two divisions. The Ulster Division had suffered five thousand casualties and won four Victoria Crosses on the first two days of the battles of the Somme, whereas the South Irish were still waiting to be fed into that attritional struggle for their share of death and glory.

Despite the generally settled weather during their time encamped at Locre the Company was experiencing its first, small taste of Flanders mud. Arthur Daulman recalls: 'While I was on guard, with a bell tent for the guard room, a lorry load of duck boards was brought in. As the load was coming in Harry Trevis, known as

"The Colonel"[7], asked Sergeant-Major Mitchinson if we could have one to put in front of the tent. It was a reasonable request as we were ankle deep in mud. The answer was "No, you can't". After unloading, the Sergeant-Major came over and said, "Now what is it that you want Trevis?" "Only civility sir." I think the Sergeant-Major just didn't know what to say, and after a slight hesitation he walked away speechless.' The last recollection of Locre is also Daulman's. 'By this time it was late summer 1916 and an Irishman, Rainey by name, was talking to the officers' cook about getting damsons and making a pie for the officers' mess. The outcome was that whoever came back with damsons would have a dinner. We knew where damsons could be found. In the garden of a cottage on the slopes of Mont Kemmel where we used to go for coffee at mid-day. Off we went. Rainey climbed the tree and shook it hard. Down came the damsons and I stuffed them as quickly as I could into a sandbag. We took them to the cook and had our promised reward but crime doesn't pay; for the next day when we turned up for our coffee at the cottage we were warned off the course. No bon, no bon, the bell did cry.'

While the Company was at Locre the wives of 'the gallant fighters' enrolled in what the Nuneaton newspapers still referred to as 'The Nuneaton Fortress Company (R.E.)' were entertained in her home by the wife of 'their popular commander Captain F.C.Cook', assisted by the Mayoress and other important Nuneaton ladies: 'A variety of amusements had been arranged and numerous prizes awarded for various competitions'. The photograph and report of this function is printed in the *Nuneaton Chronicle* (25 August 1916) directly above the list of casualties suffered by local servicemen in other units that week: 21 killed or died of wounds, 41 wounded, and one missing. The list is not complete, because Sergeant Harold Hextall was fatally wounded with the Royal Warwicks on the Somme at that time; his death was reported in the *Nuneaton Observer* a week later, alongside glowing accounts, reprinted from London newspapers, of the Warwicks' bravery in the push towards Thiepval, the German strongpoint still untaken, though its capture had been one of the objectives of the first day's bloody assault on 1 July. Harold Hextall was an elder brother of Driver Frank in the 216th Company. Another news item that day was that the Royal Engineers needed recruits so badly that men aged between 41 and 47 were to be accepted as sappers or pioneers; ordinary standards of height and chest measurement could be waived in their case.

During their spell at Locre sections of the 216th Company were occasionally detached to carry out alterations and repairs at various headquarters well behind the front line. So at the end of August my father found himself at a Divisional Headquarters on the canal between Aire and St. Omer. He recalls: 'This canal went through the village between sloping, tree-lined banks, where, on fine evenings and Sundays, most of the local male population sat, silently contemplating the tips of their inert floats slowly drifting along on the surface of the placid water. Their catches were minimal in size and quantity, but no doubt the rest did them good. Sapper Mick Cuffe, No 3 Section, had a swim in the canal every evening, and on one occasion rescued a child from drowning. This event caused some excitement in the town, and was considered to be of sufficient importance for the mayor to don his official sash, and to kiss Sapper Cuffe on both cheeks. This affair took place on the steps of the Mairie, in the presence of a few locals, including the child's relatives, and a few of No 3 Section, who wanted to see our comrade kissed officially. The mayor said a few words and then embraced Cuffe and kissed him on both cheeks; the locals clapped their hands and we applauded somewhat hilariously. This was about the only time that our leisure activities won the official approval of the French and Belgian authorities.'

'Our work here, the usual run of building, plumbing, and decorating, was completed to the satisfaction of the Divisional C.R.E., despite the delays caused by the incessant interruptions of "Squad, 'shun; eyes right or left", whenever some of our over-zealous N.C.O.s noticed an officer near us. This saluting business was the result of strict orders from the Sergeant Major, who was hoping the Company would be permanently attached to the Staff, but the majority of us were not interested in that prospect; in fact we were fed up with the sight of the place and its inmates. The estaminets were respectably dull; our usual style was cramped, and we were happy when the rumour circulated that when the job was finished we should leave. Apparently our stained and shabby uniforms and lack of smartness lowered the tone of the place.'

My father's section had a respite from C.S.M.Mitchinson's parade-ground zeal when he went off with another section to the even grander surroundings of the Second Army Headquarters in the casino at Cassel, where, my father says, he could 'enjoy another saluting holiday'. Edmund Blunden, poet and subaltern in the Royal Sussex Regiment, writes that 'the cool streets of Cassel led between ancient shop-fronts and courtyards, maintaining in their dignity that war was nothing to do with Cassel'.[8] Though they did not put it in those terms, the Nuneaton men may have had similar feelings about the place. My father writes: 'Cassel was another "starchy" place, but the chaps found a comfortable estaminet a short distance outside the town, near to their billets; in both places they were undisturbed by the "red caps" and could spread themselves. One unfortunate evening, Corporal Shelmerdine went out with a few of his section, No 2, to this estaminet, and came out at dusk too drunk to walk back to camp, and most of his companions were little better. Borrowing a decrepit handcart which was standing at the side of the estaminet, a few of the party decided to wheel Shelmerdine back to camp. Afterwards, the details of the escapade were confused and contradictory, and the collapse of the handcart, meeting with a staff car full of officers, dispersed the party. Shelmerdine was brought back to camp, and next morning lost his stripes, not so much for being drunk, but for the crime of drinking with his subordinates.' After this, the Cassel section worked on the aerodrome at St. Marie Capelle, close to the town.

The men of number 1 Section, left behind on the Somme, were now at Toutencourt, between Doullens and Albert, at the headquarters of Lieutenant-General Sir Hubert de la P. Gough's Reserve Army, better known under its later title, the Fifth Army. Perhaps they were doing what other sections of the Company were doing at Daours and Cassel: that is minor building works, such as carpentry, plumbing, and decorating. Whatever the job, the Section left Toutencourt on 25 September. The movement order issued to No.92704, Sergeant Streather on that day (one of the very few pieces of 216th Company bumf still extant) reads: 'You will proceed to Railhead (Belle Eglise). On arrival to report to R.T.O. who will notify you time of departure train. Your party is rationed up to and for 27th instant. On arrival at Destination you will report to Officer i/c of other section 216 Coy. R.E. working on Aerodrome at Clairmarais. Total strength of Party:- 26 Other Ranks. 2 H.D. Horses. 1 Officer's Charger. 2 Mules. 1 G.S. Wagon. 1 R.E. Tool Cart. 3 Bicycles. 1 Motor Bicycle. All Railway Buffets are out of bounds to troops proceeding by Rail.' Whatever Charlie Streather and his section did at Toutencourt seems not to have been appreciated. When General Gough moved his headquarters to Flanders ten months later he told Haig that he was 'delighted with his palatial residence after nearly a year in a smelly farm at Toutencourt.[9] One hopes, at least, that Sergeant Streather got to ride the officer's charger (which presumably had been Lieutenant Knox's before he left the Company).

While two sections were still at Cassel and Toutencourt the rest of the company moved, on 19 September, from Locre to Clairmarais. Some of them travelled in style in the company's own 'Berna' lorries, one driven by a London bus driver with a mate named Titterton, who was killed at Messines. Driver Hextall moved with the mules: 'did 35 kilometres; very tired'. All agreed that they had made a good move. Hextall: 'very nice place; right away from the line; nice woods; plenty of sport here; nothing to worry us; lovely weather at first, but plenty of rain afterwards; had football team'.

Clairmarais consisted of a few large farms and scattered cottages on the outskirts of Nieppe forest, two miles north-east of St. Omer, even farther from the front than Second Army headquarters at Cassel. The drivers were billeted at a farm with good stables, where, Hextall recalls, the people also were very good. The rest of the left half-company, Nos 3 and 4 Sections, were housed on the upper floor of a beautiful large granary, approached by stone steps. Arthur Daulman recalls with relish: 'This is the place where our mattresses, made with sandbags, were filled with a most luxurious filling. After the wheat had been threshed out in the barn the husks were left and these were used to fill the sandbags and they proved to be the finest filling and induced the deepest sleep of our time in France. I remember them with affection.' When at last he rejoined the Company at Clairmarais Sergeant Streather was no less pleased. He declared that the farm bedroom he shared with the Company Sergeant-Major and Sergeant Harris was 'the best billet we have ever had in France', and, despite having wet feet from continually working in long grass in the frequent rain, it was also 'the best job' they had ever had. Better still, leave was about to start. There would be a grant of six men per month, starting 1 November. If all went well his turn would come in December.

The comfortable farm billet was near to a large area of level ground which had been requisitioned as an airfield for the Royal Flying Corps; the task of the 216th Company was to put in some ten miles of land drains and construct three hangars, each 75 feet long and 75 feet wide, as well as other buildings. They were assisted by between two and four hundred German prisoners of war, captured at Thiepval, who did all the heavy work, such as digging trenches for the field drainage pipes. My father observed: 'the work was a straightforward job, and we were enjoying fine, warm weather, with a willing gang of helpers, and no interruption from Jerry or Staff Officers to hinder us'. Frank Hextall said it was 'more like a holiday': for him a holiday with souvenirs because he bought an Iron Cross from one of the prisoners for two cigarettes. The prisoners, writes Arthur Daulman, 'were kept in a "bird cage" which we erected. We had finished the wire sides and were about to put in the overhang when one very short prisoner said, "That will be plenty high enough for me". It was about 3' or 4' high at the time and I was surprised to hear a German speak well enough to make a joke.' (Actually, the regulation height for the fence of a P.O.W. cage was 8' 6" plus overhang.) The prisoners were good workers, as Sergeant Streather told his parents: 'never been shaved for a week lots of them, but my word they do work harder than I ever saw British Tommy Atkins' (6 November).

'Sundays', writes my father, 'were a holiday for the prisoners and ourselves, when we walked through the forest to St.Omer, to do some shopping at the Expeditionary Forces canteen there, a lunch and drinks at the cafés, and then a pleasant walk back in the evening, calling at the estaminets at the roadside'. Arthur Daulman is more circumstantial: 'In St.Omer were No.4 and No.6 "red lamps", and on Sundays there was a general exodus with the married men leading. I have no personal recollections of this form of recreation. I suppose I was just too young. From Clairmarais we used to go across to La Nieppe for coffee, skirting the Forêt de Rihoult-Clairmarais. There were notices in all the estaminets forbidding the sale of cognac to us, but eventually Mademoiselle, having got to know us, let us have hot milk and cognac. A very pleasant drink. I found the beer not to my taste and the vin blanc and vin rouge undrinkable.'

Two comrades found their amusement closer to home. My father writes: 'There was no estaminet in Clairmarais, and we rarely went to the village. The exceptions were Sappers Rainey and Chisholm, who became intimate with a widow known in the locality as Madame Quatre Sou, and were frequent visitors to her cottage. The rest of us spent our evenings in the estaminet in the village of La Nieppe, a mile away from our billet, where the prices were very low, and the cigars were deux sous each, and not worth that price. One evening during their return to the billet, an argument developed between Chisholm and Rainey, the woman in the case being Madame Quatre Sou, and they came to blows. Their only companion was Sapper Stevenson, a Buxton man, who was a quarry worker in civilian life and also an amateur heavyweight boxer of some local renown. On this occasion he acted as referee. He came into the billet very late that evening, carrying his tunic slung over one shoulder, and asked one or two of us to go back with him to bring home the two duellists. Corporal Ashley, the senior N.C.O. in the billet, enquired "What's the matter with em?" "Well it's like this", replied Stevenson, "We had a few drinks at Nieppe, and on the way back Rainey started arguing with Chisholm about this Madame Quatre Sou they knock around with, and one thing led to another, and they started fighting. I watched them for a bit, until I got fed up with the poor show they made, and then gave both one apiece to settle them, and laid them out in the ditch. They're only just down the road, but they'll need carrying." The two unconscious rivals were brought in and put to bed and forgotten, but the referee was awarded three days' C.B. on the following morning, for his unorthodox method of restoring order, on a charge of being drunk and disorderly.'

Sapper Rainey caused trouble of a different kind at Clairmarais. He was a blacksmith; he made rings from two-franc pieces, with "Liberté, Egalité, Fraternité" on the inside, and plain rings from aluminium shrapnel shell nose caps. One of these nose caps, recalls my father, 'exploded on the farrier's (Sapper Earp from Tamworth) forge while being melted. It went through the roof after scattering the fire, and was lost. Thereafter the practice of nosecap souvenir making was forbidden. The engraving of place-names, etc., was done by broken-off triangular saw-files.'

During the spell at Clairmarais Lance Corporal Reader and Sergeant Barker both left the Company in order to take up commissions: the first in the Royal Field Artillery, the second in the Royal Engineers. Corporal Ashley was promoted sergeant to replace Barker in No.2 Section, but remained quite approachable. My father recalls Sergeant Ashley and Sapper Clarkson cleaning mutton fat off the tables so that they could play cards. Arthur Daulman writes: 'When Sgt.Ashley had money the cards came out and candles provided the light. When he had no money it was "Put those lights out". Poor old Cpl Toogood was deaf. He enjoyed reading, as did his sleeping companion Joe Smith, my future wife's brother, and following the shout "Put the lights out" he would lean across and ask "What did he say Joe?"' It seems that Q.M.Sergeant Wheway was a stricter disciplinarian, or had a grievance against his fellow sergeants, because my father notes: 'Wheway was sleeping on Streather's bed, waiting for Mitch, Harris, and Streather, who were out late at Clairmarais. He was going to put in a charge. Lieutenant Gordon told him to forget it.'

That, no doubt, was a scrap of gossip relayed to the other ranks. My father has much more to say about their German helpers, based on first-hand knowledge. 'The P.O.W.s were easy to get along with; as one chap said, "These Jerries are bastards in their wild state, but quite decent chaps in captivity", and, with one exception, they were. The exception was a N.C.O. belonging to the Prussian Guard, who was still at war with the English: with Corporal Berry in particular bearing the brunt of this prisoner's insolent bluster, which was encouraged by Cpl Berry's mild manner. We all knew that Jerry had picked on the wrong man, and waited for him to overstep the mark; even Berry was getting over his reluctance to strike a prisoner of war, which he considered to be a cowardly thing to do. When he told us that "it was getting about time that big-bellied lump had some of the stuffing knocked out of him", we were not surprised when Berry gave someone his tunic to hold, and tucked into a very surprised German, who turned out to be better with his tongue than with his fists. The contest was short, and when Jerry surrendered, Berry told him to "mind his manners in future", reclaimed his tunic, and walked away.'

'This party of P.O.W.s included building workers and other skilled tradesmen; the building crafts workers were distributed amongst the similar tradesmen in the company. I was the foreman of a gang consisting of Hans, a skilled carpenter from Hamburg, and Otto, a watch-maker from a town near Lake Constance. As Hans had forgotten more woodworking than I knew, he automatically took charge, and Otto and myself became his labourers; in this fashion we did some first-class work and continued together throughout the job.'

'At this time our pipe tobacco and cigarette issue was plentiful but of very indifferent quality, so we bought our smoking materials from the canteen, which had then been established on the airfield. My two charges also smoked pipes, and a quarter pound of "Three Nuns" did not last very long between three of us, so I supplied them both with some of the Bird's Eye mixture issued every week, which was not very good, but at least it was tobacco. The ersatz stuff the P.O.W.s received in their Red Cross parcels from Germany resembled mouldy chaff, and smoked, and smelled like a garden bonfire. I tried a pipeful of this stuff, but, after a couple of puffs, decided to stick to tobacco in future. In return for the issue tobacco and cigarettes I was glad to get rid of, Hans, one morning, surprised and embarrassed me by presenting me with a box of cigarettes, and explained through Albert, the interpreter, that the present was sent by his wife in Hamburg in the Red Cross parcel he had received that morning. The cardboard box was decorated with a vividly coloured picture on the lid of a German battleship in immaculate condition, with every gun in action and flags flying, dashing at full speed through a disabled and sinking fleet of British battleships. Replying through Albert, I thanked Hans and his wife for the gift, and looked forward to the pleasure of smoking the cigarettes inside. Hans was pleased with the thanks but looked a bit doubtful when I mentioned the enjoyment bit. When I passed the cigarettes round in the billet, everyone there also looked doubtful, but, being curious, took one and "lit up". We found the cigarettes smoked very pleasantly, in the stove, and the verdict was spontaneous and unanimous: lousy. We had a ration of tobacco or cigarettes issued weekly; as most of the company smoked cigarettes and a lot chewed, the pipe smokers, being in the minority, had more tobacco issued than they could smoke, the plug or cake variety being greatly sought after by most of us who indulged in a "chew".'

'Albert the interpreter was a good-natured, educated young man, a native of Saxony, who was glad to be away from the fighting, which he did not agree with. He was popular with his fellow prisoners and with us and his English was perfect; his only difficulty sometimes was in trying to interpret our slovenly English words and phrases, so we had to be careful how we spoke to him. Since Hans and Otto resented my interference in the work in hand, during the time they were establishing my reputation as a skilled carpenter and joiner, I had plenty of time, on many occasions, to speak with Albert, and explain some the Midlands colloquialisms and dialect we used, in which he was very interested and puzzled at. He noted everything in a book he always carried, which he let me examine, and underline any obscene words and phrases he had innocently entered therein; he explained this book was to be used for the benefit of his pupils when he resumed his teaching after the war, and he wished it to be correct. Albert was a nice chap and I played fair with him.'

The top brass was puzzled by amicable relations between British soldiers and German prisoners. Brigadier-General Charteris at G.H.Q. mused: 'Strange to say, the prisoners are not in the least unpopular with our men. There seems no resentment on either side. So far as a mutual ignorance of each other's language admits, they confab together amicably and happily. Indeed, our men fraternize far more readily with the German prisoners than with their French allies'.[10]

The Royal Flying Corps did not have exclusive possession of the airfield. There was so urgent a need of food in wartime France that, writes the official historian, 'Cattle continued to graze on the big aerodrome at Clairmarais, unmindful of the mild excitement which they gave to pilots who were called on to avoid them'.[11] It is not known whether the left-half company played their football on the airfield, but in October both half companies had a team (and a ground), so that they were able to play one another home and away; also a full company eleven played a match at Clairmarais against the Army Workshops team. All three games were fully reported for Nuneaton readers by Sapper Joe Smith in traditional sporting style: thus the famous Nuneaton Town defender 'Billy Barratt was to the fore at back'. The reporter conscientiously avoided naming the game's venue beyond describing it as 'a nice pleasant little spot, not many miles from a place that is well known in connection with the present war'.[12]

Arthur Daulman recalls another diversion: 'By the side of the runway, which was an ordinary field levelled and drained, was a small pond, and on returning pilots would often let off a burst of fire into the pond, zoom away, then circle and land. I thought they were sometimes a bit tiddly. The bullets would ricochet off the water in a most alarming fashion, although I do not recall anyone being hurt.' On one occasion there was a more unusual example of 'friendly fire'. Late one afternoon a plane with a large bomb slung under the fuselage was taking off when the undercarriage collapsed and the nose of the plane hit the ground. The watchers, including German prisoners in ranks, ready to return to their compound, scattered. The bomb did not explode, but they were showered with volleys of what appeared to be arrows as the revolving, laminated wooden propeller blades hit the ground and shattered into long slivers. Apart from one or two scratches no harm was done to anyone; the pilot and observer were unhurt; the bomb was defused and taken back to store.

Arthur Daulman notes: 'The new Rolls Royce engines were installed on a bed for testing and run for quite a number of hours. It could have been as much as a hundred hours before use. We were told that a new model had been flown into German lines at Lille, a brand new and newly-delivered plane. The story was that it had been stolen and flown away by a German agent.' The highlight of Daulman's time at Clairmarais was when he and Sergeant Ashley were on their way to La Nieppe for a drink and a plane landed in a grass field near the road. 'We went across and found the pilot, there was no one else in the plane, which was a two-seater, had lost his way and had landed presumably to ask someone the way! We told him that an aerodrome was 1.5 miles away and then he asked Sgt.Ashley if he knew anything about a throttle. "No sir" was the answer, "but this young chap coming up, our dispatch rider, he should know about it". So I climbed into the cockpit and awaited instructions. The throttle was a simple lever on the side of the joy stick. He swung the prop on his word "Contact" and I adjusted the throttle. I must have opened it too far for the plane began to move forward. Naturally I retarded it, the plane stopped, and he took his place in the cockpit and away went the plane into the evening sky and we carried on for our evening out. I'm sorry now that I didn't take his offer of a lift to the 'drome where I believe I would have had a drink, free. However, not many can say that they have driven a plane if only for a few inches.'

Chapter Seven: Steenbecque and Morbecque, October 1916 to January 1917

The two halves of the Company left Clairmarais at different times to travel to different destinations. The left half marched to Steenbecque; the right half travelled to Morbecque, as Arthur Daulman recalls, 'in fine style, as we were carried in R.F.C. Leyland tenders which were really comfy compared to our own lorries. These same tenders took us for a weekly bath, a real bit of luxury. We used to lean out and pinch the apples off the trees as we went by.' Steenbecque and Morbecque were both small villages a few miles south of Hazebrouck, well back from the front line. The Steenbecque men camped in a field a short distance away from the village; their work was to install a pont levis bridge over a branch waterway which ran from Hazebrouck to join the Aire canal at Aire, some distance to the west.

My father writes: 'The bridge sections, together with a pile-driving hammer and mechanism, were brought by canal from the divisional bridging park at Aire; the load also included 12" x 12" pitch pine baulks, ten feet long, and a quantity of 3" x 9" timbers suitable for the construction of a pile driver. The pitch pine baulks were cut to points and shod with iron points at their lower ends, and iron collars were fitted round the tops to prevent the piles splitting during the driving. This work kept the company carpenters and blacksmiths busy until all the pile driving was finished on both banks of the canal. The banks were then built up level, and the bridge sections put together and erected, the whole operation taking about a month. What bridging stores and materials were left unused, including the timber frame we made, were returned to the bridging park, and everybody, including the local French, was satisfied.' (See illustration 41.)

The Company Commanding Officer and Sergeant-Major, who had remained with the right half company on their Second Army headquarters work, made only occasional visits to the men at Steenbecque. Those men were only too happy to remain relatively undisturbed in the charge of Lieutenant Smith, the left-half officer, described by my father as 'a capable and popular officer, who only concerned himself with the work in hand and left the N.C.O.s to supervise our leisure activities'. My father continues: 'We took the hint from the senior left-half sergeant, Harris, when he warned us: "Just mind what you get up to, you lot, Smithy don't want to be bothered with any defaulters while we're here, and I don't neither", and with the exception of one incident towards the end of our stay, no one stepped very far out of line. This incident happened when one of our chaps, stimulated by vin blanc, had a sudden ambition to ride a motor cycle parked outside the estaminet near to the bridging site, where a party had spent a bibulous evening. This sapper knew a lot about bricklaying, but nothing about motor cycles, and when his companions advised him not to "play about" with the machine, he replied, "It's easy: watch me". He got astride the saddle, and fiddled with the various levers on the handlebars, while he kicked at the starting pedal until the engine started, and he went off, wobbling from side to side of the road in the direction of the canal and the nearly completed bridge. The rider had no idea how he had started the bike, and no idea, or time available, to find out how to stop it, but very sensibly abandoned the machine before it plunged into the water. Next day, an officer and some N.C.O.s from the R.E. signals were around, enquiring about the missing machine, which we had already discovered and salvaged during our bridging work. This discovery exonerated the signals dispatch rider, who was assumed to have had no idea that the bridge was unfinished. Sergeant Harris's remark that "I'll bet some of you lot weren't far away when that bike went into the cut", was nearer to the truth than he realized, but no one contradicted him, we did not want any trouble with outsiders who had got themselves involved in our company business.'

The left half-company left Steenbecque in mid-November and marched to Morbecque, a large village ten kilometres south of Hazebrouck, whither the right half company had preceded them. My father writes: 'We arrived in the late afternoon and halted in the road on the outskirts of the village, on the Hazebrouck side, in front of a long brick wall with a narrow gateway in the centre, above which we could see the main building. Here we were inspected by Captain Cook and the Sergeant Major and a few French children. The transport was unloaded, and we carried the various loads inside the wall, where Wheway, the "Quarter bloke", indicated various lean-to buildings in which to put them. The blankets had been carried on the wagon rolled up in bundles of ten blankets and groundsheets, and these we took up to our new quarters.'

'Judging from the appearance of this place we supposed it was some sort of reformatory for delinquent French juveniles: the ground-floor windows had iron bars outside them and the large surrounding paved area was enclosed by a high brick wall. Several brick lean-to buildings against this wall provided us with lock-up stores sheds and tool sheds; the largest of these building we altered for our cook-house and cooks' billet. At the back of the main building was a lower building divided into two rooms, one containing benches with tin wash basins and taps, and the other with trestle tables with a long bench each side: sappers' ablution room and mess room. Extending the full length of the rear wall was a ten-foot wide open-fronted shed, furnished at one end with a decrepit woodworking bench and two galvanized containers with burners for carbide. This place we christened the punishment block; it was used by "John" for any defaulter undergoing pack drill on a wet evening. The ground floor of the school building was taken over by the company office, orderly room, armoury, quartermaster's stores and office, sergeants' mess, N.C.O.s' billets, and sleeping quarters for mess servants and Quarter bloke's clerks and dogsbodies. The first and top floors each consisted of a landing and one large barn-like room with few windows and a large cast-iron stove (unprovided with any fuel) in the centre; these gave ample space to accommodate the right half-company (sections 1 and 2) on the first floor and the left half-company (sections 3 and 4) on the top floor. For illumination at night we provided our own candles.'

My father and some of his mates repaired on the first evening to the nearest estaminet. He writes: 'All the soldiers inside were R.E.s who were very inquisitive, wanting to learn our business. "How long you been here?" "What are you going to do?", and so on. We could only answer the first question, which gave them an altogether wrong impression about us. "We only got here at 4 o'clock this afternoon" was not the sort of answer to impress them, and they put us down as a fresh draft, and let their imagination describe the various dangers and hardships in store for us when we should eventually "go up the line". We were amused when they disclosed they were a railway and canal company, and encouraged them to disburden themselves and tell us of their terrible experiences.' By this time the men of the 216th company were experienced soldiers. Their casualties had not been heavy, so they were not overburdened with new drafts. The pre-war regular army had been all but destroyed in 1914 and 1915; Kitchener's new armies were much thinned out on the Somme in the second half of 1916; conscription was making up the numbers, but most of the British army was still fairly raw. At the end of 1916, eighteen-year olds with nearly a year's service on the Western Front could not unreasonably think of themselves as old sweats.

My father's account of the first night at Morbecque continues: 'Closing time was about 8.30, so we called it a day and went back to the billet, and groped our way through the dark street to "kip down". Sergeant Major "Mitch" had put a sentry on the gate in the encircling wall round our establishment, who came in for some rude remarks in answer to his challenge, so we had no difficulty in passing to rest. Next morning we were aroused by the noise of heavy boots coming upstairs into the room, and a shout of "English papier; bloody good news; hospital ship torpedoed; bloody good news". He got some "bloody good boots" in reply before he had sense to retire and leave us in peace to get cleaned up and breakfasted in readiness for the day. These newspapers were very small and the news dealt mainly with the war in France, which was the last thing to interest us.'

One feature of life on the top floor that my father does not refer to is mentioned in Pioneer Daulman's recollections: 'I was on the top floor with a five-gallon drum of urine. Jock Chisholm, later to be shell shocked at Messines, came in drunk one night and was so drunk that he could not stand up, but he succeeded in knocking over the drum and the contents cascaded down the stairs.' The drivers, animals, and transport vehicles were, as usual, elsewhere: they went into the centre of the village for their stabling and billets. Driver Hextall recalls in his usual telegraphese: 'Billeted at Hotel de Ville; very nice too; decent village and people; made plenty of friends and had jolly good time; living like lords; best place we have had; good stables at hotel; mules must have thought they were prize-winners; plenty of exercise, we enjoyed it too; went to Hazebrouck a few evenings'.

My father agreed with Frank Hextall and the mules that Morbecque was a 'cushy number', where peace 'was broken only by "John's" bellowings concerning our buttons and general slovenly appearance. The other R.E. company were an untidy lot when they were out, and we agreed that a month or two under "John" would do them good and improve their appearance but not their tempers. In any case, as long as their work was up to scratch, nobody worried how they looked. Their sergeant-major was an active foreman when they had work to do, and ours was walking about on the road outside the billet, ready to salute every staff car which passed. These R.E.s were laying out a sidings, connected with the French railway system, on an acre of level ground outside the town, where it was proposed to establish a large munitions dump, and our company erected sheds and offices alongside these sidings.'

The two companies therefore were helping in their small way to further Sir Douglas Haig's plan for the next big push. The size of the forces involved meant that preparations, now well under way, for the attack on Messines ridge planned for 1917 included the laying of many miles of railway for the movement of men and other material, and the construction of new railheads for the supply of ammunition to the front. Such preparations were, of course, impossible to hide from the enemy. At Morbecque, notes my father, 'the local inhabitants were not very impressed or very happy when they saw the extent of this dump; they knew that Jerry reacted violently against these establishments, and began to clear out the rubbish from their cellars in anticipation of the wrath that they were convinced would come later on. Another thing the villagers did not care for was the fact that two R.E. companies were quartered in the village, who were not always as quiet and well mannered as they ought to be while they were enjoying the night life in the local estaminets. This circumstance, although beneficial to both companies, was unfortunate for the innkeeper whose establishment had been "rough-housed", as he could not swear to which company the delinquents belonged. In answer to any complaints, our C.O. always replied, "My men never behave in that manner, it was no doubt the other company". The other company C.O. was equally convinced that his men were incapable of such behaviour. The only people who disbelieved these assertions were the French.'

'Our first day's work, setting out the positions and extent of the various buildings, putting pegs to mark the post holes for the uprights, was interrupted by the arrival of a party of German P.O.W.s, which we were pleased to see included Albert and our other Clairmarais men. When they halted, those of them who recognized their former taskmasters did not wait to be "told off" for various jobs, but walked over to us and "set themselves on". There were a few additions, including some Prussian Guards, who were surly and quarrelsome. Corporal Berry took charge of these chaps, who were only handy as labourers. Berry's old antagonist was still with them, and Berry, calling Albert who was still interpreting, said "I'm not having any bother with that lot this time; I'll promote that chap foreman and he can sort them out"'.

'Hans and Otto relieved me of the pegs and mallet with which I had been marking the positions of the post holes, and the other chaps similarly employed relinquished their pegs and mallets, without any noticeable reluctance, to the prisoners who had formerly worked with them. While our augmented setting-out gangs were falling over each other and generally getting mixed up, the unattached P.O.W.s brought the 7" x 2" posts, rails, and purlins required for the framework of the sheds from the roadside, about a mile away, where our transport delivered them. A [narrow-gauge] railway track had been laid from the road to serve the stores area, and platelayers' four-wheeled bogies were used to move materials and other stores to the building site. Halfway between the road and the site, there was a wide and deep drainage ditch which we bridged with two 12" x 12" pitch pine baulks; the railway was dogged along the centre of each one, making a tricky path even for people in full control of their faculties.'

'We put up thirty of these sheds, spaced about fifty yards apart: open-fronted structures, fifty feet long, twenty feet deep, and eight feet high at the front, sloping to six feet at the back, the top and three sides being covered with corrugated iron sheets. The railway R.E.s put siding tracks and wooden platforms along the front of each shed. The sawn-off ends of wood we bundled up and carried back to the stoves in the billet to make our evenings comfortable, and to dry out our clothes.'

R.H.Mottram drily observed that 'the armies were provided with coal and coke and presumably intended to ignite it by holding a match to it. In result, millions of men during the five winters of the War, burnt a colossal cubage of wood.' They burned the timber intended 'for dug-outs, railways, roads, gun-pits, . . . huts, horse-lines, or billets, no great percentage [of which] ever reached its proper destination. . . . Farms, houses, public buildings were ransacked. Shelving, forms, ladders, carts, partitions disappeared. In the Belgian hop-fields the British Army alone is said to have destroyed 1,000,000 hop-poles. Who shall blame them? Shall a soldier die of cold as well as of other things?'[1] Royal Engineers in general had readier access to firewood than most soldiers and the men of the 216th Company at Morbecque had found a more than usually legitimate source of this essential comfort.

However, it was a comfort for the evenings only. The open situation of the ammunition dump, writes my father, 'exposed to a biting east wind, was an uncomfortable place, especially during the midday break, when we stood around fire buckets in the lee of the sheds, eating bully and biscuits. Douglas, Chamberlain, and I went over to a cottage, surrounded by a low hedge some distance away, on the perimeter of the dump area, hoping to get some hot coffee. The woman at the cottage, a middle-aged widow with one son who was away with the French army, made us welcome, and provided hot haricot bean soup, Benedictine, and coffee, which cost us one franc each. When we took her a tin of bully, or a tin of Maconachie's vegetable and meat ration, we were not allowed to pay anything for the soup and coffee. We lunched with the widow regularly while this job lasted, our respective Germans being perfectly happy to eat our issue midday rations and continue the work in hand without any interference from us. They enjoyed work more than we did.'

Perhaps these Nuneaton men and their prisoners were all equally happy to be where they were. Away to the south the battle of attrition on the Somme was still dragging on. It would peter out as a stalemate on 18 November in deep mud, swept by icy winds and squalls of snow and sleet, after 141 days and nights of bloodshed. The Big Push of some eight miles was made; combined British and French casualties were about six hundred thousand; the Germans lost about the same number; the war would certainly continue into 1917. This contrasted with earlier assessments of the war's duration. Many of the men who flocked to the colours in 1914 and some of their commanders (but not, as it happens, Lord

Kitchener) had said that the war would be over before Christmas. The same sentiment was expressed, with rather less conviction, in 1915. By 1916 the likelihood of a long war was accepted: so much so that on 7 September the Army Council issued from the War Office a communiqué about the supply of Christmas puddings to the troops. Members of the public were asked to contribute to the national Christmas Pudding Fund, which, for sixpence per ration, would supply a ration of half a pound of pudding for, it was hoped, each of the three million men in the army. Local initiatives were encouraged, so Mr R.C.Moon, formerly Captain Cook's civilian deputy, now Acting Borough Surveyor, collected £3.10s. from his colleagues in Nuneaton Borough Engineers' Department: enough to provide a half-pound pudding for every man in the 216th Company.[2]

While the pudding fund was swelling, its potential beneficiaries were enjoying an easy life building the ammunition dump at Morbecque. However, writes my father, 'Cheap foreign labour was the undoing of a lot of us, and jankers were more plentiful here than when we were up the line. The usual punishment was seven days' pack drill: two hours every evening, which left us free for work, but, as the estaminets closed at 8, kept the would-be delinquents sober. The incident which started this epidemic of law-breaking started one very cold wet day, when . . . a party of us accompanied by our German auxiliaries were sent back to the roadside with a bogie to meet our wagons and bring up bags of nails and other small items. As our transport had not arrived, we sheltered in the estaminet close at hand, leaving the P.O.W.s (who were not allowed in the estaminets) outside with orders to call us when the wagons came. Shortly afterwards a lorry stopped outside, and a party of Royal Flying Corps chaps on their way to get the leave train at Hazebrouck came in and, after some talk with us, offered to buy any souvenirs we had. Joe Webster replied that he had got three German prisoners outside, for sale at ten francs each: "They would be all right stuffed". They declined this offer, with a recommendation to Joe where to stuff them, so we produced a few cap and shoulder badges which we had obtained from our prisoners and traded them for vin blanc.'

Meanwhile, the wagons had come and gone, the prisoners had dutifully loaded the bogie and were pushing it back along the railway track. Leaving two of the party, Gibberd and Clarkson, in the estaminet, the other two, Sambrook and Webster set off after the prisoners. 'At the roadside were a few six-foot lengths of 7 x 2, which we picked up and carried with us after our party. Our auxiliaries were at the ditch, discussing ways and means of getting over the hole between the 12 x 12 baulks, so we caught up with them quickly. Covering the hole over with some of our load of 7 x 2, we crossed the ditch without mishap, some more unsteadily than others, remarking that if the chaps we had left in the estaminet had much more of the vin they would never cross that lot, and got back on the work site when the whistle was blown for the midday break. We went to our usual place, and I passed over the Benedictine, and had plenty of the coffee. After the break Corporal Berry asked me where the other two members of the fatigue were. "In the estaminet, having their lunch; they'll soon be back." "Not the way they are shaping at the moment. Look along the track; they won't make it here before knocking-off time." Berry turned to Joe Webster and me, and told us to go back to them: "Keep them out of sight, take them to the billet and put them in kip, and make haste before they fall into that ditch". Not liking the prospect of dragging them from the ditch, we hurried back and intercepted them while they were still making their minds up to attempt the crossing. Gibberd fell in the gully at the first step when he came to meet us, Clarkson stood stiffly upright, swaying slightly, with a happy smile on his face, looking at his companion, who was sitting on the bank with his feet in the ditch with both arms upraised. Joe and myself crossed over without mishap and pulled Gibberd out, and told them both we were to escort them to the billet without anyone seeing us, and off we went.'

The drunkards were not easy to control or help. 'We were cold when we started, but by the time we reached the billet we were sweating, and the escort were staggering and as dishevelled as the two culprits.' They had the ill luck to encounter Sergeant-Major Mitchinson at the gate of the billet. The inevitable outcome of the meeting in the Orderly Room at ten o'clock next morning between Captain Cook, Sapper Webster, and Pioneer Sambrook was jankers. My father's account continues: 'The first evening we reported to the guard room, complete with full marching order, we were greeted by 2nd Corporal Sam Hollis, who decided to hold the drill in the shed, as the weather was very wet, with a strong wind. Joe Webster was, as usual, chewing tobacco, the juice of which he ejected skilfully on any offending fly or other insect he noticed within range, usually scoring a direct hit. The illumination of the shed was provided by galvanized acetylene lights, with a naked burner on the end of a tube, and they were placed at opposite ends of the shed, sheltered from the wind. The only orders Sam knew were "Quick march" and "About turn", and having got us started, up and down, up and down, he seemed to have forgotten how to stop us for a rest. Joe was chewing all the time, and as we marched to the end furthest from Hollis he muttered "Watch that light", and squirted a jet of tobacco juice onto the burner and extinguished the flame. Sam came up at the double to relight the flare, and we about turned and marched to the other end, and Joe spit the other light out, and we rested our packs on an old carpenter's bench that stood at that end. 'Sam Hollis, a non-smoker, carried no matches, and asked us if we had any. "We have some in the billet; should we fetch them?" "No; stop here; I'll go across to the cook-house and get a light from the fire." Sam came out with a screw of paper alight, but the wind blew it out before he got halfway across the yard. He swore the only bad word he used, "Bother", and went back again. Coming out with a candle he had found, the candle was blown out half way across, and we were enjoying our punishment until a party came out of the billet, bound for the estaminet, and Sam borrowed a match and lit up again. As we had got a bit chilled sitting around we set off again. Webster muttered "Tell me when you've had enough", and soon after, Sam was astonished and disgusted when both lights went out one after the other. The coincidence of our being near the lights escaped his notice, and during the remainder of the punishment period 2nd Corporal Hollis was doing the marching: to and from the cook-house, getting about half way back, then "Bother", about turn, another light, till 8 o'clock relieved him, and he had a well-earned rest.'

At Morbecque two new officers joined the 216th Company. Captain A.D.MacDougall, a Scotsman whose home was in Canada, became Acting C.O. of the Company before Christmas. He would not become substantive C.O., in place of Captain Cook, until July 1917, but he figures so largely in reminiscences and letters (whereas Cook figures hardly at all), that I conjecture that Cook was away from the Company (doing I know not what) for much of the period from December to July. The second new officer to join the 216th Company at Morbecque was a Lieutenant Maude, so there were now three lieutenants: Smith, Gordon, and Maude.

Construction of the ammunition dump continued under new management, but not without incident, as Arthur Daulman recalls: 'This same MacDougall spent an afternoon watching Jock Mitchell putting up sheets of corrugated iron under which the ammo would be stored. At the end of the work the Capt approached the Sapper and, "Mitchell", he coolly said, "You have put up all those sheets wrong". Mitchell's reply was short and not at all sweet. "Why the bloody hell didn't you tell me before? You've been watching me all afternoon."' MacDougall seems not to have resented Mitchell's response, any more than he objected to some of the men under his command neatly painting the letters M.O. on their steel helmets (standing not for 'Medical Orderly' but for 'MacDougall's Own'): officers from the Dominions were generally less class-conscious than their English counterparts. My father thought the newcomers (rechristened 'Mac' and 'Maudie') were 'two excellent officers'. Furthermore, 'Lieutenant Maude was due for leave and bought from us the souvenirs we had picked up when working at the front. The following June at Messines he was complaining that he was kicking better stuff about for nothing.'

Arthur Daulman drove the Clyno motor cycle and side-car for Captain Cook and later for Captain MacDougall. For a while, too, he was MacDougall's servant, and so, he says, 'I was no longer conversant with the deeds and misdeeds of the working parties'. He became conversant, however, with the misdeeds of their four-legged comrades. He recalls: 'I was taking the Captain's horse to water one morning when Driver John Morton brought his mule alongside and the mule went to kick the horse with me in between. The first kick took my hat off, and the other hit my left arm which I had put up to fend off the blow. I went to see the M.O. who said, "How did you get this?" "Mule kicked me, sir." "Why didn't you get out of the road?" There was no answer to that stupid observation. A little later Corporal Mobbs cheered me up when he said "You've got to pay to learn." The M.O. gave me two days' light duty. So after two days I was back on duty with my arm very painful and getting worse. I was in agony about a fortnight after the kick. A French Red Cross worker arrived in the village and came over and looked at my arm. He shook his head and said something. I didn't know what he said but I understood his expression and went again to the M.O., who examined my arm and said, "Have I seen you before?" "Yes sir, a fortnight ago." "Get your kit, your arm's broke." I went to the hospital at Hazebroucke where I was X-rayed for the first time in my life. When I laid my arm in position I expected something to happen, a shock perhaps. Here I went to the pictures and while I was out I could hear the children saying "Beaucoup blessé". I didn't tell them I'd been kicked by a mule. Back from the hospital was an estaminet on the crossroads, where we used to go and where the sergeant-major went too, as he was very fond of the madame. One night an officer came through the door, blind drunk, clung to the bar and said, "Don't you know an officer when you see one? Stand to attention."

Some of the lads put a few coins in the barrel organ and started waltzing the officer around. Someone in the meantime had told the sergeant-major, who was jealous, and with a "Fall in two men" rushed over, and the officer was hustled away to the guard room. We never heard of any outcome.'

By now most of the Nuneaton men were preparing for their first Christmas in France. A few lucky ones expected to be on leave because the roster was for the moment operating without interruption. Charles Streather managed to have his at the beginning of December. He came back by way of Boulogne and found the transit camp there as uncomfortable as most soldiers did: 'I got wet through at B—— before we were marched to the camp and then had to spend the night in tents. My word it was cold. I was lucky enough to get down into the town on pass from 10 a.m. to 8.45 p.m. on Monday so that was much better than staying in the tents. B——— is a decent place and I had quite a good look round, and had two good finds: French fashion of course, and French prices also I may add.' He found that there had been some sickness in his absence: 'the C.S.M., Q.M.S., and all the Sergeants had a touch of the 'flu and the Captain and the other officers as well, so you see I was lucky to be away while all that was about'. Also some delinquency: 'Cox is at home and looks like getting into trouble as soon as he gets back. The last thing he did before leaving was to disobey an order, so he will be made a prisoner as soon as he arrives. Of course you must not say anything to him about it if you happen to see him.' However, 'We are going to have a fine do at Xmas I think; the officers have bought us turkeys and vegetables, fruit, nuts, beer, etc., and arranged for a concert and a regular feast and jollification. Some puddings have been sent from England, we have hired an oven at a big house, and unless something unforeseen turns up we shall not have such a bad time' (letter of 18 December).

Sergeant Streather also notes that leave has been stopped again. This was a matter of immediate concern for my father, who writes: 'Leave started for the company about the first week in December, about six or seven men at a time, in order of enlistment, to those who had been over six months overseas. My name was on the orderly-room notice board for the 19th December, which was just right for Christmas, but, two days before, Captain MacDougall came to the billet and said that there was to be no Christmas leave and I was to go on the 27th December, so I should be home for the New Year. This suited the few Scots in the Company very well, and the Sassenachs consoled themselves with the thought that our ten days were still to come, and with us not travelling at a busy time. Mac was quite chatty about leave and other little matters, then went to see the other chaps who were to go on the 27th. Capt Cook would have sent the orderly corporal, but that was the difference between Cook and Capt Mac. In the meantime we did our Christmas shopping and decorated the billets with our smalls and towels hanging up to dry. As one chap remarked, "There's nothing like a few shirts and socks hanging up to remind us of home".'

Work on the ammunition sheds went well: Morbecque remained by common consent 'a cushy number' even when, at the end of November, the winter set in with violent squalls of wind and rain, and the site soon became soft and muddy.

My father remarked that 'it made the work less pleasant, but by stopping and scraping the accumulations of ploughed field from our boots every half hour we managed very well. It was the sort of mud we got in England on a building site, but on a more generous scale.' Charles Streather, writing at the time, not sixty years later, is far more dramatic: 'The weather has been worse than awful lately: wind, rain, snow nearly every day and oh so cold.' They both describe a sensational accident to the sheds two days before Christmas. Streather writes: 'On Saturday it was the most terrible gale I ever knew. I told you we were building sheds. Three were finished, each one 200ft long, 50ft wide, and 15ft high, with an open front.[3] Well, they were lifted clean out of the ground, every stick, and blown ten feet in the air and finally deposited in a thousand pieces more than 100yds away. Luckily no one was seriously hurt, which was really marvellous considering that 250 men were on the job at the time and dozens of sheets of corrugated iron were blowing about some 100ft high and travelled at least 200yds at one go' (letter of 25 December). My father recalls: 'During one very wet spell the wind increased to a gale, blowing into the open fronts of the sheds, and was lifting them bodily up, and the corrugated sheets were working loose. We spent the morning putting extra nails in the loosened sheets but the wind was working the whole structure loose and threatening to scatter the whole dump, despite the props and reinforcements we contrived. When the whistle went for lunch break we hurried over to the widow's house where we were sure of a shelter from the wind. Before going we told Hans to watch out for tins flying about and to keep out of the way when the sheds disintegrated. As we crossed the field back to work the wind was coming in strong gusts, and as we watched a few sheets jerked loose and whirled in the air like kites, with the Germans dodging them as they nose-dived to earth. No one was hurt. One of the posts of the shed was pulled out of the ground and the whole building rolled over and disintegrated. The sergeant who reported the day's occurrence to Cook got the comforting answer: "It can't be helped; it is an act of God", so disclaimed any responsibility for failing to specify adequate footings for the posts; and the 216 commenced the reconstruction with an altered design.'

The reconstruction meant working late that day and throughout Sunday (Christmas Eve), when it snowed all day to give the troops a white Christmas. Sergeant Streather wrote to his parents on Christmas morning: 'We have just had a church service in the billet. Have got a fine spread for dinner: the N.C.O.s are going to look after the men. I have to carve up two splendid turkeys for my section. We have borrowed plates and glasses, dishes and jugs, and so on, from a French place some miles away and I think everybody will have a royal time. Our officers have turned out trumps: spent £20 on the company. That's good is it not? The only things lacking are the Xmas puddings which we should have bought if we had not received a letter to say that a large consignment was on the way, it certainly was on the way and when it arrived there were two puddings, four pounds in all, to be divided among 150 men, soldiers at that.' Perhaps he was particularly vexed about the puddings because it had been announced in a local newspaper at the beginning of November that enough money had been collected in the Nuneaton Borough Engineer's Department to provide half a pound of Christmas pudding for every man in the Nuneaton Company. My father recalled that 'Mac put a bottle of whisky on each table and wished us the best of luck. Mac had a family connection with a distillery company and used to have his whisky sent direct from Scotland, four dozen bottles at a time. The pudding was tinned, there was plenty of turkey with cabbage, and there was plenty of bottled beer and issue rum, so the afternoon was somnolent until tea time. The evening was spent in the various estaminets, which were crowded and noisy.'

'Four of us were coming back to the billet after our evening out, feeling quite merry, but a bit unsteady. My three friends were all carpenters I had known in Nuneaton, Bill Salmon, Walter Shelmerdine, and Dick Townsend, when we ran into Mitch, who stood in the doorway of the sergeants' mess, which was at the side of the main stairs up to our rooms. Mitch had had plenty to drink, and welcomed us with open arms as four "of my oldest friends", then invited us into the mess to have supper with them. We were placed at the head of the table, Salmon nearest to Mitch, then Shelmerdine and Townsend, and myself at the end. The trestle table was covered with crockery which had been hired from Hazebrouck, together with bottles of beer, rum in a jug on the floor by Mitch's chair, and vin, and, waiting for Mitch to carve, was a roasted leg of mutton, and all the trimmings. Unfortunately the Sergeant Major had been on the bottle all evening, and was incapable of doing the carving and serving, and there was no one at the table any sober enough. In the end Mitch picked the mutton up and gave it to Salmon, saying "Here, bite off what you want and pass it round the table. Taking several bites, Salmon passed the leg to Shelley, who did the same, and passed it to Townsend, who also bit some off. Opposite to Townsend Corporal Cox was sitting asleep in his chair, and the talk and laughter at this method of serving supper woke him up.' The scandalized corporal and Sapper Townsend contrived between them to overturn the trestle table and smash everything upon it, but there were no recriminations when the dishevelled company fell in on Boxing Day morning to resume work. Drunkenness was in theory a serious matter, but this was Christmas.

Frank Hextall was among the few lucky ones who, after a great deal of sweating, came home for Christmas. It was his first visit home since the death of his brother Harold (died of wounds in August) and the award of the Military Medal to his other serving brother, Cyril, who at this time was in hospital at Grantham. Captain Cook was on leave in Nuneaton at this time too; three days after Christmas he and his wife, together with a Santa Claus, entertained the wives and children of Nuneaton men serving in the 216th company.[4] Though England was quite close to the front, there was very little leave provision for British common soldiers and not a great deal more for their officers: the main difficulty was said to be finding shipping for cross-Channel transport. There was nothing unusual in the fact that most of the other ranks in the Nuneaton Company had to wait a year for their first leave.

When my father was granted his ten days from 27 December, Corporal Douglas, Sapper Chamberlain, and a few other close friends in the Company 'said they would like an apple pudding with cloves in, and have an evening party when I got back'. In Nuneaton he met Sapper Sim Fenn, who was also on leave, and they went about together. 'One day', writes my father, 'we went to get our extra coal vouchers from an office in the Congregational Chapel opposite the Police

Station in Coton Road. The minister, Rev. Masterton was the official who issued these, and we were served without delay and came out, meeting in the passage a woman who had a baby in a pram. The day was very cold and the passage was draughty, so we pushed the pram into the office, where Masterton was sitting with his back to a roaring fire, and told him the baby was cold, and left him to settle the matter himself, and went to the Red Lion for a drink. On the way there we passed by Piper's Penny Bazaar, where they were selling a large stock of enamel chamber pots, displayed in the form of a large pyramid in the shop window. With the apple pudding in mind I thought one of them would be just the thing to carry the pudding in to Morbecque, as my mother was having some difficulty in finding a basin big enough to make the pudding in, and strong enough to survive the journey to France. Having bought the pot, we continued our way to the Red Lion, where the pot was filled with Government ale, holding about half a gallon, after the barmaid had insisted on first washing the utensil, as she called it. There were one or two service men on leave there at the time, and by the time it had been filled and emptied between us the pot was considered to be clean enough for the pudding.'

'At home there was some objection to using the utensil for the pudding, but I explained that the handle was big enough to pass through the belt of my equipment, and the enamelled metal would not break during the journey, and the matter was settled to my satisfaction, and the pudding was made. There was a double thickness of pastry on top and two cloths tied over, and then part boiled, and even when cool and the covering cloths were dry, it was a hefty weight and mother wondered how I would carry it. The next day was the last of my leave, the train left Victoria at 6.30 a.m the following day, so I went on the 6.20 p.m. on the evening of the last day, with the pudding handle passed through my equipment belt. My mother thought it ought to have something wrapped round it; "You are surely not going with that thing looking like that; it looks disgraceful"; but I said it would carry quite well as it was, and, after being warned that the pudding would want further boiling before we ate it, I went off to the station, accompanied by my father.'

'When the train came in, it was crowded with troops, who, like me, were returning from leave; about half of them were Scottish, and, having had New Year at home, were plentifully supplied with whisky and were singing and shouting. My father was nervous about my travelling with that crowd and advised me to go on a later train, but I said they were O.K. and I should be O.K., and asked him to dump my equipment in the corridor of the coach. He said, "There's no room there; the corridor's full of drunks sleeping". "Put it on top of them; it won't hurt 'em", which he did. "I don't like you travelling with that lot", he repeated doubtfully, "sure you'll be all right?" "Yes; don't worry; when the train starts I shall join in the party." By the time we got to London I was slightly the worse for wear, owing to the many drams I had supped out of the various bottles handed to me. Wandering down the platform I was accosted by an old gentleman in some sort of uniform, resembling the khaki one I was wearing, who led me to a car outside driven by a young lady, and we drove off, saying something about Union Jack. I didn't care where we went, but he took us to a large building, the Union Jack Club, opposite Waterloo Station, and went inside. I said I wanted to go to Victoria. He said, "Stay here for the night; we shall see that you catch the leave train". He took me to a room which had five single beds, four of which had equipment on them, and four Canadian soldiers playing cards, and wished all of us good night, and left us. I was invited to have a drink, and did I want a hand at Nap, and the next hour or two passed quickly and pleasantly, and before we had hardly got to sleep it was time to get up and go to breakfast.'

'After breakfast we went on lorries to Victoria Station; we got a compartment to ourselves, as we had no one to see us off. The platform was crowded with soldiers and their friends and relatives, talking together or just looking at each other silently, so one of the Canadians said, "Let's have a drink; I don't feel cheerful somehow", and got a bottle of whisky from his pack; they all had two or three bottles in their packs, with a clean shirt or two and socks, nothing much else. We arrived at Folkestone about 9 a.m., and marched to some houses on the cliffs; this block of houses was surrounded by a ten-foot high fence made of sheets of corrugated iron, with sentries at the only entrance gate. Apparently the weather was too rough for the cross-channel steamers, so we remained impounded until the next day. There was not much improvement next morning, but we marched to the ship and set off for France.'

'The crossing was very rough and the men were mostly seasick, and I was told off for boat guard as I was one of the very few not affected by the weather, but the Canadians, who were also not affected, told the sergeant to get scarce. The last bottle of whisky was decanted into water bottles. We all stood round the chap pouring the whisky in the water bottles to hold him steady, and not any was spilt. During the crossing my equipment with pudding was stowed in a safe place on deck, together with the equipment of my Canadian friends. Apart from being wet with the spray and splashes of salt water, the pudding came to no harm.'

At Calais the voyagers had to report to a camp on the cliff top: 'and it was a heavy drag up the hill to it. The column was accompanied by a tribe of small French boys who were calling out "Carry your pack Tommy". They got a few packs to carry, but to the majority of us they seemed too small for the job; we were glad to reach the camp, and those boys earned their coppers. After a visit to the Rail Transport Office we went in our wagon-lits to St.Omer, and the R.T.O. there sent us on to Hazebrouck, and we walked on to Morbecque and rejoined the company. That evening we went to the house where we had arranged for the supper party. This was not an estaminet, but a private house where a few of us were in the habit of spending a short time in the evening, talking to the widow there, and drinking coffee and cognac before settling down in the estaminet where we usually spent the evening. She was very amused at the type of pudding basin, said she had a pot big enough to boil it in, and arranged for the following evening about 7 o'clock. Next evening we went there with some bully beef, a large "du pain", and found everything ready. Including Madame and a small girl, her daughter, the party numbered about eight people. Madame had made the soup, which was as usual very good. We did not have much main course, bully and bread, but Madame put away the unopened tins for her future use, and dished up the pudding. Mother's apple pudding with cloves was something quite out of the ordinary for Madame, and the little girl stuffed herself solid. There was plenty for everyone, and a bit left over. I explained how to warm it up if she wanted it for next day. We sat chatting and smoking; Madame made coffee and got from the cupboard a bottle of Benedictine. The coffee and cognac was 30 centimes and Benedictine was half a franc a very generous glassful, and we finished the evening there very contentedly. Before we went back to billets Madame asked if we required the "utensil"; we said it was no longer of any use to us, and if she wanted it she was welcome to it. She was very pleased, and said it was tres bon. Douglas said, "Let's make a formal presentation of it to Madame". As all the company was by now a bit high spirited, Douglas made a speech in French, to which Madame replied in English as doubtful as Douglas's French, and the evening finished with another round of coffee and cognac, about 9 o'clock.'

Chapter Eight: Reninghelst Road to Neuve Eglise, January to June 1917

Meanwhile there was a war to be won. Germany had made tentative moves to secure a negotiated peace and Woodrow Wilson, President of the United States, had offered to mediate between the belligerents, but the Allied governments could not countenance anything short of total victory. Their troops were still in good heart, if we may judge from Sergeant Streather's letter home immediately after his return from leave: 'What do you think of the French at Verdun? A good answer to the peace proposals was it not? The troops I saw on the way back all seem more hopeful and cheerful than the majority of the people I saw in England' (18 December). The Germans had well and truly lost their initiative at Verdun, just as the Allies had hoped when they attacked on the Somme: the event referred to by Streather was a highly successful French attack on 15 December which regained some ground at Verdun and netted many prisoners. The very fact that Germany had hinted that it wanted peace gave the Allied leadership hope that such a victory could, after all, be obtained. Also, in December 1916, a palace revolution at Westminster resulted in the energetically bellicose Lloyd George ousting Asquith as Prime Minister. Lloyd George and Haig distrusted one another deeply, but despite Haig's errors he could not be dismissed without a political storm which might also have swept away Lloyd George. King George V had given Haig the royal seal of approval by creating him Field Marshal within days of Lloyd George becoming Prime Minister.

Haig therefore remained in charge. A general must have supreme self-confidence to be able to do his job at all, so Haig made predictions about 'the great offensive' that would be launched in 1917, when 'we shall strike without respite until the German armies are totally destroyed. We have trained armies and cavalry in full working order so that defeat may be turned to rout, and so that at no moment will there be the possibility, even far in the rear, for the enemy to entrench himself. . . . There can be no peace without complete victory, for an incomplete victory, a premature and halting victory, would leave military Germany able to declare terrible revenge in the very near future. . . . All of us have with regard to peace a square jaw, that is to say, the indomitable resolve to fight to the end'.[1]

Civilians had to be square-jawed too. In February 1917 the House of Commons was told that 'Masters of foxhounds have decided on their own initiative to reduce substantially the number of days' hunting. They are shooting foxes and advising members of their hunts to shoot them, in order to prevent destruction of poultry and vegetables. More than that, they are prepared to slaughter a very large proportion of their hounds.' Also it was announced that 'realizing the urgent need for economy in food, and particularly in breadstuffs, their Majesties the King and Queen, together with the Household and servants, have adopted the scale of National Rations since early in February'.[2] The 'National Ration' was not rationing as we would understand the term: it was merely that in February the government published a scale of recommended quantities of bread, flour, meat, and sugar, per head per week, and strongly urged the public to ration themselves in accordance with this scale.

Photographs of the Nuneaton sappers reveal the range of jaw-lines one might expect to see in an average group of working-class men. Their indomitable resolve had more to do with good workmanship, personal survival, and, ideally, comfort in the hostile environment created by the enemy, the weather, and their own Top Brass. Their immediate task was to make good all the pre-Christmas wind damage to the ammunition sheds and get the job finished on time. Nevertheless they were given a half day's holiday on New Year's Day, 'on account of the acting O.C. being a "Mac"', as Charles Streather explained. Streather had also heard a comforting rumour that their next job was to be another good one: 'an R.E. dump about 8 miles from the line, so we shall be alright, and I think by what I hear we shall settle down there for the duration of the war' (letter of 1 January 1917).

His other letters in January are a chronicle of moderately comfortable survival. 'We finished our holiday programme last night with a grand smoking concert with the acting O.C. in the chair. We had quite a good night; it reminded me of the old do's in England. We have had a beautiful day today, but yesterday was a terror: a heavy wind with a cold rain. I got pretty well soaked through. . . . We have nearly twenty men sick again now, but one cannot wonder at it, really, considering the weather we are getting. I saw a German plane brought down today: a shell from an anti-aircraft gun hit it plump and it fell like a stone all in flames. The leave for the following month has been cut down from 16 to 3 so that is bad luck for the men who were expecting to go in a few days (5 January).

'We have only had one issue of fresh meat since Xmas. We have had "bully" every day this week. We have bought meat two or three times, but it is so expensive and difficult to get hold of. . . . It has been a terrible day today: snow all day long and oh so cold. We are under orders to move shortly so we had to work all day in it. I don't think my feet have been dry since I left England, it makes your socks go so bad: they only last about four days before they are in holes. The work has been held up by bad weather lately but we have done some concrete work even when it's been freezing hard. Fancy, we have actually been mixing concrete with boiling water. What do you think of a game like that? The bombardment has been somewhat quieter during the last few days, else since I got back it has been very heavy and continual. The peace talk seems to have died down again and most people out here seem to expect about another year of war yet (17 January).

'We have had six inches of snow on the ground for four days now and it has been sharp regular hard black frost. One thing, it makes it dry under foot: I have never had such dry boots since the summer. Chas Harris Seymour and four Cpls have gone on a course of bridging like I had this time last year. The Capt and Mr Gordon are also away so we are short of N.C.O.s and officers now. We finished our job tonight and move either tomorrow or Tuesday. We go about 35Ks in a north easterly direction and take the prisoners with us, so we are not in much danger again you see. We have got a good camp to go to and shall be very comfortable; the S.M. has been to look at it and says it is the best we have had in France (21 January).

On 23 January the 216th Company moved in freezing weather to a hutted camp on the road from Reninghelst to La Clytte. Reninghelst was a village in the hop-fields of Flanders, four miles south-west of Ypres. British camps, hutments, railheads and other depots were scattered thickly throughout this low country. As the pre-war drainage system had been destroyed by shell fire, this was normally very wet land, but at this time it was in the grip of a long hard frost. Flanders was suffering its hardest winter for over thirty years; the temperature sank to 20 degrees Fahrenheit for many nights on end and there was much snow. Charles Streather wrote to his parents on 25 January: 'Ashley and I have a small hut for the two of us; we have a stove and beds (homemade of course) and under normal conditions should be alright; but last night was cold. I don't think I ever was so cold before. Perhaps you can imagine what a corrugated iron hut about 12' by 8' is like to sleep in with only two blankets, and don't forget we are in clover compared with some.'

The Company were indeed in clover to be in huts, probably with the customary Royal Engineers' all-important access to firewood. For a while they even had an additional amenity in the shape of a makeshift canteen, where, writes my father, 'The drinking vessels were the 5.9 howitzers tin charge cases: this cost a half franc full. The canteen lasted about six weeks as our singing and noise disturbed our officers at their evening game of chemin-de-fer. There was also a sharp rise in the number of defaulters.' It is interesting that this canteen should have created a noise problem, for there were heavy artillery positions close to the camp. Streather wrote at this time: 'The bombardments have been continuous and very heavy for the last ten days; at times last night and today you could scarcely hear one another speak.'

My father admits that the cold weather produced some inconvenience: 'For six weeks we had a continuous hard frost, when the water in our well was frozen into a solid block. This well consisted of a large barrel without a bottom and sunk into the ground, replenished by rainfall and water seeping through the ground. During this time the water for our skimped morning ablutions was obtained overnight by knocking out with a pick sufficient ice to fill a gallon petrol can with the top cut off, put on the stove to thaw all night. This sufficed for the 22 men in each section occupying the hut. The first man up had clean water, but as each one used it, still in the tin, the last few "lie-a-beds" saved on their soap, as there was a scummy soapy liquid still available. For shaving, tepid tea, or ham rinds, when boiled ham was served, were used. I preferred the ham fat when it was available.'

Arthur Daulman was still batman to Captain MacDougall. He recalls Sergeant Ashley 'telling me that he could get a drink out of Mac to which I answered that he would not. Now each section had a hut and a sergeant in each and I was present when Sgt Ashley came to Mac to get the morrow's details. He came in scuffing, coughing, and clearing his throat. "You've got a bad cough sergeant." "Yes sir. If I were home I'd have a glass of whisky." "You shall have one. Daulman, fetch the sergeant a glass of whisky." Well, I brought in a very generous amount in a tumbler. "Do you call that a glass of whisky? Go back and fill it." I did this and needless to say Arthur had one for himself. Both Sgt Ashley and myself kept a straight face.'

Pioneer Daulman was still combining the roles of despatch rider and batman when the cold relented and the ground reverted to its usual muddy condition. He recalls: 'The motor cycles could only be reached from camp on duckboards unless you wanted to walk in deep mud. I remember telling Sapper Albert Thomas, a motor-cycle driver, that Mac had got a book in his hut on motor-cycle troubles and how to trace them. Needless to say he wanted to look at it and eventually persuaded me to bring it over to him. This I did and returning bumped into Mac whilst on the duck boards. I ducked into the kitchen but he had spotted the book and followed me. "Did I see you with one of my books a moment ago?" "Yes sir. Motor-cycle troubles and how to trace them. Sapper Thomas would like to see it." "You can read anything in the hut, but you mustn't take anything." Mac wasn't too bad.'

Daulman has reminiscences of other defaults, trivial or grave, while the company was in camp on the Reninghelst Road. Thus: 'We had regular gas respirator drill. We had three seconds to put the mask on. Mac came out on one occasion and watched. The order came to test for gas which meant "liberating the side of the mask away from the face and sniffing". Mac watched and said "Sergeant. Take that man's name. He took too long to sniff."' On the other hand: 'One morning everyone was called out on parade, cooks, batmen, everyone. We waited expectantly for we had no idea what was to come. The sergeant-major read out the number, rank, and name of an R.E. prisoner and then "was sentenced by General Court Martial to be shot". It was a complete surprise and we were shocked. The first time I was to hear such a pronouncement and I never forgot it. A month later we were on parade again. The number, rank, and name was followed by "was destroyed by General Court Martial". That upset me.' Daulman says that these were the first announcements of this kind that he had heard, so he may well not have known that at least three executions of deserters had been carried out in Mazingarbe abattoir during the month of February 1916, when the 216th Company was billeted in that village. Possibly these killings were not proclaimed to Royal Engineer companies because they were all of infantrymen (including one boy who had deserted when he was aged seventeen, and should not have been on active service in France any more than Arthur Daulman or some of his comrades).[3]

When Pioneer Daulman was Mac's batman he was not the only man with a cushy number. He recalls: 'On the strength of the permanent [i.e. headquarters] staff were various craftsmen. There were three or four tinsmiths for the plumbing. They did other work too. At that time, in January, February, March 1917, there was long frost, sixteen weeks altogether. The tinsmiths made a cooking stove for the officers' mess, a miniature kitchen range. How they nursed that job, because of course it kept them inside away from the cold. Every so often would come the sound of a hammer, especially when an officer or N.C.O. put his foot on the duck boards.'

The tinsmiths were the lucky ones, for the main work of the Company lay outdoors. Charles Streather informed his parents: 'We have moved to a new job on water supply and have to make a big dam so as to make an existing reservoir about ten times as big. The reservoir has 4 1/2" of ice on it now so we ought to have our skates. . . . The job we are on is in a valley running N.E. and the wind comes along like a knife. The ground is frozen, but in ordinary times would be a bog so perhaps we are lucky in that respect. It has been a wood and we are grubbing up all the old stumps and roots and taking off 18" of earth which has to be replaced by clay' (26 January). 'The ice is now a foot thick and the cold gets worse I think. It is playing havoc with the troops I can tell you. We are making a reservoir: it is a deep valley with a stream running through it; we are making a dam across the bottom end to hold up about 4 acres of water at an average depth of six feet. There was a small existing reservoir. I got in near the sluice while we were doing some work there and I think that is how I caught cold' (6 February). Nevertheless, he was in better health than many of his comrades. Twenty men went down with influenza in the course of one week. There was a case of measles which required the isolation of the hut in which the sick man slept and the confinement of the other men there for fourteen days. In view of the weather they perhaps didn't mind too much. Corporal Toogood went sick when he was on leave in England. As he was in Sergeant Streather's section, he called on Streather's father and gave him the impression that the war did not interest him now. The Sergeant's worried letters over some four weeks in February and March hint darkly at the very serious trouble Toogood may land in if he prolongs his stay in England.

These letters also show a serious interest in the war. 'There is a rumour about here today that America has broken relations with Germany. I hope that is right. It should help matters considerably, though I don't suppose America will be in a position to render much help on land, or sea for that matter, but I think she should help bear the financial burden and her action should influence the other neutrals. By what I make of things the war from now will be prosecuted with extreme violence by both sides losses will be great but the end will come quickly' (6 February). Leave was stopped again: 'The worst of it is that the general opinion seems to be that it will not open again before the offensive. . . they keep hammering away round about here: the fighting is continual and far more severe than last winter, though I think every week signs that the Alleman is getting weaker become more pronounced. I saw a gang of prisoners today: a poor sample — different from those we got in August and September (27 February). On the food shortages in England: 'If more attention had been given to manufacturing material of war and cultivating the land and a little less to making hats and coats and such like fancy things the war would have been over before now.' On war news: 'We seem to be getting on pretty well on the Somme just now I fancy things will move very quickly when the ground dries up a bit; at present all movement is slow because the "Western Front" is a sea of mud. The fighting round here gets fiercer every week I think, and the bombardments more intense'(9 March). 'Well: what do you think of today's advance? The war looks as if it may finish this year after all! (18 March).

The advance on the Somme which seemed so encouraging was unfortunately only to occupy land voluntarily given up by the Germans when they made a well-prepared strategic withdrawal to the immensely strong fortifications of the Hindenburg Line on a shortened front between Arras and the River Aisne. This withdrawal was virtually unhindered, thus promptly confounding Haig's prediction that there was no possibility of the enemy entrenching himself even far in the rear. The German army was now prepared to stand on the defensive while German submarines drained the Allies' strength to wage war; the question for the Allies was whether their armies could win the war before their navies lost it. As it happened, success against the submarine menace would come from the Royal Navy's belated acceptance of the convoy system; it was not contingent upon the Army capturing the (relatively unimportant) submarine bases at Ostend and Zeebrugge, though a great deal of slaughter would result in Flanders partly as the result of that mistaken belief. Meanwhile the Army's losses on the Somme and the other battles of 1916 had to be made good. There had been conscription in Britain for a year now, but it was not certain that this would provide all the bodies for the battles to come. In March 1917 it was announced that all certificates of exemption from military service hitherto granted were to be reviewed. The local tribunals who judged applications for exemption were told 'that a critical stage in the progress of the war is being reached, and that it behoves every man to do his utmost so that the military authorities may have at their disposal the largest possible number of men at the earliest date'.[4]

Back in France the 216th Company continued to play their part in providing a piped water supply for the troops currently in the front line and for all the animals and men who were to make the big push in Flanders in the coming year. The object was to provide each corps with from 150,000 to 200,000 gallons a day in advance of the old front line[5] as part of General Plumer's meticulous preparations for the capture of the Messines ridge. Plumer's staff work was better than that of most commanders; he was one of the few British generals to come out of the war with a greatly enhanced reputation. Plumer and his Chief of Staff, Major-General Sir Charles Harington, were well respected, but Brigadier-General Charteris may have been exaggerating when he wrote: 'The troops love them. When a division is rattled for any reason, either because of very heavy casualties or because it thinks it has had unfair treatment, it is sent to the Second Army, and at once becomes as happy as sandboys.'[6]

Plumer's sandboys once again included the Irishmen, Protestant and Roman Catholic, of the 36th and 16th Divisions. Sergeant Streather had been away on the Somme in the previous summer, when the 216th Company first met the Irishmen, so this was his first encounter with them. He wrote on 5 March: 'we have 400 Irishmen attached to us now. I've had English, Welsh, Scotch, Canadians, Australians, and New Zealanders, and Germans, but never Irish before and I think they are the funniest of all. One of their Sergeants was in Nuneaton and one was at Coventry with the regulars. We get them in our mess and they seem to think that Nuneaton is about the best place they ever struck.' He was intrigued to find that the Irish made as much fuss of St.Patrick's Day as we do of Christmas. Once again the 'shamrocks' from the South quarrelled with the 'red hands' from Ulster. My father reports a battle, first between two cooks, then between returning working parties from the two divisions, in which the missiles were tins of pork and beans; so that 'for two hours the battle raged in their area of the camp. Our section was not interfered with, excepting once, when our Irishman Rainey went across to join in the excitement, and was chased back by members of both parties, indignant that an outsider should presume to join in a domestic quarrel. There were some hospital cases as a result, and most of the others looked a bit battered when they joined us for work next morning.' For all their domestic quarrels, men of the two religiously-divided Irish divisions would fight very well side by side against the Germans at Messines in June.

It is this more serious topic of fighting Germans that occupies Charles Streather's letters, but he puts his parents' fears at rest by assuring them that the pipe-laying is proceeding backwards from the front to the pumping stations and reservoir: 'the fighting is pretty close but we have done the work nearest the line now and are working away from it at a rate of 350yds a day (letter of 18 March). On 31 March he wrote at more length about the comings, goings, and doings of the Company: 'Toogood arrived "home" today. He looks pretty bad and by what he says he has had a rough time, though of course he has been at home and that counts for a great deal. What do you think of the war now? It seems to me that the end is coming quickly; I fancy that August or September will see the last of it. My word, we are doing some work just now and we are short handed too. Several of the Cpls have been away on different classes; the officers have all been. Mr Smith has just been on leave and Capt Mac is on leave now, and then the whole Company has been inoculated in small batches and the work has to go on just the same. Of course all these things throw more work on the Sgts. My section has a job of its own: about eight miles of 4" pipes, filters, pumping station, pump, and 4 different lots of tanks for filling water carts. I have 20 men in the section and 100 infantry working party each day. These are scattered in small parties over about 6 miles of country. I have to go and look at all of them two or three times a day and arrange for all material, tools, and transport, so you can tell I have plenty to do. We go to the work on lorries as it is about 6 miles away from the camp. The worst of it is that whereas the men and Cpls finish about 5 o'clock the Sgts are just thinking about starting the next day's job.'

One small scattered party consisted of Charles Douglas, newly promoted to Lance Corporal, and Pioneer Sambrook. My father recalls: 'During this frost I was the rod man for Douglas, surveying ground for a new pipe line. One afternoon we came to a farm where a party of women sat in the yard lace making. "Photographie Monsieur" they asked Douglas when they saw the theodolite. "Oui Madame", and they grouped themselves to be photographed. Douglas looked through his instrument and regrouped them, put the cover on the lens, and then asked them to smile. He solemnly took off the cover for a moment and replaced it with a bow to the ladies. Then madame invited us to join them and have coffee.'

The frost mentioned here lasted with scarcely a break through March; there were frequent strong cold winds and much snow; the heaviest snowfalls of the entire winter fell on 10, 11, and 12 April; there was no improvement until 21 April, when, back at Field Marshal Haig's headquarters, Brigadier-General Charteris noted: 'Today for the first time it is real spring weather. The trees are bursting into bud and the sun has brought out the birds. War seems very futile'.[7] For the common soldier the return of spring was signalled by the minor futility of returning gloves to store. My father recalls that during the winter the men of the company 'were issued with knitted gloves, made with khaki-coloured wool. In normal everyday use these gloves lasted about a fortnight, then the fingers were worn out, and then the palms of the resulting mittens followed the fingers. Then the final tangle of wool was thrown away and forgotten, until in the following spring an order was posted on the Company Orderly board, ordering all gloves to be returned to stores. The drill was, the company paraded and filed past the Quarter bloke with the muster roll, ready when our name was called to deposit in an empty tea chest the returned gloves. Whether it was one of the gloves which had survived the winter, or an old sock, or a handful of rifle-cleaning rags did not matter at all. Wheway glanced at each man approaching the tea chest with some article clutched in his hand and then turned to his list with a smile to check the name and number of the donor. The contents of the tea chest finished up in the incinerator, and the official report was that all the gloves had been handed in, but had been destroyed by enemy action when the camp was shelled. Wheway was a very efficient Quartermaster Sergeant; his first war service was during the Boer War, where he learned all the ways and means of taking advantage of the system.' Many men would have gloves and socks sent by caring parents and wives; Charles Streather's letters home repeatedly ask for gloves and socks; Nuneaton was full of shops selling khaki gloves, socks, and wool.

More serious sartorial matters were attended to at the Reninghelst Road camp by a tailor, who, writes Arthur Daulman, 'was available for sewing on stripes, repairs to clothing and sewing on various chevrons, red for 1914/15, blue for each later completed year, a brass brooch for wound stripes in the inverted V for completed service.' About this time the earliest volunteers in the 216th Company would be getting their second year of service chevrons; there would also be a few wound stripes and rather more to come. Daulman also notes: 'a saddler looked after leather harness, a cobbler for boots, and three farriers, Sappers Montgomery, Jack Williams, and B.R.Williams, did the shoeing, and related work'.

The return of spring brought round a new campaigning season. On 6 April the United States entered the war, but the last thing the Allied generals wanted to do was to go over to the defensive until the Americans arrived in sufficient numbers to have a decisive effect. Despite the changed circumstances created by the German withdrawal to the Hindenburg Line the new French Commander in Chief, General Nivelle carried through a well-leaked plan to attack on the Aisne in April. The British and Imperial forces contributed some blood in a series of somewhat better managed battles near Arras; their greatest success being the capture of Vimy Ridge by the Canadian Corps. Nivelle's campaign ended in defeat and widespread mutinies in the French army. The main burden was now upon the British Army and Field Marshal Haig had the opportunity to make his long-meditated big push in Flanders.

Haig unveiled his master plan at a strategic conference early in May. The intention was to secure the armies' right flank by capturing the Messines-Wytschaete ridge and then rapidly advance northwards along the ridge towards Passchendaele, an as yet little-known village north-east of Ypres and four and a half miles from the nearest existing British position in the salient. As the advance gained momentum there would be a great cavalry sweep through western Belgium, which, combined with a coastal attack on Ostend and Zeebrugge, would neutralize the German submarine threat, turn the German flank, and threaten to destroy the German armies. Lloyd George did not like the plan, but was too shifty and politically weak to countermand it. Both British army commanders on the spot, Sir Henry Rawlinson (4th Army) and Sir Herbert Plumer (2nd Army) thought their Commander-in-Chief's plan was somewhat too ambitious, so Haig moved Rawlinson north to handle the proposed coastal operation, gave Plumer responsibility only for capturing the Messines ridge and covering the right flank of the main attack, and placed the main attack itself in the hands of that dashing and optimistic cavalryman, Sir Hubert Gough.[8]

General Plumer had been in command in the Ypres salient for two years now: all the time maturing his plans for an assault on the Messines ridge. Since January 1916 Royal Engineer tunnelling companies had been hard at work, driving galleries to the depth of a hundred feet beneath the German positions, placing in each completed gallery one or two huge explosive charges of ammonal. The Germans were countermining, but, in the event, British, Canadian, and Australian tunnellers placed twenty-one huge mines, nineteen of which were successfully detonated when the attack was made. Nearly five miles of gallery was excavated and the spoil hidden behind the lines, and a million pounds of explosives was primed. All this was done mainly by hand, though there were some attempts at mechanization, in one of which Nuneaton played a part. A huge tunnelling machine, costing six thousand pounds and weighing seven and a half tons, was specially built by the Stanley Heading Machine Company of Nuneaton. It was brought to the front with enormous difficulty and set to work, but became jammed after only two hundred feet of intermittent progress. It was entombed where it died, and the tunnellers reverted to muscle power.[9]

My father recalls that some of the N.C.O.s and sappers belonging to tunnelling companies 'were from Nuneaton and district, who were miners in civvy street, who often visited our camp at Reninghelst and were met in the local estaminets round about. Also a sapper named Wilkinson joined our section from hospital, who had belonged to one of the tunnelling companies then burrowing beneath Jerry, who told us quite a lot about their work. From the stories we heard from these chaps, we got the feeling that something big was coming off in the near future, and the other signs of increased air activity, tanks and guns getting into well-camouflaged positions, added to the general foreboding, or excitement, of everybody likely to be involved. "Wilky" told us when he first joined us that he thought he had "dropped lucky" in being sent to an Army Troops Company after the danger and discomfort of working underground, listening to the sound of German activity near them, and wondering which side would blow their mine first. "As long as you can hear them digging you know it's all right, it's when they stop you get the wind up", he said. The first morning we went to our job, towards Wytschaete, where we were putting in a water tank and pipe line, in a hollow out of observation from the ridge, "Wilky" began to look a bit dubious and inquired where we were going to. "You'll see", was all the reply he got, and when he did see he regretted leaving the tunnels. "It's all right and safe in there if Jerry leaves you alone", he complained. "It's all right and safe up here if Jerry leaves us alone", he was told, "shut up and keep going".'

The actions of 216th Company evidently earned the attention of British higher command as well as German gunners, because on 18 May Captain Cook's name was gazetted as mentioned in despatches; but, since no Company war diaries whatsoever survive for the entire period of his command of the 216th, we have no precise or official knowledge of the Company's activities. Charles Streather's letters during the spring sometimes refer to 'excitement' as well as work. On 29 May he brings his parents up to date on a range of activities. He apologises for not having written for three weeks, 'but I am so awfully busy. We are working night and day to get finished just at present; you will no doubt hear and understand more in a few days time. . . The C.O. was mentioned in dispatches by Sir D.Haig: no doubt he will be in for a D.S.O. or M.C. or something before long. As you say, it is only the officers who get mentioned but it's the men that do the work. I finished my [second] reservoir yesterday, but on account of the dry weather the water supply is low and we are having to clean out ditches and streams for miles to keep up the supply. It has made quite a fair head of water I can tell you. Our advance seems to have come almost to a standstill now, the Russians are doing nothing and look like doing less as far as I can see, the French are held up, the only progress is made by the Italians. . . . I think we shall be moving in the near future however; if we don't it does not look much like finishing this year any way. . . . I have several nosecaps of gas shells, various little souvenirs which it is now possible to send home. . . . The postcards I enclose were drawn by a Cpl who is attached to our company. He is a splendid fellow with the brush and has painted some first-rate pictures of trenches and troops and guns in action. These cards are of course an imitation of Capt B.B. [Bruce Bairnsfather] and quite fail to do him justice really.'

At the end of May the Company went to Neuve Eglise, where the église was now only a rag of a tower. There they occupied a few huts in a large camp established near the remains of the village on a hill overlooking the quaint old-fashioned town of Bailleul to the west. Their eastward view was dominated by the not-so-quaint Wytschaete-Messines ridge, described by John Buchan at this time as 'a low hillside seamed with white trenches, and dotted with the debris of old woods — a bald, desolated height, arid as a brickfield, rising from the rank grass and yellow mustard of no-man's land. The landmarks on it were the ruins of the White Chateau at Hollebeke, the dust-heap which once was Wytschaete village, and the tooth of the ruined church of Messines'.[10]

The 216th had been sent to Neuve Eglise for what my father calls 'the Messines do'; they were to be placed at the disposal of the Chief Engineer of II Anzac Corps; they shared their present camp with a battalion of the 3rd Australian Division. This division was commanded by Major-General Sir John Monash, a distinguished engineer in civilian life and one of the ablest new soldiers thrown up by the Great War. Monash was a careful planner and considerate commander, as too was the cautious, methodical, imperturbable General Sir Herbert Plumer, Commander in

Chief of the Second Army of which II Anzac Corps now formed a part. Australians had a reputation for fighting splendidly but taking little heed of such important military matters as saluting, spit and polish, and unquestioning obedience. My father observed that the camp that the 216th shared with the Australians 'could not be mistaken for an establishment of His Majesty's Brigade of Guards', for 'the only person in the place who kept up the Guards tradition in behaviour and smartness was our ex-Guardsman, Company Sergeant-Major John Mitchinson, whose blood pressure went up every time he saw the Aussies on parade'. The 216th had a notoriously shabby appearance, but 'our turnout was better than that of our camp mates, we always went on parade with all our uniform on. Our Australian companions came on half-dressed, and stood in some sort of a line, with pipes and cigarettes, and plenty of conversation going on; their company officers never walked up and down the ranks inspecting them, having a good idea what they looked like from the first glance at the front rank. With the smoking and tobacco-chewing indulged in there was more spit than polish, and when they were required to march off, the officers just said, "O.K. chaps, we'll get going".'

Bailleul was the headquarters of II Anzac Corps as well as being one of the places where material and troops were being gathered for the coming offensive, so it was often the target for bombing raids by Gothas. These were relatively large twin-engined biplanes with 'pusher' propellers; the recurrent beat of their engines was very different from the mosquito-like hum of British planes; they were difficult for fighters to attack because they had three gun positions: nose, midships, and belly. My father recalls having a grandstand view of some of their raids upon the many camps and dumps visible from Neuve Eglise hill. 'One night in particular we were on the edge of the camp, standing on a field track between the dump and a field of beans. Most of us were smoking, striking matches, and lighting pipes and cigarettes, watching the explosions in Bailleul. One of the planes happened to be nearly overhead. One of the Aussies was saying, "That's the stuff, Jerry, drop the load over there" [perhaps on Corps Headquarters if this man shared the usual common soldier's opinion of Staff]. Their newly-joined chaplain admonished him, telling him to "have a thought for the unfortunates being bombed". Before any more was said a loud warning swish made everyone flop down and the parson was unfortunate: he was down first, and everyone else was on top of him. There was a beanfield next to the camp, and I happened to be standing at the corner of the hut, but had no time to move before the bomb landed. In the flash of the explosion the tall bean stalks were a black silhouette, and although we did not receive any bomb splinters, there was a blast of hard ripe horse beans peppering the heap of bodies on the duckboard. As I was standing sheltered behind a corner, I never got a bean, nor did the parson, we were both well under cover.'

On another occasion, when a party including my father was erecting horse lines in Bailleul, some Gothas came over very low and threw out bundles of leaflets instead of bombs, but the planes on both sides were more frequently employed to shoot down artillery observation balloons. My father recalled: 'In cloudy conditions the aircraft of either side would dive from the cloud cover, machine-gunning the opposite observation balloons. At the first burst of fire, the two observers would jump from the basket and float to the ground with their parachutes; with very few exceptions being allowed to land without any further attack from the airmen. At first would be seen a wisp of black smoke, then a small flame from the balloon, which would begin to crumple up and sink, until the whole was a flaming mass plunging earthwards, leaving a pillar of black smoke which remained upright in the air for several minutes. On a sunny afternoon later in June a party of us working on the ridge in Messines saw eleven of these smoke columns standing up at the same time all round the horizon, five on our side and six on Jerry's side. The conditions were ideal for this sort of activity, a lot of white fleecy clouds drifting slowly along, hiding the aircraft while they stalked their targets.'

'Sometimes for a change', adds my father, 'Jerry would give his attention to working parties and transport about their business in the forward areas, and our parties got a lot of attention from them. On these occasions we took what cover was handy and fired back at them as they circled low above us, but no one was hurt in these exchanges, and after a short time Jerry flew off and the battle was a draw, no score on either side.' Once, in the Messines sector, Arthur Daulman 'was walking along a deserted road to the B.E.F. canteen, which was a converted lorry, where I could buy biscuits, chocolate, and condensed milk to sweeten the "burgoo" (porridge), when I heard about a dozen planes coming behind me. I took no notice until they overtook me, when I "went horizontal", for it was a German squadron flying red pennons which I believed was the insignia of the Baron von Richtofen's squadron. They were about two hundred feet up, not more, with the black and white crosses clearly visible. They went on their way looking for bigger game than a solitary soldier and I went on my way too. I saw dog fights and planes hitting the ground, some fleeing for their lives, and the air filled with burning twisting machines.'

During May it seemed that every available open space in the Ypres salient was filled with men, animals, stores, guns, and transport. Edmund Blunden observed: 'from Poperinghe forward the place was like a circus ground on the eve of a benefit. New roads and railways had changed the map so completely in a few weeks that one was a stranger here. The instinct revolted against the inevitable punishment to come, already tokened by those big holes now met in walls and crossings. Not the famous footprint in the sand contained a sharper shock than the shell-hole unerringly torn out by the far-off gunners "registering" his targets in the middle of some previously secure trackway'.[11]

The 216th Company performed several acts in this great circus. For about a fortnight before the attack, which started on 7 June, they laid 'corduroy tracks' in places where the ground was soft. These were made of slabs, chiefly of elm or beech, ten to twelve feet long, one foot across, and three inches thick, cut by forestry companies of Royal Engineers in the rear areas. The ground was prepared by digging side drains and filling shell holes with the spoil and any available rubble and wreckage; four or five slabs were laid lengthwise as runners and the others, laid crosswise and spiked to the runners, made the surface; half-round pine logs along each edge made a kerb, intended to keep wheels on the track. The work was done at night, all materials being cleared away and the track camouflaged before daybreak. In the unending struggle against mud and shell fire which constituted warfare in Flanders these rapidly-laid timber roads were essential for the movement of ammunition, guns, rations, and material. Men crossed the even softer ground on duckboards; the new Mark IV tanks, moving up to attack-positions at this time, could use only the somewhat rarer hard ground. My father recalls 'The tanks were stumbled on, under any cover available, and the hedges were thick with them, and batteries of 18 pounders and 4.5s seemed to thicken on the ground overnight'.

Closer to zero day the 216th strung white tapes on stakes to guide the walking wounded back from front-line trenches to the casualty clearing system, 'a couple of miles along a reasonable track', according to Arthur Daulman. The Company's main work, though, as my father recalls, was to 'put in water pipes in readiness for the transport supply wagons of the division which would capture what was left of Messines after the mine beneath it had been exploded. The water supply for this was drawn from the reservoir the company had excavated on the reverse slope of Kemmel Hill, and we put in stand pipes and wooden water troughs, made the previous winter in Reninghelst, in places near the entrances to the communication trenches, which were not seen from the German lines.' Water troughs were required not only for the all-important artillery and supply-column horses and mules but for the cavalry that always cluttered up any area close to where an attack was to be made.

The Company in fact laid two pipe lines from the Kemmel Hill reservoir towards the ridge, one in the direction of Wytschaete, the other, further south, in the direction of Messines. The southern line went over very low ground, through Souvenir Dump, St Quentin Cabaret, and Stinking Farm, where the land was so wet that 'trenches' were perforce sandbagged breastworks built up above ground level and known as the 'Chinese Wall'. My father recalls that even in midsummer 'the ground in front of the line of sandbags was waterlogged, just like a moat. There must have been millions of sandbags there, new on top of old.' Like road making, pipe laying was done at night. The men had long since developed cat's eyes, but they also located places by smell. Of 'Stinking Farm' (a place so named on the *Official History* maps) my father writes: it 'must have possessed a vintage midden, probably laid down after the 1870 trouble, and, having been battered to a heap of building rubble by shell fire, the result was noticeable and nauseous for a hundred yards around, particularly during night time.' He adds: 'The road along the front from Voormezeele, Wytschaete, to Messines, also had its decaying sign posts, usually at the places where the communication trenches ended at the road side, and the nightly ration supply wagons awaited the carrying parties from the unit holding the line. On a dark night anyone using the road, could tell his whereabouts, by the smell of decomposing horses and mules knocked over by shell fire, or caught by a burst of machine gun fire.'

During May an artillery barrage was hurled against the German wire entanglements, roads, camps, and supply dumps, so that the ridge was steadily stripped of any traces of summer greenery. From the end of the month the barrage became even more intense; then, in the days immediately before the infantry assault on 7 June, gas shells were sent over in order to compel the Germans to wear masks and lose sleep. Needless to say, the Germans responded in kind. Their guns were outnumbered by the great weight of artillery deployed by Plumer (one gun for every seven yards of front) but they still had excellent observation; they knew the roads and duckboard tracks along which men, ammunition, and supplies travelled at night; they duly dropped their shells along them, working backwards and forwards. Two days before the attack a section of the company, with a working party from the 4th New Zealand Infantry Brigade were carrying water pipes forward to Stinking Farm, on the front just below Messines village, when they were machine-gunned from the German positions on the ridge as well as being shelled as usual: Corporal Percy Keen was killed and Sapper Gilmour was wounded. My father recalls that their party carried Percy Keen 'with them when they took cover behind the ruins of the farm buildings near to a communication trench, and then brought him back to camp on a stretcher, and he was buried in a cemetery near Neuve Eglise next morning, sewn in his blanket'. Keen had been invalided home after an accident the previous November and had returned to the Company at the end of January, thanks to a routine order which enabled men to get back to their own unit.

26. Driver Enderby ('Eddie') Parratt.

Chapter Nine: Messines, June to August 1917

During the night before the attack on 7 June there was a violent thunderstorm. Afterwards the night cleared up with a three-quarter moon shining, but, writes my father, 'we did not do any night work, and spent our evening in camp. About 3 o'clock we were awakened by an earthquake, and somebody said, "That's a mine gone up". Then the guns started together, and the racket was augmented by every gas gong in the neighbourhood clanging under the beating of the various sentries; as we were already shaken out of our beds it did not take us long to get out on the parade ground, complete with rifles, ammo, and gas masks on. The sky was lit up by continuous flashes from the massed artillery barrage all along the length of the ridge from our front to the north towards Ypres. Jerry was sending up yellow and green Very lights, calling for artillery support. We stood for some time waiting for Capt MacDougall, who presently came across to us, appearing unusually agitated; we wondered a bit at that, but in the sudden alarm he had put his gas hood on inside out, and consequently he had great difficulty in breathing, as the valve was on the outside. The Sgt Major went to meet him, and took his hood off. Mac thanked him, and then called to his batman, "Eddie" Parratt: "Parratt, I can't find my box respirator. Will you go and look for it for me". After some time, as there was no gas about, we were dismissed back to bed, and lay listening to the noise of artillery, and discussing what the situation would be when we went to work in the morning, until we all eventually dropped off.' Perhaps Captain MacDougall was in difficulties because he had forgotten how to fit the old-fashioned gas hood. This had now been superseded by the box respirator (temporarily mislaid by MacDougall), which had a canister carried in a satchel, slung around the neck, connected by a flexible rubber tube to a face-piece with inlet and outlet breathing valves; the canister contained granulated charcoal and other chemicals capable of filtering out a number of poison gases.

While the 216th were taking their rest the guns continued to pound away and the infantry advanced to capture the ridge in a matter of hours, making the battle of Messines a victory won 'with a swift completeness beyond that of any previous major operation of the British Armies in France and Flanders'. The battle of Messines, with its tremendous artillery bombardment and its record explosion of land mines containing nearly a million pounds of high explosive, 'was a triumph of organization and of co-operation of the artillery and the engineers with the infantry'.[1] The most dramatic engineering contribution to Messines was, of course, mining, but the pre-arranged water supply was hardly less important. In the winter and spring before the long-planned attack on 7 June over 180 miles of piping were laid in the Second Army area, with reservoirs and pumping stations capable of supplying a million gallons of treated drinking water a day, together with half a million untreated gallons for animals.

Once the attack had succeeded the water supply system had to be extended forward. On the baking hot June day of the attack itself it was business as usual for the 216th Company: some men were patrolling the pipe lines to repair bursts caused by shell-fire; others continued the pipe lines forward, now assisted by working parties from the 171st Tunnelling Company, R.E., for the tunnellers had done their work beneath the ridge and the New Zealand infantry were otherwise engaged. As the engineers worked, large groups of dazed German prisoners were being escorted back and cavalry could be seen winding their way to the crest north of Messines. 'Although this and other attempts to employ mounted troops at such a stage was due to a groundless anticipation of open warfare, the spectacle increased the general cheerfulness'.[2] The attack had gone so well that the entire ridge from Wytschaete to Messines was captured by 9 a.m. An Australian officer described the scene as more like a picnic than a battle: 'Behind was a ploughed-up wilderness of shell holes and battered trenches, with a litter of tangled wire, broken rifles and abandoned equipment; it reached back as far as a clean-cut line in the original No Man's Land, beyond which grass still grew. In front, however, was a green countryside, with woods of leaf-covered trees, and the gentle sloping grassland was intersected by tree-lined hedgerows. The lower half of this eastern slope, where lurked most of the German batteries, was out of sight owing to its convexity; but in the distance could be seen the towns, woods and water meadows for many miles along the Lys valley. This panorama slumbered under a bright sun which already gave promise of an exceptionally hot day'.[3]

For my father, 'the day was largely taken up with moving stuff from Abeele, and it was not until late in the afternoon we went to Messines with a load which we dumped in the trench. The front line was deserted and the sandbags and wire had been removed from across the Wulverghem-Messines road. When the transport turned back, some of us, myself included, walked up to the village. The first thing that struck us was the range of the view Jerry had enjoyed over the roads and trenches of our side. At the entrance to the village the road disappeared into a huge crater, and the place was littered with damaged machine guns and other weapons and ammunition, but very few bodies. There was the odd one or two about, mostly in the corners of practically obliterated trenches: where the craters were exploded were only a few remnants. A mine a short distance away had gone up under a "pill box" concrete strong point, which was thrown up to the surface. The late occupants were inside, with their machine gun and ammo; the blast of the explosion had knocked them out; as far as we could see they had no wounds whatsoever. Souvenirs were plentiful: Luger pistols, bayonets, and personal belongings of the late garrison were lying about, but, apart from collecting a few for the young Church Army parson, who had established a coffee and "wad" stall in a roadside dug-out near the old front line before the "push" and was still with us unscathed, we left the things lying where they were. Despite the warm sunny weather at this time, the devastation was too complete, and it was depressing to walk about looking at it.'

Coming back towards Neuve Eglise my father saw that 'One of the tanks which crossed the front line at zero hour on June 7th got no further than the front line. The front line here on the right side of the Wulverghem road to Messines was built up on the surface of the ground by a mass of sandbags, eroded by weather, shell fire, and continually built up and repaired to a height of about 7 ft. This tank had successfully crossed the swampy rubbish dump at the parados (the rear side), and the trench, when the weight of the tank had bent the walls from rear to parapet together, to form an arch. Then, going down the front slope of the parapet, had dug its nose into the pool of mud and water which had collected there for about two years of churning up, and got stuck. There was also a field kitchen, standing in the middle of the road, which was actually nothing more than a track. Both were undamaged, and were removed two days later.'

After their stunned retreat on the morning of 7 June the Germans fought back, particularly with their artillery, most of which they had managed to withdraw before their positions on the ridge were taken. During the rest of the month the 216th Company, with the help of Australian and New Zealand working parties of sometimes over two hundred men, laid water pipes up to and along the ridge, and installed the usual pumps, tanks, and water points. Thanks to the work of this and other R.E. companies in the space of one week pipe lines had been laid across the captured and completely devastated country and were delivering water into what had been German positions at a rate of 600,000 gallons a day. It is doubtful if existing German pipe lines were brought into use: Captain MacDougall inspected them, but reported to the Chief Engineer, II Anzac Corps that they were of little value.

My father was with a party digging a water tank in the shelter of a ruined German strongpoint amid the rubble of Messines. In this case the tank would probably have consisted of a square hole in the ground, lined with tarpaulin pegged to the surrounding bank, with a canvas cover over the top. Surrounded by enemy souvenirs, able to 'kick them around', they remembered the needs of the Church Army chaplain. My father writes: 'The Church Army parson was a tall good-looking chap, who gave tea or coffee and buns to every service man who passed along the road where he lived in his dug-out, which was residence-cum-canteen for about six weeks. He was relieved by another Church Army man every day and night in shifts, but we rarely saw his relieving companion, as we also went up at varying times during the day or night. Our young friend was interested in warlike weapons, and used to ask his customers to bring anything in that line when they returned, and before many days had passed he was dispensing tea and buns girded with German Luger automatic pistols, with a Mauser rifle or two over the bunk at the back of the dug-out; he lacked ammunition, so he particularly requested us to look out for an ammunition belt for him, which we promised to do, and enquired what kind of ammo he would like. "Anything will do", he replied as we moved off.'

'We were excavating for a water tank at the end of the pipe line in the shelter of the remains of a cottage, which job kept us busy most of the day. As we were preparing to leave, someone remembered the ammo belt we had promised to get. On our way back we kept our eyes open, and two fully-loaded machine-gun belts were picked up. The cartridges were similar to our 303 small-arms ammo, with the difference that in place of the rim on the base of the brass shell the German ammo had a groove for the ejection fitment on the bolt engaged. Cpl Toogood said, "Well, never mind, this lot will fit the Mauser", so we presented them to the Church Army parson when we called on the way back to camp. Next morning when we called at the dug-out the young chap was draped by two fully loaded machine gun belts crossed over his back and front, with some round his waist with a pistol in a holster on each side. One of the Aussie party going up with us said,

"I don't like the look of you, Cobber; you put the wind up me". The parson said, "Don't mind me; I'm collecting them for a friend of mine. I'm a man of peace, old chap". "That's all right by me; you look dinkum, Cobber".' My father ends respectfully, 'But he was close to the front line'. The self-image of a soldier in the third year of his service emerges in my father's reference to 'our young friend', though a parson, whatever his appearance, would certainly have been older than my father's nineteen years and three months.

My father's age is a factor in another anecdote concerning the water tank in Messines village. He writes: 'Going up one particularly fine evening, we were followed by the ration wagons of the Aussies, led by a sergeant riding a large grey horse. The wagons were unloaded at the old front line trenches to be picked up by the fatigue parties later during the night. The sergeant, however, rode on up to the top of the ridge, and for a time rode his horse to and fro, looking towards the German positions, where no doubt the German observers, seeing a horseman cantering about, silhouetted against the bright western sky, were also very interested. When the Germans got interested about something unusual going on, everybody except the fool of a sergeant knew what the result would be. The transport drivers knew without any doubt what would happen, and while unloading the rations loudly and obscenely discussed the bastard of a newly-joined sergeant. Luckily for the sergeant, nothing happened, and after a last look around the horizon he came down to his party and they turned round and went back to camp.'

'That night a large party of us were taking the pipe line over the ridge, together with the water tank, to finish getting the water supply into what was virtually the front line at that part, and our wagons came up soon after which we unloaded and sent back. The tank was left in the trench, with spare pipes in our usual dump, and we went up to the village with the few pipes required, and the picks and shovels, when it began to get dark. On the way one of the chaps remarked, "I bet Jerry will send some stuff over tonight. I'm thinking about that bloody fool riding about earlier on. I'll bet we get the backlash." For about an hour and a half we were not molested, and a few Australian carrying parties were bringing up their rations, and we were digging narrow slots in the rubble for the pipes, and then started joining them together, and burying them as we went along. While doing this we stood at intervals in the trench, holding the pipe level and turning it to screw the socket together. There was just room for our legs and the pipe in the slit trench, and when the first whizz-bang came over, all we could do was to bend our bodies over face down on the ground. We felt the wind of that one, which burst a few yards away. "That one couldn't have been more than a couple of foot up when it passed over", somebody said. One of the chaps laying out the pipes on the top ran away, and we lost him for quite some time. The shelling now was very heavy, whizz-bangs, 5.9s, and gas shells were coming over all mixed together, and after counting heads we found Jock Chisholm was missing, and split up into small groups to find him. Stumbling about amongst the ruins and wrecked German trenches, mine and shell craters, and the heavy continuous bombardment, none of us felt like heroes, and everyone was relieved, after some time searching, that Jock was found crouched in a corner of a trench by a party who heard his piping, and Streather gave the order to quit. Jock gave a realistic imitation of the bagpipes by holding his long nose and moaning, usually after a dose of rum and vin blanc. Chisholm was badly shell shocked, and was led away to the dressing station by Sergt Streather and a few others, the rest of us were told to split up into small groups and make our way back to camp as best we could. Everyone got back without further casualties, except Clarkson and myself who started back together.'

'Halfway down the track from Messines we stumbled across a carrying party lying under a bank. Thinking they were resting while things got quiet, we stopped and spoke to them, but got no answer, so we went closer to see what was wrong. There were six in the party, and the rations, in sandbags, were thrown about around them, and at a second look we realized they were all dead. The last one we came to had two jars of rum[4] tied together with a sandbag over his shoulder, and we decided to help ourselves to a tot or two apiece, so we pushed in the cork of one of the jars with the sharp end of a trenching tool, took a mess tin from one of the other members of the carrying party, and sat under the shelter of the bank and had a drink. After a drink or two we decided that where we were was as safe as anywhere else, and stayed there. Finally Clarkson stuffed a bit of rag in the neck of the jar and wedged it upright so the men would not lose their rum ration, and we went to sleep, oblivious of shells, gas, or our companions. I woke up lying on a stretcher in a bare Nissen hut and wondered where I was. Not feeling too good I lay quiet for a while listening to someone snoring next to me. Rousing up, I saw Clarkson also on a stretcher lying on his back snoring. Then I noticed a large card with a broad diagonal red stripe across attached to one of the buttons of my tunic, and also one on Clarkson's tunic. On examining this card I learned that we were both on the danger list, severely gassed, and wondered if we had been put by ourselves in this empty hut while the gas finished us. Anyway, I didn't feel gassed, so I woke Clarkson up and told him we were gassed. He couldn't see it, and while we were speculating about where we were and how we came to be there, an orderly came in, and was astonished to see us sitting up and talking. We disregarded his orders to lie down and keep quiet, and asked him about some breakfast. He told us we would have nothing to eat or drink until the doctor had seen us, and then left us.'

'We were taken to see the doctor about an hour afterwards, who we found to be a young, pleasant-mannered officer. After talking to us for a while, he suddenly asked Clarkson how old he was. Clarkson, who was turned fifty, and had been in the South African 1899-1902 war, gave his age as 45 years, and in reply to a similar question from the doctor, I gave my age as 21 years, which was two years above my correct then age. The doctor looked at both of us for a few moments and then said: "I'll forget you have been brought here. Go and join your company." So we escaped the charge of being drunk in face of the enemy, to which we were liable. If this charge was universally applied, the forces in the line would have been reduced somewhat, as a tot or two of issue rum took the rough edge of our conditions off slightly. We walked back to camp at Neuve Eglise about four miles away, after stopping at a roadside estaminet for eggs and coffee, and reported to the orderly N.C.O. Our kit and personal belongings had been taken to the Quarter Stores and we reclaimed them and went to our section, and as usual that evening we went back on the job.' The stretcher party's mistaken diagnosis is easy to understand when read about men killed by gas, whose 'faces were calm and showed no trace of suffering'.[5]

It is likely that such tales of drink, unsoldierly conduct, and the humours of gas could be paralleled in any British army unit. They crop up refreshingly in the journal of General Sir Henry Rawlinson, commanding the Fourth Army. He wrote on 19 January 1917: 'It is not often that anything funny comes out of Ypres, but I have been roaring with laughter over stories of two distinguished generals. W. had selected a day in the festive season to inspect one of his brigades. Just as he came on parade it was discovered that one of the men was too drunk to stand up, so he was hastily smuggled out of the ranks, put on a stretcher, and rolled up in a blanket behind the rear rank. W. in his inspection passed behind the line, and, seeing a body on a stretcher, halted in front of it, stood to attention, and saluting with much ceremony, said: "I salute the honoured dead". A thick and muffled voice replied from the blanket: "What's the old b—— say?" On P's front, there are strict orders that all troops beyond a certain line are invariably to wear gas masks. P. one day was visiting his front, and found he had forgotten his mask. Meeting a man coming down from the front, he borrowed his mask-case, which the man handed over with considerable hesitation. On reaching the front, P. ran into a subaltern emerging from a dug-out without a mask-case. Having rated him soundly for his disobedience to orders he went on: "Why, sir, I don't believe you even know how to put a mask on. Here, take mine, and let me see." As soon as the transfer was made, P. roared out, "Now, *gas*!" The trembling young officer with fumbling fingers undid the case, and drew out a pair of dirty socks'.[6] For all that, gas was a real danger: in the 216th Company war diary for 11 June Captain MacDougall records that Sapper Bishop was 'wounded (gas)'.

My father's experiences at Messines were all 'near misses', whether by night or day. He writes: 'One night a mule belonging to our company was left to taint the air on the road between Wytschaete and Messines. We had a dump of water pipes at the reservoir at Kemmel Hill, and were taking a G.S. wagon loaded with some of these to a small dump near Messines, which we had in the old front line trenches near the track, but away from the battery. The Second Army Engineers stores dump was at Abeele, from whence all the water-supply material we required was brought to Kemmel in the day time and taken during night work to the forward area dump as required. The road running parallel to the ridge got a lot of interference from Jerry and mix-ups with dead mules and wrecked carts were frequent. We were going along this particular night about 2 a.m. in the G.S. wagon, carrying a couple of dozen cast iron water pipes with six of us riding on the load. The night was quiet, and there was not much traffic about, so we jolted along at a good pace. The cart had iron-shod wheels which rattled on the cobblestones and shell holes roughly filled; the iron pipes rolled from side to side with us holding our feet up to stop them being pinched; there was such a racket you couldn't hear a thing. We had nearly reached a part of the road where a slight rise gave plenty of cover for the rest of our journey when one of the leading mules suddenly dropped forward to the ground, and we then heard a machine gun and shots coming over, and everybody was off the wagon, helping the two drivers to sort the other three mules out. There was not much of a tangle as the driver on the box had put the brake on, and the machine-gun fire died down after a few shots wide of us. The dead mule was untackled and we heaved it to the roadside and started slowly on, and got under cover without further trouble. After dumping our load in the trench we returned to camp and reported our casualty. The only comment on the episode was made by Cpl W.Barratt of the drivers' section: "Well, we ain't going to send Cutter Moreton to fetch it in". Cutter Moreton was the horse knacker in Nuneaton.'

On another occasion, 'One evening I was left behind to wait for a tin of red paint needed for the camouflaging of the cover to the water tank, which had been excavated in the village [Messines] amongst the ruins. The cover was a comparatively light framework of scantling covered with canvas, on which Sapper Patfield displayed his artistic talent. At the entrance to the village was a large crater, which had been partially sandbagged up to make the road good. I was opposite this hole, hugging the paint keg, when I had the split-second warning of a shell getting tired, and flopped into the ditch. The crater had deepened the ditch to about twenty feet, and I rolled down the retaining wall of sandbags, and the paint keg following me without the lid on and shedding paint as it came, I got my share of paint when it caught up with me at the bottom. It was difficult to scramble out, but fortunately, owing to the dry weather, there was no water in this hole, so I rescued what little drop remained of the paint, and went to the tank. Patfield told me the camouflage was supposed to be on the cover, not on me, so I told him where to find the rest of it and what to do with it when he found it. After scraping me down, and daubing the scrapings onto the cover, Cpl Toogood, who was in charge, called it a day and we all left for camp.'

'The road we were on went through Wulverghem and on to Neuve Eglise. Near Wulverghem a large ammunition dump was established, called Souvenir dump, screened by a small clump of trees. As we approached this place, Jerry put a few shells into the dump and set fire to it, so we sat in the ditch under a very high hedge and waited until quieter times, in this instance about four hours, until nearly 10 o'clock. It was a dark night and the fires and the exploding shells and small-arm ammunition were flying about everywhere, some of them dropping near and some dropping beyond us. This was the first time I had the opportunity of studying the glow worm, the particular spot where we lay was alive with them. When the excitement ended we went across country round the smouldering dump and back to Neuve Eglise, arriving there a long time after lights out. As far as we knew there were no casualties amongst the people in charge, they got out into cover when the first shell came over. Wheway, the "Quarter bloke", fitted me out with a second-hand tunic, one of a corporal's cast offs with the stripes removed, the cloth which the stripes had covered was still like new, but the rest of the garment was faded by use and weather'. My father needed a new box respirator too, because, having obeyed the order to wear the respirator case open at all times in the front area, his was full of red paint.

Another ditch figures in another story. 'From the old British front line in the valley below the old German positions on the ridge above, the road from Wulverghem went obliquely uphill to the right to about half way to Messines, and then turned to the left and on up the slope to the village. At the outside of the turn halfway up the slope stood a large four-wheeled farm cart between four upright posts which had at one time supported a thatched roof over it. From a distance, the wagon looked to be intact, and in good working order, but closer inspection revealed that every part was so chipped or perforated by bullets and shell splinters, and was bored through and through by wood worms as thick as pencils, that it was amazing the vehicle was able to stand up so long; it was like a colander, and was certainly not the sort of cover to shelter under when caught out between the lines in any action. It had stood here since the beginning of the war, and looked likely to stand for some time to come, unless it stopped one of the "whizz-bangs" that Jerry was beginning to send us whenever their observation spotted any movement on the slope.'

'The end of this relic came on a warm sunny afternoon, about a fortnight after the capture of Messines, and Cpl Toogood and myself were at the turn of the road opposite the wagon when it had a direct hit by a 5.9 howitzer shell. There was a narrow drainage ditch cut on the side we were walking, and we dived for this scanty cover at the last-second warning swish of the shell. We had a sixth sense for German shells: a long whistle meant it would miss, but a short whistle meant it was close. I lay wedged face upwards in this ditch; there was a clatter when the shell burst and I watched the large elm hub from one of the rear wheels, with splintered spokes, cartwheeling up into the clear blue afternoon sky, apparently over the spot where I was lying. I did not observe its descent, as I shut my eyes and waited for the tremendous thump as it landed. It missed both of us by a few yards and when we looked out the wagon was scattered all over the place. A few more shells came over, so we retired down hill to the shelter of the old front line trench, which was now occupied by a battery of 18 pounder field guns. We were lucky we had done so, because we had scarcely reached the trench when a De Haviland scouting plane of the Royal Flying Corps came low over us, with two planes of Baron Richthofen's Red Circus squadron in pursuit, firing their machine guns. The gunners of the battery opened up with German Mauser rifles and ammunition they had picked up, and we all had a crowded half hour, exchanging shots with the aeroplanes and dodging round the traverses when Jerry got too close to us. There were no casualties on our side and no apparent damage to the German planes; the R.F.C. plane got safely away and Jerry went back over the ridge.

About a week later, on another hot and cloudless day, as my father recalls, Corporal Toogood, Sapper 'Manny' Taylor and he were taking a cast iron waterpipe up the slope to Messines. 'I was carrying the front end, walking with Toogood, Manny was following under the other end. Manny heard something heavy about to settle and threw the pipe off his shoulder and ran for it. When his end hit the ground my end bounced up and nearly stunned me and I stood dazed when the shell burst. There was a queer, loud, moaning sound, and I remember thinking it's the nose-cap, when something flashed over my foot, which proved to be the copper band from a 5.9 shell. I threw down the end of the pipe and joined the retreat, but first retrieved the band as a souvenir. It was twisted into a spiral shape, and red hot, and as I went down the slope I tossed it from one hand to the other. The foot it went over happened to be in a hollow between two tussocks, which deflected it.

When the band was fashioned into a paper knife and engraved with the name Messines it proved to be one of the best shell-band paper knives made in the Company; later on it was changed into a shoe horn. I brought it home with me the first leave afterwards.' A standard length (15ft 6in) of four-inch screwed pipe weighed 132lbs: so it was heavy enough to give a good clout behind the ear.

Throughout the preparations for and the immediate aftermath of the battle of Messines the Company worked seven days a week. Their first respite was on 17 June; on the following day Charles Streather wrote home: 'We had the first day off we have had for six or eight weeks yesterday. I tried to get a motor bike to go and see Wilf [his brother, whose R.E. company was nearby] but I am not attached to H.Q. of the Coy so I could not go; the poor fellows who have nothing to do but loll about camp were in need of a change and rest so the C.S.M. and Fenn had to go.

27. Sapper Thomas Henry Wright.

They ran into Wilf as it happens. . . I would have gone down on a horse only I had to go to work again at 8 p.m. so it did not give me time to get back. I have just changed shifts again ; I work from 8 p.m. to 4 a.m. now, all in the dark except the walk there and back. I am lucky to have a fair pair of feet but it plays havoc with some of the men I can tell you; 5½ miles each way over rough ground, railways, shell holes, trenches, barbed wire, and dead men and horses is no joke. We got complimented again by the C.E. of the army we are in yesterday and a day or two ago by the C.E. of the Corps to which we are attached. No doubt you will be seeing F.C.C.'s name again before long, and when he comes back he will be decorated with all sorts of medals I suppose.' The compliment referred to is recorded in the war diary of the Chief Engineer of II Anzac Corps, Brigadier-General A.E.Panet: 'during operations in connection with the capture of Messines Ridge', all the work carried out by the 216th A.T. Company, R.E. 'reached a very high standard of efficiency. Progress in each case was exceptionally good, although work had to be carried out under heavy shell fire for prolonged periods'.[7] Driver Frank Hextall's report on their activities is, as usual, very brief: 'In the stunt at Messines. Rather hot.' One of the few recorded memories of Sapper Thomas Wright of Nuneaton is of the time his party sheltered from machine-gun fire behind a pile of cast-iron water pipes: 'noisy but effective shelter', he said.

Despite the stunning success of Messines, Sergeant Streather was not too happy about the course of the war in general: 'I am afraid things do not look very hopeful for us according to the papers, as far as I can see Russia might just as well be counted neutral and the French I fear are not up to par. The only thing we have to hope for is a revolution in Germany I think.' As for food shortages at home: 'I hear new potatoes are 1/- a pound. I reckon men selling at that price should be sent straight out into a front line trench and kept there on no pay for the duration of the war.' His idea of the war's likely duration is revealed by a comment on leave allocation: 'leave has started again: we are sending 10 men during the next fortnight. There are still about 40 men of the old company who have not been yet, then there are about 70 men of the various drafts to go, and we start to go round again; so if leave goes on with no more than the usual stoppages I should be home again for 10 days sometime during 1920.'

Sergeant Streather's assumption that medals for gallantry went only to officers proved to be mistaken. On 27 June he wrote to his parents: 'The Company was complimented for good work by the Duke of Connaught yesterday and you will be surprised to hear that Sgt Ashley and Sgt C.W.Streather were both awarded the Military Medal.' He says nothing about the actions which earned these awards and no details are recorded in local newspaper reports. The *Nuneaton Chronicle* of 6 July merely printed photographs of the two sergeants, noting that Streather was formerly a Nuneaton schoolteacher and Ashley was formerly a foreman for Mr Taberer, builder of Queen's Road, and that the medals were awarded for 'good work accomplished in the recent push'. The awards were made on 24 June; perhaps the presentation was made by Field Marshal the Duke of Connaught, uncle of the King and Inspector-General of the Armed Forces, who, as it happens, had begun his military career nearly fifty years earlier as a Royal Engineer subaltern.

The rest of Charles Streather's letter is devoted to the usual topics of weather and food: 'The weather has been very changeable during the last few days: several nights were quite cold and we have been wet through half a dozen times. One night we went up and the trenches were all dust at 8 p.m. When we came down in the morning they were ankle deep in mud and water. I thought I had seen some mud before but I came to the conclusion that I had not seen real mud till then. I fell into about 50 different shell holes and by the time I landed in camp looked a picture I can tell you. The night was so black you could not see a hand in front of you; the only way of finding holes and trenches was to tumble in and then tell the next man not to fall on top of you. . . . I was pleased to get the socks and the cakes and lemonade. We never get cake and not a lot of bread now. We get plenty to eat but we are getting a lot of biscuit just at present.'

Capt Cook formally handed over command of 216th Company to Capt MacDougall on 2 July, but, for whatever reasons, it seems that he had spent little time with the Company for the previous six months. Promoted Major, he took command of the 209th Field Company, R.E. on 8 July, and commanded it until the end of the war, by which time he had earned the M.C., D.S.O., and Croix de Guerre. After his departure there was a far more generous grant of leave to other ranks in the Nuneaton Company, which, rightly or wrongly, the men believed was a matter of cause and effect. Charles Streather wrote on 19 July: 'we have sent a lot of men on leave. You see what the departure of F.C.C. does in one direction any way. We have 28 men away now and shall have far more by the end of next week.' On 25 July: 'I suppose that you have heard that a lot of the Coy are on leave. We are getting a splendid allotment at present but you must not be looking for me again just yet you know. All the men going now have been in the country more than twelve months without one and it is only eight months since I had mine.'

In fact it was not long before some members of the Company were enjoying a second spell of leave in their eighteen months abroad. Streather himself was on leave in August; my father probably went about the same time, though he says virtually nothing of the leave during which he displayed his new shell-band paper knife. Pioneer Daulman says more: 'I came home with Harry Trevis who had been running a crown and anchor board and had made some money. When we got to Victoria, I said, "Let's get the Underground". His reply was, "We don't want no Underground. TAXI!" And we crossed to Euston in style. We got out in Nuneaton and he said, "You know where I live, my lad. If you run short of money come and see me."' Trevis was nicknamed 'The Colonel', perhaps because his air of authority could, as we have seen, even abash the Company-Sergeant-Major on occasions. A fragment of his crown and anchor patter is recorded by my father: 'You all know me, gentlemen. Been connected with the turf ever since I joined up. I have straddled some of the finest mules that ever looked through a bridle. Put your money on. You come in rags and go away in motor cars. Nobody else? All done? Right. Shake em up and tip em out. Oh, hard luck.'[8]

When they were working, the company continued to be split up on various sites in the II Anzac Corps area. Some men were constructing a new concrete reservoir at Kemmel, excavating catchwater ditches for it, and fencing in the catchment area.

Others were taking the Messines pipe line further forward, erecting a pumphouse, and setting up water supply points for man and beast. Others, a little further south, were laying water pipes to Hill 63, between Kemmel and Armentières. This was where Pioneer Daulman found himself when he returned from leave: at Ploegsteert, in some natural caves, extended by Australian tunnellers into vast dug-outs capable of accommodating two battalions and called the 'Catacombs'. He recalls: 'A cave roof had been penetrated by a large shell which had not exploded. Someone had set it up on its base. It was either a British 4.5 or a German 4.9. I did not examine it closely. We worked here on a water supply to Hill 63, where we put an elevated tank over the caves. The water supply was interconnected, one branch coming from the River Lys and the second branch from a reservoir on the back side of Kemmel, so that a complete break in the water supply was made less likely.'

In their various jobs the Company was assisted by very large working parties of Australian and New Zealand infantrymen and was hampered by frequent German shell fire. Sapper Sol Walker was wounded on 5 July. On 11 July a shell wrecked one of the Company's lorries, killing the Army Services Corps driver, together with three members of the working party, and wounding several more. Sergeant Streather, who was in command of the working party, described it to his parents on 19 July as 'a nasty knock', but immediately added that they had finished that job. He wrote: 'I have lost my sore feet now that I don't have so much marching every day. Old Fritz blew a lot of our work down and I have had to go and put that up again but I have finished up there now and handed over to a party to keep it in repair, so if it happens again I shall not have the job to do it. I have started a new job today . . . on "Home Service" about eight miles behind the line so I am nothing to do with the war for a time.' He does not say what the job is. Possibly he was supervising the dismantling of H.Q. huts at Bailleul, as this is the most rearward job among those listed in Captain MacDougall's war diary at this time. Though Bailleul was a long way from the excitements of Messines it was, of course, shelled and bombed. Sergeant Streather, who in the space of eighteen months had learned to respect the French, reflects: 'Jerry is just beginning to let some of the men round the bases and soft jobs behind the line know that they are at war. They make a fine fuss over the raids on London. I wonder what they would do if they were like some of the French and Belgians. Plenty of the towns out here are shelled regularly and yet the people stick it and say nothing, and the poorer people had to be turned out of their homes only a few weeks ago quite near the line in lots of places a couple of miles in front of our heavy guns and not more than a mile from the German trenches. Plenty of them have had the roofs knocked off and the houses practically destroyed and then they stick it in the cellars. They get a living by selling coffee and bread and butter and eggs to the troops. Of course thousands have been killed one time and another. Those that are left never grumble; they sometimes say "no bon the war", but that is about all; they all look pretty miserable but quite resigned to fate whatever it may be.'

Meanwhile preparations continued for the Big Push for which Messines had been only a preliminary nudge. On 19 June, in London, Field Marshal Haig 'spoke not only of capturing Ostend and Zeebrugge, but of crossing the Scheldt, persuading the Dutch to abandon their neutrality, and, in co-operation with the

Dutch army, driving the Germans out of Belgium'.[9] Haig's most highly-placed supporter, King George V, was in France in early July, when Sergeant Streather caught sight of him and thought he 'did not seem any too comfortable in a "tin hat": he was quite close up and had a good look round our part of the front'. My father also saw the King. The circumstances were that, a few days after his escapade of being drunk, believed gassed, my father 'came back about 4 a.m. with the working party and, feeling queer with stomach trouble, I went with the sick parade to see the doctor who had diagnosed the previous condition of Clarkson and myself. This time I received a more sympathetic reception and was told I had a dose of "trench fever" and he was sending me to the Casualty Clearing Station at Bailleul for a week or two. The rest of our chaps had been given a few days of light duty, and when they went back with the orderly corporal were unanimous that I was a "jammy bugger". This hospital was staffed by Australians and the place was comfortable and the cooking was excellent; the only snag was that the medical orderly in the hut where I was was very concerned about the state of our bowels, and was continually hovering around with castor oil, telling us that it was "the best stuff to get folks back on their feet". No one in the ward believed him, so he was reduced to the experiment of mixing his oil with rum. Several of the more active, up and about patients, myself included, fell for this, and took what we thought was a very generous tot of rum, realising too late we had been dosed. During our stay here we had a few night visits by German aeroplanes, Gothas, who came over bombing the town and adjacent military places. In the ward there was a chap with shell shock, and when the bombing started we had to get him out of bed and put him underneath it, and put his tin hat on him, before he would calm down. One day everything in the ward was tidied up, and card parties were interrupted, and we were all put to bed, washed and brushed, to receive a visit by King George, of whom we caught an occasional glimpse, between the accompanying generals and staff. We were not impressed and I don't think King George was either.'

Trench fever, also called P.U.O. (pyrexia of unknown origin), was a disease carried by lice, though this fact was not known in 1917, in which year it accounted for 15% of all cases of sickness in the British Army. It was never fatal, but treatment required a few weeks off duty; no cure was found until 1918. R.H. Mottram writes of trench-fever cases: 'Here, on stretchers or in blankets on the grass, lay some eighty of the battalion, all with the new disease called everything from "para-typhoid" to "cold feet"; known not by its symptoms but by its causes — standing up to the waist in filthy water without food or sleep, or "resting" in cattle trucks or barns, still wet'.[10]

On 15 July the British began a heavy bombardment which was intensified a week later along the entire Flanders front. Over four million shells, weighing altogether a hundred thousand tons were hurled into waterlogged ground. The main infantry attack was launched on 31 July by Gough's Fifth Army north-east and east of Ypres, with Plumer's Second Army in support on the right flank. Little headway was made against German defences; heavy rain set in that evening and continued for three days and nights almost without a break; after four days the leading divisions of the main assault had suffered 31,000 casualties and were less than half way to their first day's objectives. The ground to be crossed was a two-mile-wide swamp of shell holes full of semi-liquid, clayey mud; horses and mules sank to the belly and wounded men drowned; it was a nightmare to bring up artillery, ammunition, and supplies, and to evacuate the wounded.

In the middle of August the rain stopped long enough to allow two more largely unsuccessful and costly attacks, but by the third week of August the total exhaustion of his troops was such that Gough 'informed the Commander-in-Chief that tactical success was not possible, or would be too costly, under such conditions, and advised that the attack should now be abandoned'.[11] Haig, though, needed to maintain an offensive in order to continue to distract German attention from the French armies among which there had been widespread mutinies that summer; he also believed that the Germans' morale was low and that one more good push would start them sliding towards collapse. He now handed responsibility for the main attack over to the Second Army, so there was a pause in the action while Plumer made his preparations.

Chapter Ten: Kemmel to Zillebeke Lake, September 1917 to January 1918

While the battle which later would be called Passchendaele was getting under way the 216th Company continued making reservoirs at Kemmel and Lindenhoek — forming dams, making sluice gates, building pump houses, fencing catchment areas, washing sand for filters, etcetera — and laying pipes for the forward water supply, installing tanks and water points for men and transport. Infantry working parties on these tasks were quite large: several times in August they numbered over three hundred men. Captain MacDougall's diary records that the company's work this month was much hampered by shell fire and 'inclement weather'. On 1 September the company left II Anzac and rejoined IX Corps, whereupon they moved back to a tented camp on Kemmel hill. My father recalls that he 'made a sleeping place in a long green canvas-covered meat safe'. From it he enjoyed a view over Ypres and the back areas and could trace the front line by puffs of bursting shrapnel picking out the trenches. Perhaps 'meat safe' was the recognised name for a kind of bivouac: an undated list of one day's duties for Sergeant Streather's section includes the note that Corporal Dunton and Sapper Pearce were responsible for 'meat safes'.

The company now handed over upkeep of the Hill 63 and Messines pipe lines to the 554th (Dundee) Army Troops Company. During the handover some of the Nuneaton men, writes Arthur Daulman, 'went to the Dundee Company for three days to help them out. We finished in one day and the captain said he had ordered three days' rations, so the next two days' were ours. I went shopping at Steenwerck, not far from Armentières, and bought a silk scarf for my lady love.' For their part the 216th Company now took over from the 4th (Royal Monmouth) Siege Company the upkeep and extension of a pipe line from Dickebusch Lake, via Brasserie Corner, Dead Dog Farm, and Moated Grange up to Damm Strasse. At the same time they began to build a new reservoir, sluice gate, and pump house, and lay a new pipe line at Kim Road, close to Kemmel, with branches to Devon Camp and the R.E. park at Siege Farm; also they began to build a hutted camp at Kemmel. Later that month they took charge of the Bomb Shop in Bailleul: on 24 September L/Cpl Haigh and four sappers were detached there to supervise French civilians in a workshop making hand grenades. Also two mechanics were detached to Kemmel saw mills.

Most action occurred in the extension of the Damm Strasse pipe line. The Damm Strasse itself had once been an ornamental drive leading to the White Chateau, once the summer palace of the Belgian King, on the ridge north of Wytschaete. Now the chateau was a heap of pink and white rubble and the drive was a waterlogged, cratered depression, littered with pill boxes and German corpses. The corpses provided good pickings for souvenir traders, but the captured pill boxes were of problematical value; their entrances faced the present German positions; also, as my father writes, 'the Germans were well aware of the exact position of each, so kept them under accurate fire'. His rough notes on the Damm Strasse read: 'Pack mule bogged down, helped drivers to get it out.

Artillery panniers canvas three 18-pounder shells a side. Jerry had a high velocity gun shelling this area. Took cover in German "pill box" and found some cocoa, so brewed up. Tables were Portland cement barrels dated 1915. Battery Sergt on corduroy shot a runaway horse while getting a gun in position at side of track.' (One wonders how German imports of Portland cement evaded the British blockade.)

On 18 September the Damm Strasse pipe line was extended over the Ypres-Comines canal, to be taken, by way of Spoil Bank, to Battle Wood, where a tank was installed; water was supplied from the pump house at Dickebusch. Captain MacDougall's war diary records the ongoing work and the continual repair of shell damage to existing works. On 18 September he reports that Sappers Bartley, Woodfield, Daintry, and Duley, and Pioneer Davies were wounded in action. Bartley died of his wounds on the following day.

Woodfield, a plumber from Stockingford who was to be killed later, believed in the cause for which he was fighting. Two weeks before he was wounded he wrote a very long reply in the *Nuneaton Observer* to a letter by an anonymous 'Progressive Worker', a coal-miner and union officer, justifying strikes to support claims for better working conditions and higher pay. Woodfield gently protests that 'Progressive Worker' nowhere mentions the fighting men, 'the very men upon whom England places her reputation and honour', though they are 'the very men upon whom you will have to rely when peace comes again'. He concludes: 'I can assure you that as surely as they are fighting for the cause of humanity, home and

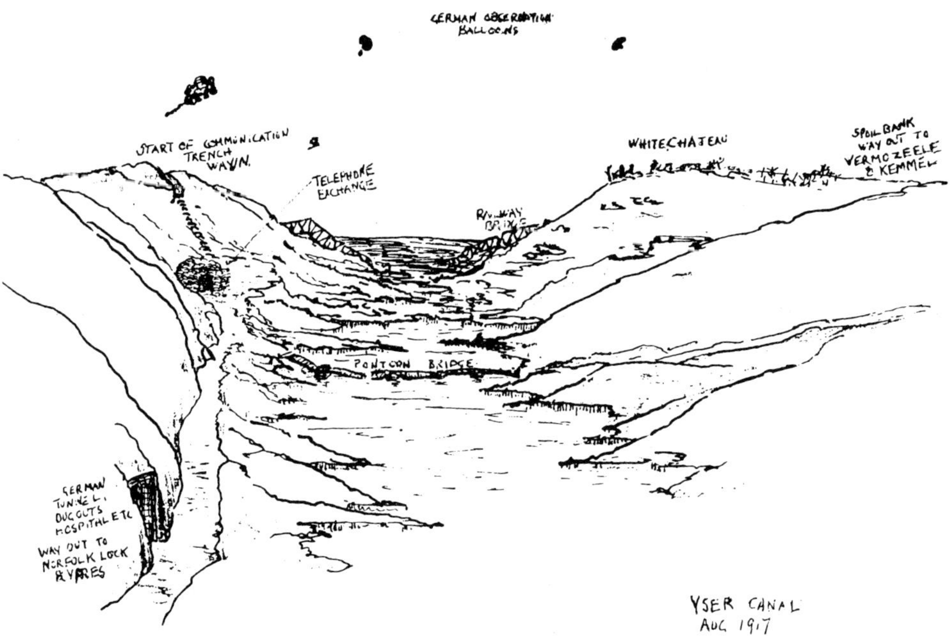

28. Arthur Sambrook's drawing of the Yser Canal in August 1917: 216 Company laid water pipes to White Chateau (top right) and across the canal.

beauty, so surely will they return to fight and achieve what is right and fair. . . . We are fighting for our homes and for the emancipation of civilisation. We are not grousing. We are out to see it through, and thousands of our wives and children are bearing their share of it too. They do not get a rise each time you people get a 25 per cent advance on the present rate of wages, but still they stick it and stand it nobly. . . . The revolution of mankind is in sight and will prove victorious. I think you have all done fairly, and have not the slightest cause for dissatisfaction. You have not been robbed of the society of your dear ones and the comfort of your homes, and I think your claims have been met fairly up to date, so I would beg of you to give the soldiers' wives and children a chance, who do not get an allowance of coal monthly, and no percentage on their present allowance on the occasion of the necessities of life being raised in price, and who in spite of all do not grouse'.[1] Sapper Woodfield was married, with two small children; his trust in the ultimate workers' revolution and in the humanity, home, and beauty that were so little in evidence in the Ypres salient is impressive.

My father's thoughts of home were far less eloquent, but he does speak of being caught in a barrage coming back one day from Spoil Bank, when 'we sat in a shell hole near the crossroads on our way back to Kemmel; we ate bully and I showed them a photo of Nuneaton Market Place to cheer them up.' On the occasion when Sapper Bartley was fatally wounded, writes my father, 'Clarkson left his gas mask on the job; I went back with him to recover it and lost the heel of my boot by a shell splinter'. Someone else going back and forth between Kemmel Hill and Spoil Bank at this time was Edmund Blunden. He writes: 'A view of the then notorious Spoil Bank under these conditions is in my mind's eye — a hump of slimy soil, with low lurching frames of dug-out entrances seen in some too gaudy glare; a swilling pool of dirty water beside it. . .; tree-spikes, shells of waggons, bony spokes forking upwards; lightnings east and west of it; dingy splashes of searchlights in the clouds above; drivers on their seats, looking straight onwards; gunners with electric torches finding their way; infantry silhouettes and shadows bowed and laden, and the plank road, tilted, breached, blocked, upheaved, still stretching ahead. The plank road was at once the salvation and the slaughter-house of the forward area in this battle. To leave it was to plunge into a swamp, to remain on it was to pass through accurate and ruthless shell-fire.'[2]

Frank Hextall, perhaps one of those drivers looking straight ahead, described their work at Spoil Bank and Battle Wood in his usual laconic style as 'a very hot shop'. My father recalled the constant bombardment, so that they were endlessly replacing the 4" cast-iron pipes which took water right up to the support trenches. In the dark they had to feel their way along for leaks and replace broken pipes from piles dumped well up front. The hottest times in Hextall's 'hot shop' arose from German retaliation to the enormous barrages that accompanied Plumer's three successful 'bite and hold' attacks on 20 and 26 September and 4 October which captured most of the ridge due east of Ypres (notable victories which were soon eclipsed in public memory and imagination by the subsequent failure to make a decisive advance). As the rainy October dragged on Field-Marshal Haig accepted that a break-through was unlikely but he wanted to continue a battle of attrition in the belief that the Germans were suffering more casualties than his own men. The

German common soldier had as little relish for fighting in these conditions as his attacker and his morale was, if anything, lower, but the German army remained unbroken. Eventually, on 10 November, Haig called a halt to the battle which came to be known as Passchendaele from the name of the last-stormed heap of rubble, once a village. There had been nearly a quarter of a million casualties in his armies: more on the German side. The mud became a legend: bad as it was in August, it was indescribably worse in October and November.

Captain MacDougall's official war diary records 4 October as 'Zero Day' (for an attack) and notes that after a dull morning the weather was stormy with heavy rains in the afternoon and evening, then, for the next ten days records similar weather: 'showery', 'very cold and stormy later', 'stormy at times', 'heavy storms at night', 'boisterous, heavy showers'. The activities of the Company on a typical day, 1 October, were as follows: on the Kim Road pipe line, 14 sappers and a Working Party of 2 officers and 75 other ranks of the 7th Battalion East Lancs Regiment excavating site of tanks, excavating and filling in trench for and laying pipes for horse and ablution service; at work on the new camp, 37 sappers; at the Bailleul Bomb Shop and Kemmel Sawmill, 6 mechanics and 2 mechanics respectively engaged in workshops; on the Berthen pipe line, 2 mechanics superintending the laying of water mains; on the Moated Grange-Damm Strasse pipe line, 6 sappers making alterations and additions to water points, erecting water troughs for horses, and building a dam, also 13 sappers patrolling and repairing bursts. MacDougall also reported air activity around Kemmel during the previous night, with six bombs dropped near Kemmel dam. (The fifty or so members of the company not in this list would presumably include headquarters staff and drivers, amongst others.)

Arthur Daulman was with the party at Kemmel, erecting huts for what would be called Gibraltar Camp, and could hardly believe his good luck when they were allowed to move into 'the beautiful camp' themselves. He writes: 'Whilst building we lived under canvas and never thought we would be fortunate enough to use the camp. We were the first in however. We laid down a "corduroy" road of timber, a semi-circular road right round the inside of the perimeter. There were four huts, one for each of the sections of thirty men, another for the drivers, another for the Officers' Mess, and one for the kitchen. They were Nissen huts of corrugated iron. There was a properly appointed kitchen and dining room with tables, benches, and plenty of water. Each officer had his own hut, called an Armstrong, consisting of canvas stretched over a wooden framework, with a stove inside. Incidentally, the Signals had a refuge hut for their linesmen which we called a "baby elephant". Made of corrugated iron to hold five, it was so low that it was impossible to stand. We would use it until turned out by the signalmen.' The invention of Captain Nissen, R.E., was warm and weatherproof, but the baby elephant, being designed for forward areas, was stronger and therefore a more popular refuge.[3] British attacks on the ridge never overran German gun positions, so the British back areas continued to be regularly shelled.

Charles Streather's letters in October express continuing contentment with camp, continuing discontent with the weather, and growing unease about the Big Push. 'We have got quite comfortably settled in our new camp now, though we are still working on it. We just moved in time for we have had several wet days this week and it has been quite cold today. It is to be hoped that winter does not set in right away as it will hamper operations so much and we seem to be giving him some hard knocks just now' (6 October).

'Our camp is at least six miles from the line. We have a hut for the N.C.O.s mess and we Sgts have a hut to ourselves for a billet. . . we are right away from any civilians; we never leave our camp from one week's end to another except to go to work. We have never been quite so much on our own since we came out and the time seems to hang more than ever it did. We are kept pretty busy too; we do an extra hour's work every night after dinner now and we never get a full Sunday off. The fighting gets worse every day I think, but I believe it gets more one-sided and I don't see how ever Fritzy can stand the hammering much longer. We don't seem to make a lot of progress on the map but he must have terrible casualties from our bombardments and the air at times is thick with planes which swoop down with bombs and machine guns and never give him a moment's rest. I can tell you I am mightily pleased I am this side the line. The weather this week has been atrocious: winter seemed to set in in five minutes; it has been very cold all the week and wet every day; the trenches are an indescribable sea of mud and iron from shells and debris of fortifications. It is quite common to see men in shell holes well over their knees in water and at least a foot of mud; to walk a mile over the "crater field" is like a day's march on a road, and this is after one week's rain which has been preceded by a month's drought' (14 October).

'The mud defies description. One would never know that it was dry land: it looks far more like the sea in many places where the traffic is heavy. . . . Air raids are a regular occurrence here now. Our planes are constantly bombing; we often see them, especially at night. Air fighting increases in violence every fine day we get. I saw over fifty planes fighting a day or two ago. We have quite settled down in our new camp and shall be comfortable here even if we get a winter like we had last year. I hope we are lucky enough to keep it till winter is over. I thought this time last year that we should not be fighting through another winter but it looks very much as we have a long way to go yet' (23 October).

At the beginning of November Sergeant Streather was lucky enough to be sent, along with Captain MacDougall, on a course at the Aire Bridging School. This Royal Engineer training centre operated in the winters of 1916-17 and 1917-18 especially to give instruction in the erection of heavy steel bridges: by early 1918 30% of the officers and men in all the Army Troops R.E. companies on the Western Front had been trained there.[4] Streather wrote home from the Aire School on 1 November: 'I have just arrived at a pleasant little French town far away from the line where the roar of cannon and chatter of rifles and machine guns seem to be a trouble of another world. The only thing to remind us of the war is the distant row of specks in the sky: our observation balloons. I shall be here for 14 days, so that will be a good holiday; my billet is on a big barge on the river which is much bigger than the canal at home.' The mud at the front still haunts him: 'We have been rather far forward for the past few weeks: not a nice job at all, but thank goodness it is finished now. The mud is absolutely awful. We were wearing thigh boots, but several times during heavy shelling we were in water and mud up to the waist. However we pulled through with very few casualties and none among our own men.'

Back with the Company, writing on 16 November: 'I had a good change down on the barge: it is less disturbed by the war than any place I have been at. It is not a large town, but there are some fine buildings. On the Sunday afternoon I had a look round the Cathedral; some of the work is really beautiful. We had a gentle reminder of the fact that we were at war the second day I was there: Fritz sent two souvenirs close to where we were at work. I can tell you it was some surprise considering we were about twenty kilos from the line. . . My word the mud out here gets worse: it absolutely defies description. The roads are getting a lot better, but on the works one has to be careful or one would get shoulder deep in liquid mud. We do not seem to make much progress do we? I thought this time last year that we should have done with by now, but I am afraid we still have a long way to go.'

Most of the 216th Company were still engaged on water-supply works: the patrols and repairs continued; Driver Eddie Parratt and Pioneer William Benson were wounded; Captain MacDougall reported (9 October) that, without his knowledge, a branch pipe had been put into the Moated Grange-Damm Strasse pipe line. On 20 October work was begun on a new pipe line from Zillebeke Lake south-eastwards to Spoil Bank, providing this sector of the front with a supply additional to that from Dickebusch Lake, for as battle for Passchendaele was pushed doggedly northwards the Company's work moved with it. However, it was now tacitly recognized by higher command that the forward water supply would not be going very much further forward, because on 25 October the Company was ordered to bury existing pipes deeper as a protection against frost: the crown of the pipe 2ft 6in from the surface of the ground. This work was done by very large working parties in a ratio of one sapper to ten or more infantrymen. Sappers were also detached to work on various hutted camps, including one named after Brigadier-General Panet, Chief Engineer of II Anzac Corps, and, of course, their own 'beautiful' Gibraltar Camp.

Working parties of infantry were large, but not necessarily efficient: their disadvantages were eloquently set forth about this time by Brigadier-General C.H.Foott, Chief Engineer, Australian Corps: 'Daily working parties are very unsatisfactory. The men are changed daily and the Officers and men do not take much interest in their work. They necessarily come on the job without knowing anything about what they are required to do. This has to be explained to them and just as they are becoming useful their shift is up. They seldom, if ever, see a job completed. There is always great difficulty in getting working parties out on time, up to strength and at the place required and provided with the necessary tools and materials. This is due to the fact that before the transport, materials, the supervision and the labour can be brought together at the required place, at the required time, arrangements have to be made with several organisations. The work is naturally very distasteful to the men as it must be carried out under adverse circumstances of weather and hostile fire. While the Sappers are responsible for the quality of the work performed the Infantry Officers in charge of the working party must be responsible for the quantity of work performed, and experience shows that the young Infantry Officers, under the circumstances denoted above, seldom produce the necessary results as regards the quantity of work completed. In fact there may be many reasons why the Officers may be inclined to sympathise with the men. It is safe to say that under these conditions the average man does not do 25% of the work he might fairly be expected to accomplish. His fighting efficiency is also considerably reduced for the work is very tiring.'[5] The Commander, Royal Engineers, 3rd Australian Division, agreed that 'the attaching of Infantry to R.E. is a makeshift that should not be necessary after so many years of a world war'.[6]

In mid November the 216th took over the upkeep of another pipe line from Zillebeke Lake, north-east by way of Valley Cottages, Maple Copse, and Zouave Wood, to Hooge on the Menin Road, though the Company soon received instructions not to try and maintain the extension to Hooge in view of appalling mud and excessive damage by shelling. This was a notoriously bombarded place: the Australian war historian writes: 'At Hooge, where the front had lain for some years near the point at which the Menin road began gently to mount to the main ridge, all marks on the original surface were completely erased. Through that village even the road was untraceable, and the village site was only marked by a cluster of mine-craters'.[7]

After Passchendaele the Fifth Army was sent south to the Somme, the Second Army settled down to hold the now-elongated salient, and the 216th Company continued its usual jobs. On 1 December, for instance, when their effective strength was 3 officers and 137 other ranks, and the weather was dull, with rain at intervals and a high NW wind, their tasks were as follows. Kim Road pipe line: 2 men repairing leaks etc. Dickebusch Lake-Damm Strasse-Battle Wood pipe line: 10 men on picquet at, patrolling and repairing bursts etc; 4 men making alterations etc for laying 4" and 2" water mains from Transport Farm to Spoil Bank Tunnel; 22 men digging in pipe line as protection against frost. Zillebcke-Spoil Bank pipe line: 6 men digging trenches etc; 5 men digging and relaying 4" pipe etc from No 2 Pump House Zillebeke Lake to Transport Farm; 7 men on picquet at, patrolling and repairing bursts. In Gibraltar Camp: 5 men engaged on works for Dickebusch Lake-Damm Strasse-Battle Wood pipe line; 2 men re- erecting huts. Bailleul Bomb Shop: 7 men engaged in workshops. Panet Camp: 2 men engaged in saw mills; 4 men engaged on other works. Zevecoten R.E.Park: 1 clerk engaged in office. Siege Park, Kim Road: 1 man superintending erection of huts. IX Corps Area: 2 surveyors surveying and preparing plans of hutted camps etc. Hallebaste Corner: 4 men engaged on works. Working parties of 158 other ranks from the 52nd and 136th Labour Companies (with one officer) assisted in the various diggings. This was a new source of unskilled help for the Nuneaton men. From their arrival in France their working parties had consisted of either British or Anzac infantrymen or German prisoners of war; but after 4 November some, and after 25 November all, their working parties were drawn from the British Labour Corps. This reflected a general changeover in British practice on the Western Front in the second half of 1917, as arguments like those of Brigadier-General Foott, above, were accepted and as the supply of non-combatant labour grew.

For smaller jobs the 216th Company, my father recalls, 'was split up into groups to keep the various pipe lines and tanks we had installed in working order. These systems of water points were scattered about in the forward areas east of Ypres. I was included in a party of six sappers and two N.C.O.s stationed at the side of Zillebeke Lake. The artillery of both sides had considerably altered the contours of the lake from the contours shown on the map, and it was now a morass and lake combined, irrigating the surrounding country by haphazard shell craters. We walked from Hallebaste to Zillebeke Lake via Vermozeele, past "Swan and Edgar", a large isolated deserted house.'

This little party had to forgo the luxury of Gibraltar Camp, so lovingly described by Arthur Daulman; they usually had to work in mud and rain, wet to the skin and chilled to the bone; but they devised some home comforts near the shores of the morass, in the shape of a shelter made of elephant iron covered with sandbags. My father writes: 'The mound of sandbags piled over the corrugated iron and the thickness of the sides made us safe from a hit by whizz-bangs and would have softened a hit by 5.9 howitzers, and we were safe and comfortable tenants. There was sufficient sleeping room for all of us, four heads on one side and four heads on the other side, with the corresponding feet between the opposite heads. The only trouble here was occasioned by someone groping their way outside at intervals, suffering from the effects of too much vin the previous evening. The groper's knee on one's stomach, or a heavy hand pressing on one's face brought out a profane and uncomplimentary remark in reply to the offender's "Sorry, mate". At the end of the dug-out, opposite the door, we had made a stove from a five-gallon paint keg. The chimney was made from pork and beans tins, with the tops and bottoms removed, and the tins were pressed into each other, and made a very shaky and insecurely joined tube. This chimney went through the sandbags horizontally from the back of the stove, by this arrangement the weight of sandbags gave some stability to our rickety contrivance. There was no danger of fire as there was too much water percolating through the sandbags; any gaps in the tins just caused a faint haze of wood-smoke to mingle with the copious tobacco smoke when we were all "kipped in".'

'No night work was attempted on this job, as the ground was mainly knee-deep or waist-deep mud, well watered, or just deep slurry, almost impossible to get out of. As the tanks at the front end were filled every day, if the pipe was damaged by shells it could wait until daylight for repairs, and the valves at intervals along the pipe prevented much water going to waste. Our duty equipment was two men with a six-foot long duckboard apiece, two men with any pipes needed for replacements, and two men with "Stelson" grips and shovels, Corporal Stone in charge, who was too finicky about the muck and mire we worked in to be of any practical use. The odd man out was cook and general orderly, with 2nd Cpl John Brunt in charge of the billet.'

The latest battle having ended where it did, there were of necessity many artillery positions around Zillebeke Lake, even though the ground there was too sodden for stable or well-hidden gun-platforms, or safe dug-outs for the gunners. Artillery positions were always prime targets for return fire; these were particularly vulnerable. Edmund Blunden observed that the 'gunpits hardly looked strong enough to store potatoes. Not much better were the numerous shanties and holes, all in a row, along the Zillebeke Lake dam'.[8] The gun-platforms consisted of double-decked beech slabs, nailed together, on a foundation of fascines; plank roads were built from each platform to the main roadway so that ammunition could by brought up by pack mule; shells generally arrived so mud-plastered that each one had to be cleaned before loading.

Relations between the Zillebeke pipe-line patrol of the 216th Company and local artillerymen were not harmonious. My father writes: 'About a week after we got settled in, a smart new battery of 18 pounder field guns were to come round us. We laid down corduroy bases where the guns and limbers were positioned, and put bits of shelter up for them. This place was a very bad place for chaps just out of Larkhill camp. They were all "wet through and windy", "like a lot of duck's farts", as one sapper remarked. We did not welcome them very effusively, because they had put an end to our peaceful existence, but consoled ourselves that we were safer and drier than they were if they should be foolish enough to fire their guns to annoy Jerry and bring down his return fire. The Battery Sergeant-Major and Quartermaster Sergeant paid us an uninvited visit and demanded that we leave our dug-out, as they said we had no right in the midst of the battery and they wanted the place for their billet. They were the senior N.C.O.s and had got to be safe to carry out their duties. The reception these two big-headed youngsters got astonished them and after some remarks made to them they realized that their "say so" carried no weight further. Jack Brunt closed the discussion by telling them both to "Get out, and get your breeches wet, you windy pair of bastards". As they left the S.M. said, "You'll see, we'll have you out of here and you'll have to put a place up somewhere else". Brunt replied, "There seems to be plenty of room around, put one up for yourself".'

'Our rations and stores came up to us every three days by G.S. wagon, coming as near as possible, and we fetched them to the billet ourselves. Corporal Stone sent a report to Captain MacDougall about this incident and he came to see us the following morning. After hearing what had been said, he went across to the battery officers' shelter with Brunt, and, after some talk, learned that the officers knew nothing about the affair, so he took Brunt with him to interview the Battery S.M. and Quarter bloke. Both of these N.C.O.s had a very uncomfortable ten minutes listening to Mac's mildly expressed opinion of them, and he ended by telling them they would be wise to consider the matter closed. Jack Brunt told us all about it after Mac had left. "Mac took the shine out of them good and proper, you know what Mac's like, they wondered what they'd got hold of, and when Mac finished they nearly forgot to salute him." Soon after this the battery opened up and sent a few rounds over to Jerry, who in answer gave them a very hot return fire: whizz-bangs and a few 5.9 howitzers mixed with the lighter stuff. The ground was too soft and squashy for the shells to burst on impact; they penetrated deep into the earthy water, scattering large globs of slosh over men and guns when the explosion occurred, which made a mess of the shiny guns and new uniforms. We told them they did not know how lucky they were, being posted on such soft ground, but some of them seemed a bit doubtful about any benefits which came their way as a result.' Despite the alleged harmlessness of German shells the artillery Q.M.S. came to an arrangement whereby he exchanged rum for shelter in the baby elephant hut during bombardments.

December frosts made walking easier on the daily routine of pipe-line inspection; also, as the front was relatively quiet, there were not too many repair jobs. The 216th Company continued to maintain their water installations, patrolling and repairing bursts, digging in pipes more deeply against frost damage, making alterations and extensions in the forward areas and laying pipes to horse-watering, drinking, washing, and bathing points in the back areas, while their officers went and came. On 3 December Lieutenant Gordon was replaced by Lieutenant T. Walker, the two officers being cross-posted; on 7 December Captain MacDougall and Lieutenant Smith went to the Aire Bridging School to see the demonstration launch of a Hopkins Bridge, and on the following day Captain MacDougall went on to the R.E. School of Instruction at Blendeques, near St.Omer. The Company began to think of Christmas. Charles Streather wrote home on 8 December: 'Xmas is almost with us again and the war is still on, and I believe it looks worse than it did this time last year. I was at home then and quite thought it would be over by this time. We had winter with a vengeance for nearly a week: it was quite sharp; we had a little snow but it did not lie for long. . . We are working pretty hard just now; it has been three months since we had a half day off. . . We lost Mr Gordon this week; he has been with us just over eighteen months. The new man is quite a good sort but I would far prefer to carry on without the changes. We had Major Cook to see us the other day: he is quite well and I think would like to be back in the Company. . . The O.C. Capt MacDougall is away for a few days but he has shelled out well for Xmas: he has bought us some turkeys and left the money for vegetables, fruit, and beer, so we should have a good time unless Fritz has made other arrangements for the 25th.'

Most days in December were frosty, with a fierce east wind; snow fell on 16 December and on most days to the end of the year, including Christmas Day. On Christmas Eve Corporal Stone's little party was still on piquet at Hallebaste Corner, near the Royal Field Artillery battery, patrolling the water pipe-line to Zillebeke in a heavy fall of snow. They checked everything carefully that day because they had been told to get back to Gibraltar Camp at Kemmel early on Christmas morning to spend the day with the rest of the company. Even so, they found time not only to purloin more rum from the artillery Q.M.S. but to 'liberate' two dozen bottles of lager intended for the artillery officers. Their meal in the elephant-iron shelter that Christmas Eve, cooked over the stove made from an old paint tin, was rum and porridge. My father recalls that 'Cordingley, a Yorkshireman from Batley, didn't care for it, so he took the top of the stove off and tipped in the contents of his mess-tin, whereupon a jet of blackened porridge shot up to the roof, spread out and dripped down on the half dozen men fighting to get out of the narrow doorway.'

On Christmas morning they had to make their none-too-steady way some five miles back to Kemmel to join the rest of the Company. There were ditches on each side of the snow-covered road; when someone fell in a ditch the others went to help and fell in too. Passing Kemmel Chateau, they observed that the Australians billeted there had set fire to it during their Christmas festivities. Back at Gibraltar Camp they all had tinned turkey, which came out in large cubes, and tinned Christmas pudding. Sapper Wilkinson celebrated Christmas by performing a Zulu war dance on the table with an axe until someone cut the cords of the trestles and floored him, and Bill Higham fell forward on the hot stove and burnt his hair while nodding off. On his way to the latrine my father fell over; half an hour later some of his comrades-in-arms came to look for him, fell over a heap of snow, and found him underneath it. As Sapper Joe Smith wrote of their Christmas at Buxton two years earlier: 'the evening was spent as only Nuneaton men know how to spend it'.

Captain MacDougall was with the Company for Hogmanay and treated the men to whisky, which arrived in bulk from Scotland, from a distillery largely controlled by his family. Not all of it went to comfort the Royal Engineers, though. My father recalls: 'Any horse or mule down with colic during the winter months was doctored with a very select brand of Scotch whisky. The drivers had their own remedy for getting colicky animals back onto their feet. One cold day at Kemmel in the winter of 1917-18 a mule was lying down with colic. Mac went with Corporal Barratt to his hut for a bottle of whisky. Barratt came back with the bottle and told the drivers to "give the mule a kick in the slats and get it onto its feet, and they would empty the bottle between themselves". Unfortunately Mac had followed him and remarked "the whisky is for the mule Corporal".' Let us hope that the mule was appreciative: whisky retailed at 7s. 6d. a bottle, that is more than four days' pay of an ordinary driver.

A far more cultivated soldier than Billy Barratt was toasting the New Year. At midnight on 31 December Edmund Blunden stood with some acquaintances in camp 'finely overlooking the whole Ypres battlefield': they might well have been on Kemmel hill – not so far from Corporal Barratt's mules. Blunden writes: 'It was bitterly cold, and the deep snow all around lay frozen. We drank healths, and stared out across the snowy miles to the line of casual flares, still rising and floating and dropping ... bullying salutes of guns in brief bombardment, echoes racing into space, crackling of machine-guns small on the tingling air. . . . All agreed that 1917 had been a sad offender. All observed that 1918 did not look promising at its birth'.[9]

Certainly the omens were not good. The French army was still in the field but no one knew how fully its morale had recovered from the mutinies in the summer. The Italian army had been heavily defeated at the end of October, so that some French and British divisions had to be sent, with General Plumer, from the Western Front to hold the line in northern Italy and prevent further disaster. The Russian army had been effectively knocked out of the war in September; by December the Bolsheviks who had taken power were negotiating a separate peace with Germany. The Germans would now be able to bring as many as fifty divisions from the east to mount a great offensive long before the Americans could possibly arrive in sufficient numbers to tip the balance of Allied strength against them. British manpower on the Western Front was running short because Lloyd George was unwilling to give Haig more young men for more battles of attrition similar to Passchendaele; also Lloyd George had conceded to French demands that more of their front should be taken over by the British. Haig recognized that his business in the foreseeable future would have to be the unfamiliar one of defence.

On New Years Day it was business as usual for the 216th Company R.E. Captain MacDougall's diary records their effective strength at the usual figure of 3 officers and 138 other ranks. Of their number 10 men were on picquet at, patrolling, and repairing bursts on the Dickebusch Lake-Damm Strasse-Battle Wood pipe line; 6 were on the Kim Road pipe line, digging and laying a 2" extension for horse watering to Devon Camp; 15 were laying a 2" branch from the Ridge Wood 2" main to Ridge Wood Camp and fixing up washing water points. On the Zillebeke-Spoil Bank Pipe Line 7 men were on picquet, patrolling, and repairing bursts, and 16 were digging a trench for laying 4" and 2" mains from Transport Farm to Spoil Bank tunnel. 5 men were comfortable in Gibraltar Camp, engaged on work (perhaps plumbing or carpentry) for those pipe lines. 7 men were still in the Bailleul Bomb Shop; 6 bricklayers were building a dug-out for artillerymen; 4 men were engaged on 'works', perhaps of a similar nature, at Hallebaste Corner; others were scattered around camps and workshops in the rear area. The day was fair and freezing. For the rest of the month MacDougall's daily weather record rings the changes on cold, rain, sleet, frost, and snow.

The army in which the 216th Company served had now been temporarily renamed the Fourth Army, its commanding officer was currently General Sir Henry Rawlinson because Plumer was still in Italy. Such matters of high command were probably of little concern to the Nuneaton sappers but they were affected by some shuffling much lower in the pack when, on 12 January, the 216th was transferred, along with such other flotsam as half a Tramway Company and two Sections of Canadian tunnellers, from IX Corps to the Australian Corps. On that day the Bailleul Bomb Shop was handed over to the 567th (Devon) Army Troops Company, R.E., and Captain MacDougall made a reconnaissance of Hill 60 with a view to altering captured German pill boxes there. Hill 60 was the Nuneaton men's northernmost workplace on the Messines-Passchendaele ridge. They patrolled a newly-acquired pipe line there and continued to work as usual on all their other pipe lines and in workshops, camps, and battery positions; they also built a concrete observation post at Damm Strasse. All this was soon to change: on 23 January their works were handed over to the 236th Army Troops Company, R.E., and the 216th prepared to move. It was raining.

Chapter Eleven: Péronne to Ham, January to March 1918

On 24 January the Company left Kemmel and marched to Bailleul, where their train was waiting. After loading the animals, transport, and gear, the men settled into spacious 'Hommes 40' for the usual stop-and-start leisurely journey, which included an eight-hour delay in Abbeville and one of eighteen hours at a place which Driver Hextall recorded as 'Romans Copse'. Eventually they detrained at La Chapelette, because their ultimate destination, Péronne, was, writes Arthur Daulman, 'frequently strafed, so considered too risky for the railway engines and coaches'. At La Chapelette was the Divisional dump, including the R.E. stores dump for this part of the front, and a compound for Indian labourers. My father recalls 'an Indian labour battalion unloading wagons on the railway sidings and loading R.E. transport with their supplies. There was a sergeant R.E. in charge of them, who was tolerant towards his charge but not enthusiastic about their efficiency.' From La Chapelette the company marched to Péronne, where they arrived before noon on 27 January. It was two years to the day since they had left Buxton for France.

My father recalls: 'Péronne was a small pleasant town in Picardy, very compact inside the old walls and their several gateways, ruinous in places, but still an interesting feature of the town. It was undamaged, apart from a few demolitions which the Germans did when they withdrew from the town, chiefly to the walls and gate towers.' Edmund Blunden, who passed through the place at this time recalled 'old round towers standing firm; but perhaps the extraordinary German strongholds built in concrete under the station and elsewhere looked firmer. There were warning notice-boards outside these, and German bombs and boxes of explosive were still lying about in the entrances of some. Civilian life was as yet inactive in Péronne, nor could I find an estaminet open. This city had been in the same state, perhaps, after Waterloo'.[1] Driver Hextall briefly observed: 'Town all smashed up, but found a very decent billet'. The drivers' section, along with the company headquarters staff, occupied some outbuildings at the chateau, where they had ample stabling facilities for the horses and mules, with a plentiful and convenient water supply drawn from a deep well in the yard (of which more anon). The rest of the men were billeted in some unoccupied houses in the town. Sergeant Streather wrote home on 1 February: 'we have settled down in our new billet, we are in several old houses and quite comfortable. We have a good open fireplace and can get plenty of fuel which is quite a change for this country. The town we are at is about [——] Kilos behind the line.' (The number of kilometres had been blue-pencilled out by Lieutenant Smith, who censored this letter.)

When the 216th Company were last in the Somme area eighteen months earlier, Péronne had been behind the German lines and now it was behind the British. It had not been captured from the Germans, but voluntarily relinquished by them when they withdrew to the strong defences of the Hindenburg Line in March 1917, giving up then a tract of land some six times the area taken from them so bloodily in the battle of the Somme. The calculated devastation that accompanied their withdrawal was still evident in the countryside around Péronne. Blunden wrote: 'The civilians had not yet attempted to resume their properties and all the farms for

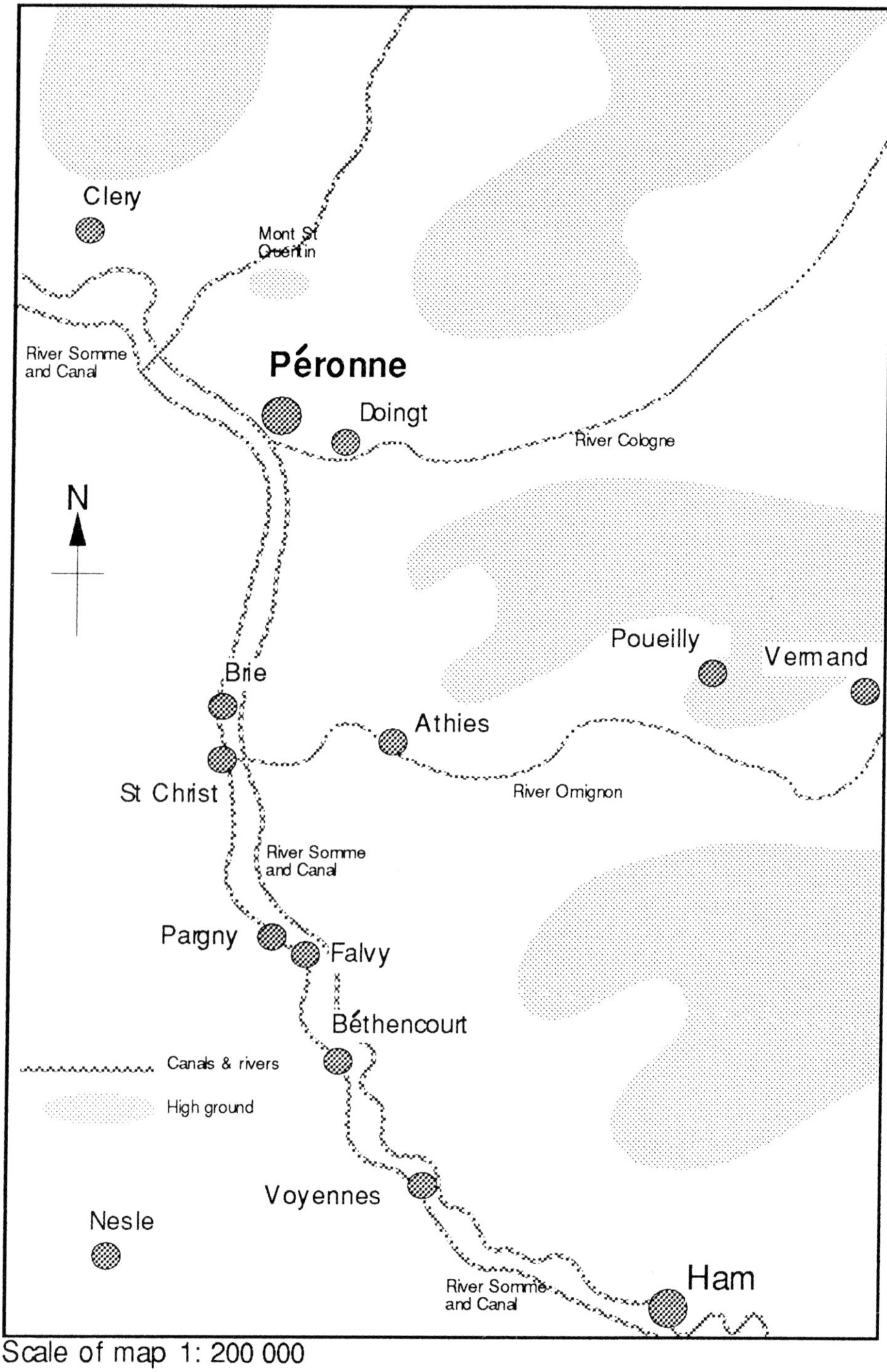

Map 6: Péronne, Ham, Vermand, 1918

miles were only shells of brick'.[2] There is more detail from the historian of the 34th Division, which came to Péronne in July 1917: 'All the villages round here have suffered the same fate. Practically every house ruined . . . certainly every one has had a charge fired in it, and many of them have been burned. . . . A village wrecked by continual shell fire is a melancholy sort of sight, but it is a very different one from one destroyed after careful preparation, and with a certain fiendish sense of humour. It forces you to the conclusion that a live Boche is a mistake. . . . Wrecking farmhouses, cutting down ornamental shrubs, smashing farm implements (all laid out in a row for the purpose), sawing through spokes of farm carts, fouling ponds and water supplies, were all items of the official programme, but I think that breaking *one* wheel of each perambulator must have been a spontaneous burst of humour on the part of individuals'.[3]

For all that, Péronne in fine frosty weather at the end of January 1918 was a great improvement on Flanders mud. It was an improvement not least because the armies were not shooting at one another very much. The British Fifth Army, in which the 216th Company was now a bit player, was in the process of taking over part of the front from the French army to the south, an extension forced on an unwilling Haig by Lloyd George: 'offensive spirit' was temporarily in abeyance while this reorganization took place and defences were being prepared against the anticipated German attack. The Germans, for their part, were not disposed to be troublesome just yet, for they were too busy extending roads and railways, building new hospitals, aerodromes, and bridges, moving troops forward (including many from the now peaceful Eastern front) and training them for attack.

Field Marshal Haig chose to concentrate the bulk of British forces in Flanders to cover the vital Channel ports, so the Fifth Army was very thin spread: at the end of January it had 10 infantry divisions for 42 miles of front, whereas there were 47 divisions in the three armies holding the remaining 84 miles of British front. The plan was that if any ground was to be lost it should be east of the Somme in the Fifth Army area, where French reinforcements would be close at hand in case of need. Instructions for an elaborate three-line defensive system were issued from G.H.Q., supplemented by instructions about a bridge-head to protect Péronne and a further defensive line along the river Somme. Existing defences were poor. A Frenchman wrote: 'the sectors taken over had been quiet fronts, and were in a neglected state. A tenant who knows that his lease is up does not bother to repaint his house or install more bathrooms, and so the French Third Army had left the line with little evidence of defensive preparations for their successors — all the work remained for the Fifth Army to do'.[4] General Sir Hubert Gough, commanding the Fifth Army, remarked upon the situation in the second week of February: 'To complete all these defences with support and reserve lines and supporting redoubts entailed digging about 300 miles of actual trenches and erecting the necessary wiring — a stupendous amount of fortification'. . . . 'No amount of labour — nothing short of a fairy wand — could have prepared all those defences in a few weeks'.[5]

At the end of January the Fifth Army had 32 Royal Engineer companies (compared with 178 altogether in the other three British armies on their smaller fronts) and a Labour Corps strength (racially and untactfully distinguished in

G.H.Q. orders as 'Indian', 'Chinese', 'Italian', 'White', and 'Prisoners of War') of 21,000. By the time the Germans attacked , seven weeks later, the number of R.E. companies had risen to 56 and the Labour Corps strength to 48,000, but it would prove to be too little far too late. Front-line defences were not the only need: depots, dumps, railways, roads, and bridges were also required now that lines of communication would be with the British armies to the north. Indeed, most of the Labour Corps was engaged on such work under the sixteen Army Troops companies of Royal Engineers which had arrived by March: the miles and miles of trenching and wiring that was needed had to be left to overstretched 'resting' infantrymen.

General Gough's orders from G.H.Q. were that, 'in the event of a serious attack', his policy should be 'to secure and protect at all costs the important centre of Péronne and the River Somme to the south of that place'; the river crossings in this area were therefore to be protected by a bridge-head that would require some 25 miles of defensive works and several new bridges. Gough pointed out to Haig on 9 January: 'In view of possible eventualities, great importance attaches to early provision of ample facilities for passage of Heavy Artillery and Mechanical Transport across the Somme at West and South of Peronne. These facilities do not exist.' Existing facilities, he explained, were either heavy bridges which are single-way and subject to great congestion or duplicate bridges suitable for horse-traffic only. He continues: 'The extensive programme of bridge construction obviously necessary and urgent, could only be completed expeditiously, in my opinion, by an Army Troops Company, R.E., supplemented by a Labour Company detailed for bridge work only. I am not in a position to provide these Units from among those now or about to be at the disposal of this Army. I urge therefore, that they may be allotted as an addition to this Army with as little delay as possible.'[6]

This was the request that had brought the Nuneaton men to Péronne. A history of R.E. bridging in the Great War describes activity on the Somme during February and March: 'Existing bridges were doubled on the main routes, others strengthened to carry Tanks, and new ones erected. This work was organised by the C.E. Fifth Army, and was all carried out under the general supervision of the G.H.Q. Bridging Officer by the 216th A.T. Company, and two Companies of American Engineers. The 216th Company was specially picked out for this work on account of the O.C. and senior Subaltern of the Company having both passed specially good courses at the Bridging School. The American Army had asked to be supplied with various type spans for instructional purposes, and willingly agreed to a suggestion that they should instead send Units to assist in practical work on the Somme'.[7] The senior subaltern was Lieutenant Smith. Presumably both he and Captain MacDougall were among the tiny minority of officers who obtained marks of over 80% at the Aire Bridging School and were therefore specially recommended for employment on bridging work.

Their first major job was on the river Somme and its parallel canal, close to the walls of Péronne on its southern side. It was, writes my father, 'to construct Hopkins girder bridges to replace wooden bridges which were the earlier replacements of the original bridges destroyed by the retreating Germans'. The heavier of the two prefabricated bridges they built at Péronne, known locally as 'Bristol Bridge', was understood by Arthur Daulman to be 'the first bridge specifically designed to take heavy tanks. Before building we were lectured by an officer, using a blackboard and easel, on how it was to be put together.' Perhaps the officer with the blackboard was the designer of the bridge, Captain Hopkins himself: he was the Bridging Officer at G.H.Q. and was often to be seen at bridge sites. As tanks had been in use for some considerable time before January 1918, the bridge at Péronne could not have been the first to carry them, but it may have been an early example of the new, heaviest Hopkins 120 ft Type Span (see illustration 42).

Captain MacDougall's war diary records daily progress on his Hopkins bridges. There were no rest days; for instance on Sunday 3 February, a mild, fair day, 66 men were working on Péronne Bridge No.1 (Bristol Bridge) 'off loading material from lorries and carrying to site, preparing bank seats and anchorages, tackle winches, etc. Masons working on abutments.' Smaller parties were five miles upstream at Brie, surveying existing bridges with a view to repairs and off loading and carrying materials for a new bridge. It was a similar routine for about two weeks: one or two sections of the Company worked on Péronne Bridge No 1 while other parties started other works upstream (i.e. to the south); Captain MacDougall was often examining bridge sites further upstream, sometimes accompanied by Captain Hopkins, the steel bridge designer. The Company's handiwork was inspected by the Chief Engineer of the Fifth Army, Major-General Philip Grant, on 30 January and again on 13 February when the big Péronne bridge was launched.

The canal spanned by this bridge was the major waterway throughout the whole area south of Péronne where the 216th Company were to work. The following description is from the *Official History*. The canal 'is 58 feet wide at water level, and six feet, six inches deep. The valley is from half to three-quarters of a mile wide, with gently sloping sides; its marshes and water meadows lie about a hundred feet below the general level of the surrounding country. The river itself is a small stream, 24 to 30 feet wide, sometimes split up into several channels; in March 1918 it was wadeable in some places, as the water was low. On its eastern bank there were dotted patches of small poplars, willows, and undergrowth. The obstacle which the marshes presented to movement was increased by a number of small ponds or chains of water-logged holes, from which peat had been cut for fuel. Practically, the valley was only passable at the causeways, which cross the waterways by a series of small bridges. These causeways are very ancient. In 1415 the French sought to obstruct the passage of the Somme by Henry V at Voyennes by digging holes in them, and he was delayed for some hours whilst the holes were filled up with any material to hand.'[8]

By all accounts the work of the engineers who were now improving a Somme crossing some five-hundred-odd years later went smoothly. Charles Streather was pleased to be able to tell his parents that 'the work is close to the billet and is the most interesting job we have had since we came out here. This particular job will not last long but I hope we shall carry on with the same class of work for some time' (1 February)). My father found the job interesting too, but recalled one small hitch in its smooth running. He writes: 'The Hopkins bridge was made up of standardized units of girder sections, they were put together on one of the banks of the obstacle, on baulks and rollers, and then winched across to the opposite bank, slung from a heavy block and tackle fixed to the top of a derrick pole, with scotches nailed to it, which Sapper Higham usually climbed: cf illustration 40 (b). This particular bridge was 120 feet long and the men detailed off to turn the winch handles had a very heavy and laborious job. The rest of us prepared the 12" by 12" pitch-pine baulks, bedded on the repaired stone abutments of the original bridge, or were stationed at the guy ropes attached to the derrick and the bridge. These baulks and the underside bolts of the bridge were coated with hot tar to preserve them; it was during this operation we had the only excitement during our stay in Péronne. A drum of tar was put on a fire near one of the baulks and when melted was lifted from the fire, but the bottom of the tin had melted out and the hot tar caught fire and spread to the baulk nearest to it. The heat made it difficult to get near to smother the blaze, and shovels were used to throw earth onto the baulk and tar drum, and eventually both were pushed into the river and the job went on.'

He sums up: 'After the mud and desolate appearance of the Ypres salient Péronne was so peaceful that at first we did not feel quite at home. Having an interesting job for the daylight hours and spending your evenings in the streets and estaminets with plenty of people about seemed quite out of our usual lot. There were no gun flashes or exploding shells, and on the horizon all round not a Very light could be seen.' The town was even safe for British civilians. It was reported to General Gough that a civilian who was touring the front climbed upon a wagon in the streets of Péronne, and from this extemporized platform addressed all and sundry who were in the streets of that ruined town. He told the soldiers there that 'every one at home was fed up to the back teeth' and that 'if only the soldiers would refuse to fight there would be peace'. Needless to say, the soldiers regarded such speeches as sceptically as they regarded the tub-thumping bellicosity of Horatio Bottomley.

The 216th went on bridging, their only excitement apart from burning tar being a glimpse of hidden treasure in the well at the chateau where the Company's horses and mules were stabled. My father writes: 'After a week or two the water was considerably lowered and a number of bundles were noticed at the bottom of the well. Sapper Trevis went down and sent these bundles up, when they were found to contain a collection of pistols, swords, and other old weapons. They belonged to the chateau and had been wrapped in waterproof material and sunk in the well to conceal them during the German occupation of the town. Before the souvenir hunters could get their hands on any of the antiques, Captain MacDougall got to hear of the find and notified the French authorities, who came with the owner's inventory and claimed the lot. Some of them were already decorating the walls of the sergeants' mess and the drivers' billet, but eventually the mayor and his squad of gendarmes cleared the lot.'

On 7 February one section of the Company moved a further eight miles upstream beyond Brie, to offload bridging materials at Voyennes. By now it was known that the Yanks really were coming: on 8 February Captain MacDougall interviewed the Town Major of Voyennes about billets for U.S.Engineers there, and on the following day he and the ubiquitous Captain Hopkins inspected the camp allotted to the Americans at Doingt (a place known to the British as 'Doing It'), which was close to Péronne, on a tributary of the river Somme. Engineers were among the first combatant Americans in France; as late as May 1918 they accounted for over half the total of U.S. forces training with the British. The contingent which joined the Fifth Army in February 1918 was composed of the 6th, 12th, and 14th Regiments of Engineers. General Gough was very pleased to see them. He writes: 'I went over one morning to their billets and inspected them — a fine body of tall, strong, active men — and afterwards I had a talk with their officers, not only about their own work, but on our general situation as well. Their experiences during the time they were with us were as exciting as they were varied, and gave them a vivid insight into war and battle. Their first job was to build a bridge over the Somme, but even as they were completing it they had to prepare it for demolition, and eventually when we fell back to the line of the river they blew up their own bridges'.[9]

On 13 February, the day that Péronne Bridge No 1 was launched, U.S. Engineers began work on another bridge at Péronne, two at Brie, two at Voyennes, and two at Doingt. In all cases, some men of the 216th Company were on hand to assist; their attitude to their new allies was as friendly and patronising as was their General's. My father writes: 'An American Engineer company was sent to work with us to get experience of this type of bridge; they were very enthusiastic about being at the front, as they thought, and carried their rifles and ammunition about with them wherever they went. They were surprised that we always left ours in the billet. They were a decent lot of chaps, and we got on very well together while they worked with us during the week or two we remained in Péronne to finish the job.'

Immediately after the decking of Péronne Bridge No 1 was completed and the road approaches to it made good the 216th Company, with the exception of its headquarters staff, moved to Pargny, a small village in a hollow, sheltered by trees, about ten miles upstream from Péronne. Here they remained for four weeks (17 February to 17 March) under the command of Lieutenant Smith. Sergeant Streather was pleased with the place and the people. He informed his parents on 27 February that he had so comfortable a billet close to the canal that he 'should not mind if we could spend the rest of the winter here. It is the best place we have ever struck as far as being safe goes. We are twenty miles from the line, there is no railway or big town or dump anywhere near, and we are the only troops about, so we are safe from both shells and bombs. I was very busy for a week fixing up the billet. Harris and I put six different stoves in before we got a good one. Some would not burn, others smoked us out, the one we have now we carried nearly a mile: it is a Jerry and a good one too. . . . Our work is progressing wonderfully well and I suppose we shall not be here more than another three weeks. That is a pity as it is such a decent place. Of course I don't suppose you would think so if you saw it, for on all sides one sees signs of the wanton destruction of the Hun. In the village not a building stands complete: only one has a roof and there is not half a dozen gables left; the church is a complete ruin. A handful of French civvies have returned: they live in neat little huts built by the government; they tell fearful stories of the atrocious conduct of the Germans and are far more obliging than most of the people we have met.'

My father recalled Pargny as having few inhabitants. 'The fruit trees in the gardens had been cut down by the retreating Germans and some of the village wells filled up, and other wanton damage was done. There were some unoccupied houses and barns where we made ourselves comfortable and had a look round for the estaminet, but Pargny was dry. The only estaminet was at Falvy, about a mile away by road. At one end of the village was a large German cemetery which had been laid out during the German occupation of this district. Judging from the area and the number of granite headstones, standing in ranks, carved with the names and units of the deceased, there must have been a large casualty clearing station here. At the entrance was a large granite statue of Germania, complete with eagle and sword. This statue had been toppled over by the French but not damaged in any way and the rest of the cemetery was left undisturbed and neglected. Near this place, on a patch of waste ground, was the remains of a large bonfire, and scattered about were a quantity of half-burned German leather helmets and brass eagles and spikes belonging to them, but no complete helmets, which we wanted for souvenirs; some of these badges were picked up, but were not considered worth bothering with by the majority of us. There were also half-burned fragments of letters, other documents, and clothing, etc.'

There were more useful objects to be picked up at Pargny, as Sergeant Streather noted in his letter of 27 February: 'We live close beside the canal and two nights ago we "found" a boat, so yesterday and tonight we have been afloat with two German shovels for oars. There is a big river close handy and some of the fishermen are having some fine catches.' My father recalled: 'the river and canal were only about a hundred yards apart here: swampy ground covered with undergrowth and tree stumps intervening, and the canal was banked up on that side about twelve feet'. Both waterways had to be bridged, the canal by a pont-levis (drawbridge); the swampiness of the ground on both sides of the river made it necessary to lay corduroy approach roads and drive piles to make the banks solid for the bridge seating; also some existing bridgework had to be dismantled and slewed across. A pile driver was constructed on site, its 15 cwt. monkey (hammer) being wound up by a winch, which, writes my father, 'was a job no one cared for'. He adds: 'We were somewhat hampered by the lack of a boat, until someone remembered seeing one tied up near a cottage on the other side of the river. As there was no one about the cottage an expedition was organized to capture the boat after we had finished work for the day and carry it across the swampy part and launch it on the canal. Taking a roundabout way over a bridge we got the boat across the river, using shovels as paddles; then, putting poles underneath, the carrying party stumbled over to the canal and floated down to the village.'

Two days after the boat was 'found' Sapper Trevis was lost. Sergeant Streather wrote home: 'You remember Trevis who joined the company the same day as me. He fell down a well 40ft deep today and hurt himself considerably, I don't know exactly how. He was alone at the time and was not found for more than an hour.

Luckily the well was empty or he would have drowned.' My father recalled this episode in greater detail. 'At the bottom of an overgrown, deserted garden, at the back of an unoccupied cottage which had been taken over as the sergeants' mess, was an old well covered by a heavy trapdoor. Harry Trevis, No.2 Section, had been acting as sergeants' mess orderly here and at Péronne, and while walking round the garden came across the trapdoor among the weeds. He was interested in exploring wells after the one we found at Péronne. After prising the trapdoor open, which was very heavy and solid, he stepped forward to throw it back and fell down the shaft; the door dropped back into place, Trevis was trapped, and his shouts were not heard. Luckily, a small French boy was watching what he was doing and saw the mishap, and went next door to the sergeants' mess and told Sgt-Major Mitch, who took no notice, owing to inability to understand the boy's tale and being too busy swearing about the absence of the cook at dinner time. After some time, about one and a half hours, the boy fetched someone who could speak a bit of English, and Trevis was discovered and rescued, the well being dry and a heap of refuse at the bottom. When they pulled up the cover one of the rescue party shouted "Who's down there", getting the reply in return, "Sapper Trevis, who the 'ell do you think it is: the C.R.E.?". Trevis's back was injured by his fall; he was taken to hospital and sent back to England; he never rejoined the company.' Trevis's reply to his rescuers is given some piquancy by the fact that the C.R.E. (i.e. the Chief Engineer of an Army Corps) of the area where they were working rejoiced in the name and style of Brigadier General H.G. Joly de Lotbinière.

Sometimes one, sometimes two sections of the Company worked at Pargny; after a week, one, later two sections were detached to nearby Falvy in order to dismantle and replace two bridges and construct a third. Meanwhile other, smaller parties were from time to time with the Americans, bridging at Béthencourt, Cléry, Athies, Flamincourt, Brie, Voyennes, St.Christ, Tincourt, Sancourt, Moislains: all places on the Somme, south and east of Péronne. The Fifth Army Chief Engineer's plan was for the 216th and its associated American companies to erect 62 bridges, of which 51 were to be completed before 21 March. 'Work proceeded smoothly and rapidly, and the opportunity that it offered for progressive training to the Units engaged was most valuable. The very high standard of efficiency attained by these Companies in a comparatively short time showed clearly the results that could be obtained by training and practice, and this was fully borne out by the work of the 216th A.T. Company in the intensive bridging operations during the Autumn of 1918.'[10] As each bridge was built it was prepared for demolition along with the other two hundred bridges or thereabout in the Fifth Army area. 'Lists of all the bridges in each corps area were drawn up and the corps engineers instructed to inspect them and place the necessary charges, fuses, etc., in position in weather-proof covers'.[11] Throughout this rush of bridge building the weather was generally fine and dry: this was convenient for the engineers' work, just as the low water level in the river Somme would be convenient for the Germans when they came to cross it in March

There were no rest days for the 216th, but evidently there were some free evenings. My father writes of the boat captured by the carpenters who built the pile driver: 'It was very helpful for the job, and was in great demand for fishing parties in the evenings, when we found the best bait was a Mills bomb with the pin out. After the explosion the surface of the water was covered with stunned fish; all we had to do was to paddle round and pick out the best. For paddles we used German entrenching spades found lying about. It was also useful for our evening trips to the estaminet at Falvy, the next village, where Sapper Bill Higham, No.3 Section, played his mandolin at the sing-songs. We walked along the tow-path, a short cut of about two miles, the boat followed ("light engine" as an ex-railway driver said) to bring back the chaps who had doubts about the walk back to billets along the tow-path. At Falvy there was another R.E. company, and one of the sappers was a Nuneaton man named Pallett. Before we left Pargny, after the bridge was completed, we decided to have a grand fishing party on the Somme, and Pallett, with a few of his friends, came to fish with us, bringing his own bait. The bait was a slab of gun-cotton and primer and detonator. The boat's crew was Sergeant Ashley, No.2 Section, Corporal Berry and myself, No.3 Section, and we had to collect the stunned fish. Pallett threw his gun-cotton, it landed very close to the boat, and we were nearly swamped by the water thrown up by the ensuing explosion. When the boat had been cleared of water and we had time to look round, the surface of the river appeared to be solid with all the varieties of fish in the vicinity. There was enough of and to spare for both companies, and for the village people of Pargny and Falvy, and the original owner of the boat, together with his boat returned.' Explosive methods of fishing seem not to have been very unusual. General Sir Henry Rawlinson, always full of delighted praise for the Australians under his command, recounted this tale of their ingenuity in April 1918: 'They are certainly original fighters, and up to all sorts of dodges, some of which would shock a strict disciplinarian. I hear that during the battle of Villers-Bretonneux the village of Corbie was being shelled by 5.9s. Some of the German shells were falling short into the pools of the Somme river, and exploded under water. Two Australians spent the day in a boat, rowing about and watching for a shell to explode and then picked up the stunned fish. They wore their gas masks to prevent recognition'.[12]

When General Gough wrote to G.H.Q. on 9 January concerning the need for more bridges over the Somme on his ill-provided front, he asked not only that an Army Troops Company specially detailed for bridging work (i.e. the 216th) should be sent, but that its establishment should be increased temporarily by attaching to it two R.E. officers trained in heavy bridging. This would enable work to proceed simultaneously on more sites. On 2 February he also asked G.H.Q. to 'send a Labour Company to work with the 216th A.T. Company' because the two companies of U.S.Engineers 'assisting in work on the Somme bridges are liable to recall at short notice'.[13] The Labour Company never arrived but one officer was eventually provided, when, on 15 March, 2nd Lieut. J.D.Brand joined the 216th from the R.E. Base Depot, Rouen. It would appear that this was not his first spell of service with the Company, because his name appears as censor of a letter written by Charles Streather from Villers-au-Bois in May 1916.

On 17 March the detachment under Lieutenant Smith moved from Pargny to Ham, eight miles further upstream and closer to the front. Their new billets were in a large empty warehouse near the railway and a large casualty clearing station.

Most of the men continued to work on bridges but some were sent some miles forward to help prepare trenches as a support line in the 'rear zone', that is the third line of defence behind the 'forward zone' and the 'battle zone'. There had been so little time for preparation that, at this date, the defences of the rear zone consisted of no more than a ribbon of trench, seven feet wide and a foot deep, with occasional small belts of wire; the sites for machine guns and strongpoints were marked by notice boards.[14] My father recalls: 'We travelled by lorry and G.S. wagon. There was an old castle outside Ham which we passed daily, partially blown up during the war of 1870. The weather was pleasant during most of the day, but foggy and frosty at night.'

As usual, he has more to say about leisure pursuits than work. 'The evening before the German attack, a chap in No.3 Section was teaching Chamberlain, Clarkson, and myself to play poker, at which we did so well that our tutor, Wilkinson, lost his patience along with his francs. "Wilkie" was a very excitable fellow, who had joined the Company, along with another sapper named Simmons, at La Clytte the previous year. They had both spent a few years working in Canada and it was amusing to hear them reminiscing about the various places they had worked in, at that time unknown to each other. Simmons was a Salvation Army man. Wilkie told him quite often that he was a bloody fool to swap that army for this one, but when they were discussing the towns they had worked in Simmons's landmarks were the churches, chapels, and citadels, and Wilkie found his way round by the public houses and other places of entertainment, but they both got round the place in time.'

The Germans were playing poker too. Their manoeuvres deceived the French into believing that they were to be the object of the main attack, with the result that when the blow fell on the British the French refused help at first. On the front of the real attack the Germans took great precautions to conceal their immense gathering of men and guns. General Gough, as it happened, could read the German hand but had no aces up his sleeve. On 19 March he wrote to his wife: 'I expect a bombardment will begin to-morrow night. last six or eight hours, and then will come the German infantry on Thursday, 21st. Every one is calm and very confident. All is ready.'[15] In view of the sketchiness of the defensive line, the thin spread of front-line troops, and lack of reserves, his last remark is a brave overstatement.

Ham was the headquarters of XVIII Corps, which consisted of the 36th (Ulster), 30th, and 61st Divisions, spread over a front of nine miles astride the valley of the upper Somme, looking towards St.Quentin. On the morning of the attack these three divisions had to oppose fourteen German divisions. At 4.40 a.m. on Thursday, 21 March, the German bombardment opened with a single shattering crash from nearly ten thousand howitzers, guns, and trench mortars ranged against the Fifth and Third Armies. The shelling was mixed in the proportion of $4^1/_2$ gas shell to 1 of high explosive against artillery and 1:1 against other targets; 'the effect was devastating; in many places the entire defending force in the Forward and Battle Zones was annihilated.' Five hours later German infantry attacked in thick fog. In the Fifth Army sector, 'where the defenders were very thin on the ground, continuous trenches were virtually non-existent, and rear positions pious hopes rather than military realities, great store had been set by mutually supporting machine-gun posts. To be effective, however, these needed to communicate, and preferably to see each other; the bombardment cut out communication, the fog blotted out vision. The German tactic of infiltration succeeded in these circumstances beyond all the dreams of its devisers: British battalion headquarters found the enemy infantry upon them before they were even aware that the attack had begun; posts were surrounded; gunners became aware of close-by shadows in the murk on which they had to fire over open sights. The front crumbled like plaster; each probe loosened a little more for its neighbours'.[16]

Loss of communication, fog, and general confusion under the overwhelming weight of the German assault ensured that it was many hours before the General Staff learned exactly what had happened to the front line. The 216th Company knew, of course, even less of what was going on. My father writes: 'On the morning of the 21st, about 4 o'clock we were all roused by a tremendous barrage, something quite beyond the usual uproar. Our sympathies at the time were for the unfortunate Germans: Alf Chamberlain said, "Jerry is getting some stuff now, I wouldn't like to be under that lot". When we turned out in the morning we soon found out the boot was on the other foot. Jerry was doing the sending. The town was very lively, and the gendarmes were all out, knocking on doors and telling the people to leave; the people were excited, and commenced packing bundles and putting furniture and bundles on carts and wheelbarrows, hastened by a few heavy shells which were dropping on the town.' These civilians had been in German hands from early in the war until February 1917; now they had to turn out before a further invasion.

It was still business as usual for the trenching party. My father continues: 'As usual we went to our digging but had some trouble getting there as the roads were crowded with carts and pedestrians coming back towards Ham. There was one incident that struck me when we were working on the line near the road, which made me realize the miserable condition of the civilians hurrying away from the forward zone. Two old women stopped near us, one with a wheelbarrow loaded with a large bundle wrapped in bedclothes, the other was leading a nanny goat, which lay down at the roadside and refused to continue walking. One woman sat on the wheelbarrow while the other was trying to get the goat to move, and then they had a quiet discussion, and the bundle was placed on the grass verge and the goat on the wheelbarrow, and away they went with the crowd. Infantry were going up across the fields in single file and the noise of gunfire was loud and continuous, making us all wonder what was going on, but we kept to our work until midday, when we were ordered back to Ham. The civilians there had nearly all left; the shelling continued, but fortunately our billets and the hospital were well away from the area where the heavy stuff was dropping. A hospital train stood near the level crossing, and we were told off to load up the wounded, staff, and supplies.'

In mid-afternoon, while the R.E.s were loading the hospital train, General Gough visited the Corps H.Q. in Ham, where he found the Corps Commander, Lieutenant-General Sir Ivor Maxse and his Staff 'cheerful, active, and confident'.[17]

Even so, it was clear by now that the Germans were pressing their attack with great vigour and vastly superior numbers and that the best the Fifth Army could do was to 'fall back fighting in order to maintain a continuous front, using every means of delaying the enemy's advance: put in the simplest language, the Army would make the best fight it could by day without getting overwhelmed, and then slip back at night to a new selected line, the engineers destroying bridges and roads; it would repeat the process day after day until reinforcements arrived'.[18] It is always a severe task to conduct a fighting retreat. Gough had lost a quarter of his infantry on the first morning of a battle that would, in the event, last for two weeks; the German assault units were still largely intact and behind them were many fresh divisions that could be brought into action day by day, while Allied uncertainty about German intentions would deny him any British or French reinforcements for several vital days.

Chapter Twelve: In Retreat, March 1918

After the Ham detachment had loaded the hospital train they were ordered to stand by but not to go far from the billet; they had a meal and their last drinks in the nearly deserted cafés. 'After about an hour of this', writes my father, 'we all went back to billets, where our transport was, and company stores were loaded up and our packs were also put on the wagons. We fell in and commenced to march out, in skeleton equipment — haversacks, water bottle, and ammunition — back to Nesle; one or two who were unfit to march were laid out on top of the baggage. This would be about 9 o'clock, a foggy, frosty night, but a bright full moon above the mist. Our inebriates were soon recovered, and glad to get down and march with the rest of us.'

Nearly everyone else in the area was on the move. Confused by orders from on high and in the inexplicable absence of their Corps Commander, the headquarters staff of XVIII Corps were going back to Nesle too, while the front-line troops of the Corps were retiring behind the right bank of the Somme, north-east of St.Simon, five miles from Ham. Seventy-five bridges over the Somme and its canal were blown up by R.E.s that night, sometimes under fire: in one particularly hazardous and courageous operation of this kind Lieutenant C.L. Knox, brother of the Lieutenant Knox formerly with the 216th, earned the Victoria Cross.[1] The retirement of the Ham detachment of the 216th Company, R.E., was fortunately unexciting. Only one incident is recalled by my father: 'Some time that night we were all a bit startled to hear a crowd of people rushing up the road towards our column and shouting and yelling in a foreign language, so we halted and separated to either side of the road to let them come up to us, when we found out they were a Chinese labour gang, about a hundred strong, with a sergeant R.E. who was trying to control them. The sergeant told us they had panicked when all the inhabitants had cleared out; some of the German shells fell near their compound and away they went. Where they finally finished up we never knew or cared. These Chinese were a picturesque lot, very big and strong in physique, with a fondness for large women's hats with plenty of feathers on, skirts, and brightly coloured jackets. Their boots were tied together and hung round their necks; they preferred to wear their sandals for walking.'

Nesle is about seven miles west of Ham and away from the river Somme. There the Ham detachment were rejoined by the Company C.O. My father writes: 'Arriving at Nesle some time in the early morning, we fell out in the square near the church. It was a small town with a very large Gothic church: "more church than houses" someone said. The place was deserted, and we had our bully, biscuits, and tea while Mac went somewhere for orders. As usual at this time of day there was a thick cold fog, the kerb stones and church steps were cold seats, but we made the best of it and got what rest we could, as the estaminets were out of bounds after our lapse at Ham, and we were kept in the square until Mac returned, fell in and set off for Péronne. The roads were paved with setts in the centre part, leaving a comparatively smooth gravel surface each side, and every so often the ranks of four men each were changed round, sometimes easy going on the gravel, then the tiring "bashing the pavé". As the fog lifted, the day became warm and pleasant; there were no refugees about and very few other army units. The noise from the direction of the line was not so noticeable, although we were marching parallel to the old front, but had no idea as to whether Jerry was liable to cut us off.' There was in fact no danger of their being cut off: the fighting was ten miles away to their right where infantry of the XIX Corps were holding out in the redoubts that dotted the 'battle zone', inflicting heavy casualties on the Germans, and giving ground slowly. XVIII Corps to the south of them was being pushed back somewhat further and faster by the German attack.

The 216th R.E. contingent reached Péronne in the afternoon and went back to the billets they had occupied in January. My father recalls: 'The only people in the town were a few small army units; no civilians anywhere; estaminets closed but capable of being opened via the windows after darkness. One of the chaps in the section was knocked up by the late marching; he was one of the older men, a Nuneaton man, Bill Salmon, a carpenter. Alf Chamberlain and myself were sharing a small room with him and we decided to get him something to drink. There was an estaminet just outside the walls, near the bastions of the old gates, where we had put a bridge across the canal nearby. The estaminet was deserted, so in we went, lit a bit of candle we had with us, had a drink, and found an enamel bucket, and half filled it with beer and a few bottles of vin blanc, and went back. Bill was asleep, so putting the bucket down by the bed we slammed the door going out to wake him up and watched through a crack in the door. Rousing up, he noticed the bucket, looked in, and reached for his mess tin and tasted the drink. Then he smiled, made himself comfortable, and took a long drink. We went back to the estaminet. While we were there two soldiers came in; we blew out the candle when we heard them approaching and they ran out when we spoke to them. After about an hour we went back to see how the invalid was going on. We found him quite recovered and singing, so, helping him to drain the bucket, we got down for the night.'

On the night that this mild looting occurred in Péronne Captain Herbert Read, poet and art-critic, was retreating with the remains of his battalion of Green Howards through Ham. He recalled: 'Ham, as we walked through its cobbled streets, seemed very hollow and deserted. The last time we had seen it, it had been a busy market town, full of civilians. Now only a few sinister looters went about the empty houses with candles. We saw one fellow come out of a door with a lady's reticule [handbag] and other things over his arm. We should have been justified in shooting him, but we were far too tired. We just noticed him stupidly'.[2] The looters in Ham and Péronne alike might have been surprised had they known that Field Marshal Haig had confided to his diary on 3 March 1918: 'Really the absence of crime in this army is quite wonderful'.[3]

While the Nuneaton men were sleeping the sleep of the not-so-just, much of their handiwork and that of their American comrades was being blown up by other R.E.s. One of the last of their bridges to go during that night and the following morning was at Ham. 'This, a temporary double lattice girder bridge of 84-foot span, taking the place of one destroyed by the Germans in 1917, crossed a lock, its undersurface being only 6 feet above the level of the lock walls. It was fired at 8 a.m. on the 23rd just as the enemy was gaining a footing on it. The explosion cut the girders in the centre, but their shore ends stayed on the abutments and the hanging ends fell on the lock walls, so that the gap was small. As the enemy was getting very near, nothing more could be done' Even when bridges were more thoroughly demolished than this one at Ham there was always enough debris standing out of the water to enable infantry to cross, and it was reckoned that the passage of the enemy's field artillery would be delayed by no more than two hours unless the site of the bridge was kept under rifle or machine-gun fire at close range. It was realized too late that the British in this area might have been better advised to follow and improve upon the example of the French in 1415 by making holes in the Somme valley causeways, because 'To fill up large craters made by explosives in a causeway is a slow process, as material — if to hand — cannot be got to the second before the first has been dealt with, and so on'.[4]

The destruction of these bridges was made necessary by the somewhat premature withdrawal of XVIII Corps to the left bank of the Somme (i.e. to the south and west of the river). Part of XIX Corps also withdrew behind the Somme immediately south of Péronne, but two divisions (24th and 50th) remained five miles or so east of the river, tenuously holding the Péronne bridgehead. However, neither flank of this latter force was in touch with other British troops so it would not be long before it too came back to new defensive positions behind the Somme. Thus it was that the following morning, 23 March, found the sobered-up Nuneaton R.E.s from Péronne digging trenches at La Chapelette, just south of the town, but, writes my father 'a staff officer came along with some infantry and ordered us away to Chaulnes and the infantry carried on with the trench digging'. This infantry probably belonged to the 66th (East Lancashire) Division, which had lost three-quarters of its fighting strength in heavy fighting over the previous forty-eight hours; the survivors had retired across the Somme about 3 a.m., so could have had very little rest before they were called upon to dig in yet again. The best that could be said was that after a very cold night the day was warm with brilliant sunshine.

To get to Chaulnes, ten miles away to the south-west, the 216th Company had to cross the old Somme battlefield, where movement away from roads was difficult and where the roads themselves were now full of the transport of retreating (and occasionally advancing) Army units and ambulance columns evacuating the wounded, together with refugees. In the later stages of their march the Nuneaton men would have come across remnants of the 24th Division which had just retired over the bridges at Pargny. A nursing sister, caught up in the retreat, observed Major-General A.C.Daly, commanding 24th Division, 'sitting on the road-side' outside the Orderly- Room tent of a casualty clearing station, 'with a few of his Staff, and the Divisional Flag stuck up in the field, using our telephone as his Divisional H.Q. His Division was practically napoo for the moment — they did wonders afterwards — masses of his transport were spread out opposite and a steady stream of everything flowed past us all day the wrong way'. About 5 p.m. the wounded were evacuated by road and rail: ambulance cars took some of them 'through Chaulnes, over battlefields with pill-boxes in them, and ghastly wrecked woods and villages'; the roads were being shelled. At this time 'The Boche was 4 miles this side of Ham, just into Péronne and three miles from us — 13 miles nearer in 2 days. We were trying to hold them at the Somme at St.Christ, the little place we walked to the other day 3 miles away, with the blue lake where the Yankee sappers were building a bridge. I'm glad I've seen Péronne. The 8th Warwicks marched in on March 19th, 1917. The Germans will take down our notice board on March 23rd, 1918, and put up theirs'.[5]

The German attack continued with unabated vigour all this day and the exhausted, continually thinning Fifth Army was still losing ground. At 5 p.m. there was an order from G.H.Q. that 'Fifth Army will hold the line of the Somme river at all costs', and, with the Third Army, maintain Péronne as a pivot of the defence'; but by then 'the line of the Somme had been lost, the right of the Péronne bridgehead was being evacuated, the last troops were struggling through the streets of the town', and 'eight out of the eleven divisions of the Fifth Army originally in the front line, and three brigades of the remaining divisions had suffered such heavy losses that they were only "remnants" of their former selves'.[6] Some French divisions were beginning to reinforce the hardest-pressed British on the extreme right of Gough's army, but the French would always see the need to cover Paris as more important than conformation with Haig's strategy for the British front. The Germans were already uncomfortably close to the French capital: this was the day on which it first came under fire from a German long-range gun.

By the end of the day every bridge built by the 216th R.E. and their associated American companies had been destroyed. Pargny heard rather more explosions that afternoon than were heard during Sapper Pallett's fishing trip the week before. Five bridges on the road from Pargny to Falvy (where the estaminet was) were blown up while some British cavalry were on the far side: 'Most of their horses had to be abandoned, as they could neither use the wrecked bridges nor swim across on account of the boggy banks'. At Péronne there was a bonfire much bigger than a burning drum of tar: the detonators on Bristol Bridge were destroyed by a bomb, so 'petrol was then sprayed over the bridge, and it burned all night'.[7] This was after the badly-mauled 16th (Irish) Division — old acquaintances of the 216th R.E. — had crossed between 3 and 6 p.m. At Brie there was a bonfire earlier in the afternoon, when 'five British tanks appeared on the eastern bank intending to cross. They could not do so; for even the larger bridges — "A" class, built of lattice girders used as "through" spans — although sufficiently strong, were too narrow to admit of a tank crossing with its sponsons on. [Sponsons are the protrusions on each side of a tank that enable its guns to be pointed fore and aft.] There was no time to take these off, so the tanks were set on fire and abandoned. All the charges in the bridges were then exploded. It was subsequently found that the rear guard of the 1/4th Green Howards had been cut off, but it managed to cross by the debris of the bridges'.[8] There were similar incidents to these at many of the bridge sites.

In the late afternoon the 216th Company reached Chaulnes, and, writes my father 'came to a large American stores dump, which was deserted, except for a train of empty wagons and two R.E. sappers, driver and fireman, on the engine. The evening was drawing in, misty and cold, and they were glad to see us instead of Jerry, who was not very far away. We loaded the wagons as much as could be stacked on, and they drew away, and we had a scrounge round for something to eat, and got clean underwear and new boots, and then soaked the rest in petrol and tar and set fire to it. There was also a sugar factory burning nearby, and a staff officer came along with some machine-gunners and infantry, and posted them to get full advantage of the light, and told them, "There's your target; help yourselves", so we supposed Jerry was not far away.' The 216th climbed into their lorries and left; behind them fighting continued along the Somme by moonlight. Shortly after midnight the Chief Engineer of the Fifth Army, Major-General P.G. Grant, penned an order to Major Owen, Officer Commanding the 353rd Electrical and Mechanical Company, R.E., at Chaulnes: 'I find that no message can be sent by telephone to you and that owing to congestion of traffic, a message from this Office would take a long time to get through. . . . I must leave it to your discretion as to the appropriate moment in case of necessity to burn and destroy buildings and stores. . . . This should only be done if Chaulnes cannot be held. . . . You will readily realize that firing ones own buildings and stores is not good for "morale" of troops fighting in front, or in reserve in the neighbourhood, or moving forward.' Grant's diary for 24 March notes: 'Major Owen had however retired on Moreuil after firing the Dump before these orders arrived about 3 a.m.[9]

The Germans were less than five miles from Chaulnes when Major Owen gave his fire-raising orders, but they were meeting stiff resistance from the Fifth Army. In the event it was not until 26 March that they captured the place, so General Grant's misgivings about too early a burning were justified. The historian of the 20th Division observes darkly: 'The work of the [Divisional] R.E. was made particularly difficult at this time, as someone had set fire to the R.E. park at Chaulnes long before the enemy got anywhere near it. In consequence, for two or three days hardly any shovels or R.E. stores could be obtained. Parties went to the park with lorries but were unable to do very much good, owing to the great heat and to the impossibility of getting at much of the most necessary material.'[10]

During a bitterly cold night the 216th Company marched some seven miles westwards from Chaulnes over the low plateau called Santerre, through Rosières, to Caix. My father recalled Caix as 'a small village which we had all to ourselves. We fell out for breakfast and afterwards wandered round the place. On a patch of grass a very ancient cow was tethered, all skin and bone; the little quantity of grass it could reach was finished, so, thinking to put the animal out of its misery and thereby also to have some beef, we shot it. The beef was there ready for the cooking, but having nothing but bayonets and jack-knives to get to it, nothing we could do would pierce its tough hide, so the beef was off. Some rations came along shortly after, and we were served with several large tins of prefried bacon, which was as tough as the cow, and I think we left the rest of it at Caix. I don't remember any other time that bacon was issued. These wagons left us and went back to the ration dump, wherever that was.'

This was the morning of Palm Sunday. The Nuneaton men were lucky to be struggling with prefried bacon while a far more desperate struggle was being resumed behind them. 'The divisions of the Fifth Army were now fighting and moving in small bodies, often composed of men of different units, frequently with parties of Germans mixed up with them, so that it was almost impossible for the corps or divisional staffs to ascertain the position of the front line. After three days of battle, with each night spent upon the march or occupied in the sorting out and reorganization of units, the troops — German as well as British — were tired almost to the limit of endurance. The British, at any rate, were short of food and often of ammunition: rations and ammunition were duly sent up, but as the troops were so rapidly changing position and constantly coming under different commanders, the issue of supplies was a matter of extreme difficulty. As a rule they were dumped, and units drew from them as they passed'.[11]

My father's account continues: 'Leaving Caix, we marched all morning, and in the early afternoon came to a village called Beaucourt en Santerre. The country in this part was not so undulating; this village was somewhat isolated, just a row of houses and a small church, the road passing through the middle. As we came in the place looked deserted, except for a barricade halfway along the street which was built up of furniture, mattresses, farm carts, etc., left behind by the inhabitants: no sandbags, but some shovelfuls of earth chucked among the cartwheels. This barricade consisted of two overlapping leaves, with a space in between so that retreating English soldiers could file through. When we got through, we found that the place was occupied by a small force of infantry and a company of R.E.s, who were fortifying the place, getting plenty to drink from the estaminets to fortify themselves at the same time, having barrels of beer and vin blanc in the streets, upright with the end knocked out. A staff officer met us here and took away Captain Mac, officers, and N.C.O.s to set out some trenches round the place, to make a strong point, where we were to stay and reinforce the chaps already there. As we had become part of the garrison we shared in the amenities, so the result was that, when the officers returned, about half the company were the worse for wear, but in high spirits.'

The company began digging, but, writes my father, 'The arrival of some fresh infantry to occupy this place caused a change of plan. These chaps dug themselves in and we were set on the move again, going to another village farther back, where some lorries were waiting, and before evening we found ourselves at Moreuil, a small country town. After the evening meal we went to a café and spent a very pleasant evening in the company of some French infantry who arrived about an hour after us. They piled arms in the square, and came into the several estaminets for a drink while their soup was stewed up. After their meal they came back, and we all made a night of it. Moreuil was still inhabited, and it was quite a change after the deserted places we had recently passed through.' They would not have known this, but, while they were fraternizing with French infantrymen, the Nuneaton men, along with most of the Fifth Army were about to come under French command. At 11.20 that evening Haig issued an order that all British troops south of the Somme would pass from his command to that of General Fayolle: units of the Fifth Army north of the Somme would be transferred to the British Third Army. General Gough was still in post and received no orders from Fayolle: the change of command was a device by which Haig hoped to maintain a continuous line between the British and the French, for if the French followed their inclination to withdraw south-westwards and cover Paris a fatal gap would open for the Germans to exploit.

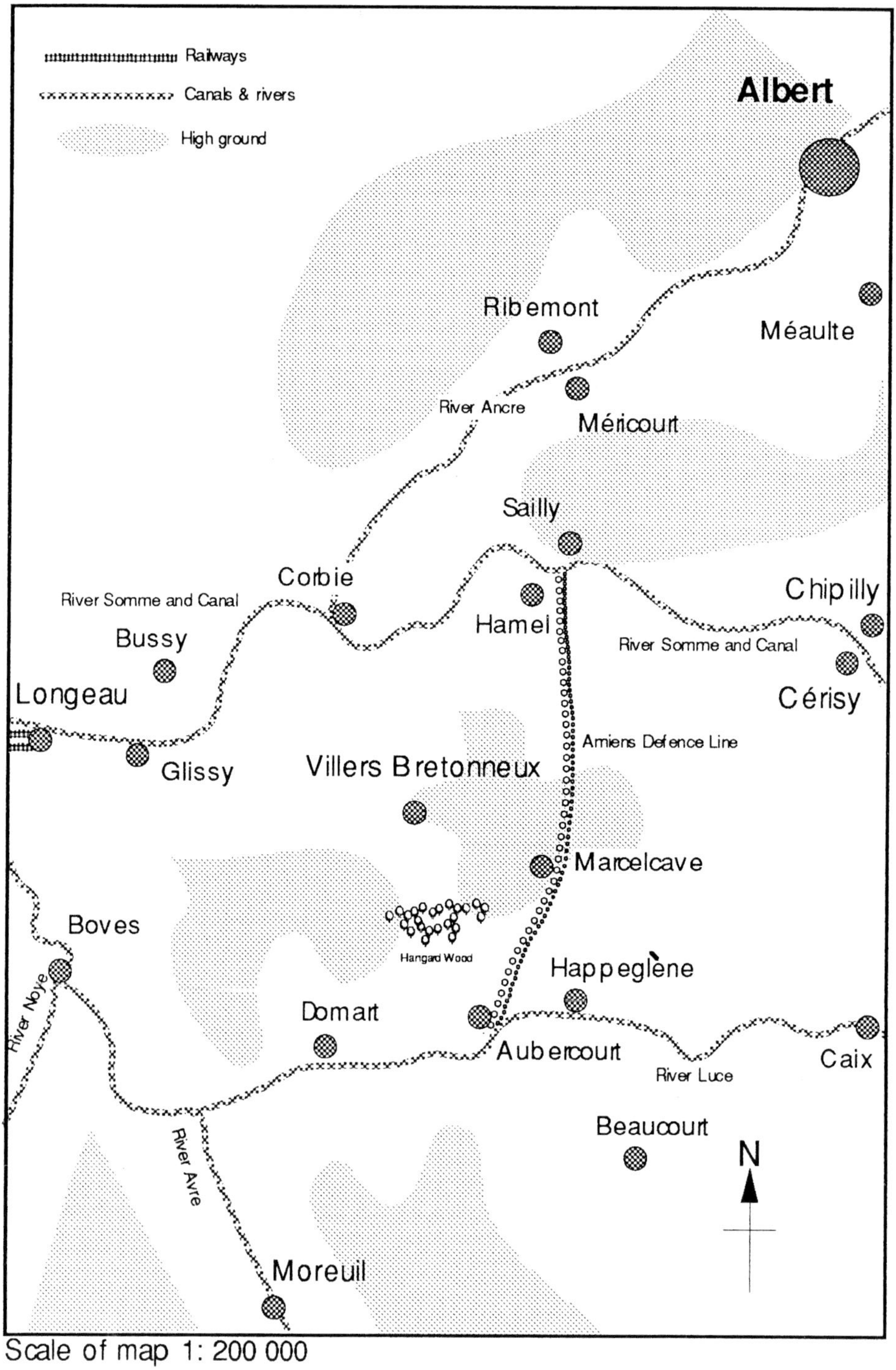

Map 7: Albert and the Somme east of Amiens, 1916, 1918

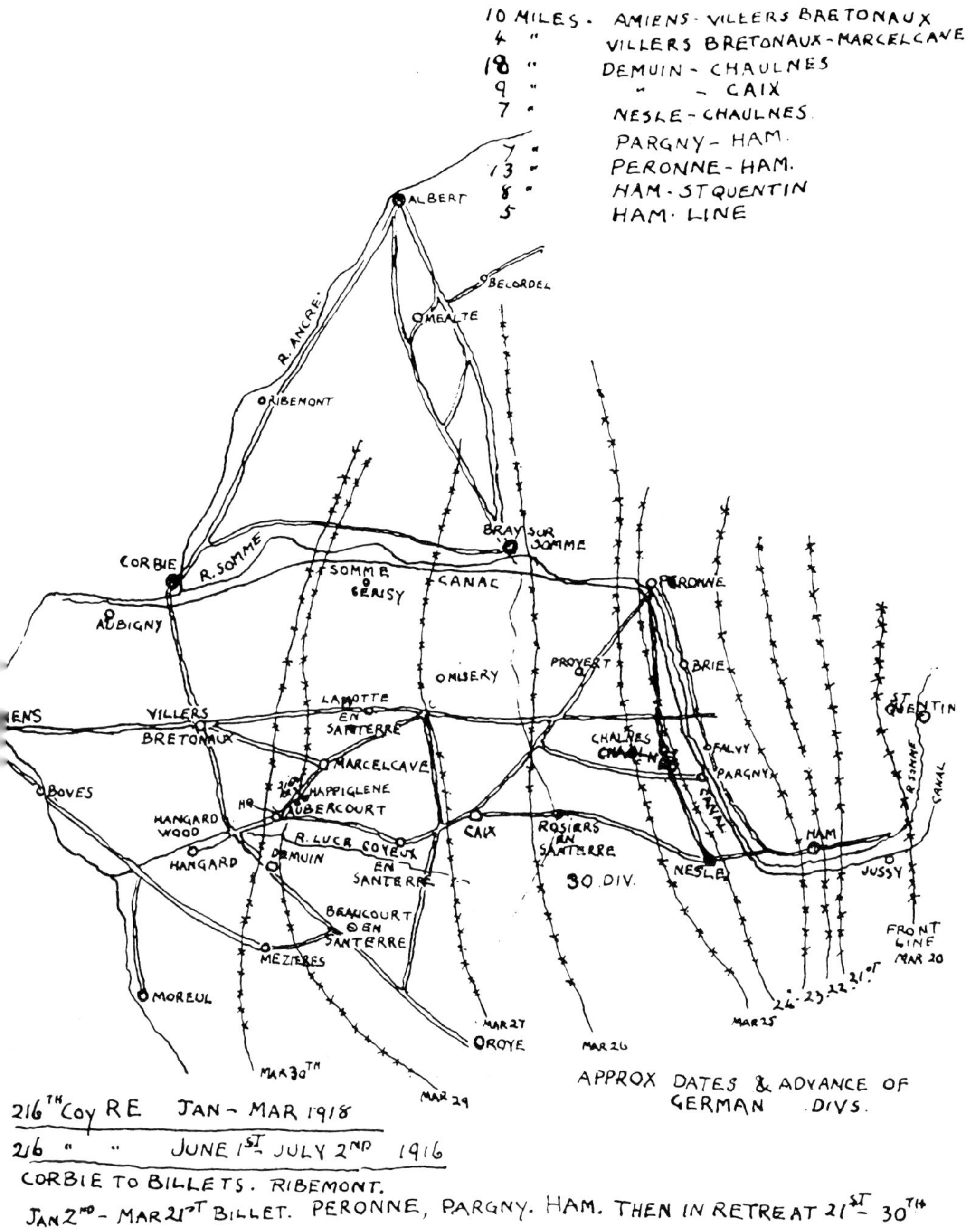

Map 7A: Arthur Sambrook's sketch map of 216 Company's billets and works around Albert and the Somme east of Amiens

On the following morning, Monday, 25 March, the remnants of XIX Corps still held the line of the Somme from near Péronne southwards to a point three miles short of Pargny. Their position was now outflanked and untenable because both the Third Army to the north and the mingled British and French force to the south had been compelled to retreat under heavy German assaults on the Sunday. So Monday was a day of general, and generally hard-fighting, retreat. By that night XIX Corps had been pushed five miles back from the Somme to a line running north-south through Chaulnes, where the German front line had been two years' earlier; on its left the Third Army had retreated some five miles further again, all the way to the line of the river Ancre. In the old XVIII Corps area, where the 216th Company, R.E., was, the arrival of the French had, if anything, speeded up the retreat, but the weary remnants of XVIII Corps were still available to plug the now-opening gap between British and French. At 5 p.m. on Monday the headquarters of XVIII Corps were moved to Moreuil, where the 216th had spent a day furiously digging trenches in readiness for the next stage of the retreat. The 216th left that evening. My father writes: 'Where we slept that night, or when, I have no recollection; we probably returned to the lorries, not being required there, as the French were coming in force when we left, apparently coming all night, judging from the numbers about when we left.'

The experience of the Nuneaton men, marching back and forth, waiting for orders, digging a little, then moving on, was commonplace. Orders were constantly miscarrying or being countermanded, now that a system of communications and a chain of command that had been devised for static warfare was breaking down under the pressures of a retreat. A brigadier, returned from leave and going forward to find his brigade somewhere near the Somme on 26 March, was struck by the number of 'officers, even including senior ones, Colonels and Majors', who 'were just standing about in a hopeless sort of way, doing nothing'.[12] For all the confusion Captain MacDougall seems at least to have kept his Company together, unlike the 567th (Devon) Army Troops Company, R.E., which had been working close to the 216th on the Somme. During the retreat sections became detached from one another, 'no officer had a map of the district and one section might have been taken prisoner but for the fact that one Sapper was pretty good at reading the stars in the sky, and detected that they had turned in the wrong direction and were heading back towards the advancing Germans'.[13]

The French were still coming, but they brought no artillery and only as much small arms ammunition as each infantryman could carry, so, for the present, could make no more than a token resistance before joining and, indeed, accelerating the general retreat on the right wing of the remains of the Fifth Army. As the Third Army, north of the Somme, was also falling back it was likely that General Gough's men would have to continue their retreat, so, on the night of 25th/26th March, Gough organized what it was hoped would be (and what more or less proved to be) the last defensive line for the Fifth Army. This stretched for eight miles northwards from Demuin on the river Luce to Sailly le Sec on the Somme, running on a slight curve three miles in front of Villers Bretonneux, a key position which enjoyed commanding observation over all the valleys converging on

Amiens, some twelve miles to the west. A line had been constructed here by the French in 1915 for the defence of the vital railway junction at Amiens, the purpose for which it was now more urgently required again. In 1917 the local peasantry had begun to remove wire and fill in trenches in order to cultivate the land, but Gough, when he arrived on the Somme in December, had put a stop to this premature return to peacetime conditions: it was well that he had done so. Haig, with his 'offensive spirit' took little interest in defences: late in 1917 he told his fortress engineer at G.H.Q., 'Your old back lines aren't going to be any use'.[14]

The 'Amiens Defence Line' was now to be restored, strengthened, and manned by any odd troops possessing rifles who could be found, all the Fifth Army's infantry reserves by now being expended. The task of gathering and organizing these troops (most of whom were engineers) was given to the Fifth Army's Chief Engineer, Major-General P.G. Grant; Grant was soon needed for his proper duties, so, from the evening of 26 March, the improvised force was under the command of Brigadier-General G.G.S.Carey, who happened to be passing by on his return from leave. Though, thanks to Lloyd George, 'Carey's Force' became the best-known, it was by no means the only force hastily improvised during the March retreat. 'It was a larger version of the many scratch bands that had been fighting alongside the front-line infantry since the battle started, and it had the advantage, which none of them enjoyed, of more than a day's freedom from the attentions of the enemy and an opportunity to get organised and entrenched'.[15]

'Carey's Force' numbered about 2,900 officers and men from the following units: the 144th, 213rd (Leamington), 216th, and 217th (Glasgow) Army Troops Companies, the 253rd Tunnelling Company, the 353rd Electrical and Mechanical Company, No. 4 Army Workshops Company, R.E., the Fifth Army Field Survey Battalion (45 officers and 650 other ranks), two companies of the 6th Regiment of U.S. Railway Engineers (500 men in all), detachments from the Fifth Army Infantry, Sniping, and Musketry Schools, three companies formed from the III and XIX Corps Schools, and a detachment of Fifth Army Signals. Retreating stragglers and officers and men returning from leave were also collected as occasion arose to add to the force. On 27 March it was reinforced by 400 officers and men of the 2nd Canadian Railway Engineers. 'The force provided, what was so often lacking during the retreat, a visibly occupied line on which the remnants and stragglers from the worn-out divisions could rally'.[16] On the best military principles, Carey's Force was divided into three sectors, right, centre, left, running northwards from the Luce to the Somme. The Right Sector, from Demuin for two miles to Marcelcave, was manned by the 216th Company and detachments from the Field Survey and III Corps School; at first the 353rd Company and U.S.Engineers were in this sector too, but on the 27th they were moved to the Left Sector where there was a more immediate threat from a German advance along the north bank of the Somme. Right Sector was commanded by Lt.Col. N.M.S. Irwin, who had found himself without a command because the remains of his own infantry battalion (8th Leicestershire), along with other fragments of 21st Division (VII Corps) of which it had formed a part at the beginning of the retreat, were now absorbed into another improvised formation, called McCulloch's Force.

My father describes the arrival of the Nuneaton men on the morning of 26 March to take their place in Carey's Force: 'Early next morning we came into a village called Demuin, where we found panic and confusion. People were loading up, the local gendarme was wheeling his bicycle up and down the street, urging the folks to load their belongings and get out quickly. The Company fell out in an orchard at the side of the road to get out of the bustle, and when only one or two carts were left we went into the estaminet. While we were in the orchard Mac ordered us to fall in, and read an order from Haig to all troops. Mac started off; "Men, your backs are to the wall, there is nothing behind you, between you and the Channel ports; each man must stand and fight".

Haig's famous order, including the words 'with our backs to the wall and believing in the justice of our cause each one of us must fight on to the end', is dated 11 April, so it would seem that my father must have remembered some other last-ditch order. He was not the only one. The historian of the 47th Division, in the Third Army at that time, noted: '27 March: received Haig's famous order that, at last, the withdrawal was to cease. The present line was to be held at all costs. Our backs were to the wall'. Also, Private Bert Bishop, serving with the Australian Corps, says that 'Haig's famous message' was read to his unit on Sunday, 24 March: 'It was the last few words that really hit us. "With our backs to the wall, believing in the righteousness of our cause, we fight to the end."'[17] Conceivably, all three had confused Haig's later, more famous, order with General Gough's special order of the day on 26 March, thanking his troops: 'We are fighting for our lives, our existence, our honour, and in your hands all these are safe.' 'Backs to the wall' was a common feeling. General Rawlinson wrote in his diary on 26 March: 'Gough is to be sent home, and I am to reconstruct the remnants of the Fifth Army as the Fourth Army. . . . Our losses up to 6 p.m. tonight are 80,000, and this is what worries me most. We are short of men and of divisions. It is quite evident that the Boche means to get to Amiens, and if he does he will cut the British Army off from the ports of Rouen and Havre, as well as separating us from the French Army. . . . Anyway, we shall have some ding-dong fighting, but, with our backs to the wall, we shall, I know, give a good account of ourselves. The Boche reserves are not unlimited'.[18]

The intended wall for the backs of the 216th Company was north-east of Demuin on the river Luce. My father's account of 26 March continues: 'At dusk we moved to the left of Demuin in the direction of Marcelcave, on a low ridge; we waited under a clump of trees while the officers and N.C.O.s marked out the trenches. Several of us dropped off to sleep and were left when the rest moved off to start digging. There was a severe frost and mist, which whitened the grass with hoar frost; there was a full moon above the ground mist. On waking, I had one side white with frost and on the grass was the outline of the other side. The others were rousing up and we were all so cold that we could not get a pick and shovel quick enough to get warmed up; higher up the slope we could hear the sound of digging, and found the company, and got busy. Corporal Fenn was singing "Will you not come to the ball", an aria from "The Quaker Girl". At daylight we found a hamlet at the foot of the slope, round four crossroads, two cottages on the outskirts of which became the headquarters of the mixed crowd digging in, composed of units retiring a few at a time, groups sent up from the rear, cooks, clerks, and other odds and ends. A company of R.E.s arrived, a surveying company who had rifles, but no bayonets, and were not used to their rifles, but were quite ready to have a go. Some of the infantry groups were Northamptons, and various Scots regiments, and a few Lewis machine guns: about two hundred men in all. This hamlet was called Happiglène, between Aubercourt and Marcelcave.'

Happeglène is on the river Luce, east of Demuin and Aubercourt. The Luce at this time was described as 'a small, water-cress, stream, four to eight yards wide, and generally fordable. Like other rivers in this part of France, it has pools and swamps along its course. The valley bottom is flat, and there are trees, chiefly poplars, planted nearly along it to a width of 200 or 300 yards'.[19] The trenches being dug (in heavy clay under a chalk topsoil) by the 216th Company were on the gentle ridge above Aubercourt and Happeglène, east of Hangard Wood and looking south over the river; this was the extreme right flank of the position occupied by Carey's Force. The Company dug and then waited: six hours on guard and six hours off, turn and turn about, sleeping in the open beside the trench. Arthur Daulman recalls, 'The order was to be careful not to fire on our infantry but we saw none'.

As the 216th Company dug their trenches the battle of retreat gradually grew closer. The Third Army, strengthened by substantial British reinforcements provided by Haig, held firm to its position covering Arras, so preventing a rolling-up of the British front northwards, but on 26 March its right wing unnecessarily withdrew along the northern bank of the Somme. This movement exposed the flank of XIX Corps, into which had now been assembled most of the surviving Fifth Army troops. On the following day the Germans were able to cross the river and compel the outflanked XIX Corps to swing back its left wing until it rested on the centre of the Amiens Defence Line. Thus it was that the battle was brought to the Left and Centre Sectors of Carey's Force before nightfall on 27 March. To the south of XIX Corps the newly-arrived French had taken over much of the former Fifth Army front, but they were still retreating; by the evening of 27 March they had given up Montdidier, south of Amiens. The Germans had advanced forty miles in less than a week; foiled at Arras, their immediate objective now was to capture Amiens. On the morning of 28 March the French north of Montdidier and XIX Corps were in a pronounced salient which they retired from gradually during that day: 'There was no hurry or serious confusion, but a steady flow of British and French troops drifting westward at a slow pace'.[20] As night came on, black with drenching rain, all the remnants that made up XIX Corps were either in Carey's line or in reserve behind it; the French were in a southwards extension of this line; the junction of the allies was at Demuin; their orders were to cover Amiens 'at all costs'. It was now time for the Right Sector of Carey's Force to see action.

Early on the 28th the General Commanding Fifth Army had telephoned from Amiens to ask Lieutenant-General Watts, the Commanding Officer of XIX Corps, about the situation. Watts 'in a cheerful voice replied: "they may well get us by lunch-time and you by tea-time"'.[21] The Fifth-Army General concerned was not

Gough but Sir Henry Rawlinson, who had replaced him on the previous day, for forced retirements were occurring not only at the front. The event immediately leading to General Gough's dismissal was a politico-strategic conference between President Poincaré, Prime Minister Clemenceau, Lord Milner (the British Minister at Versailles), General Foch and Sir Henry Wilson (Chiefs, respectively, of the French and the Imperial General Staff), Haig, Pétain, the French Commander-in-Chief, and their advisers. Pétain feared that the British would retreat to the Channel ports and Haig feared that the French would fall back to cover Paris: in either case a vast gap would open between their armies and the war would be lost. Haig noted in his diary: 'Foch seemed sound and sensible, but Pétain had a terrible look. He had the appearance of a Commander who was in a funk'. Wilson, however, 'reported that Haig was cowed, saying that unless the whole French army came up, the B.E.F. was beaten'.[22] Whichever Commander-in-Chief was the more fearful, the upshot was that Foch was appointed to co-ordinate all the actions of the Allied armies on the Western Front. Foch now decreed that more French divisions would be switched to support the British, though not just yet; Amiens would be defended at all costs.

During the conference Pétain had said of the British Fifth Army: 'Alas it no longer really exists, it is broken'. Neither Gough nor Fayolle, his nominal superior, had been invited to the conference, so, in default of reliable information, Pétain's opinion was accepted. In fact, Gough had 'fought well with the meagre forces allocated to him by Haig, had conformed at all times with the policy laid down by Haig, and had made the best of the almost impossible circumstances in which he and his army found themselves'.[23] Nevertheless Sir Henry Wilson on 27 March ordered that Gough should be 'rested' and superseded by Rawlinson. Wilson said privately: 'Hubert Gough has got to go because he had lost the confidence of his troops',[24] but it is doubtful if most ordinary soldiers had any opinion on the matter. The decision to deprive Gough of his command was political. Lloyd George disliked Gough as much as he disliked Haig, holding, as he did, both men responsible for the slaughter at Passchendaele: he dared not strike at Haig, but Gough was fair game. Wilson, too, disliked Gough, his junior, who had been promoted to an army command over Wilson's head; Gough had no influential friends at court. From London the retreat of the Fifth Army looked like a total disaster, so its commanding officer was an obvious sacrificial victim. Haig was not responsible for the sacking of Gough, but it is said that, after the war, he admitted that 'after considerable thought, I decided that public opinion at home, whether right or wrong, demanded a scapegoat, and that the only possible ones were Hubert or me. I was conceited enough to think that the army could not spare me'.[25]

The creation of a unified command under Foch altered the course of the Great War but it is unlikely that the motley band digging trenches near the river Luce were aware of that stupendous fact. The change of command in the Fifth Army on 28 March did not impinge upon my father, who, as it happened, was celebrating his twentieth birthday, being shelled in icy cold rain on that day as he and his comrades continued work on the Amiens Defence Line. At dawn on 29 March, Good Friday, writes my father, 'Sapper Tom Burdett and myself were detailed off to be company runners between headquarters and the 216th position on the ridge above Happeglène, the other R.E. company officer was in charge of Headquarters. Tom Burdett and myself had a small semi-detached cottage to ourselves, and the other larger one was taken over by the other company with about thirty men.

By now nearly all of XIX Corps had retreated behind the line prepared by Carey's Force, though 20th Division was obliged to take over two miles of front south-west of Demuin which was lost by the French on 29 March. Most of the exhausted infantry were put into reserve, rest, or work on yet another defensive line, five miles to the west, but some came into Carey's line. Thus 39th Division, reduced to two composite battalions, came to share the Right Sector with the Engineers on the night of the 28th; it was sent into support and replaced on the following day by 66th Division, reduced to one composite battalion of about five hundred men. On that day shell fire killed the commanding officer of the 39th in Demuin and wounded the commanding officer of the 66th in nearby Domart. Some Canadian machine-gunners came into the Right Sector, and other infantry, including all-important machine-gunners, came into the other two sectors of the line. 'By 29th March, there was mixture of troops from many divisions among whom Carey's Force began to lose its identity, but the original units still held, and by digging and improving trenches helped to stiffen the line, and added their quota of rifle fire to the defence'.[26] The Germans were now very close, so the 216th Company's horse transport, under the charge of Lieutenant Brand, was removed to Demuin; later that day it retired to Ailly-sur-Noye

My father's recollections of that Good Friday continue: 'In the afternoon we were sent up to the company with a message to Mac; while chatting to the fellows we looked across where the Germans were and saw them coming across some open country in extended order and massing in a wood a couple of miles away. It was a lovely warm afternoon, with bright sunshine, and everything looked peaceful until the small black figures of the Germans, crossing from the cover of one wood to the cover of the nearest one, were noticed, giving promise of a nasty day tomorrow. A few light shells came over and one or two people were knocked out. Mac wrote a reply and added a note for artillery support, gave us the message and sent us off. The trench system was a series of short trenches with a short space between each one, with no supports for communication, for retiring, or for any supports to come under cover. "None for us either", commented Burdett, "It'll be nice going up there again in the open with Jerry shooting".'

'Reporting back to headquarters, we were dismissed with orders to stay next door until we were required, so we began to think of having something to eat. Scrounging round the billet, we found a cellar underneath, with the remains of a store of potatoes and carrots, with a small barrel about one quarter full of cider. The cider was sweet and strong, and we prepared the vegetables, lit the stove, and put the dinner on to boil while we had a look round for something else. We had earlier noticed a rabbit hutch in a corner of the small back yard and put a sack over it, so that the Survey people wouldn't see that it contained a large blue beveren rabbit. "Here we are: rabbit for dinner", said Tom, opening the door to drag out the animal. The animal was not so tame as it was supposed to be and Tom got a nasty bite, and the rabbit hopped out of the hutch and took cover behind a big water butt standing there in the corner of the yard. After poking with our bayonets each side of the angle of the walls, the rabbit was killed, but could not be got at, and our supper stayed where it was. Then we noticed a smell of burning in the kitchen, and when we got back to the stove our vegetables were burnt black, so the saucepan and its contents were flung outside.'

'A few small shells dropped near us, as the Germans were trying to find the crossroads, so we took our equipment and rifles and went to the cellar. Tom thought cider was a good cure for a rabbit bite, and after a few trials it was agreed that cider was good for a lot of our troubles, including the loss of our supper. There was some excitement next door, some infantry had found two Germans, either captured or deserters, one of whom was bleeding at the side of the head; the only dressing available was the one I carried, and without thought for the morrow I handed it over. Come to think about it, the morrow did not concern us greatly, with a very few exceptions: the infantry just dug little foxholes, or a bigger one to take a Lewis gun, and the rest in slit trenches, each holding a few men, and waited to see what turned up. Meanwhile, as dusk was drawing in, cold and misty as usual, Tom and I decided on bed; we took the sheets off a large bed in the back room and changed the sheets and blankets. Putting our rifles and equipment to hand, each on his side of the bed, we climbed in, boots, puttees, and all, and after congratulating ourselves on lying on a straw bed, instead of the ground, had a good night's sleep.'

Captain MacDougall's war diary for 29 March records that the Company was 'in action in right sector'. There is no further record of that action, but the citation of the award of a D.C.M. to Sergeant Harris of the 216th much later in the year reads, in part, 'On the night of 29th March previous to the enemy attack on Aubercourt Ridge, during heavy shelling, he kept together all the men of his own section, together with some stragglers, who were manning a trench. He maintained the discipline and morale of all around him and so materially helped to hold up the enemy's advance'.[27] The troop movements observed from the 216th Company's trenches and the night bombardment gave warning that the German push towards Amiens would come in the morning. Ground conditions would be good for fighting. It rained, 'but as the ground, open corn-growing country, dotted with small villages and woods, had not previously been fought over, operations were not greatly influenced by the weather'.[28]

The morale of the two Company runners down in Happeglène was good enough to enable them to sleep. My father's account continues: 'The window in this room faced east, and just before dawn we were awakened by a burst of machine-gun fire from the ditch outside the house, so we slipped on our equipment and went out. There were a dozen French machine gunners in the ditch, loosing off into the usual thick fog, but we could see nothing moving, so got into the ditch close to the wall of the cottage. The other headquarters company came out, and we brought out and opened some ammunition boxes. When the French saw us ready they packed up and went back behind the ridge in our rear. After a few moments we could see the German machine gunners coming through the fog; their legs were going like toy dancing bears under their long greatcoats, and their packs were jogging up and down on their backs; the chaps carrying ammunition boxes, one hanging from each hand, bent down as they ran. Tom and I opened up and may have knocked over some of the men who were carrying the guns.'

'The R.E. captain, whose name was Kitchen, took half the party, about twenty men, in a counter attack towards the Germans, but they were all killed or wounded before they had gone many yards. The other officer, a lieutenant, was in the middle of the road, cursing us for opening fire without orders; his men were lying idle, watching the Germans get set, and waiting for the order to fire. The first burst of shots knocked some tiles from the roof, which fell near the officer, so he jumped into the ditch and shouted to his chaps, "What the hell are you waiting for: shoot the bastards", which we did for the next half hour or longer. After some time we found Jerry had got round to our right, where we thought the French were, and the ditch was not so safe.'

'The lieutenant gave orders to retire and they retired in a body up the road at our rear, up hill for about thirty yards, where were two cottages. Tom and I stayed put and watched as they got shot down by machine-gun fire from our front. When the firing stopped, we decided to make a dash ourselves, to see if we could work round to the left, to rejoin our company. We got half way up the hill before Jerry opened up on us, and bullets were knocking bits off the pavé and twigs from the trees at the side of the road; I noticed white marks all round us, where the shots were hitting the road, but we got up to the houses at the top before I was hit. We passed the other crowd, who all appeared killed. We had reached the first cottage when I got a violent blow on the right elbow, which knocked me over against the door. Luckily it was not fastened and I fell inside. Tom came in from the garden; he had gone through an orchard at the side of the road (I was in too much of a hurry to notice the gate), and said he would work round the back of the ridge to rejoin the company if possible. Tom met up with the company later in the day.'

'We had a smoke and waited for things to quieten down, and I decided to leave my greatcoat and equipment in the cottage, as we still had about twenty yards to go before we were over the brow of the ridge, and then made a dash and got over before anyone started shooting. The other side was very steep, with bushes and saplings, and a brook at the bottom. Our late allies, the French machine-gunners, were dug in the other side of the brook in a ploughed field. I did not think it a very safe position for them to be in without much cover, but plenty for Jerry to take advantage of on top of the ridge. I went past them, nursing my elbow, and continued across open country. There was firing to the left, where the company and infantry were, and before I got very far the firing started again at the rear and on the right.'

'There were a few walking wounded coming back, and a few stragglers amongst them, but after about a mile back, we were stopped by a staff officer and two cavalry orderlies, who were turning back anyone not wounded. I showed my arm, like a piece of old unravelled rope, with the muscles and sinews all torn. I got cursed for giving away my field dressing the previous evening, and one of the orderlies got down and tied my elbow up; they had a lot of spare ones with them, and the officer told me "Keep on over that way to Villers Bretonneux, where you will find the hospital", so off I went. My late companion, who was unwounded but said he had lost his spectacles, was turned back towards the line. After walking for nearly an hour I arrived at the railway sidings at Villers Bretonneux and joined half a battery of Horse Artillery who were having breakfast, which they invited me to share. Tea with rum, biscuits, and bully went down very well, and I stayed chatting with them until they limbered up and moved forward. These guns were thirteen pounders.'

So my father was happily out of the action before breakfast. The Germans came through Happeglène and Aubercourt and captured Demuin, further down the river. From high ground above Demuin on the south bank they directed flanking fire upon the 66th Division and the Right Sector of Carey's Force, including the 216th Company on the Aubercourt ridge; then, working around to the right, they compelled the British to retreat, about 11 a.m., to Hangard Wood on the next ridge, a mile or so to the west, where the remnant of the 39th Division was in a support line. My father's account of the action is based on the recollections of his friend Alf Chamberlain: 'The company and the various units came into action with Jerry after our affair at the crossroads was finished. They were mixed in with the infantry in isolated trenches on the ridge. Our Section, No.3, was under Sergt Streather and Corpl Douglas and some of the Northamptons on their right. Lieut Walker, Right Half Company officer was in another trench on their left. The Germans worked round to their right (possibly some of the lot that attacked us earlier in the morning) and took the Northampton trench, and set up a machine gun over the end of it to enfilade the trench occupied by Streather, who sent Tom Norman across to Lieut Walker and then shot the machine gunner and kept the others engaged until Walker had received orders from MacDougall to retire. Sergt Ashley, No.2 Section, was wounded and carried off the field on a gate by Alf Chamberlain and Edgar Dunton, and got another shot through the backside. His bearers told him to stop kicking and be still, else they would dump him. They were getting machine gunned badly during the start of the withdrawal, crossing open ground without any cover. The Company fell back to Hangard Wood.'

Tom Norman, reported as 'missing' in Captain MacDougall's diary was wounded and captured. Sergeant Streather's brief account of the action in a letter home reassuringly notes that the wounds of some of the Nuneaton N.C.O.s, Ashley, Hughes, and Corporal Fenn, were not life-threatening. By 8 May he reports: 'Fenn is about better I think. He is close to the Forth Bridge in Scotland; you may be seeing him in Nuneaton soon. He was pretty tough in the line; he must have fought for at least two hours after he was shot before he went to the dressing station and even then he helped carry a badly wounded Australian.' As for their officers: 'We had every reason to be very proud of our officers during the scrap. They turned out trumps, especially the new one, Mr Walker: he is the best we have ever had. In civvy life he was an architect and seems to be more popular than even Mr Knox used to be' (letter of 5 April).

Arthur Daulman's section was mixed in with some of the Canadians. He recalls: 'We were supported by Canadian machine guns and two 18 pdrs. Then we saw the Germans working round behind us but we stayed until ordered to retire by a Canadian officer. We left the ridge and went back to the next one about a mile away, where we reformed under Smith. We laid down in the open and waited, reflecting glumly that the Germans were in our trenches whilst we had none. We were attacked again and although we had lots of casualties the Germans must have been pretty bad shots, because we had no cover and were out in the open. My webbing brass on my neck was hit, and then I felt as though someone had hit me on my left arm with a red hot hammer. I had been hit by a bullet in my upper left arm. I told Lieut Smith who was next to me that I had been hit and was told to get back. I went on all fours down to a sunken road to a Red Cross Station for my first dressing. They directed me to the next station, but it was full, as were the others. I must have walked ten miles until I was attended to.' Evidently the Casualty Clearing Stations had overfilled since my father had passed through in the morning.[29]

The Company and other odds and ends of infantry and engineers held on in Hangard Wood until late afternoon, when they were relieved by a fresh, strong battalion of the Australian 9th Brigade. My father writes of the arrival of the Australians and the departure of the Nuneaton men: 'They came up in skirmishing order, and Mac met the officer and said he would go along with them and show them the position of things. The Aussie officer said "That's all right. We'll find the bastards. If you chaps want to help, look after the wounded." So the Company acted as stretcher bearers, getting the wounded to the hospital at Villers Bretonneux. Mac, Sergt Harris (No.4 Section), Sergt Streather, and Sapper Edgar Dunkley adjourned at dusk to a deserted estaminet, and there spent the night and made their supper with champagne.' It is obscurely reassuring to have this evidence that mild looting, so habitual to the common sapper, extended to the very summit of the 216th Company's chain of command.

The action was probably more confused than those narratives suggest. The historian of another R.E. company, the 253rd Tunnellers, which was originally in Carey's Centre Sector but found itself over on the right near Hangard on the morning of 30 March, writes: 'the various units became hopelessly mixed, and any sort of cohesion was impossible. . . . 253rd Company became so scattered that small groups of men attached themselves to any unit, however fragmentary, in their vicinity. A disjointed battle developed and continued until dusk, when reliefs began to arrive. The Company were ordered to Boves . . . and here the survivors eventually gathered'.[30] It is likely that the experience of the 216th Company was similar. Their casualties, in addition to those already mentioned, were: killed, L/Cpl A.J.Money, Sappers W.C.Pearce, W.Roberts, and W.J.Taylor; wounded, Corporals O.G.Lago, F.Follett, Sappers W.Benson, H.Jones, H.Patfield, H.Pierpoint, R.Potter, H.Robinson, F.Sherriff, and R.Stewart. The effective strength of the Company on 31 March was 4 officers (Captain MacDougall, Lieutenants Smith, Walker, and Brand) and 112 other ranks.

This day was Easter Sunday; the weather was cold and showery; the 216th Company were relieved and retired to Boves on the river Avre, about five miles south-east of Amiens. There was fighting on the spur between the Luce and Avre; north of the Luce there were no infantry attacks but the opposing artilleries were busy all day: for the first time since the retreat began the British infantry on the Somme were being given really good artillery support. With the relief of most of the engineer companies Carey's Force was disbanded, but some of its units remained in the line for a few days longer, under a new commanding officer, as part of 'Whitmore's Cosmopolitan Force'. General Rawlinson noted in his diary on 31 March that 'the Old Guard' (as he called Carey's Force) had 'been in the line for five days and have just tided over the dangerous period, but the guns are not yet working very well with their barrage, and things are still rather upside down. However we are beginning to get them into some sort of order.'[31] The Amiens Defence Line was holding firm, albeit dented a little in the centre at Marcelcave and on the right at Hangard. Without early or substantial reinforcement the survivors of the Fifth Army had fought to a standstill a German force three or four times more numerous than they. The French had retreated a little further to the south but were now generally firm because their artillery, arriving later than the infantry, had come into action in force for the first time on 30 March. The British Third Army was still firm in front of Arras. The Allies had suffered nearly a quarter of a million casualties between them: the Germans about the same number.

Chapter Thirteen: The End of the War, April to November 1918

Though the retreat gave rise to enormous alarm and anger in London, it does not appear that British morale at the front was much broken: the Germans were, if anything, more despondent after a forty mile advance than were their enemies. B.H. Liddell Hart suggests that one reason for their failure was 'the physical effect on ill-nourished troops of breaking into an area full of well-filled depots, and the psychological effect of discovering that the enemy is so much better fed and equipped than themselves — that they have been nourished only with lies, about the result of the U-boat campaign and the enemy's economic condition'. He quotes a German officer's diary on 27 March: 'Now we are already in the English back-areas . . . a land flowing with milk and honey. Marvellous people these, who will only equip themselves with the very best that the earth produces. Our men are hardly to be distinguished from English soldiers. Everyone wears at least a leather jerkin, a waterproof . . . English boots or some other beautiful thing. The horses are feeding on masses of oats and gorgeous food-cake . . . and there is no doubt the army is looting with some zest.' Liddell Hart notes: 'anyone with personal experience of war knows how the thought of food and of civilized comfort fills the soldier's horizon', and, returning to 1918: 'Once this plunder was exhausted the reaction was all the greater and the contrast of their own paucity with the enemy's plenty the more depressing. As hopes of military success fade and with them the hope of again nourishing their stomachs, and souls, on the enemy's supplies, a moral rot sets in rapidly.'[1]

The Germans acquired a great deal of loot in the thousand or so square miles of ground they captured, but achieved neither their first objective, which was to break the Third and Fifth Armies and roll up the British front northwards, nor their second, smaller objective, which was to capture Amiens. Even so, the retreat was an alarming reverse for the British. Recriminations began early. On 27 March Brigadier-General Charteris at G.H.Q. blamed the politicians for not providing enough men: 'If only the truth were known in England of the way we have been starved of men and made to increase our commitments with dwindling resources, how every protest was fobbed off with fine phrases, there would be some free hanging in England. But no doubt shortly the politicians and the L.G. peers will turn and rend the soldiers.'[2] It was Lloyd George's decision that the British should take over more of the French front, and either his or the Chief of the Imperial General Staff Robertson's decision that extra troops should not be sent to France so that this front could be manned fully. It was Haig's decision to keep the main British strength in the north. Neither he nor Pétain realized early enough that the March offensive was not a diversion but the Germans' main blow. In the early stages of the battle Haig was, as usual, over-optimistic and somewhat out of touch with what was happening on the ground. As we have seen, Gough was made a scapegoat for what was perceived in London as a disaster. Lloyd George made a notoriously ill-informed speech in the Commons on 9 April, putting all the blame, by innuendo, on Gough, but giving extravagant praise to Carey's Force.

After Carey's Force was disbanded the 216th Company was ordered into the back area to reform and refit. While the men were in their trenches on Aubercourt ridge the horse transport had been taken through Moreuil to Ailly sur Noye, thence over the river to Jumel, and subsequently a little further west to St.Sauflieu. On 1 April it was rejoined here by the rest of the Company, which then moved further south (it is not clear why) to Ferrières, some thirty miles from Amiens. On 2 April they came all the way back to the river Somme, ten miles downstream from Amiens, to join other ex-Carey's Force R.E. units assembled at La Chaussée and Picquigny for refitting. Here the Company made up the stores, tools, and equipment lost in the retreat and perhaps received new drafts to replace the casualties of 30 March: certainly they were back to full strength by the end of April. Here also Sergeant Streather had his first chance to write home since the retreat had begun. On 5 April he wrote: 'You will not be surprised to hear that we have been at war during the past ten days. We got relieved on Monday and now we are on rest at a quiet little village twenty miles behind the line. This is the first possible chance I have had of writing a letter... We have a queer sort of billet just now. Harris, Taylor, and I sleep in one bed in a dark attic which we get into through a hole in the wall. Here we get a better idea of the French peasants as they were in peace time, except that the war has cast an everlasting look of sadness over every face. The people in England have something to be thankful for I can tell you; they will never understand the position of the French and if they did there would be no talk of peace and no strikes or troubles at home.'

On the first three days of April there was very little fighting. The French took over some of the British line as far north as Hangard; two companies of the British 18th Division made an unsuccessful attempt on the evening of 2 April to retake the old 216th Company position on Aubercourt ridge. In an infinitely more rarefied region of military events the Fifth Army passed on that day from the high command of General Fayolle back to Field Marshal Haig. It was now renamed the 'Fourth Army' because General Rawlinson and his staff had formerly commanded an army with that numbering; the change of title gave some colour to Pétain's myth that the Fifth Army had been annihilated. On 4 April the Germans again made a determined attempt to push towards Amiens; there was savage fighting all day in the rain around Villers Bretonneux and Hangard, but the attackers gained only a little ground and at great cost. On the following day the attack petered out.

These events brought the 216th Company back to Boves on 5 April, initially to prepare more trenches but subsequently to resume bridge-building, for bridges over the Avre near Amiens were needed in case of further retreat. Driver Frank Hextall approved of Boves. He writes: 'This village was abandoned by the civilians who left all their furniture etc in the houses so we made ourselves pretty comfortable. However the Company were engaged "up the line" for a few days and the transport moved back to Vers on the 6th where, after a few days, we were shelled from our lines and forced to move away from the buildings. The glorious part of the few days (and it was worth risking a few shells) we had plenty of rations and therefore the first decent meal for about three weeks. From here we made daily journeys to Longueau to cart material for the steel girder bridges which the

Company were erecting.' Hextall's remarks about food remind us of the enormous difficulty of providing regular rations for an army in retreat and perhaps provide a context for his comrades' desperate struggles with tough cows and fierce rabbits.

Between 6 and 12 April the Company erected three Class A steel bridges at and near Boves: one was a thirty foot span, the other two were sixty foot spans, one of them replacing a pontoon bridge which they moved upstream and reassembled. For a bridge of 60ft span, standard girder sections were bolted together on site to make a pair of heavy Warren girders; the 30ft span consisted of standard steel joists laid side by side in the number necessary for the traffic to be carried: see illustrations 39 and 45. The decking of both kinds of bridge was made of 9"x4" timber baulks. 216th Company had at this time the help of large working parties from the 90th Labour Company to unload trains in the huge army sidings at Longueau, just east of Amiens, and to labour on the three bridge sites; the familiar figure of Captain Hopkins, the bridging officer at G.H.Q., was seen on site again. 45 railway wagon loads of bridging materials arrived at Longueau on 10 April to provide a forward dump for future work in this area: incidentally confirming that British High Command was confident that there would be no further retreat in this area (the German attack switched to Flanders on 9 April). Even so, as soon as 216th Company completed each bridge they prepared it for possible demolition.

One familiar figure not on view was C.S.M.Mitchinson. He was on leave in England before the retreat began, so he missed all the excitements; the Company had moved so frequently that he still had not rejoined it on 13 April, when Sergeant Streather wrote home: 'Most of the wounded seem to have got to England, so probably you have heard more about them than I can tell you. The only one missing is poor Tom Norman and we know nothing whatever about him, but hope he is alright. The C.S.M. has not joined the company yet and we don't know where he is, but expect he will turn up in a day or two as things are getting more settled. Well, our rest did not last long; we went back up the line again the day I wrote last [5 April] and we have been at work hard ever since. Have done 18 hours several days and really never get time to write. One thing we have good billets: house completely furnished; have beds and everything. The village is about 4 miles from the line and the work not much nearer. The work is very urgent and we are not up to strength and that makes us have to do long hours. There are no civvies in the village and nowhere to buy anything so for the first time since we have been in the country we are short of cigarettes. There is plenty of bacca but no cigs, and matches are almost like gold. The rations are good and plentiful.

On 15 April the 216th shifted camp three miles northwards to Boutillerie, a move which took them closer to the Fort Manoir crossing over the river Avre, where they had begun work on another sixty-foot steel bridge the day before. On 20 April the 216th were transferred from the Fourth Army to III Corps for administration and work; on the same day Captain MacDougall was promoted Major and transferred to command the 1st Siege Company (Royal Anglesey) R.E., being succeeded in command of the 216th by Captain P.H. Sanders. 23 April brought a reward to humbler members of the Company for their exploits as part of Carey's Force, in the shape of Military Medals for Cpl Anderton, Cpl Douglas,

2nd/Cpl Walters, Spr Baldwin, and Spr Key. The official history of Royal Engineer bridging in the Great War stresses the importance of the work done east of Amiens during April and notes that it 'was carried out under considerable difficulties immediately the line stabilised'.[3] Neither MacDougall nor Sanders makes reference to difficulties in the Company diary, but one imagines that they may have included disruption of communications and loss of stores, due to the retreat, and current German shelling.

On 9 April the Germans attacked in Flanders, where they battered away for three weeks in an attempt to smash the British army; as on the Somme in March, they took back most of the territory they had lost in 1916-17 and some more. Incidentally, they captured all the water installations set up by the 216th Company: one wonders how they treated them in the light of a description of German plundering which says that they 'ruin sources of supply invaluable to the maintenance of their own advance — wrecking waterworks for the sake of the brass taps'.[4] As on the Somme they failed to make a strategic breakthrough, but, as on the Somme, they inflicted (and suffered) many casualties and created a great deal of alarm. Also, they were still capable of giving a nasty surprise on the Amiens front. Early in the morning of 24 April there was a heavy bombardment of the front and back areas, including gas shells, as usual. It was probably on this occasion that Sapper Lathbury of the 216th Company was gassed: the *Nuneaton Chronicle* of 7 June reports that he was then in Rugby hospital. The Germans attacked with tanks as well as infantry and captured Villers Bretonneux, but a counter attack by the Australians during the following night turned them out of the place. In the following few days there were smaller, unsuccessful German attacks; then relative quiet settled over the Somme country. The 216th took no part in this action beyond constructing and manning a reserve line at Glisy on the Somme, four or five miles behind the fighting. Here, recalls Frank Hextall, 'we were daily shelled and nightly bombed'. An officer of another R.E. company, also in the Glisy trenches at this time noted in his diary on 24 April: 'Stood to all day but had little news of front. Late afternoon a British plane came over our position and pilot waved hand, indicating that German attack had failed.'[5] On that day the 216th Company's transport was removed from Boutillerie to Amiens. Driver Hextall continues: 'we moved back to Amiens which was now little more than a wreck. Here, along with other R.E. units disorganised in the retreat, we billeted in old French hospital huts on one of the boulevards. The company were working shifts in the line. Whilst here the station (a fine building) was set on fire by the Boche incendiary shells.'

When things had quietened down a little around Amiens, III Corps handed over the whole of its line to the Australian Corps and, on 27 April, went back to rest in the Fourth Army reserve. At this point the 216th Company was transferred from III Corps to the Second Army in Flanders. On 28 April they entrained at Ailly sur Somme, a short distance down-river from Amiens; their destination was Watten, a small town on the Aire Canal, six miles north of St.Omer, where they arrived, after the usual leisurely train journey, on 1 May. They were billeted in Serques, close by. There, writes Frank Hextall, we 'began a well earned rest. The country round here was delightful and we enjoyed some glorious rides and weather. We were engaged (on and off) widening and strengthening old French bridges over the canal and erecting new bridges.' As soon as they arrived at Serques a Lieutenant Wise, R.E., was attached to the unit. After a kit inspection in the forenoon and a route march in the afternoon of 2 May, while the officers conferred with Captain Hopkins, the Bridging Officer from G.H.Q., the Company rested for two days.

Work restarted on Sunday, 5 May, with the strengthening and redecking of three wooden bridges at Serques, Lieutenant Smith in charge. On 8 May Lieutenant Rows, R.E., was attached to the Company for duty, after which the four subalterns now available each commanded a detachment of bridge builders or repairers on a different site: Smith at Henmuin, Walker at Shipstaat, Brand at Fort Brionelles, Rows at St.Momelin. The detachments under Lieutenants Walker and Brand were erecting emergency Portal Bridges: see Appendix, p.236.

Sergeant Streather wrote to his parents on 8 May, probably from Henmuin: 'We have seen a bit of the country during the last six weeks but I think we have settled down for some time now. We spent the last six days in a splendid little village: had very little work to do, plenty of enjoyment and the very best of living. The people there were very good to us; in fact they treated us better than the Indian troops were treated in Nuneaton. I think it is the first time I have seen that in this country; the pity was that we could not stay. We moved yesterday to our present billet; we have a big job to do many miles behind the line but it is very urgent, so I suppose we shall be kept pretty busy. The place is like a big town but has been made entirely by the army and there are only one or two isolated farms about where we can meet the civvies. Of course there are some splendid canteens, Y.M.C.A.s, Church Army huts, cinemas, and suchlike places here, and the camps round about are kept just like they would be at home. The funny part of it is that nearly all the men you see down here have been here for months and they do nothing but grumble. I never heard so much grumbling and quarrelling all the time I have been up the line as I heard in this place last night. Everybody I met said what a rotten job he had and how fed up he was, and nearly all wished they could get up the line. So they said, but I know where I would rather be. . . Some of the gardens out here are looking grand just now. The weather has been nice and warm with an occasional wet day so the things have grown by magic almost. During the course of my travels I met a little girl. I want you to send her one of those little R.E. badges. Her address is Mlle Madeleine Lefebvre, Serques par Moulle, Pas de Calais. She is only nine years old. . . I was once billeted in their farm and had a good time there. There is only number 3 section on this job so for the time being I am commander in chief. Cpl Douglas, Cpl Berry, and I have a tent in an orchard so we are quite comfortable. The other Sgts are all away on different jobs with their own section and headquarters are in a village about equal distances from all the works.'

There was some night bombing and long-range shelling of bridges in the area where the Company were working, but they suffered no casualties by enemy action. There had been no serious fighting in Flanders for over a week, but Haig could not be sure that it would not flare up again. The Germans had not reached their main objective, the railway junction at Hazebrouck, but they had penetrated to within thirty miles of the sea. In May the British were reducing or moving rear installations (a hospital and a mechanical transport repair shop at St.Omer were, for instance, removed all the way to Normandy); they were constructing emergency defences to cover Dunkirk and they even had plans for a possible evacuation of the Second Army through Dunkirk. Where the 216th Company were now working, the lines of the rear defensive system ran on both sides of the Aire Canal; if ever these defences should be needed emergency bridges would be needed too.

Company headquarters remained at Serques for over a month, with the four sections working on various bridges round about and enjoying fine weather for most of the time. Sergeant Streather wrote home on 16 May about the activities of his own section: 'We have been very busy again during the past week but we are in a very quiet place on a river many miles behind the line so we don't mind work here: it is better than up the line I can tell you. . . We are working two shifts and as I am the only Sgt I have to be out a large part of the time on both so that has made me so busy I have not had a chance to write. I have 35 of my own men and 30 labour men attached so you see I have quite a family. . . Leave is not open nor is it likely to be while this German offensive is in progress. . . We have quite a lot now who have been out twelve months and I have only been back nine so am well down the list. . . We have set a lot of new officers on lately. We have nine with us at present I think. They were not anxious to work for us when up the line but they stick now I can tell you. I only hope they will and keep us back here for duration.'

The 'labour men' mentioned by Streather were not 'resting' infantrymen, such as those who provided working parties for the Company in 1916 and 1917 and whose units are recorded meticulously in Captain MacDougall's war diary. The war diary of the far less informative Captain Sanders (April to November 1918) never once mentions a working party; but Streather's remark about labour men allows us to make the reasonable supposition that much of the Company's bridge building during the period of Sanders' command was done with help of Labour Corps personnel, who were increasingly taking over the unskilled engineering labour once performed by infantrymen. The war diary kept by Captain Sanders's successors in command of the 216th during 1919 reveals that a working party was attached to the Company on every day they were building or repairing bridges. These working parties were drawn almost invariably from the 90th Labour Company, so I conjecture that the 216th might have had an equally regular band of helpers (perhaps even from the 90th Labour Company) between April and November 1918.

From Captain Sanders' otherwise rather uninformative war diary we learn that Lieutenant Rows left to rejoin his unit (whatever it was) on 26 May and that Smith, Brand, and Walker and their detachments rejoined the rest of the Company one by one, but there is no mention of nine officers. The Company's own officer establishment in May and June was four, i.e. Sanders, Smith, Walker, and Brand; the war diary mentions just three officers (Lieutenants Wise, Rows, and Fothergill) attached for various periods in those two months; the only other attached officer named is Captain Skerry of the 'U.S.A. Engineers' in July; but an 'E.J.Stone' who censored a letter written by Sergeant Streather on 26 June might be an otherwise unnoticed attached officer. Streather is unsure of the number of new officers because the Company's workforce at any one time is spread over bridge repair and construction work on four or more different sites and men are working in shifts. He refers to the new officers condescendingly and implies that, for practical purposes, he is the head of his 'family' of 35 sappers and 30 'labour men'. I conjecture therefore that some, perhaps all, the new, briefly attached, officers were 'set on' to learn about heavy steel bridging from the experts in the relative peace and quiet of the back area. There is some evidence (see p.210 below) that Captain Sanders refused to employ strange, half-trained officers when there was urgent work to be done close to the line.

As the prospect of a wholesale British retreat grew fainter, the task of building and improving bridges between the front line and the Channel ports became less urgent, but its importance did not diminish. The accumulation of heavy steel bridging material and the long-continued training programme in its use during three years of largely static trench warfare indicates that the British High Command was fully aware of the importance of motor transport. The speed and success of the advance, when it came, would depend upon supplies brought mainly by road: therefore it would depend to a degree upon the number, strength, and width of bridges.

On 1 June congratulatory messages were received from General Rawlinson for 'Capt D.A.MacDougall, R.E, Cpl Anderton, L/Cpl Douglas, L/Cpl Walters, Sappers Key and Baldwin', from which it would appear that Douglas had lost a stripe since winning the M.M. On 3 June L/Cpl Salmon was injured in the head, owing to a pulley chain breaking, and was admitted to hospital. One by one the new bridges were completed, painted, and opened to traffic. On 6 June the Company were engaged on infantry training, on 7 June kit inspection and sport, on 8 June they were preparing to move, on 9 June cleaning billets. The only activity recorded on 10 June was that Capt Sanders and Lt Wise visited G.H.Q. to receive instructions. It was indeed a very quiet time for the Nuneaton men.

It was a relatively undisturbed period for British troops in general, apart from five unlucky battle-mauled divisions which were posted to a so-called 'quiet' sector of the French army's front only to find themselves involved in the fierce battles that ensued when the Germans attacked there on 27 May. Fighting on the French front, at first along the river Aisne, then along the Marne, involved another four British divisions and (fighting for the first time in any significant numbers) three American divisions, but the French took the brunt of the German attack. The Germans had attacked with the intention of drawing reserves away from the north, and then coming back to Flanders for a third and, it was hoped, final blow to knock out the British. This was not to be: on 18 June the French began a series of successful counter-attacks which soon began to show that the tide of war had at last turned. With the pressure off them for weeks on end the British armies in Picardy and Flanders revived their spirits and replenished their numbers. Lloyd George sent more troops from England and the Middle East; the age limits for conscription were extended in both directions; civilians in essential industries were 'combed out' for the army; the shipment of American troops was accelerated. Time was against Germany. The German army realized that it could not win the war and the German ruling class realized that the likeliest outcome of prolonging an unwinnable war would be a Communist revolution in their country. Germany's war aim henceforth was to fight strongly enough to earn a negotiated peace.

On 13 June the Headquarters section of the 216th Company moved to Arques, between St.Omer and Hazebrouck. Driver Hextall recalls briefly: 'We moved to Arques to dismantle and re-erect bridges. Rather dreary place — except for a few stray shells'. The Company was split up again. The right half company, under Lieutenant Brand built an emergency Portal bridge and four other, unspecified, bridges at or near Arques. The left half company, with Lieutenant Smith, departed 'by Motor Bus' on 13 June for Montreuil, then went to Beutin (between Montreuil and Etaples) where their first task was to erect an 85 ft Class A steel span bridge at a nearby place called Enocq; they were in what was formally 'G.H.Q. Area', so were now perhaps under G.H.Q. rather than Second Army orders. Lieutenant Wise went to Bourbourg (close to Gravelines, between Calais and Dunkirk) in order to make a reconnaissance of bridges in the Northern Area of the Second Army. Lieutenant Walker went on leave. At one stage work on all bridges stopped for a day pending authority from the French, and once Captain Sanders was constrained to have an interview with Major Bostock, Inland Water Transport, 'as to hurrying Pile Driver'. Otherwise the work went smoothly in uniformly fine weather. Presumably the laggardly pile driver was a petrol or steam driven machine, mounted on a raft and therefore the responsibility of an Inland Water Transport Unit: the 216th Company was quite capable of building an ordinary bankside pile driver. On 25 June No 2 Section (Sgt Henley in charge) left Arques for Beutin by road; on the following day the Headquarters Section and the Mounted Section, including Frank Hextall, followed them. Hextall writes: 'We moved to Beutin, making a three day road journey in glorious weather and country, undoubtedly the best move we had made. We were encamped on the banks of a tidal river: as work was rather scarce could visit Etaples and Paris-Plage and indulge in sea bathing.'

This tidal river is the Canche. Work may have been scarce for the mule-drivers, but Capt. Sanders's diary indicates that a certain amount of bridging work was done. Their 85 ft steel span bridge at Beutin took six days to erect, deck, and open to traffic; the bridge had two spans, which were bolted together and launched by the cantilever method; three sections of the Company were employed on this work. The other section (No.1) was at Arques, loading dismantled bridges onto a barge for dispatch to Guines, near Calais, then erecting and launching what is described as an 'experimental' bridge. After the whole Company was reunited on 13 July, they erected another seven steel span bridges in the area. Capt. Skerry, U.S. Engineers, was attached to the Company from 1 July until some unknown date. It is not known what happened to Lt. Wise when he went away on his Northern Area bridges reconnaissance. Another Lieutenant, perhaps Brand, must also have left the Company about this time because Capt. Sanders's diary reports both the establishment and the actual strength of officers on 1 August as three. (Wise and Brand are not mentioned again in any record of the Company.)

The strength of other ranks on 1 August was healthily 137, against an establishment of 138. The diary on that day reports: 'Company employed heavy bridging in G.H.Q. area. Nos. 1, 2, & 4 Sections employed on Bridge F.D.4 at ENOCQ. Two 85' spans Class A with 30' shore bay on North Side. No.3 Section on Bridge F.D.6 at Nempont.' Except for six wet days, the weather was fine throughout the Company's refreshingly long stay in the back areas. Sunday, 4 August, was one of the rare wet days and the one day on which it appears that the whole Company was 'resting'. It was the fourth anniversary of the outbreak of the Great War. The 216th completed their various bridges in the following week; by 7 August one section was still working on a bridge at Airon Notre Dame while the rest of the Company was cleaning up the sites and painting.

Sergeant Streather wrote on 6 August: 'I am back with the company again now but I think I shall be going away again tomorrow. I rather like this game; it is alright for the summer but it would be a bit of a terror in winter. We had two more leaves come in today, Thomas and Cpl Walters, you may see them; that puts me 69th on the list so if they continue at the present rate I may be home early in 1980. What do you think of the news lately: not so bad is it? Well, this August is not such a good one for me as I had last year though we have a far better job now than we had then and I think it will continue for some time yet. The S.M. has just come into the tent he tells me that some more men will be going on leave in a day or two so hope a rush sets in. Has been very stormy again this last week; we have been wet a good many times but we get used to that nowadays: one thing, one soon gets dry this weather.' The 'not so bad' news was the French armies' success in the Second Battle of the Marne. The British would soon be on the move and the current job of the Nuneaton men would not 'continue for some time yet'. On 9 August they were taking material and appliances to the railway station. Where the next move would be was only a matter of rumour: the British army was about to go on the offensive and secrecy was the order of the day. At the beginning of August a printed notice was pasted into every man's pay book: it was headed 'KEEP YOUR MOUTH SHUT' and went on to warn men not to talk about operations in which they were engaged or to question men in other units about their operations.

On 10 August, a fine hot day, the 216th Company entrained at Beutin; on the following day they reached the huge army sidings at Longueau, just east of Amiens, from where they marched about eight miles to Bussy les Daours on a small northern tributary of the Somme. Their arrival coincided with the last stage of the battle of Amiens, in which a well-planned surprise attack by British, Canadian, and Australian troops, with over five hundred tanks, penetrated the German line south of the Somme by up to twelve miles, netted over twenty thousand prisoners, and, as subsequent events would show, badly damaged German morale. Ludendorff, the German Commander-in-Chief wrote after the war: 'August 8th was the black day of the German army in the history of the War'. Such a decisive turn of events was, of course, not yet clear to the troops on the ground: by 12 August German resistance had stiffened; their reserves were in place and their artillery was becoming effective again. On the Allied side, troops needed rest, and roads, railways, and bridges had to be repaired before artillery and tanks could be brought forward; so there was a pause in the front-line fighting.

There was never a pause in engineering on the Western front, however. The Australian Corps, to which the 216th Company was now attached, had units on both banks of the Somme in the area where it flows east-west with the Somme Canal alongside; this canal was needed as a supply route forward and for the evacuation of the wounded. (In May 1917 Wilfred Owen was one of many patients carried 'six miles down the beautiful tree-lined canal on a steam tug' from the casualty clearing station at Gailly, an experience that prompted his sonnet 'Hospital Barge at Cérisy'.) Before the canal could be brought into use it was necessary to clear it of a vast accumulation of both floating and sunken debris, to repair lock gates, and to replace wrecked bridges with new ones, including some capable of taking tanks. The 216th Company, along with two other British R.E. companies was placed under the Chief Engineer of the Australian Corps, Brigadier-General C.H.Foott, for the purpose of carrying out this work.

They began immediately on 12 August: while the Right Half Company was fixing billets and drawing material from the station, Left Half Company was bridging at Bouzencourt, between Sailly-le-Sec and Hamel, where they erected three reinforced-steel-joist girder spans on wooden trestles, capable of carrying motor transport. They continued working without respite for the next twelve warm, sunny days, at Bouzencourt, at Gailly, further east, and at Chipilly, further east again. At this last place they put the finishing touches to a remarkable undertaking by the 3rd Australian Pioneers. 'Two high level steel lattice bridges existed before August 8th, one a French civilian and the other a French military bridge, the latter being of a longer span than the former. Both bridges were blown at one end by the enemy. The length of the military bridge left undamaged was found to be sufficiently long to span the civilian bridge abutments. The bridge was picked up, a few new members made, and was placed in its new position in four days, producing a first-class single way bridge for all loads except Tanks'.[6] On 18 August four officers and 64 other ranks from the 254th Tunnelling Company, R.E. were attached to the 216th in order to gain experience in bridging.

The work at Gailly was probably typical: it entailed repair of the existing masonry abutments to demolished wooden bridges and the erection of one 60ft span Class A Mk II Hopkins Bridge, one 30ft span, two spans of 21ft 6in and one of 16ft, all capable of carrying all loads, including tanks. All five steel spans were brought from dismantled bridges at Blangy, now well to the rear of the Australians' advance: the 60ft span erected at Gailly was over the main stream of the Somme, the others were over a lesser stream, a weir, a canal lock, and a ditch.[7] On 25 August the 216th were clearing up the bridge sites and removing canal debris at Bouzencourt and Gailly; on the following day they were packing in readiness for the next move.

Meanwhile the Australians had resumed their eastward advance on both sides of the Somme. In a moonlit attack on the night of the 23rd they took Bray-sur-Somme; by the evening of 26 August they were beyond Suzanne to the north and Cappy to the south of the river. More heavy bridges were needed to enable the Corps tanks to manoeuvre on both sides of the canal and river, and, more importantly, facilitate the movement of heavy artillery, without which the advance could not continue, so the 216th moved forward too. On 26 August Sergeant Streather took his first opportunity to write home: 'We have been so busy that I have been glad to get to sleep every spare minute we have had. . . I was without mail for 14 days on account of our big move. We have once more gone back to the line but we are not too close and Jerry so far has been fairly kind to us, in fact he's had little chance to be otherwise. . . We are getting glorious weather and it is a good thing too for we are having to rough it pretty badly. The country we are fighting in is absolutely desolate: completely destroyed by shell fire and there are no huts or houses, not even trees. Men live in shell holes covered with tarpaulins if they are lucky, but generally with the big blue sky for a roof. My word, you should see the battlefields; they are absolutely beyond description: nothing but ruin desolation and death for miles and miles. When ever will all this end? The heat has been most trying at times but we have been at the river side all the time so we have been able to bath twice most days, and of course we get plenty of drinking water, which is a great trouble in many parts. My word, a bath means something nowadays. I often thought no conditions could be worse than the seas of water and mud we saw last year but I think they are little worse than the blinding dust we get now: the slightest breeze or movement stirs up clouds of it. We breathe it, eat it with our food, and drink it in our tea, we walk about in it all day and sleep in it at night; not a particle of our body escapes. One thing I am pleased to say I never felt healthier or stronger in my life, so no doubt the open air does not hurt one. You no doubt would be surprised to see the troops in the forward areas. The war is fought by half, no, three-quarters naked men. For more than ten days I have only worn boots, trousers, vest, tin hat and gas helmet, and many wear less than that.. Nearly everyone is sunburnt. I am nearly black, especially the neck and arms.'

On 27 August the Company moved to Froissy Lock, where the Somme Canal cuts straight across a low-lying tongue of land as the river takes a great hairpin loop northwards to Bray. Here, in less than twenty-four hours they erected a 22ft steel span tank bridge: see illustration 45. On 28 August they were preparing the site and unloading materials for an Inglis Bridge of 84ft span, suitable for all traffic except tanks, at Bray itself, when, for the first time in three weeks, it was raining. The Inglis steel bridge consisted of a series of identical rectangular bays, formed of weldless steel tubes; it was easily portable and could be erected and dismantled more rapidly than the Hopkins bridge: see illustration 43(a). The Inglis bridge that the 216th were erecting at Bray had previously been in use at Vaire lower down the river towards Amiens; at Bray it would later be replaced by rolled-steel joist spans on piles, so that it could be re-erected again for the crossing of the Selle river in October. Re-use was essential because Inglis bridging was slow to manufacture (and expensive), so only a a limited amount of it was available in France by the summer of 1918.[8] Three sections of the 216th Company worked on the Inglis Bridge and some smaller bridges at Bray while No. 3 section was repairing a bridge upstream at Cappy; all at some time or other took a hand in removing debris from the canal. On 31 August the Company was resting, except for 'inspection of arms, etc.'

Sergeant Streather wrote from Cappy on 2 September, describing their life as 'all work and move on': 'we find ourselves in new surroundings every few days.

At present Sgt Harris and I occupy a snug little dug out many feet below the ground. Until Wednesday it was the home of a certain Herr J.C.Kraumer, a quiet gent with long flaxen hair and a big moustache just like the Vikings of old. He lay outside for a couple of days but we buried him one night after a hard day's work. That's the way we go on. Really the war gets worse, surely it must end before long. One thing, we are doing well now and certainly our men are far superior to the Jerries we are capturing now. . . We lost one of our officers again last week and have just set a new one on: don't know what he is like at present. Smith is on leave but we have three with us and two Aussies attached in addition. It is a different war now. The old days when we first got out here were like holidays compared to these stunts; we could get away from the line into quite comfortable quarters but now everywhere is like a wilderness; there are no civvies within 35 kilos and only odd houses which are not absolutely demolished. My word, the people at home will never know what war really means or what the French have had to put up with.' The name of the 'lost' (i.e. posted away) officer is not recorded: perhaps it was Lieutenant Brand. The new officer was perhaps Lieutenant D.B.Wilmot, whose name appears occasionally in the Company war diary from September onwards. The 'three with us' may have been from the 254th Tunnelling Company, part of which was still attached to the 216th on 1 September, or they may have been from the 2nd Australian Tunnelling Company, reported as working with the 216th on 10 September[9]. There was no need for tunnellers during the advance, so they were retrained for other duties, including bridging.

One reason why the men of 216th Company hardly ever rested was that they were seemingly able to draw upon a never-ending supply of heavy bridging steel and other bridging material, despite ever-lengthening lines of communication across the wilderness of the Somme battlefield. Despite the loss or destruction of 17,000 feet of heavy bridging material during the March and April retreats, there was (except in the case of Inglis bridge sections) ample steel in reserve. The Engineer-in-Chief placed a huge order for additional material in May 1918, with the proviso that 25% of new bridges should be wide enough to accommodate tanks with their sponsons out, but the war ended before most of this material was received at the front: virtually all the steel bridges actually used in the advance between August and November had been gradually accumulated during the preceding three years.[10] Delivery to the front was more difficult than supply to the base, but, judging from the experience of the 216th Company, it appears that delivery was reasonably well handled. Bulk transport of anything was never easy on the overworked railways and roads of northern France. The historian Cyril Falls points out that ammunition was generally given precedence over engineer stores when the daily allotment of trains was determined by the Quartermaster-General's branch at G.H.Q., because the need for ammunition was more obvious to fighting men, despite the equally obvious fact that artillery could not be moved if material for building bridges and roads was not available. Also 'artillery was an easier "customer" than the engineers', because the needs of the latter were not so predictable day by day: sometimes mostly road metal would be needed, at other times bridging material, then water pipes, barbed wire, sandbags, timber of different kinds, etc.[11]

As for the stores that the 216th Company needed mostly in 1918: heavy steel spans were held at the R.E. Base Park, Le Havre, and could be delivered to railheads at 72 hours notice; other bridging stores were held in army R.E. parks and corps R.E. parks and dumps sited on the standard-gauge railway system. It was the responsibility of army and corps Bridging Officers to arrange the delivery of all this material to the railhead most convenient for the bridging site; it was the responsibility of the Company doing the bridging to unload and carry material to the site.[12] All the 216th Company's bridging between January and July had been carried out quite close to an intact (albeit very heavily used) railway system, so it would not have been too difficult or time-consuming for them to collect heavy steel sections from a railhead in their own two Berna five-ton lorries and seven-ton trailers, and collect lighter bridging material in their own mule-drawn G.S. wagons. On at least two occasions when they were on the river Canche (28 June, 2 July) canal barges were used to take away dismantled bridges; also, parts for a pont levis were brought by canal direct to the site where a section of the company was bridging in October 1916. However, conditions would have been quite different from August 1918 onwards, when the Company was bridging in places where roads and railways had been destroyed and waterways blocked either in battle or by retreating Germans.

Captain Sanders's war diary is enigmatically brief on all matters, so it gives hardly any detail about supply of bridging material in general or railheads and motor transport in particular, but there are references to unloading material at railheads in Longueau (just east of Amiens) on 12 August and in Vecquemont, only four miles further east, on 5 September, by which date the haul from railhead to bridge site must have increased by more than twenty miles, over a recent battlefield, on roads crammed with all manner of supply vehicles. Surprisingly, only one 'broken-down lorry' is mentioned in the diary (23 September). Undoubtedly, the Company would have been obliged to make ever-longer and more difficult hauls by road during the Allied advance, so it is possible that they sometimes had the use of road transport in addition to their own two lorries and trailers. The Engineer-in-Chief had twelve Berna lorries and trailers to be allocated where needed; similarly, the Chief Engineer of each army and corps could allocate pontoon wagons and trailers from his own mechanical-transport pontoon park. A pontoon wagon could carry most standard sections of steel bridging; a Berna trailer could carry the very heaviest sections; so could a Berna lorry, which was also adapted to carry girders and timbers up to 32ft long, because it was fitted with a transom behind the cab and a roller and winch at the rear of the chassis.[13]

Orders to 216th Company and to another attached R.E. Army Troops Company (the 574th) from the Chief Engineer, Australian Corps, on 11 August note that 'additional transport in the form of Pontoon trailers and F.W.D.. Lorries' may be obtained from the Chief Engineer, and name the member of his staff who 'will keep in close touch with the work being done, and will assist the Companies to obtain transport, stores, etc.' Presumably the 216th Company's own motor transport was reinforced from some such source for their biggest and most urgent jobs, for instance at Brie and Bellenglise in September. Even so, the Chief

Engineer noted on 1 September that 'had it not been for the discovery of some enemy engineer dumps during the recent advance, it would have been impossible to keep on with' the transport at his own disposal.[14] Also, material could sometimes be found to hand during the advance through an area where bridges had earlier been built and destroyed by both sides: the Company war diary sometimes refers to the construction of bridges from 'salved stores'.

Amazingly, it is not until 29 October that Captain Sanders records that his men are having to 'stand by' for three days awaiting bridging materials. The near-continuous programme of heavy-steel bridging carried out by the 216th Company during the three months of Allied advance testifies to the speed of R.E. platelayers and roadmakers who rebuilt supply lines, and to the strikingly efficient staff work of Chief Engineers and their specialist Bridging Officers in the armies and corps in which the Company served. Arguably, heavy bridging was the most important duty of Royal Engineers from August 1918 to the end of the war, because the pace of the infantry's advance depended upon the volume of supplies that could be delivered by a hugely expanded fleet of motor vehicles[15] and upon the speed with which heavy artillery could be brought forward: (tanks were unimportant weapons compared with big guns).

Engineering rarely figures in war reports or histories (unless it goes badly wrong), but the scale of engineering work in the last three months of the war may be inferred by the rate of advance and the forces involved. Before the end of August Field Marshal Haig was orchestrating a general advance of all British armies: the Third Army mounted a major attack on 21 August; the First Army followed suit five days later; then a daring attack by Australians on Mont St.Quentin, north of Péronne, enabled the Fourth Army to capture the town on 2 September and outflank the Germans' hoped-for defensive line behind the south-north course of the Somme. On 22 August Haig impressed upon his Army commanders the desirability of resolute offensive action: 'The enemy has not the means to deliver counter-attacks on an extended scale, nor has he the numbers to hold a continuous position against the very extended advance which is now being directed upon him... Risks which a month ago would have been criminal to incur, ought now to be incurred as a duty... The situation is most favourable; let each one of us act energetically, and without hesitation push forward to our objective.'[16]

The enemy saw the writing on the wall (or at least the carriage door). Crown Prince Rupprecht, an German Army Group commander, returning to the front on 2 September observed the inscription on a troop train: 'Slaughter cattle for Wilhelm and Sons'. The aim of Germany's military leaders was now to hold out for a negotiated peace that might enable them to retain some of their gains in the war: to that end Ludendorff decreed an orderly withdrawal to the strong defences of the Hindenburg Line, beginning on 3 September. On the Somme front a rearguard was left to hold the river and canal crossings, but several of these crossings were forced on 5 September. At Brie it was a battalion of the Royal Scots (32nd Division, attached to the Australian Corps) who waded across under machine-gun fire that morning: their capture of seven prisoners and eight machine guns implies that the Germans were quick on their feet. Later that day the Chief Engineer of the Corps was on the scene. He noted in his diary: 'Bridge across the Somme and its canal at Brie must now be taken in hand and it is proposed to allot 216 A.T.Coy to this work'. He chose this company because it had achieved 'some excellent results in very good time' during the August bridging.[17]

On 5 September the 216th Company were loading material for a second Hopkins Bridge they were preparing to erect at Froissy, but the Chief Engineer's change of plan sent them to Brie on the following day. His original order of 5 September was that the Company should 'arrange to transport the 90ft Hopkins bridge from Daours and re-erect same where main Bray road crosses the Somme canal'[18], but according to the Company war diary the longest span they built at Brie was of 60 feet. The 'bridge at Brie', which carried the Roman road from Amiens to St.Quentin, actually consisted of a causeway with eight separate bridges at irregular intervals; the five longest of these had been destroyed. The 216th Company erected two steel spans of 60ft, one of 30ft, and two of 21ft 6in as replacements. The bridges were erected as 'deck spans', i.e. with side girders below the roadway, rather than in the usual place above it, in order to allow tanks to cross with sponsons out. 'This meant a considerable amount of extra work, as approach ramps had to be built up at each end. The first spans were delivered at the sites on the 6th, and all five bridges were completed and opened for traffic on the 9th.'[19] This completion time of four days may be compared with the seven days needed to bridge these same gaps in March 1917, when British troops were following the Germans retiring to the Hindenburg Line: on that occasion seven days (instead of the original estimate of nine) was thought to be so rapid that the Royal Engineers concerned received a special message of congratulation from Sir Douglas Haig himself.

On 10 September, when the Australian Chief Engineer came to inspect the Company's handiwork, they were salving materials from the destroyed bridges, under orders that they were to devote their attention 'to the duplication of the Brie bridges for "A" Class loads, using as far as possible materials found locally or drawn from the Corps Dumps', and to 'the reconstruction of the St.Christ bridges for "A" Class loads.' The orders further stipulated that the 216th 'will have attached to them the whole of the 254 Tunnelling Coy R.E. who will give them every possible assistance in this work. O.C. 254 Tunnelling Coy will detail continuous patrols for the Brie and St.Christ bridges, relieving the men of the 2nd Australian Tunnelling Coy now guarding the St.Christ bridges. These patrols will at once remedy any minor defects occurring, paying particular attention to the junctions of the road with the bridges, and will immediately report any serious damage to O.C. 216 A.T. Company R.E. and to the Traffic Control on the bridge.'[20]

On the following day the 216th Company was transferred to IX Corps, which had just arrived to take over part of the front from the Australians, but its orders remained the same: the Company continued bridging at Brie and at St.Christ a mile and a half to the south. Apart from five wet days between the 8th and the 12th the weather was fine. The two sections of the 254th Tunnelling Company (not, apparently, the whole company, as specified in the order of 10 September) that they had instructed at Gailly and who had helped them at Bray continued now with them at Brie. The 221st Army Troops Company, R.E. was also attached to the 216th very briefly, perhaps for some particularly complicated job. The officer commanding that company wrote aggrievedly in his diary for 13 September: 'All men put onto Brie bridges. No officer allowed on job, 216 Coy being far superior!!! Officers now have nothing to do. Weather fair.' The 221st, a Kitchener New Army company raised on the Isle of Wight, had been trained at Buxton at exactly the same time as the 216th, so this comment may reflect an old rivalry. The bridging programme being now continued under the Chief Engineer of IX Corps provided a doubling of the crossings at Brie, one for tanks and one for motor transport, and a crossing for heavy motor transport (17 ton axle loads) at St.Christ: this entailed five more bridges at Brie, bringing the total to ten, and four at St.Christ. The 574th (Cornwall) Army Troops Company, R.E., of the Territorial Force, was also involved in this work. At Brie 'The second series, consisting of three 60 ft spans, and two made-up rolled steel joist bridges, were delivered at the site on the 14th, and completed alongside the first series on the 18th. The rapidity and smoothness of the whole work was striking proof of the value of the training these companies had received.'[21]

Captain Sanders's war diary records the rapid completion of these bridges, together with work on road improvement, clearing debris, and salving bridging materials. On 20 September the Company constructed an A Class bridge from 'salved stores'. On 22 and 23 September half the Company were doing such odd jobs as excavating ground for huts or salving material from a broken-down lorry; the other half had moved on. One small but useful piece of salvage work undertaken by the Company was the retrieval of cork floats. These were bales of cork slabs tightly bound in wire netting which provided highly buoyant piers for rapidly assembled footbridges: unlike petrol cans cork bales were virtually impervious to shrapnel, splinters, and bullets. 'The supply of cork was never equal to the demand. . . . Chief Engineers were asked in the early summer of 1918 to give an estimate of the amount they were likely to require during the rest of the year. The total estimate amounted to under 50 tons, — 100 tons were actually ordered and made up into floats, and the whole of this was issued and used during the first few weeks of the advance. Further supplies had to come from overseas, and owing to shipping difficulties could not be obtained in time to be of much use. So valuable were these floats considered by many units that, in spite of their weight after being any length of time in the water, they were frequently lifted and carried forward for re-use. Floats made of oil tins were lighter to carry, but were easily punctured and sunk.'[22] The floats left bobbing about on the Somme Canal after the infantry had crossed were to be used at the next great water obstacle, the St.Quentin Canal.

Brie was the most important Somme crossing: it was used by both the Fourth Army and the French First Army operating on its right. As soon as the bridges were open Haig sent a general message of 'high appreciation of the good work done by Engineer units of the Fourth Army in the construction of temporary and permanent crossings over the River Somme during the recent operations'. Passing this message on to the Commanding Officers of the 216th and those of other engineer companies in the Australian Corps, Brigadier-General Foott added, as a democratic Aussie touch, 'It would give me pleasure if you could see your way, when promulgating this message, to say that it is fully realized that the credit is due entirely to the Officers, N.C.O.s, and Sappers who actually did the work'. As the 216th War Diary is so lacking in detail, whether kept by Captain Sanders or (as is occasionally the case) by Lieutenant Walker, we do not know how much of the Somme bridging was done under fire, but the undated citation for Sergeant Harris's D.C.M., after referring to his conduct on the night of 29 March, adds: 'During the recent advances on the Somme up to the present time he has shown great coolness and resource in forward bridging operations, and by his cheerfulness and disregard of danger under all circumstances has largely contributed to the success of the Company's work'.

The movement of one Half Company of the 216th on 23 September, followed by the other two days later took them to Vraignes and then Poueilly, two small villages just off the Roman road from Brie to St.Quentin: the latter was nine or ten miles away and still in German hands. Both villages were ruined of course, because the Germans had for a second time devastated the area from which, for a second time, they were withdrawing to the Hindenburg Line. The Roman road went over high, rolling land parallel with the river Omignon to the south; this river descended to join the Somme at St.Christ, through a wide, marshy, tree-covered valley, where in two places its waters were transformed into the (now-ruined) ornamental lakes of chateaux. It was near one of these that a Half Company of the 216th erected an Inglis bridge in a day and a half. For the rest of their time and for the rest of the Company, the work was mainly on water supply for camps in the IX Corps area at Brie, Catelet (south-east of Doingt), and Montigny Farm (north of Poueilly) as troops assembled for the next stage of the advance.

No one doubted that the advance would continue. 12 September saw the launch by the American First Army of a successful attack against the St.Mihiel salient away in the east beyond Verdun. On the Fourth Army front the Australian Corps and, a little later, IX Corps secured a footing in the outposts of the Hindenburg line to the west of the St.Quentin Canal. Generalissimo Foch proclaimed 'tout le monde à la bataille' and fixed the timetable for a general offensive from the Meuse to the North Sea. On 26 September the French and Americans attacked between Reims and Verdun; on the 27th the British First and Third Armies attacked a strongly defended section of the Hindenburg Line behind the Canal du Nord in the direction of Cambrai; on the 28th, in Flanders, Plumer's Second Army and the Belgians pursued an already retreating enemy so successfully that in two days they retook all the ground as far as Passchendaele that had cost months of blood to win in 1917.

The turn of the Fourth Army came on 29 September, when its task was to break through the strongest part of the Hindenburg Line behind the St.Quentin Canal. 'Line' is perhaps a misnomer to describe a defensive system ten miles deep, consisting of trenches, underground barracks, concrete machine-gun posts, deep thickets of barbed wire, anti-tank ditches, and a wide canal at the bottom of a steep-sided cutting. Nevertheless, after a forty-eight hour bombardment in which nearly a million shells rained down on the German positions, the 46th Division, with three

Staffordshire battalions in the lead, stormed across the canal around Bellenglise on the morning of the 29th. In the crossing they used three thousand life-belts commandeered from cross-Channel ferries, scaling ladders, collapsible boats, and the invaluable bridges on cork floats.

As soon as they were over, a number of Royal Engineer companies, including the 216th, were ordered up from Poueilly to begin the repair of existing bridges and construction of new ones. The 216th erected an 84ft Inglis bridge, which opened for traffic on the afternoon of 1 October; two days later they completed another Inglis bridge on another site nearby; then, between 5 and 9 October, they built a permanent girder bridge, using 60ft standard Class A spans with short rolled-steel joist extensions supported on wooden trestles (see illustration 44). While they were bridging at Bellenglise the Company headquarters was at Vadencourt where there was another ruined chateau alongside more shattered ornamental waters on the Omignon river. Between there and Bellenglise was the line of a Roman road the British called 'Watling Street' (a homely name for the Nuneaton men) and the unhomely rusting, weed-covered wire, and sagging trenches of the 1917 British front line. From time to time as the 216th worked they would see the British cavalry, summoned up from their bivouacs near the Omignon to be 'put through' to exploit an advance, then sent back because they were too vulnerable to German machine-gunners. Most of the traffic was of more present use: artillery, ambulances, prisoners of war, lorries and wagons carrying supplies, rations, and ammunition; for ammunition alone, fifteen ammunition trains had to be cleared daily from the Fourth Army railhead at Templeux le Guerard, five miles west of Bellenglise.

Sergeant Streather missed the bridging at Bellenglise because he was on leave. He joined the Company beyond the Hindenburg Line in October and wrote to his parents: 'arrived "home" early this morning. Had quite a good journey, managed to sleep all the way to London and then four of us had a first class carriage to Dover so slept again, by 9.30 we had marched to a rest camp, dumped our kit, and got out into the town where I got a good breakfast. Crossed over about two, sea was quite calm and I got some more sleep, so you see I made up for the sleep I missed at home. Next day we spent twelve dreary hours in a cattle truck, had the night in one of our old camps and moved up to company H.Q. on Saturday. . . Had the night with the S.M., Q.M.S., and Taylor and at 4.30 this morning joined my section. We are billeted in one of Jerry's elaborate works nearly 200ft below the ground and I am settled down quite comfortably to wait for the end of the war. The army have done great things during my absence: it is nothing short of wonderful how they have overcome the great difficulties in so short a time. The company have had their fair share of horrors, in a way I am sorry I missed this job and yet I was lucky to be out of it. The job was rather a big one and carried right under Jerry's nose and by great good fortune without a single casualty among our own men. Every one is excited over the peace proposals and many officers seem to think that the end is very near.'

Between 10 and 14 October the 216th Company was scattered between various jobs: some dismantling an old bridge at Bellenglise; others making and writing sign-boards, making rakes and scrapers, and dismantling a water tower at Vermand, west of the St.Quentin Canal; others hutting at Magny-la- Fosse, east of the Canal. The weather, which had been fine while they were building their bridges at Bellenglise, had now turned wet. By 15 October the Fourth Army was well clear of the rearmost Hindenburg defences and was near Le Cateau, fifteen miles on from Bellenglise in a region that had not seen fighting since 1914. If the men of the 216th were not to have a rest, they were briefly to have a change from bridging. On 15 October they moved westwards, well to the rear, to Roisel on the Cologne river, to work on water supplies in the Second American Corps area, where for the next eight, mostly wet, days parties worked at Péronne, Doingt, Tincourt, Margaux, and Roisel itself; also, between 19 and 22 October, one section was at Bellicourt, on the St.Quentin Canal, for water supply. On 23 October the Company was ordered to be transferred to the First Army. Between 25 and 27 October they marched to Arras, luckily in three days of fine weather; one night on the march was spent in Bapaume (a place-name made notorious in the 1916 battles of the Somme).

From Arras, on the 28th, they moved forward to begin heavy bridging on the river Scarpe at Marchiennes, but after two days they were split between three bridge sites: one section at Marchiennes, one near Vred to the west, the other two further west again in the historic town of Douai, where they and another Royal Engineer company erected a Hopkins bridge of 120ft span. They continued thus until 5 November. On 7 November one section was bridging at Denain, on the river Schelde or Escaut, west of Valenciennes; the other three sections were at Marchiennes, 'standing by for material'. It is not surprising that R.E.s were short of material at that time. In three months since the beginning of the British advance on 8 August, Royal Engineers in France had erected no fewer than 330 steel bridges (compared with just 180 in the preceding four years) as well as over 200 heavy timber bridges, but the accelerating speed of advance in November made it increasingly difficult for bridging material to be brought forward from base and from redundant bridges being dismantled in the rear. The section of the 216th at Denain could carry on perhaps only because the railway had been reopened to that town, whereas it was not yet open to Marchiennes.

By then the Germans were in full retreat. Their rearguards of field artillery and machine-gunners were still inflicting casualties, but the biggest problem for the British armies was, as ever, to transport supplies, ammunition, and rations from distant railheads along roads and across bridges destroyed by the Germans. As usual, German pillage and devastation extended beyond mere military need. In Douai, for instance: 'Everything of value had been removed and such things as had been left — furniture, crockery, pictures and the like — had been smashed to atoms'.[23] It is not clear whether such conduct was in defiance or in furtherance of the request for an armistice that the Germans had made as early as 5 October. At that time German armies were still fighting so effectively that they had not given up hope of a negotiated peace well short of surrender, but by November such hopes had gone: the armistice which came into force at 11 a.m. on 11 November was on the Allies' terms.

Chapter Fourteen: Aftermath, November 1918 to June 1919

Most infantry and artillery units had a restful and celebratory Armistice Day, but for the engineers, at once the aristocrats and the drudges of the Army, it was an ordinary working day. Materials had come to hand, so bridging at Marchiennes continued. Sergeant Streather told his parents on 14 November that he had 'about settled down to semi-peacetime soldiering now. It makes little difference to the amount of work we get but of course the danger is over and the air seems clearer and we can look up at a bright moon without a shiver. How are the munition workers going on: have they stopped yet? I have no doubt many have the wind up now they see the likelihood of losing the best jobs they ever had in their lives. I wish I could lose mine straight away but I suppose there is little hope of that for six months at least. . . You seem to have this wretched influenza very bad in Nuneaton, it's very prevalent out here but I have kept wonderfully well myself. We are getting some beautiful weather lately; it has been fairly cold at night but nice and clear and sunny during the day time. Of course we shall no doubt always be sure of a good billet now and we get made quite a fuss of by the people. It is a good thing in a way that there is no drink about, otherwise we should be getting lively times. I hear things have been pretty rough down the line in the old quarters. The O.C. is back and Mr Wilmot has gone on leave. Smith and Walker are still in hospital so we still have only one officer. . . Haven't things moved at a pace since I left home; it really seems years since I saw you instead of five weeks.

On Sunday, 17 November, he wrote again: 'I am away from the company again on my own with my section; we are nearly 40 miles ahead of the Coy in quite a large town which is full of civvies and my word they do love the Boche. . . Sometimes we hear that peace is about to be signed and sometimes that Jerry has broken the terms of the armistice and that fighting will start again. Big and little Willie have both been murdered two or three times, the latest is that they are in England. . . The people up here are fine and proud, you should have seen them today, all togged up in their fine clothes, the mayor and corporation out in full uniform with umpteen flags and banners and two of our bands. I should think everybody went to church except the gallant lads and of course we had to work.' Sergeant Streather's section was not working every day. There appears to have been a kind of shift system by which one, two, or three sections worked on bridges, while the other sections 'rested' (sometimes taking their rest in the form of a route march), turn and turn about. Their bridge sites in this period were at Marchiennes and Vred, as before, at St.Ghislains on the Condé Canal, west of Mons, and at Douchy and Triant on the Schelde, south-west of Valenciennes. The Company headquarters was sometimes at St.Ghislains and sometimes at Aniche, between Denain and Douai.

Streather thus had ample time for letters home. On 25 November he wrote: 'I have been away from the company with my section a good deal. . . The censorship regulations have been relaxed and I may tell you that this morning I joined the company at a little village called Aniche half way between Douai and Denain, east of Arras. We had a fifty kilo ride here in lorries from St.Ghislain in Belgium where we had been at work for nearly a week. Previously we have been in Mons,

Valenciennes, Denain, Douai, and several smaller places during the past month. I was glad we reached Mons which is quite a nice town and not knocked about except round the station... The 1914 people left very little trace of their activities along the line of their retreat. I saw about 120 of their graves and that is the only mark of the battle. Lately we are always billeted in houses, sometimes with the civvies and sometimes in empty houses, but they are always furnished. At St.Ghislain we lived with a big wholesale grocer on the canal side where the British fought for 26 hours in '14. He told us the whole story of the battle time after time: how 200 Tommies held up several thousand Boche from 10 a.m. on the Sunday till noon on Monday. 13 of our men were killed and 20 wounded but they left over 1000 Boche dead. The dead Boche were buried in big graves of 50 men but the crosses erected only say 10. The civvies round that quarter think a wonderful lot of Les Anglais. "Bon, Bon, Bon, Soldat" they say. They will do anything for you and make you as comfortable as possible and nearly drown you with coffee which has neither sugar nor milk. They have had a terrible time during 1917 and 18, even now are on the verge of starvation but food is rapidly being sent to them. The Germans have subjected them to every possible cruelty and robbed them of everything of value; both men and women and children have been forced to work for him and have been removed from their homes without the slightest hesitation; heavy fines and long imprisonment have been imposed for small offences. For giving a cigarette or a piece of bread to an English prisoner people have been fined 200 marks, for hiding wine, cognac, or food 1 or 2 thousand marks, all of which had to be paid in gold and the mayor of the place had to find the gold: the person fined would actually pay the mayor in paper money. You talk about things being dear in England but you have no need to grumble. In Mons a 3d tablet of soap would cost 8 francs, stuff they sell for butter is 10 francs a pound, meat about 8 or 10 francs a pound, boots 200 or 300 francs a pair. Of course with things at these prices no one except the very rich can buy anything and you can safely say that for 2½ years the great majority have lived on coffee, bread, and vegetables. They mostly look pinched and thin and no wonder. Probably the worst sufferers of the whole war are our prisoners. I have seen a good many and they are pitiful to behold, many are close on death from starvation, they are ill-clothed and have been worked like slaves, often being harnessed to waggons of late. Even now many are being left by the Boche without food or blankets to get back to us as best they can. My word, we have something to be thankful for that it is all over now, and I think every man, woman, and child in Germany should be made to pay for all this, for they seem to have studied the crime of cruelty and applied it in its worst form at every opportunity.' (Perhaps the 'coffee' drunk by the French and Belgians under occupation was a substitute made of acorns.)

On 30 November two sections and Company headquarters moved to Anzin, the twin town to Valenciennes, just across the river Schelde. They were followed soon afterwards by the remaining two sections from Douchy: the exact date is uncertain because the Company diary for December is missing. One may assume that the men's thoughts were primarily on demobilization. Sergeant Streather wrote: 'They have been taking particulars ready for giving us our discharge, hope they make haste and sign peace and send us all home. By all accounts we shall have quite a little fortune when we are paid off... I have heard that 5/- a week is to be allowed to all mothers who have sons in the army who enlisted before they were 21. . . We are still at the same place, have had a day off today, we have nothing to do now for a few days until some material arrives' (27 November). 'We are at Valenciennes now, have quite comfortable billets and are likely to remain here until well after Christmas as we have quite a big job to do (1 December).

On 1 January 1919 the Company was still almost at full strength, with 4 officers and 125 other ranks compared with 3 officers and 137 other ranks on 30 November. It would seem that about a dozen men whose civilian jobs were thought to be important had been demobilized in December. Charles Streather wrote on 27 Nov that Lieutenant Smith had 'gone to Blighty', one assumes to be demobilized. His replacement is not named: perhaps it was Lieutenant Hughes, who emerges as Officer Commanding in the following April. Captain Sanders left some time in January. As he was replaced as O.C. by Lieutenant Wilmot, not Lieutenant Walker (who was senior to Wilmot), it may be assumed that Walker left the Company in January also. Effective strength is not reported in the Company diary between 1 January and 31 March; the slow trickle of demobilizations is recorded, but names are not given. We may assume that, as with other army units, demobilization dates had no reference to length of service, but only to the needs of civilian employers, channelled through the Ministry of Labour to the War Office. The Government's fear of civil unrest ensured that policemen were among the first to go home; agricultural workers and miners also had priority. Charles Streather obtained a relatively early discharge, in January, to return to his post as a schoolteacher. Back in France, an army was still required, for no peace treaty had been signed and the country was still theoretically at war. So the Nuneaton men each had to wait his turn, while the slowly-shrinking company remained at Anzin-Valenciennes for six months or more.

Their work at Valenciennes can best be described as post-war reconstruction in an area where the retreating Germans had destroyed road and rail bridges and made canals impassable by destroying locks, making dams, and cutting the banks upstream of these dams. One of the tasks of the 216th was to rebuild the bridge over the canal between Anzin and Valenciennes and dismantle the old trestle canal bridge. A more improvised and less pleasant task was to clear the blockage in this canal: it was unpleasant because the Germans had mixed dead, and now very putrefying, horses with the bricks and rubble they had used to block the waterway; but the major difficulty was that the Germans had felled twenty large trees and dropped them into the canal. 'Work of clearing was first started by cutting the trees up into sections by the use of German stick grenades. A 2 ft 6 in diameter tree could be broken in half by four of these grenades lashed round it, and fired simultaneously. The tree sections were then hauled out by winches found in the neighbouring mills or workshops. After a few days a caterpillar tractor was obtained by means of which whole trees 40 ft to 50 ft long easily pulled out.'[1]

The rest of the Company's work was in and around Valenciennes railway station. They removed the remains of the old bridge over the railway, which had been wrecked by the Germans, and built a new bridge 350 feet long: probably the longest they ever built (illustration 46). Like much of their bridging, it combined old and new technology: the piers consisted of wooden trestles, made according to the way the 216th were taught on the Heavy Bridging Ground at Buxton and not much different from those built by ancient Roman military engineers, but the roadway was laid on rolled-steel joist spans that came into widespread use only in 1918. They also restored a level crossing at the station and attended to the water supply at the station bridge

These tasks occupied them until 4 March. From 27 February, while some of the Company were still clearing the canal at Valenciennes, a detachment was building a new bridge and dismantling an old one at the ancient fortress town of Maubeuge on the river Sambre, west of Charleroi; this work, the 216th Company's last piece of bridging, continued until mid March. At Maubeuge the circularity of war had brought the Nuneaton men to the very place where the British Expeditionary Force had first assembled after its arrival in France in August 1914. It is not known exactly how many bridges the Company built in France, but their heavy bridging was commended by several Chief Engineers and by the anonymous historian of R.E. bridging in the Great War. Oddly enough, it seems that after they left Buxton the 216th only once (in April 1918 on the river Avre, south-east of Amiens) had occasion to build, or, to be exact, reassemble, a traditional, trademark R.E. pontoon bridge, like those with which they spanned the ornamental waters of the Pavilion Gardens, or (as they were told at Buxton) like the one that the engineers of Darius put across the Hellespont in 480 B.C.

Every few days during the work at Valenciennes and Maubeuge one or two, rarely as many as four or five, men were demobilized: altogether 34 went in January, 52 in February, and just 12 in March, by the end of which month the Company's effective strength was reported to be two officers and 55 other ranks. One of the officers was Lt. D.B.Wilmot, who succeeded Sanders as Commanding Officer in January, was promoted Captain in mid-February, and was posted away to command another R.E. company on 1 April; the other was probably a newcomer, Lt. J.R.Hughes. A Lt. J.B.Templeman was with the Company between 31 January and 18 March, the day all their bridging work virtually came to an end. The shrinking of the 216th was matched by that of their labour gangs, usually drawn from the 90th Labour Company, which were often over a hundred strong in January, but averaged less than thirty in February and March. Between 18 and 22 March the only real work recorded in the diary is of three sappers repairing abutments at Maubeuge Bridge, assisted by three other ranks from the 90th Labour Company; the rest of the 216th were overhauling and cleaning Company stores and equipment.

From 24 March to 17 May, except for Sundays and the long Easter week end (18-21 April) the whole Company was reported to be overhauling and cleaning stores and equipment: a remarkably long spell of bull by any measure. The only excitements recorded for April were L/Cpl. Lock transferred to the 10th Pontoon Park, Royal Army Service Corps, and 'Pioneer Snell evacuated to U.K. (sick)'. And, one imagines, tired. Only seven men were demobilized in the seven weeks between 28 March and 18 May, but 23 other ranks were posted to the 133rd (Army Troops) Company, R.E., on 19 May, after which the 216th is described as 'resting'.

On 1 June their strength is one officer (Lt. Hughes, Commanding Officer since 1 April) and 21 other ranks. On 10 June the Company moved back to Denain, where they had been on Armistice Day; thirteen other ranks were demobilized there on the 13th; in the following week the transport was put on a train to be taken away and stores and equipment were handed over to the Corps store in Anzin; between 26 and 28 June the men were 'resting' for the last time; on the 29th the last officer and the last seven other ranks were demobilized and the 216th (Army Troops) Company, R.E., was disbanded. This was the day after the Treaty of Versailles was signed and the war was officially over.

Driver Frank Hextall, a Lance Corporal since February, was one of these very last seven. His journey home first took him to Boulogne, where he spent the four days required for delousing, a bath, documentation, and embarkation. He spent another night in camp at Dover and two more in the army dispersal centre at Fovant. He reached Nuneaton on 7 July. On 31 July the 216th had a reunion dinner in the Peacock Inn with the Mayor of Nuneaton as guest of honour. There was no grand ceremony like the Company's departure, with the band playing, four years earlier: these men were all civilians now, but they did 'jubilate' as the Mayor's predecessor had promised. As far as I can tell, the Nuneaton newspapers ignored the return of the 216th Company, in striking contrast to their treatment of its departure in 1915. Indeed, there are very few references to the Company in any local newspaper after 1916: casualties at Mazingarbe were headline news, but those at Hangard Wood, for instance, two years later, went entirely unnoticed by the gentlemen of the press. By 1918 death in battle was yesterday's news.

The officers and men of the 216th returned to their professions and trades, and to such employment as could be found in the 'land fit for heroes' promised by Lloyd George. This band of Nuneaton surveyors, carpenters, bricklayers, plumbers, and the rest, had killed and wounded some Germans; some of them had been killed and wounded in their turn; they had earned a few medals and the occasional congratulations of a major-general or brigadier at headquarters; but they were never militarized. What is often said of Kitchener's extraordinary army of over two million volunteers — that they were civilians in uniform — may be said with greater truth of Royal Engineers, for these men continued to practise, amidst the intolerable destructiveness of a battlefield, their own familiar civilian construction skills. Their incessant and ubiquitous building work was exactly complementary to the demolishing activities of the Royal Artillery, with whom they shared the motto 'Ubique'. After the decimation of the pre-war professional British army in 1914-15, 'the Royal Engineers', says Cyril Falls in the *Official History*, 'constituted probably the most efficient arm of what was now in effect a hastily trained citizen army, because they brought from civil life technical knowledge of their tasks which left them less dependent than their fellow-soldiers upon training and experience in warfare. As their casualties were relatively light, they had also fairly good opportunity to profit by this training and experience.'[2]

Royal Engineers were different from the common run of soldiers. Though their numbers grew proportionally more than those of any other fighting arm, there was never enough of them on the Western Front; they were a scarce resource which had to be husbanded by commanders. Infantry were more easily expendable. In respect of both Kitchener and conscript troops this was partly because the High Command, at least initially, could think of no better strategy than attrition and no better tactics than frontal assault; also because it was believed that semi-trained infantry could not be treated as if they had intelligence and initiative, but must be ordered to advance in well-aligned rows, whatever the cost in casualties. The importance and nature of engineers' work meant that they would not be sacrificed in this wholesale way: their casualties generally came in penny numbers, when, scattered between their various constructions, they received the attentions of enemy artillery. We do not have complete casualties figures for the 216th Company, but at least nineteen other ranks were killed and at least fifty wounded during the course of the war, out of a normal full strength of three or four officers and about 135 other ranks. These are minimal figures. The record of the Company in newspaper reports, War Diary, anecdotes, and letters is so fragmentary that it is not possible to determine how much higher the true figure is likely to be, but it is reasonable to suppose that, except for the unusual feature that apparently no officer was killed or even wounded[3] when serving with the Company, these are unremarkable figures.

The men of the 216th were assured by their instructors at Buxton that Royal Engineers were supposed to be different from all other soldiers because brains lay behind their cap badge; this was why their rate of pay was so much higher than the infantryman's. They were expected to work without close supervision from their officers: so for much of their time in France the Company was divided into very small parties engaged on individual tasks, for instance a man-and-boy surveying team, a corporal and small party installing a water-pump, a lance-corporal and four men making bombs, two men supervising the erection of huts, some tinsmiths cunningly stretching out a cushy indoor job in the cold weather, and so on. For heavy labouring jobs the 216th generally had the help (however grudging) of working parties of 'resting' infantrymen, prisoners of war, or Labour Corps personnel. Their working parties for bridge-building and repair in 1919 were drawn almost invariably from the 90th Labour Company; Captain Sanders' war diary in 1918 never mentions working parties, so we cannot be certain whether or not the 'labour men' under Sergeant Streather's command in May of that year were from a Labour Company with a similar long-term attachment to the 216th, but, if they were, it is likely that those labourers would have acquired skill and speed with practice in the erection of steel bridges to complement the engineers' expertise. Whether semi-skilled or unskilled, working-party members usually outnumbered sappers (on some jobs by a ratio of ten to one), so an Engineer N.C.O. was expected to have the technical knowledge, organizational ability, and authority of a foreman in more than one trade.

One has the impression that the men of 216th Company were, on the whole, good workmen: certainly they earned commendation from on high for their collective, new-learnt skill in heavy bridging. (Their emergence as an élite steel bridging company illustrates in miniature the wartime technical advance of the Royal Engineers: the Company's bridging training at Buxton was all in wood). It seems that civilian talents of craftsmanship counted for more in their estimation than any soldierly quality, so a German prisoner of war was admirable when he proved to be an excellent carpenter and a sergeant-major who was an efficient foreman was more highly respected than one whose main interest was order, good military discipline, polished buttons, and smart salutes. When Sergeant Streather writes of 'setting on' a new officer he adopts the attitude of a craftsman towards an apprentice or management trainee who still has to prove his usefulness to the firm.

These men defined themselves primarily, as working men always have done, by manual skills. Unfortunately, there is no comparable, first-hand evidence of how their officers regarded themselves. The Company war diary during the period of Captain Cook's command is lost, but had it survived it probably would have been no more revealing than the cold factual summaries in his successors' war diary. What glimpses we have of the officers, the all-important management of the firm, are for the most part only in the 'worm's eye' view of their men, the workers. The sappers, driver, and even the sergeant, who provide the main sources for this history were very young men, two of them only seventeen on enlistment, though in due course they both liked to pride themselves on becoming old soldiers. Their education was no doubt improved by genuine old soldiers, such as Sapper Clarkson, a veteran of the South African War, who figures in several of my father's less morally improving tales. They all acquired a degree of emotional toughness as they became accustomed to flyblown corpses, stinking mud, and fear, so their allusions to death are as marginal and off-hand as Sapper West's understatement about the 'very noticeable' smell of fragments of dead *poilu* at Cabaret Rouge or Sergeant Streather's hard-boiled reference to the corpse of Herr J.C.Kraumer, former tenant of his snug little dug-out near the Somme. It is the breaks from the sweating routine of work and shell fire that they all mostly remember; they all remember drink of course and food, but when they refer to food it is particularly to the sweet things that appeal to a boyish palate — most especially fruit puddings.

The 216th Company, in common with so many other units of Kitchener's army, was locally raised. Over the four years of its existence it was diluted by drafts, but to the end it was essentially the product of Nuneaton and the surrounding area. These comrades in arms had been workmates and would be workmates after the war. They read Nuneaton newspapers at the front (though, ironically, those newspapers for the most part ignored their existence after 1916), they wrote jokey letters offering roof-repair jobs to a Nuneaton builder, and they were cheered in a shell hole by a photograph of Nuneaton market place. The civic sense of community in which the Company was formed seems obscurely to have helped to sustain its members, even though they hardly ever spoke of their motives in joining up. Avenging the Lusitania, rescuing poor little Belgium, and protecting the British Empire probably counted for little. Perhaps some enlisted because they had been brought up in Victorian notions of honour and duty, sharpened by a patriotism developed in their parents' generation during the internationally anxious decade that preceded the war. Perhaps others were motivated by a less conscious sense of solidarity and enlisted because their workmates did.

The Great War did not end war, ensure the peaceful self-determination of small European nations, preserve the British Empire, or even halt German militarism for long. The war aim of most ordinary soldiers was to come out alive on the winning side, but perhaps there was more to it than that. The only member of the Company who ever published his notion of what he was fighting for was Sapper Walter Woodfield, the plumber who was to be killed in March 1918 and so would never return to his wife and children in Stockingford. In the mud and slaughter east of Ypres in September 1917 he believed that he and his fellows were fighting for 'the reputation and honour' of England and for 'humanity, home, and beauty'. Whatever our opinion of war (or of humdrum, unbeautiful Midland towns) this is a belief that commands respect. These patient, good-humoured, resilient, level-headed craftsmen-turned-soldiers did believe that there was such a thing as society. They have, perhaps, more right than we to speak of England's honour and reputation.

29. Rowing drill on the lake in the Pavilion Gardens, Buxton, October 1915: from bows Spr Trevis, 2nd Cpl Toogood, Sprs Phillips, Douglas, Gibberd, and Dyer; Lieut Smith steering.

30. Pontoon and barrel-pier bridge, Pavilion Gardens, Buxton: shore end (standing, from the right, Sgt Luxton, unknown, Lieut Knox, Lieut Smith, C.S.M. Mitchinson, Sgt Seymour, Sgt Lee).

Appendix: 216th Company and Military Bridging

[Note: information about the types of bridges the Company built under training at Buxton and Newark, and illustrations 32-3, 35, and 37-8 are from the War Office manual, *Military Engineering: Part IIIB, Military Bridging — Bridges* (1914); information about heavy steel bridging, and illustrations 39 to 46, are from the *Royal Engineers Journal*, vols. 30 and 31 (October 1919-January 1920), reprinted in *Work of the Royal Engineers in the European War, 1914-1919: Bridging* (1921).]

Photographs of the 216th Company in training at Buxton show four types of bridge that they might have been expected to construct in the field during the early stages of the war: pontoon, barrel-pier, trestle (light or heavy), and single span with made-up girders.

Illustration 29 (rowing drill on the lake in Buxton Pavilion Gardens) shows a standard service pontoon. The pontoon consists of two parts: a bow piece, 11ft 6in long, and a stern piece, 9ft 6in long, each weighing 5cwt. Under normal conditions, whether being carried on a pontoon wagon or in use on the water (as here), the two pieces are fixed together with phosphor bronze couplings. Each pontoon piece has four carrying handles on each side (seen just above the water-line in this photograph). In use, a saddle beam is set fore-and-aft in the centre of the pontoon across the thwarts (seen here between the rowers). There are cleats on the upper surface of the saddle beam to receive the baulks, i.e. the longitudinal road-bearing timbers of the bridge, when the pontoon is moored in position.

The roadway constructions of a light and a medium pontoon bridge are shown in illustration 32. For a light bridge the pontoon pieces are used separately and the roadway is carried on three bearers; for a medium bridge complete pontoons are used and there are five road-bearers. The road-bearing baulks are supported on the saddles of the pontoons and on a shore transom (a device similar to a pontoon saddle) on each bank. The flooring of the roadway consists of wooden planks (called chesses) placed across the line of the bridge, resting on the road-bearers. On top of the chesses, near their outer edge, timbers known as ribands are fixed lengthwise.

A bridge built by the 216th Company in Buxton Pavilion Gardens, shown from the 'shore' end in illustration 30 and from the opposite, 'head' end in 31, is a light bridge, suitable for infantry. Most of the piers upon which the roadway is supported are bow and stern pieces of pontoons used separately and alternately, but barrel-piers are used at the head of the bridge. There are three road-bearers; standard 10ft chesses are laid diagonally and nailed to the outer road-bearers; the ends of the chesses are lashed to pontoon oars which act as ribands. At bottom right of illustration 30 the oars-for-ribands, diagonal chesses, road-bearers, and part of the shore transom are visible.

Barrel piers (see illustrations 31 and 33) were made up on land by tightly lashing rows of casks to timber cross-pieces called gunnels; these were launched and floated or paddled into position in much the same way as pontoons. Pontoon

31. Barrel-pier and pontoon bridge, Pavilion Gardens, Buxton: head end (Company billets in background).

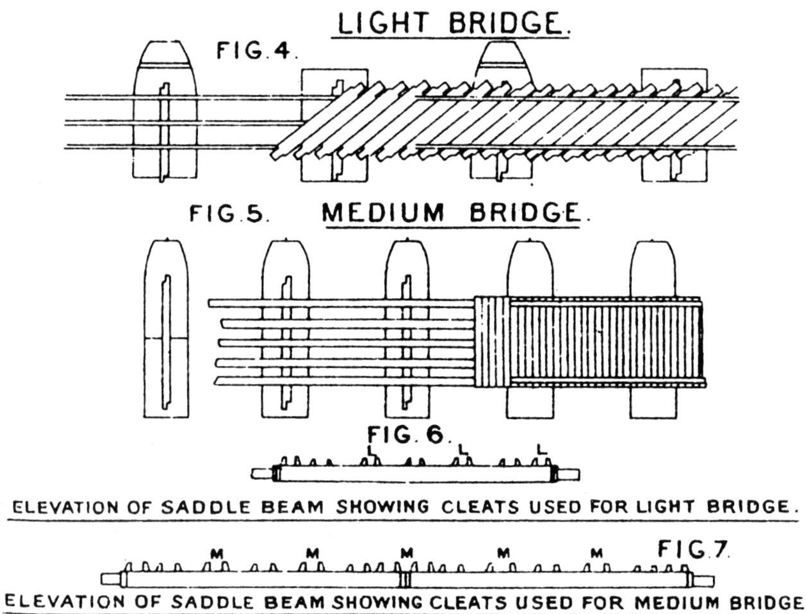

32. Light and medium pontoon bridges.

bridging was rapid: Corporal Streather, training at Newark, said that he was in a gang of 42 men who built a medium pontoon bridge for artillery, a hundred yards long, in 23 minutes. Barrel-pier bridging was obviously slower, but barrels had some advantage over pontoons in that they were far less likely to be holed if they grounded on a rough bottom under a heavy load.

Illustration 34 shows some men of 216th Company on the heavy bridging ground at Lightwood Road, off the Manchester Road, where they practised building timber trestle bridges over a deep gully. The wooden girder spanning the gully above and behind them is presumably their handiwork. The two booms running the entire length of the girder are 'laminated', i.e. made up of shorter timbers fastened together with bolts or dowels. Upper and lower booms are joined together by vertical wooden struts, so that the girder is divided into panels approximately five feet square. Each panel is braced diagonally (the central panels double braced) by iron rods, passed through auger holes and fitted with nuts and bearing plates. The finished work is an 'N' pattern girder.

In the background is a lattice girder with diagonal wooden struts and vertical bracing members, some of which apparently are iron rods and some timber. Between the two girders is a heavy trestle (cf illustration 35). The girder in front of the trestle appears to be about 60ft long; the trestle is perhaps 15ft high, unless what we can see is only the substructure of a two-tier trestle. Before the 216th Company left Buxton, they built a heavy bridge with girders 70ft long and 6ft deep, with booms 18in wide, which they lifted onto a 28ft high trestle they had built. The girder weighed over three tons and could carry a 22 ton locomotive.

Illustration 36 shows a light trestle bridge for infantry, built by the 216th Company perhaps in the Pavilion Gardens. The trestles were made on land, using spars lashed together with rope: see illustration 37, noting that both tips and one butt of the diagonal spars are on the opposite side of the legs to the transom (upper horizontal spar), the other butt being on the same side. In 36 two trestles have been positioned, road-bearing spars have been laid on their transoms and the plank roadway has been laid. A third trestle, loosely lashed to two longer spars has been floated out to the head of the bridge: the long spars will be used to position the feet of the trestle while the trestle top is raised; they will then be left as longitudinal braces, like the two that can be seen extending from the transom of the first trestle into the water around the feet of the second trestle.

33. Barrel piers.

34. Heavy bridging ground, Lightwood Road, Buxton

12″ × 12″ Timber.

Fig. 1.

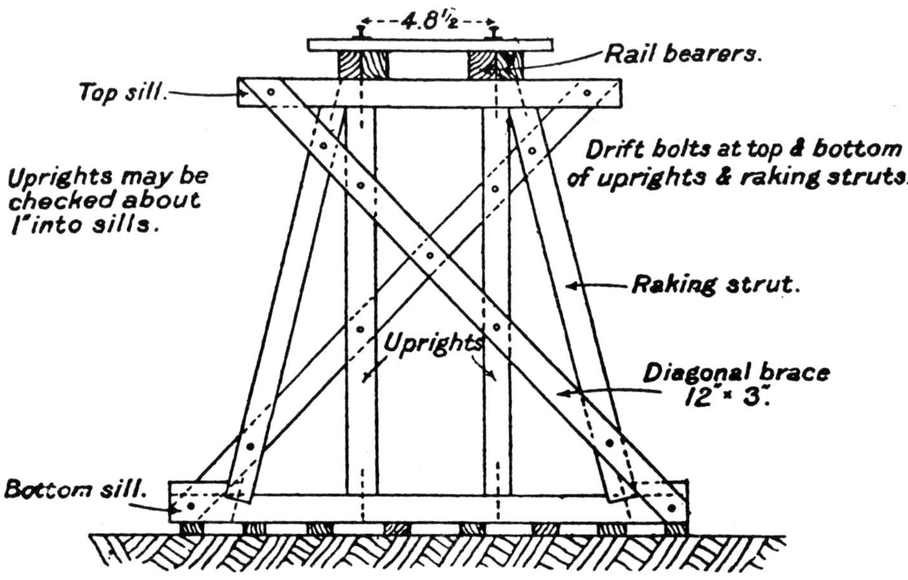

35. Heavy trestle.

36. Light trestle bridge at Buxton (Lieut Smith and Sgt Lee on left).

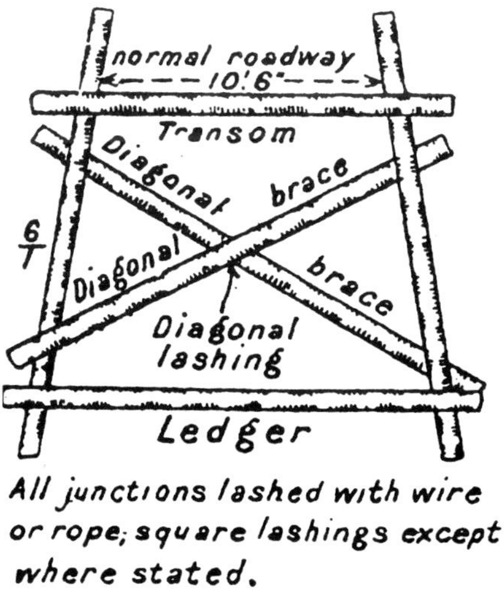

37. Light trestle.

There is no information about the Company's training on steel bridges in February and March 1916, when they were in France, beyond my father's statement that the duty of the men at Minx was to acquire skill and speed in putting together and taking apart steel girder bridges, and Corporal Streather's letter from Le Havre telling how the N.C.O.s under training there launched steel girders, 90ft long, weighing 17 tons for a bridge that would carry 33 tons. It is likely that in both cases the bridges were assembled from standard girder sections bolted together on site to make heavy girders of the 'Warren' pattern (i.e. a girder divided by its struts into a series of equilateral triangles). These girders were assembled on rollers, then launched and winched across the gap to be bridged, with the aid of a derrick on the far bank: i.e. the same method as for wooden girders, as shown in the War Office manual, illustration 38. Cross members were bolted to the girders with double angle brackets; lateral bracing and decking then followed. Illustration 39 shows a 60ft long portable Warren girder bridge, each girder of which consists of five sections; the four rectangles marked 'cover plate' on the side of each boom show where the sections were bolted together on site, before the girder was launched. The heaviest member of a 60ft 'Class A'

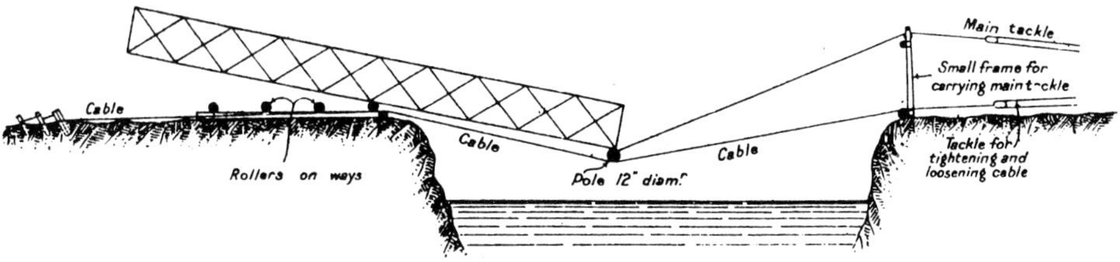

38. Launching a girder.

bridge, such as this, weighed 28cwt and one completed girder weighed just over six tons. A Class A standard steel girder bridge could carry a maximum axle load of 17 tons, such as a heavy howitzer or six-inch mounted naval gun. There was also a Class B steel girder bridge, made of lighter materials and capable of carrying a 13 ton axle load.

The monster referred to by Streather is perhaps a standard 85ft heavy Warren girder bridge (see illustration 40[a]), or some modification of it. The carrying capacity mentioned is far beyond the 'Class A' maximum, so perhaps the bridge was for railway use, but tanks were under trial by February 1916, so it is not inconceivable that prescient engineers at Le Havre were already trying to devise a portable bridge that would carry a thirty-ton tank over a wide river. Certainly, by the time that the first tanks came into service in France in 1916, the design of some Class A bridges had been modified to carry the extra load; these bridges were designated Class AA. In the case of the 60ft Warren girder bridge the only modification needed was to increase the size of the bolts. Other types and spans were more difficult to adapt, including the 85ft Warren girder: a type that was never popular 'owing to the great weight (66cwt) of a single section' (*Royal Engineers Journal*, vol.30 (1919), p.169). The problem of combining portability with the capacity to support a tank over some distance was not overcome until the bridge invented by Captain Hopkins became available at the front in 1917, and even then the width of a tank in full fighting order could sometimes be a problem.

It is not known what bridges 216th Company built in the field in 1916 and 1917. My father's recollections speak of his half-company building a pont levis (lifting bridge) near Steenbecque in October 1916. Arthur Daulman's reminiscences and Charles Streather's letters do not mention any bridging in France (apart from training) before 1918, but we should not expect an exhaustive catalogue of the Company's doings from any of these three sources — particularly as the Company was often split up and widely dispersed over a variety of jobs. The Company war diary for the period before July 1917 is not extant.

Illustration 41 shows the general arrangement of a Mark II pont levis. The two columns are erected on a pier of rolled steel joists which serves to tie them together; the columns are tied near their tops by a transverse girder; the bridge proper is hinged at the base of the columns; the lifting arms swivel at the top of the columns. The lifting arms carry a counterweight between them at one end; the bridge is suspended

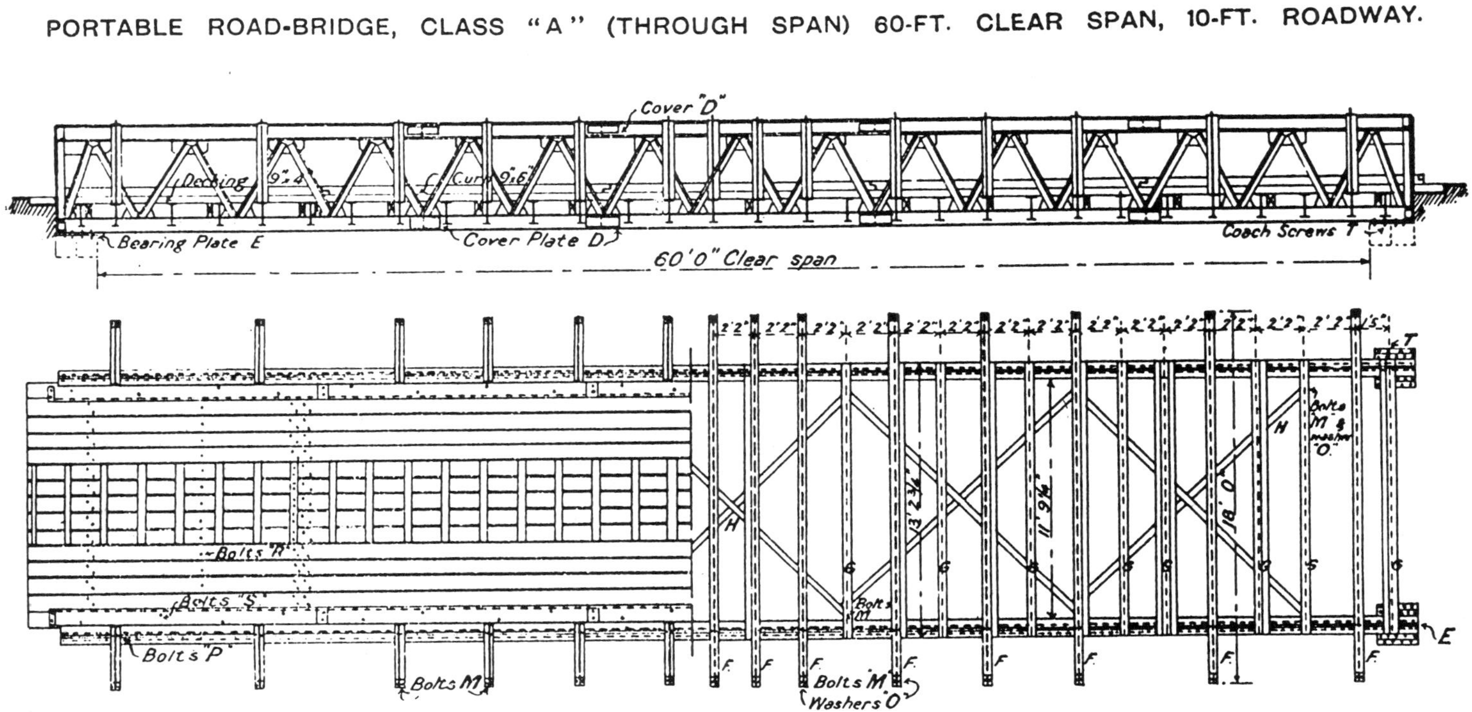

	T.	C.	Q.	L.
Weight of Bridge........	32	12	2	3
" " 1 Girder......	6	3	3	21
Heaviest Member........	1	8	1	17

39. Portable road bridge, class A, 60ft clear span (Warren girder): plan and elevation.

by wire ropes at the other end and is raised by means of wire ropes through pulleys on the arms and tower top, thence down to a winch. The standard pont levis had a span of 21ft 6in: just sufficient to bridge the widest French and Belgian canal lock. The parts for it were prefabricated in France to the R.E. design.

From the war diary it would seem that 216th Company suddenly emerged as a specialist heavy steel bridging company in January 1918. In the course of the following year they built in the field most types of portable steel bridge available to the British army and achieved an expertise that came to the attention of Chief Engineers and post-war R.E. historians. There is hardly any information about their training, but it is known that Captain MacDougall, Lieutenant Smith, Sergeant Streather, and other unnamed N.C.O.s and men took courses of instruction in heavy steel bridging at the R.E. Bridging School on the Aire Canal in northern France during the winter of 1917-18. The war diary also notes that on 7 December 1917 MacDougall and Smith went to the Aire Bridging School to see the demonstration launch of a Hopkins Bridge.

The Hopkins bridge (illustration 42), named after its designer, a Royal Engineer captain who was Bridging Officer at G.H.Q., consisted of standard steel girder sections, bolted together, which could be made up in any multiples of 15ft spans to make bridges of up to 120ft long, capable of carrying tanks. The girders were 16ft 3in high overall, with overhead bracing. Ten feet of clearance between the side girders provided ample room for tanks with their sponsons turned in, but not when they were turned out: this last limitation would have unfortunate consequences during the March retreat. The Hopkins bridge was stronger but somewhat lighter than earlier girder bridges and it was more easily portable because its heaviest single member weighed only a little over 10cwt. The effect of increasing the number of component parts was to 'admit of a large number of erectors being employed simultaneously, but, owing to the time required to make the bolted connections and the method of launching, the time required for construction is long'. It was reckoned to take forty men a hundred hours to construct a 120ft long span.

The standard method of erection was to assemble the bridge, less flooring, on one side of the gap, and to haul it into position by means of winches and derricks on the opposite side: see illustration 40(b). As the steelwork of a 120ft. span weighed about sixty tons, heavy reducing tackle and a strong, well-anchored winch were required : not surprisingly, my father notes that the men detailed to turn the winch handles had a very heavy job. When the bridge was fully launched and bedded on the further side of the gap, 'tarpaulins were slung under the bridge to give the men confidence while fixing the deck beams and to protect traffic passing along the bed of the canal from any material that might be dropped accidentally' (*Royal Engineers' Journal*, vol.35 (1922), p.222; vol.30 (1919), pp.265-6.)

216th Company unloaded materials for their first Hopkins bridge on 30 January 1918 at Péronne; they completed what, apparently, was their last on 6 November at Douai. In August and September they built at least three of the new Inglis bridges, along with a larger number of older types of steel bridges. (One cannot be certain of numbers because the company war diary often fails to specify which type of bridge is currently being built.)

40. (a) 85ft class A span (Warren girder).

40. (b) Launch of a Hopkins bridge.

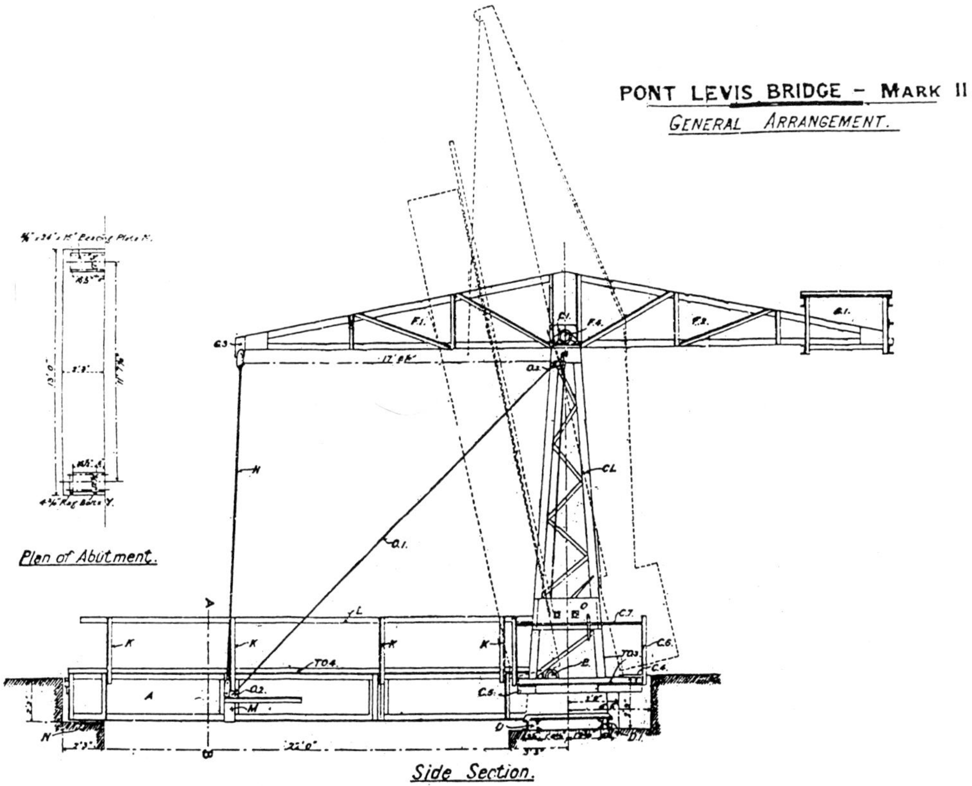

41. Pont levis: elevation and cross section.

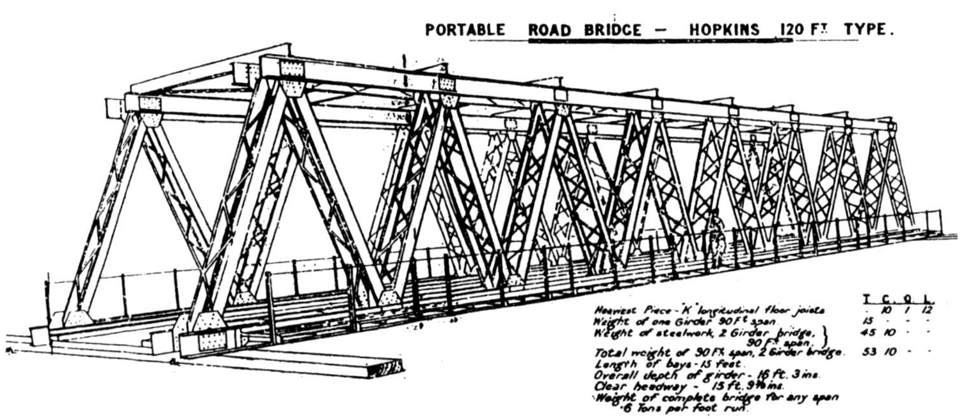

42. Hopkins bridge: perspective drawing.

The Inglis steel bridge (invented by Temporary Major C.E.Inglis, Professor of Engineering at Cambridge) consisted of a series of identical rectangular bays, 12ft long, 12ft wide, 12ft high, formed of weldless steel tubes; it was easily portable, could be erected more rapidly than the Hopkins type of bridge, and could also be dismantled more quickly than the Hopkins and moved to a fresh site as soon as a permanent bridge was completed: see illustration 43. The improved type, available to 216th Company in 1918, was not strong enough to carry tanks and was too low to allow for the passage of motor buses, but it could carry Class A loads

43. (a) Strengthened Inglis bridge.

43. (b) Inglis bridge being dismantled for erection elsewhere.

(17 tons) over 96 feet and Class B loads (13 tons) over 108 feet. With ingenuity its capacity could be increased. The Chief Engineer of the Australian Corps, after recording that in the 'bridging of the Somme Canal above Corbie some excellent results were obtained in very good time by 216 and 574 Companies', adds: 'The great value of the Inglis bridge as a means of rapidly bridging any stream up to 84ft from bank to bank was amply demonstrated. It should also be noted that if it is desired to adapt a long span of Inglis bridge to carry a weight which could only be carried by a shorter span it may be quite easy to do this by applying under each end of the Inglis bridge a cantilever up to say 10ft long, which thus reduces the span by as much as 20ft, and therefore correspondingly increases the weight-carrying capacity of the bridge' (War Diary, P.R.O., Kew: WO95/1000). With later modifications, including a strengthening to enable it to carry tanks, the Inglis was so successful a design that it remained the British standard steel military bridge until superseded by the more versatile Bailey bridge in 1941.

In 1918 Inglis bridges were in short supply because they were slow to manufacture and expensive, so re-use was essential. The 84ft Inglis bridge erected by the Company at Bray-sur-Somme, for instance, had previously been in use at Vaire lower down the river towards Amiens; at Bray it would later be replaced by rolled-steel joist spans on piles, so that it could be re-erected again for the crossing of the Selle river in October. At Bellenglise the Inglis bridge built by the Company was dismantled and sent forward when the permanent girder bridge, using 60ft standard Class A spans with short rolled-steel joist extensions supported on wooden trestles was completed: see illustration 44.

44. Bridges built by 216 Company at Bellenglise, October 1918: from foreground to background may be seen — (a) a German-built dam surmounted by a narrow walkway; (b) a partially-built permanent steel girder deck-span bridge resting on a wooden trestle; (c) an Inglis bridge resting on a pier of steel cubes; (d) an earlier bridge demolished in the German retreat.

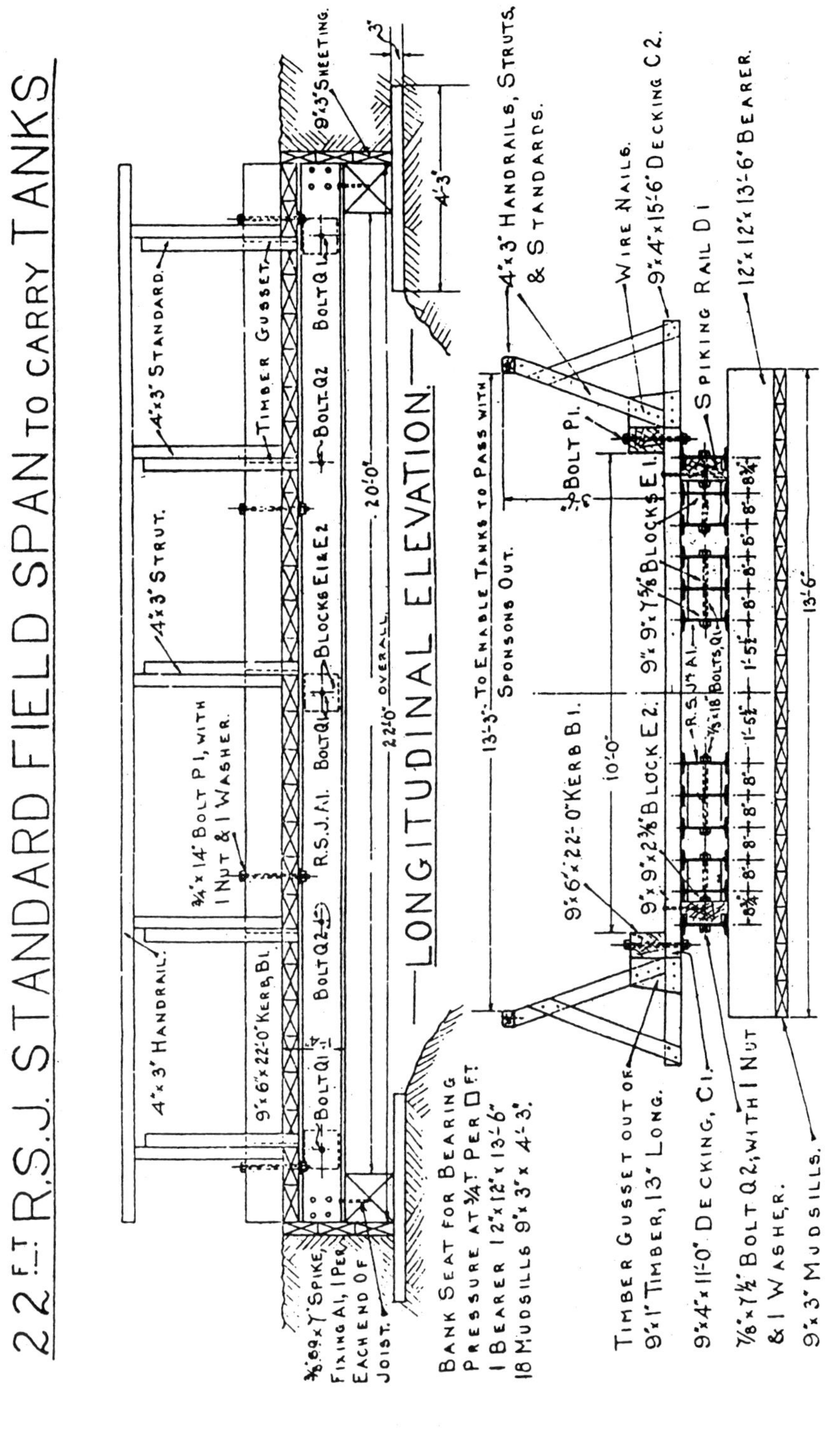

45. 22ft rolled-steel-joist span for Tanks: elevation and cross section.

Older steel bridge types, from stores accumulated since 1915, continued to be used alongside the Hopkins and the Inglis types. In June and July the 216th Company built several 85ft Class A heavy Warren girder bridges. The longest, over the river Canche at Enocq consisted of two 85ft spans with a 30ft shore bay: a total length of 200 ft. What the two piers were made of is not specified in the company diary: photographs of their later bridging work show both timber trestles and piers made of mild steel cubes, 3ft high: see illustration 44. 60ft Class A Warren girder bridges are mentioned at various dates between April and October, including some described as capable of carrying tanks (though the official term 'Class AA' is not used). At Brie, on the low banks of the Somme, 60ft bridges were erected as 'deck spans', i.e. with the roadway resting on the upper booms of the girders, rather than as 'through spans' with the roadway fixed between the lower booms (as in illustration 39). Erection as a deck span allowed tanks to cross with sponsons out, though it meant a considerable amount of extra work because approach ramps had to be built up at each end. When the Company replaced their Inglis bridge at Bellenglise with a more permanent composite bridge consisting of a short span of rolled-steel joists and a 60ft girder span resting on trestles, the girders were erected as a deck span; but this was over a deep cutting on the St.Quentin Canal: see illustration 44.

Spans of 30ft length and less are often mentioned in the diary. They would have consisted of standard 12in by 5in rolled-steel joists laid side by side in the number necessary for the traffic to be carried: i.e. six joists for Class B loads, eight for Class A, and twelve for a 30 ton tank (see illustration 45). These short bridges are essentially simple beams, withstanding stress by the strength of the road-bearing joists; the side members shown in the drawing are merely handrails, splayed in this case to allow room for the sponsons of a tank. (In a girder bridge, by contrast, the stress is distributed by struts and ties over the web of the girder, between the top boom in compression and the bottom boom in tension.) The decking of all types of heavy steel bridge consisted of timber baulks, 9in by 4in or larger.

Two types of steel lifting bridge were built by the 216th Company in 1918: the pont levis (see above) and the Emergency Portal bridge. The latter consisted of four steel columns, braced together with girders or standard rolled-steel joists at their tops across both the roadway and the canal. The bridge proper was not hinged at one end like the pont levis, but was lifted horizontally at each of its four corners on wire ropes through pulleys at the top of each column to a worm-gear arrangement with a hand-chain for working it. The lifting arrangement was weak, four men were required to raise and lower the bridge, and it could jam if not raised or lowered evenly; consequently it was erected only in places where it could normally remain down, being raised only in cases of emergency. The Emergency Portal bridge could carry 12-ton axle loads; like the standard pont levis, its span was just sufficient to bridge a 21ft 6in wide canal lock.

Though they were primarily a specialist heavy steel bridging company during the 1918 advance, the 216th built at least one pontoon bridge and occasionally built wooden bridges. One of their last jobs was a 70ft long trestle bridge over the canal at Valenciennes in January and February 1919. Their 350ft long bridge at Valenciennes railway station was supported on a large number of wooden trestles; the spans, however, were rolled-steel joists: see illustration 46.

46. 350ft-long bridge at Valenciennes railway station, built by 216 Company early in 1919, consisting of standard 22ft rolled-steel joists resting on numerous wooden trestles.

NOTES

Chapter 1: Nuneaton

1. Borough Council Minutes, 31 March; *Nuneaton Chronicle*, 2 and 16 April, 1915;
2. *Locally Raised Units*, War Office, 1916; *Nuneaton Chronicle*, 6 November 1914, 16 April 1915.
3. *Nuneaton Observer*, 4 and 11 December 1914, in the course of complaints about a slackening of recruitment in Nuneaton: the number of recruits had fallen from 294 on the best day (1 September) to 10 in the worst week (ending 6 November).
4. *Private Papers of Douglas Haig, 1914-1919*, ed. Robert Blake (1952), p.84.
5. *Nuneaton Observer*, 4 February 1916.
6. *Nuneaton Chronicle*, 27 November 1914.
7. Weekly lists of names of recruits in Nuneaton newspapers usually do not specify the military formation in which a volunteer enlisted, except in the case of the Nuneaton Fortress Company, R.E. In the ten weeks required for the raising of this Company, from April to June 1915, its recruits accounted for about one fifth of the total number of Nuneaton men recruited into the New Army (85 out of 436 names printed: the first figure certainly and the second figure probably too low). The majority of Nuneaton army recruits before, during, and after the raising of the Nuneaton Fortress Company enlisted in the Royal Warwickshire Regiment.
8. *Nuneaton Observer*, 7 May 1915; the caption to a photograph of the victorious Nuneaton Town XI in this issue gives Barratt the dignity of his army rank of Sapper.
9. *Nuneaton Observer*, 30 July 1915.
10. *Nuneaton Chronicle*, 9 and 30 October 1914.
11. *Engineer Training* (1914), p.2.
12. *Nuneaton Observer*, 2 July 1915.
13. *Engineer Training* (1914), p.149.
14. Large shallow earthenware bowls.
15. *Nuneaton Observer*, 9 July 1915. 'K'nut': Showy young man.
16. *Nuneaton Observer*, 13 August 1915.
17. *Nuneaton Chronicle* 13 August 1915.
18. 'Blue Sky School': optimists.

Chapter 2: Cosham and Buxton

1. *Buxton Advertiser*, 14 November 1914.
2. A person who sells fruit, vegetables, etc. from a street-barrow.
3. A cattle truck or box wagon which carried troops or horses on French railways: each truck could hold 'Hommes 40' or 'Chevaux 8'.
4. Notes on the bridging techniques illustrated in these photographs may be found in the Appendix, pp.222-37.
5. *Military Engineering: Part IIIB* (1914), pp.34-8.
6. *Buxton Advertiser*, 5 December, 21 November 1914.
7. Cf *Engineer Training* (1914), p.20: 'bridging at night must be practised, silence and celerity being aimed at'.

8. H.L.Pritchard, *History of the Corps of Royal Engineers*, vol.5 (1952), p.232. Pritchard does not mention heavy steel bridging, which eventually became the 216th Company's special skill.
9. 'Now the Line's but a man with a gun in his hand,
An' Cavalry's only what horses can stand,
When helped by the Engineer,
Her Majesty's Royal Engineer,
With the rank and pay of a Sapper!

Artillery moves by the leave o' the ground,
But *we* are the men that do something all round,
For *we* are the Engineers,
Her Majesty's Royal Engineers,
With the rank and pay of a Sapper!
(Kipling, 'Sappers', in *Barrack-Room Ballads*.)
10. *The Sapper*, October 1915, p.73.
11. *Nuneaton Observer*, 3 September 1915.
12. The other newcomers are named by my father and Arthur Daulman as Sapper Irvine and Corporal Snow from Nuneaton, Sappers Godwin and Stevenson from Buxton, Sapper Islip and Driver Smith from Northampton, Sappers Barrier, Brophy, and Hallsworth from Chesham (Bucks.), and Dan Firbank from Guernsey, There was a draft of eight, all from Fenny Compton according to Daulman, though my father gives them various places of origin: Alf Brackley, Bill Draper, Edgar Dunton, Bill Gibberd, Joe Harris, Jack Hunt, Percy Keen, and Bert Money.
13. *Nuneaton Observer*, 3, 24 December 1915, 7 January 1916.
14. Others who left the Company at Buxton included Sappers Dyer, Ludford, and Rose, and Driver Orrill. Harry Ludford's discharge may well have been connected with the fact that he married a Nuneaton girl on 19 September; the best man was Sapper Dick Townsend; there was no honeymoon because Ludford had to report back to Buxton the following day (*Nuneaton Chronicle*, 24 September 1915). Sappers Ross, Davies, and Kinsey were transferred to another company; Len Brookes was discharged with tuberculosis; Sapper Williams, writes my father, 'was in clink at Knutsford and we were glad to be rid of him'.
15. *Nuneaton Observer*, 7 January 1916.
16. *Engineer Training* (1914), p.7.
17. *Nuneaton Chronicle*, 28 January 1916.
18. R.M.S.Mauretania, 16,800 tons, was launched in 1906 and won the Blue Riband for the fastest crossing of the Atlantic on the eastbound leg of her maiden voyage in 1907. Early in 1915 she carried troops to the eastern Mediterranean, but in September of that year she was repainted in the red and white colours of a hospital ship and made three voyages bringing home men wounded at Gallipoli: the Nuneaton men saw her at the end of her last such voyage. After this she was given a camouflage of dazzle-paint and was employed as a troopship again, carrying Canadian, and later United States, servicemen across the Atlantic. In 1919 she returned to passenger service; she remained the fastest liner on the Atlantic crossing until 1929; she was scrapped in 1935.

Chapter 3: Mazingarbe

1. R.H.Mottram, *The Spanish Farm Trilogy* (Penguin, 1979), p.191; Henry Williamson, *The Wet Flanders Plain* (1929), pp.35-36.
2. *Nuneaton Chronicle*, 11 February 1916.
3. *Ibid.*, 11 February 1916.
4. George Coppard, *With a Machine-Gun to Cambrai* (1969), p.29.
5. Charles Douie, *The Weary Road* (1919), pp.110-11.
6. *Cahiers de l'abbé Joseph Varret, curé de la paroisse* (Comité historique, Mazingarbe, 1992).
7. *Nuneaton Chronicle,* 11 February, 3 March 1916
8. On 2 July 1915, while the 216th Company was still in the town, the *Nuneaton Observer* printed a photograph of a bullet-pierced pocket book given by the Minister of Manor Court Baptist Church, Nuneaton, to a colour-sergeant in the Royal Warwicks. The accompanying story told how the bullet which tore the pocket book was deflected so as to wound but not kill the sergeant.
9. Charles Carrington, *Soldier from the Wars Returning* (1965), p.177.
10. Quoted in John Ellis, *Eye-Deep in Hell* (1986), p.129.
11. J.E.Edmonds, *Military Operations: France and Belgium, 1915*, vol.II (1928), p.173.
12. C.H.Foulkes, *"Gas!" The Story of the Special Brigade* (1934), pp.52-3, 307-9; J.E.Edmonds, *Military Operations: France and Belgium, 1916,* vol.I (1932), pp.79-80.

Chapter 4: Bouvigny-Boyeffles

1. 'In 1914 the six-division British Expeditionary Force possessed 1,200 lorries; . . . the five armies constituting the mobile right wing of the great German advance through Belgium had only 500 between them': John Terraine, *White Heat: The New Warfare 1914-1918* (1982), p.25.
2. *Royal Engineers Journal*, vol.30 (1919), p.164
3. *Royal Engineers Journal*, vol.30 (1919), pp.166-7
4. The other replacements were Sappers Chisholm (Glasgow), Clarkson (Stockport), Cordingley (Bradford), Gledhill and Glieb (Bradford), Heston (Wigan), Rainey and Williams (Liverpool), and Stewart (Dundee).
5. W.G.Grieve and B.Newman, *Tunnellers* (1936), p.198. Paddy Griffith adds: 'it was "at least highly probable" that no such spying really took place. For example it did not need the guiles of a Mata Hari to work out that a large chateau just behind the lines might be earmarked for a brigade HQ.'
6. Lieutenant Vivian da Sola Pinto, Siegfried Sassoon's second in command, wrote a parody of Flecker's 'Golden Road to Samarkand' in 1917:

    Have we not bully tough and biscuits hard,
    McConochie's tins of horsemeat boiled in glue,
    And strange pink jams by Thomas Tickler jarred,
    Spurned by the delicate lords at G.H.Q.?

    (Pinto, *The City that Shone, An Autobiography* (1969), p.223.
7. H.R.Sandilands, *The 23rd Division, 1914-19* (1925), pp.56-7.
8. Richard Holmes, *Firing Line* (Penguin, 1987), p.249.
9. Sheldon appears in a photograph of some members of the 17th Battalion

(Football), Middlesex Regiment, reproduced in *The History of the Football Association* (1953), plate XLIV. He enlisted on 23 July 1915 (*Nuneaton Observer*, 30 July 1915). The Football Battalion was a Kitchener New Army unit, now incorporated into the old regular army 2nd Division.

10. Everard Wyrall, *The Die-Hards in the Great War*, vol.I (1926), p.236.
11. J.E.Edmonds, *Military Operations: France and Belgium, 1915*, vol.II (1928), p.187.
12. Philip Gibbs, *Realities of War* (1920), p.31.
13. J.E.Edmonds, *Military Operations: France and Belgium, 1916*, vol.I (1932), p.156.
14. i.e. loaves of bread.
15. Robert Graves, *Goodbye to All That* (Penguin, 1960), p.150.

Chapter 5: Villers-au-Bois and Ribemont

1. A.H.Maude, *The 47th (London) Division, 1914-1919* (1922), p.52; J.E.Edmonds, *Military Operations: France and Belgium, 1916*, vol.I (1932), pp.212-13.
2. H.L.Pritchard, *History of the Corps of Royal Engineers*, vol.5 (1952), p.458.
3. J.E.Edmonds, *Military Operations: France and Belgium, 1916*, vol.I (1932), p.213.
4. Algerian light-infantrymen.
5. F.C.Hitchcock, *Stand To* (1988), pp.196-7; E.L.Spears, *Prelude to Victory* (1939), p.296.
6. J.E.Edmonds, *Military Operations: France and Belgium, 1916*, vol.I (1932), pp.210, 212.
7. A.H.Maude, *The 47th Division* (1922), pp.53, 55, 57.
8. J.E.Edmonds, *Military Operations: France and Belgium, 1916*, vol.I (1932), p.80.
9. Cyril Falls, *Military Operations: France and Belgium, 1917*, vol.I (1940), p.327.
10. Charles Carrington, *Soldier from the Wars Returning* (1965), pp.103-5.
11. Monk Gibbon, *Inglorious Soldier* (1968), p.191.
12. Charles Carrington, *A Subaltern's War* (1929), p. 27.
13. John Charteris, *At G.H.Q.* (1931), p. 149.

Chapter 6: Second Army and Reserve Army

1. Leon Wolff, *In Flanders Fields* (1979), p.114.
2. J.E.Edmonds, *Military Operations: France and Belgium, 1917*, vol.II (1948).
3. Henry Williamson, *The Wet Flanders Plain*, pp. 47, 97.
4. Cf *Military Engineering: Part V* (1914), p.34:' . . . a layer of fine gravel should be placed between the sand and the charcoal, otherwise the sand will choke the pores of the charcoal. Charcoal acts more quickly than sand, but the water should take at least four minutes in passing through the layer. To ensure this, it must be not less than 6 inches thick, and powdered and rammed very tight, or the water will pass between the pieces of charcoal instead of through them.'
5. Philip Gibbs, *Realities of War* (1920), p.67.
6. Denis Winter, *Death's Men: Soldiers of the Great War* (Penguin, 1979), pp.152-53.

7. Sapper Trevis's Colonel-like bearing may be judged from illustration 29: he is in the bows of the pontoon.
8. Edmund Blunden, *Undertones of War* (Penguin, 1981), p.208
9. A.Duff Cooper, *Haig* (1936), II, 116.
10. John Charteris, *At G.H.Q.* (1931), p.221.
11. H.A.Jones, *The War in the Air*, vol.II (Oxford, 1928), p.185.
12. *Nuneaton Observer*, 20, 27 Oct., 3 Nov. 1916.

Chapter 7: Steenbecque and Morbecque

1. R.H.Mottram, *The Spanish Farm Trilogy* (Penguin 1979), pp.306-7.
2. *Nuneaton Observer*, 20, 27 October, 3 November 1916.
3. These sheds are much larger than those in my father's description of the Company's work on the Morbecque ammunition dump. Perhaps they are different sheds, or perhaps they shrank after sixty years in my father's memory, or perhaps Charles Streather was exaggerating to impress his parents.
4. *Nuneaton Chronicle*, 5 January 1917.

Chapter 8: Reninghelst Road to Neuve Eglise

1. *Nuneaton Observer*, 16 February 1917. (Haig still emphasises the importance of cavalry.)
2. Michael MacDonagh, *London during the Great War* (1935), pp.177, 188.
3. Anthony Babington, *For the Sake of Example* (1983), pp.72-4, 77.
4. *Nuneaton Observer*, 16 March 1917.
5. J.E.Edmonds, *Military Operations: France and Belgium, 1917*, vol.II (1948), p.40. I do not know how many miles of water pipes were installed in total by the 216th Company. The laying of cast-iron water pipes was certainly a major engineering task on the Western Front: 291 miles of four-inch piping and 162 miles of two-inch piping were issued to R.E. companies in 1916; the figures for 1917 were 703 miles of four-inch and 407 miles of two-inch (*Work of the Royal Engineers in the European War, 1914-1919: Supply of Engineer Stores and Equipment* (1923), p.103).
6. John Charteris, *At G.H.Q.* (1931), p.226.
7. *Ibid.*, p.218.
8. J.E.Edmonds, *Military Operations: France and Belgium, 1917*, vol.II (1948), pp.15-20.
9. Lyn Macdonald, *They called it Passchendaele* (1993), pp.21-2.
10. John Buchan, *History of the Great War* (1922), III, 574.
11. Edmund Blunden, *Undertones of War* (Penguin, 1981), pp.191-2.

Chapter 9: Messines

1. J.E.Edmonds, *Military Operations: France and Belgium 1917*, vol.II (1948), pp.87, iii.
2. C.E.W.Bean, *The Australian Imperial Force in France, 1917* (1982), p.609.
3. J.E.Edmonds, *Military Operations: France and Belgium 1917*, vol.II (1948), p.72.

4. The pottery jars in which rum was carried were marked 'S.R.D.', standing for 'Special Rations Department', but rumoured to mean 'seldom reaches destination'.
5. C.H.Foulkes, *"Gas!" The Story of the Special Brigade* (1934), p.143.
6. Frederick Maurice, *The Life of General Lord Rawlinson of Trent* (1928), p.185. There is a variant of the socks-in-the-box-respirator story in C.H.Foulkes, *"Gas!" The Story of the Special Brigade* (1934), pp.258-9.
7. War Diary, Chief Engineer, II Anzac Corps, June 1917 (P.R.O., Kew: WO95/1035: Crown Copyright).
8. Crown and anchor is a gambling game played with three dice, each bearing a crown, an anchor, and the four card suits, and played on a board similarly marked. There is an example of a crown-and-anchor banker's patter in Henry Williamson, *The Patriot's Progress*: 'Lay your money single and pick up double. You lay and we pay, the good old Sweaty Sox, out since Mons, often bent but never broke, the rough and tough, the old and bold. If you don't speculate you can't accumulate. Come along gentlemen, you are not on parade. Who fancies the lucky old Major? Copper, silver, and gold. You come in rags and ride away in motor-cars' (1968 edn., p.142). 'Major' (sergeant-major) is the crown.
9. Llewelyn Woodward, *Great Britain and the War of 1914-1918* (1967), p.285.
10. R.H.Mottram, *The Spanish Farm Trilogy* (Penguin, 1979), p.188.
11. Hubert Gough, *The Fifth Army* (1931), p.205.

Chapter 10: Kemmel to Zillebeke Lake

1. *Nuneaton Observer*, 7 September, 1917.
2. Edmund Blunden, *Undertones of War* (Penguin, 1981), pp.211-12.
3. The 'baby elephant', so named from its appearance, was semi-cylindrical, like the Nissen hut, but made of heavier iron, with larger corrugations (3in. wide, 4in. deep) than ordinary corrugated iron.
4. Cyril Falls, *Military Operations: France and Belgium, 1917*, vol.I (1940), p.131.
5. Australian War Memorial, AWM4, 14 / 4 (reel 334).
6. *Ibid.* AWM4, 14 / 9 (reel 341).
7. C.E.W.Bean, *The Australian Imperial Force in France, 1917* (1982), p.739.
8. Edmund Blunden, *Undertones of War* (Penguin, 1981), p.173.
9. *Ibid.*, p.263.

Chapter 11: Péronne to Ham

1. Edmund Blunden, *Undertones of War* (Penguin, 1981), p,265
2. *Ibid.*
3. J.Shakespear, *The 34th Division, 1915-1919* (1921), p.134.
4. Paul Maze, *A Frenchman in Khaki* (1934), p.265.
5. Hubert Gough, *The Fifth Army* (1931), p.225
6. *Ibid.*, p.235; War Diary, Chief Engineer, Fifth Army, January 1918 (P.R.O., Kew: WO95 / 534: Crown Copyright).
7. *Royal Engineers' Journal*, vol.30 (1919), p.213.

8. J.E.Edmonds, *Military Operations: France and Belgium, 1918*, vol.1 (1935), p.338.
9. Hubert Gough, *The Fifth Army* (1931), p.239.
10. *Royal Engineers' Journal*, vol.30 (1919), pp.213-14.
11. Hubert Gough, *The Fifth Army* (1931), p.244.
12. Frederick Maurice, *Life of General Lord Rawlinson of Trent* (1928), p.220.
13. *Military Operations: France and Belgium*, 1918, Appendices (1935), p.46.
14. J.E.Edmonds, *Military Operations: France and Belgium, 1918*, vol.1 (1935), p.123 n.
15. Hubert Gough, *The Fifth Army* (1931), p.251.
16. John Terraine, *To Win a War* (1978), p.60.
17. Hubert Gough, *The Fifth Army* (1931), p.267.
18. J.E.Edmonds, *Military Operations: France and Belgium, 1918*, vol.1 (1935), p.207.

Chapter 12: In Retreat

1. J.E.Edmonds, *Military Operations: France and Belgium, 1918*, vol.I (1935), p.212.
2. Herbert Read, *Annals of Innocence and Experience* (1946), pp.173-4.
3. *Private Papers of Douglas Haig, 1914-1919*, ed. Robert Blake (1953), p.291.
4. J.E.Edmonds, *Military Operations: France and Belgium, 1918*, vol.I (1935), p.280 n.1; Appendices (1935), p.126 n.
5. K.E.Luard, *Unknown Warriors* (1930), p.260.
6. J.E.Edmonds, *Military Operations: France and Belgium, 1918*, vol.I (1935), pp.368-9.
7. H.L.Pritchard, *History of the Corps of Royal Engineers*, vol.5 (1952), pp.350-1.
8. J.E.Edmonds, *Military Operations: France and Belgium, 1918*, vol.I (1935), p.350.
9. Chief Engineer, Fifth Army, War Diary, March 1918 (P.R.O., Kew: WO95 / 534: Crown Copyright).
10. V.E.Inglefield, *History of the Twentieth (Light) Division* (1921), p.226.
11. J.E.Edmonds, *Military Operations: France and Belgium, 1918*, vol.I (1935), p.400.
12. Tim Travers, *The Killing Ground* (1987), p.229.
13. A.J.Comins, *History of the 567th (Devon) A.T. Coy* (typescript in Imperial War Museum.)
14. Tim Travers, *The Killing Ground* (1987), p.227.
15. Gregory Blaxland, *Amiens 1918* (1968), p.89.
16. H.L.Pritchard, *History of the Corps of Royal Engineers*, vol.5 (1952), pp.356.
17. Bert Bishop, *The Hell, the Humour, and the Heartbreak* (1991), p.147
18. F.Maurice, ed., *The Life of General Lord Rawlinson of Trent* (1926), pp.213-14.
19. J.E.Edmonds, *Military Operations: France and Belgium, 1918*, vol.II (1937), p.48 n.
20. *Ibid.*, p.50.
21. *Ibid.*, p.51 n.
22. *Private Papers of Douglas Haig, 1914-1919*, ed. Robert Blake (1953), p.208; Tim Travers, *How the War was Won* (1992), p.68.

23. Martin Middlebrook, *The Kaiser's Battle* (1978), p.356.
24. J.E.Edmonds, *Military Operations: France and Belgium, 1918*, vol.II (1937), p.28 n.1.
25. Anthony Farrar-Hockley, *Goughie* (1975), p.324. Lloyd George in his *War Memoirs* (1933-36) fully exonerated Gough and openly blamed Haig for British reverses in March 1918. The *War Memoirs* were published after the death of Haig (1928) and after publication of Gough's *The Fifth Army* (1931), a self-defensive book in which blame is thrown upon Lloyd George, rather than Haig.
26. H.L.Pritchard, *History of the Corps of Royal Engineers*, vol.5 (1952), pp.357-8.
27. Undated clipping from *Nuneaton Chronicle*.
28. J.E.Edmonds, *Military Operations: France and Belgium, 1918*, vol.II (1937), p.87.
29. Neither Arthur Daulman nor my father returned to the 216th Company. Accounts of their service after March 1918 may be found in the typescript Great-War memoirs of each man: Daulman's deposited in The Institution of Royal Engineers, Brompton Barracks, Chatham, and Nuneaton Public Library; my father's in those two depositories and in the Imperial War Museum.
30. W.G.Grieve and B.Newman, *Tunnellers* (1936), p.264. There is a brief account of the action of another R.E. Company near Hangard Wood on 30 March in the War Diary of 234 Field Company (P.R.O., Kew: WO95 / 2575: Crown Copyright).
31. F.Maurice, ed., *The Life of General Lord Rawlinson of Trent* (1926), p.216.

Chapter 13: The End of the War

1. B.H.Liddell Hart, *The Real War* (1930), pp.427, 429.
2. John Charteris, *At G.H.Q.*, p.294.
3. *Royal Engineers Journal*, vol.30 (1919), p.214.
4. B.H.Liddell Hart, *The Real War* (1930), p.428.
5. A.J.Comins, *History of the 567th (Devon) A.T. Coy*, t.s. in Imperial War Museum.
6. *Royal Engineers Journal*, vol.30 (1919), p.263.
7. Australian War Memorial AWM4, 14 / 4 (reel 334): Engineer Instruction 7, dated 11 August 1918.
8. *Work of the Royal Engineers in the European War, 1914-1919*: Bridging (1921), p.19
9. Australian War Memorial AWM4, 14 / 4 (reel 334): Engineer Instruction 19, dated 11 September 1918.
10. *Ibid.*, p.15; J.W.S. Sewell, 'The Supply of Bulk Stores in War', *Royal Engineers Journal*, vol.36 (1922), p.24
11. Cyril Falls, *Military Operations: France and Belgium, 1917*, vol.I (1940), pp.546-7.
12. *Work of the Royal Engineers in the European War, 1914-1919: Supply of Engineer Stores and Equipment* (1923), p.105; *Ibid*: *Bridging* (1921), p.24.; Cyril Falls, *Military Operations: France and Belgium, 1917*, vol.I (1940), p.131.
13. *Work of the Royal Engineers in the European War, 1914-1919: Bridging* (1921), p.25. Steel bridging spans were sometimes carried by horsed trestle

wagons belonging to divisions: see Cyril Falls, *Military Operations: France and Belgium, 1917*, vol.I (1940), p. 132.

14. Australian War Memorial AWM4, 14 / 4 (reel 334)
15. The number of motor vehicles employed by the British Army rose from 1,485 at the outbreak of war to 121,720 at the Armistice: John Terraine, *White Heat: the New Warfare 1914-18* (1982), p.26.
16. J.E.Edmonds, *Official History: France and Belgium, 1918*, vol.IV (1947), p.588.
17. Australian War Memorial AWM4, 14 / 4 (reel 334).
18. *Ibid.*
19. *Royal Engineers Journal*, vol.30 (1919), p.264.
20. Australian War Memorial AWM4, 14 / 4 (reel 334).
21. *Royal Engineers Journal*, vol.30 (1919), p.264.
22. *Royal Engineers Journal*, vol.31 (1920), p.62.
23. J.H.Boraston and E.O.Bax, *The Eighth Division in War, 1914-1918* (1926), p.267.

Chapter 14: Aftermath

1. *Royal Engineers Journal*, vol.31 (1920), p.152.
2. Cyril Falls, *Military Operations: France and Belgium 1917*, vol.I (1940), p.546.
3. Ernest Harold Loam joined the 216th Company probably at Buxton. By March 1916, when he accompanied Corporal Streather to the Havre bridging school, he was a corporal. He left the Company probably in 1916, was commissioned as a Temporary Second Lieutenant on 24 February 1917, and was killed in action, serving with the 56th Company, RE., on 5 May 1918.

Bibliography

Babington, Anthony, *For the Sake of Example* (1983).
Bean, C.E.W., *The Australian Imperial Force in France, 1917* (1982).
Blake, Robert, ed., *Private Papers of Douglas Haig, 1914-1919* (1952).
Blaxland, Gregory, *Amiens: 1918* (1968).
Blunden, Edmund, *Undertones of War* (1928: Penguin edn. 1981).
Boraston, J.H. and E.O. Bax, *The Eighth Division in War, 1914-1918* (1926).
Boyd, Derek, *The Royal Engineers* (1975).
Buxton Advertiser.
Carrington, Charles, *Soldier from the Wars Returning* (1965).
Charteris, John, *At G.H.Q.* (1931).
Comins, A.J., *History of the 567th (Devon) A.T. Coy* (typescript in Imperial War Museum.)
Edmonds, J.E., Cyril Falls, and others, *Military Operations: France and Belgium* (eleven volumes, 1926-47) ['*Official History of the Great War*'].
Ellis, John, *Eye-Deep in Hell: the Western Front, 1914-18* (1986).
Foulkes, C.H. *"Gas!" The Story of the Special Brigade* (1934).
Fussell, Paul, *The Great War and Modern Memory* (1975).
General Staff, War Office, *Engineer Training* (with amendments, 1914).
General Staff, War Office, *Military Engineering* (five parts, 1914-15)
General Staff, War Office, *Manual of Field Engineering* (1911).
Gibbs, Philip, *Realities of War* (1920).
Glubb, John, *Into Battle* (1978).
Gough, Hubert, *The Fifth Army* (1931).
Graves, Robert, *Goodbye to All That* (1929: Penguin edn. 1960).
Grieve, W.G., and B.Newman, *Tunnellers* (1936).
Inglefield, V.E., *History of the Twentieth (Light) Division* (1921).
Maude, A.H., *The 47th (London) Division, 1914-1919* (1922).
Maurice, Frederick, *The Life of General Lord Rawlinson of Trent* (1926).
Middlebrook, Martin, *The Kaiser's Battle* (1978).
Montgomery, Archibald, *The Story of the Fourth Army in the Hundred Days* (1926)
Mottram, R.H., *The Spanish Farm Trilogy* (Penguin, 1979).
Nuneaton Chronicle.
Nuneaton Observer.
Official History: see Edmonds.
Osborne, John, *The Voluntary Recruiting Movement in Britain, 1914-1916* (1982).
Pritchard, H.L., *History of the Corps of Royal Engineers*, vol.5 (1952).
Quigley, Hugh, *Passchendaele and the Somme* (1928).
Read, Herbert, *Annals of Innocence and Experience* (enlarged edn., 1946).
Reith, John, *Wearing Spurs* (1966).
Royal Engineers Journal.
Sandilands, H.R., *The 23rd Division, 1914-19* (1925).
Sapper, The.
Shakespear, J., *The 34th Division, 1915-1919* (1921).
Simkins, Peter, *Kitchener's Army: The Raising of the New Armies, 1914-16* (1988).

Terraine, John, *White Heat: The New Warfare 1914-1918* (1982).
Travers, Tim, *How the War was Won: Command and Technology in the British Army on the Western Front, 1917-1918* (1992).
Varret, Joseph, *Cahiers de l'abbé Joseph Varret, curé de la paroisse* (Comité historique, Mazingarbe, 1992).
Williamson, Henry, *The Wet Flanders Plai*n (1929).
Work of the Royal Engineers in the European War, 1914-1919 (eight volumes, 1921-24): [reprinted from the *Royal Engineers Journal*].
Wyrall, Everard, *The Die-Hards in the Great Wa*r, (1926).

Index